RESPONSIBILITY

DICKENSON TITLES OF RELATED INTEREST

Reason and Responsibility: Readings in Some Basic Problems of Philosophy, Third Edition
  edited by Joel Feinberg

Principles of Ethics: An Introduction
  by Paul W. Taylor

Problems of Moral Philosophy: An Introduction to Ethics, Second Edition
  edited by Paul W. Taylor

Understanding Philosophy
  by Tom Regan

Moral Philosophy: An Introduction
  edited by Paul Fink

Philosophical Problems of Causation
  edited by Tom L. Beauchamp

Individual Conduct and Social Norms: A Utilitarian Account of Social Union and the Rule of Law
  by Rolf Sartorius

Freedom and Authority: An Introduction to Social and Political Philosophy
  edited by Thomas Schwartz

Philosophical and Religious Issues: Classical and Contemporary Statements
  edited by Ed. L. Miller

The Logic of Grammar
  edited by Donald Davidson and Gilbert H. Harman

Philosophy of Law
  edited by Joel Feinberg and Hyman Gross

RESPONSIBILITY

edited by
Joel Feinberg
and
Hyman Gross

DICKENSON PUBLISHING COMPANY, INC., ENCINO, CALIFORNIA,
AND BELMONT, CALIFORNIA

ISBN-0-8221-0171-8
Library of Congress Catalog Card Number: 75-21402

Printed in the United States of America
Printing (last digit): 9 8 7 6 5 4 3 2 1

Cover by Jill Casty

Originally published as Part 4 of *Philosophy of Law,* edited by Joel Feinberg and
Hyman Gross, Dickenson Publishing Company, Inc., © 1975. All rights reserved.

CONTENTS

THE DICKENSON SERIES IN PHILOSOPHY

Philosophy, said Aristotle, begins in wonder—wonder at the phenomenon of self-awareness, wonder at the infinitude of time, wonder that there should be anything at all. Wonder in turn gives rise to a kind of natural puzzlement: How can mind and body interact? How is it possible that there can be free will in a world governed by natural laws? How can moral judgments be shown to be true?

Philosophical perplexity about such things is a familiar and unavoidable phenomenon. College students who have experienced it and taken it seriously are, in a way, philosophers already, well before they come in contact with the theories and arguments of specialists. The good philosophy teacher, therefore, will not present his subject as some esoteric discipline unrelated to ordinary interests. Instead he will appeal directly to the concerns that already agitate the student, the same concerns that agitated Socrates and his companions and serious thinkers ever since.

It is impossible to be a good teacher of philosophy, however, without being a genuine philosopher oneself. Authors in the Dickenson Series in Philosophy are no exceptions to this rule. In many cases their textbooks are original studies of problems and systems of philosophy, with their own views boldly expressed and defended with argument. Their books are at once contributions to philosophy itself and models of original thinking to emulate and criticize.

That equally competent philosophers often disagree with one another is a fact to be exploited, not concealed. Dickenson anthologies bring together essays by authors of widely differing outlook. This diversity is compounded by juxtaposition, wherever possible, of classical essays with leading contemporary materials. The student who is shopping for a world outlook of his own has a large and representative selection to choose among, and the chronological arrangements, as well as the editor's introduction, can often give him a sense of historical development. Some Dickenson anthologies treat a single group of interconnected problems. Others are broader, dealing with a whole branch of philosophy, or representative problems from various branches of philosophy. In both types of collections, essays with opposed views on precisely the same questions are included to illustrate the argumentative give and take which is the lifeblood of philosophy.

Joel Feinberg
Series Editor

PREFACE

The appearance early in 1975 of our book, *Philosophy of Law,* prompted the suggestion from many quarters that each part be published separately in paperback form for readers with a narrower range of interest. The selection of readings and cases in this volume introduces the many faces of responsibility that intrigue and baffle both lawyers and philosophers. The viewpoint is contemporary, though the puzzles are ancient. Limitations of space and a concern to avoid overly technical presentations have led us to omit some favorite pieces. What we have included we believe will convey to the reader the richness of the subject and a large measure of its excitement.

Joel Feinberg
Hyman Gross

RESPONSIBILITY

RESPONSIBILITY

Critical judgments about what people do occupy a very large place in our daily life. Philosophers want to make sure that these judgments are valid, and so seek principles under which the judgments may in turn themselves be criticized. There are urgent practical reasons for making sure that our criticism of conduct is sound. We live our lives in a community of persons each of whom pursues his own interests, yet each is required to respect the interests of others in order to make possible the benefits of life in a civilized society. Since disinterested benevolence is not a regular feature of social life, people must be encouraged to avoid harming others as they seek their own ends. When harm is done, it is important that acceptable remedies be applied to undo the harm as much as possible. It is also important to take steps that will reduce the likelihood of harm being done in the future. This requires holding to account those (and only those) who properly are accountable when something untoward occurs. It is a matter of some importance also that those (and only those) who are entitled to recognition for good works receive it, so that encouragement of socially valuable activities is provided. What we need, then, are ways of criticizing conduct that are rational and fair. Theoretical work concerned with responsibility seeks to increase our understanding of our critical practices, and through better understanding to make our critical conclusions more reasonable and just.

Legal theory is nowhere more generously endowed with philosophical substance than in those parts that address questions of responsibility. It is also true that the law offers more promising material than any other human endeavor to the philosopher who seeks to develop a theory of responsibility. This happy coincidence makes the subjects sampled in this part of the volume preeminent among concerns of legal philosophy. It is the criminal law that presents the most philosophically important questions, for a just system of criminal liability requires as a foundation principles of responsibility that are just. Civil liability, and especially the law of torts, also poses many similar questions under such textbook headings as fault, negligence, causation, and strict liability. Regarding criminal liability, we want to know when punishment is warranted. Responsibility of the accused is always the first (and sometimes the only) consideration in deciding that. In considering civil liability, we want to know when a loss suffered by one person is to be made up by another; and that often (though not always) involves issues of responsibility, sometimes to the exclusion of all other questions.

"A Plea for Excuses," which appeared in the 1950s, is one of a small number of pieces by J. L. Austin to be published in his lifetime. A leading figure in modern Oxford philosophy, Professor Austin here not only illuminates the method of linguistic philosophical investigation that is so prominent in much of modern Anglo-American philosophy, but also shows how an understanding of the important questions of responsibility at the intersection of law and moral philosophy is to be advanced by it. The small-scale, low-level questions are the rewarding ones, and one must be prepared, in Austin's work, not for global theories employing the grand concepts but rather for an uncovering of those innumerable and subtle differences in the details that together present a picture of human intelligence at work passing judgment on human actions. Professor Austin makes clear how extensive is the law's involvement in this critical practice—indeed the very lives of accused persons often turn on such judgments. While legal cases provide an endless supply of specimens for philosophical dissection, each in some respect different from any other, there are some caveats which Austin notes. Both philosophers and legal theorists should beware of sterile legal jargon and barren appeals to naked legal authority. The utterances of judges and legislatures not uncommonly contain appalling misuses of crucial terms (which Austin illustrates with the case of *Regina v. Finney*); or even worse, they contain faulty attempts at theory which then serve to mislead those who rely on the authority of what is said in deciding subsequent cases.

Even the little that has been said about responsibility so far will likely have created an impression in the reader's mind that the very subject of the discussion is not entirely clear. Just what is it that those who speak of responsibility are speaking of? H. L. A. Hart distinguishes the separate though related ideas concerning responsibility that are marked by different forms of expression and different contexts. There are four major categories, and within them a considerable number of important distinctions. As this sorting of expressions makes clear, much in critical practice and in its theory depends upon recognizing differences among expressions that on their face appear alike. This reminds us of J. L. Austin's observation that "words are our tools, and, as a minimum, we should use clean tools: we should know what we mean and what we do not, and must forearm ourselves against the traps that language sets us." Even more important, through work like Professor Hart's we become clear about the word and as a result of that learn about responsibility itself. Again Austin put the point sharply. "When we examine what we should say when, what words we should use in what situations, we are looking again not *merely* at words (or 'meanings,' whatever they may be) but also at the realities we use the words to talk about: we are using a sharpened awareness of words to sharpen our perception of, though not as final arbiter of, the phenomena." One may profitably consider here what the "final arbiter" is, with reference to responsibility as it is dealt with in Hart's analysis. If one wishes to understand what responsibility is, is there anything further that must be understood after one has exhaustively analyzed characteristic correct uses of the term? The value of Professor Hart's analysis is apparent to anyone who has experienced the confusion of responsibility and liability that permeates legal literature. Setting inappropriate requirements of responsibility for some legal liability, and imposing legal liability on some inappropriate occasions of responsibility, have both frequently resulted from just such confusion.

In ordinary life or in legal proceedings, whenever we assert that a person is responsible for some harm, we may be challenged on grounds of causation. It often counts conclusively against responsibility that what was done by the accused did not cause the unhappy event for which we wish to hold him liable. Yet clear as that is, there is hardly a more difficult task for the theorist than that of spelling out principles which determine in any given case whether the act was or was not the cause of the harm. At the heart of the difficulty is understanding what we *mean* by a cause when the cause is an act. Formidable difficulties about causation arise when general accounts of the relations among events of the physical world are attempted, and these difficulties are often imported into the special cause accounting that issues of personal responsibility call for. But should they be? Causation in a theory of responsibility may be very different in important respects from causation in a theory of scientific explanation or in metaphysics. Many things which are singled out as counting for or against the causal status of one event in relation to another seem not really to matter, as it turns out, when we are talking about *acts* (as acts) and their consequences. Who can deny that in some sense an ancestor's act of reproduction was a cause of the death of the person that his descendent murdered, yet who would assert that the act of reproduction caused the death? Even more revealing, perhaps, is the fact that *doing* harm and *causing* harm are quite different notions, yet an act which is the *doing* surely is in some other more general sense a cause of the harm, every bit as much a cause as another act which is spoken of as *causing* it. This strongly suggests that there is indeed something special about conceiving acts as causes, quite unlike conceiving viruses or volcanoes as causes.

Professor Hart and his Oxford colleague, A. M. Honoré, undertake to clarify causation as it bears on questions of responsibility in the law. In the first part of this selection from their book *Causation in the Law,* they consider the similarity in the concept of causation to be found in law and in morality. This can be accounted for by the common concern of both law and morality to ascertain responsibility. In this part they also point out certain differences, not in the very concept, but in the rules that are used by both law and morality to decide whether an act truly caused a harm. Considerations of legal policy require that the rules the law adopts be suited to the purposes the law must serve, and it is this that accounts for the difference. In the second and larger portion of this selection, the authors take up the master problem of when (ignoring such special restrictions) the consequences of an act can rightly be said to have been caused by it.

Three sorts of problematic cases are analyzed. All of them deal with intervening or supervening events but for which the harm would not have occurred. If what was done would not have resulted in the harm but for something subsequent which was quite usual, the subsequent event does not deprive the act of its causal status. If, however, there is an intervening voluntary act (subject to two major exceptions and certain qualifications), that deprives the earlier act of its causal status. Finally, in cases in which the harm is a result of mere coincidence of the consequence of the act and something else, the act is deprived of its causal status (though once again there is an important exception). After reading this selection, it seems appropriate to pose again and extend the question raised earlier. Is it the concept of causation one finds useful in explaining the physical world that is really germane to issues of responsibility? Have these authors been unduly influenced at any point by the problem of physical causation? And what, in any case, is it really that makes responsibility depend in part on whether one's act was the cause of the harm?

Robert E. Keeton shifts attention to risks in deciding whether or not an act caused harm. In "The Basic Rule of Legal Cause in Negligence Cases," Professor Keeton expounds a risk rule of causation which draws on the insight that causation issues in the law resolve themselves into issues about whether in acting one ought to have regard for some possible harm. The insight is not without its difficulties, however. One may wonder whether the modest claim that A is the cause of harm B has not been unduly enlarged in risk theory. It is not normally thought to be an objection to such a claim that act A was not negligent, for one who causes harm need not be at fault in doing so. Risk theory, however, seems to suggest the contrary. It suggests that when harm occurs and certain conduct caused it, the conduct is the cause of the harm because it created a risk of the harm and the harm was one that falls within the hazards of what was done. But creating a risk of the sort of harm that falls within the risks of what one is doing is (at the least) negligence. The challenge presented by risk analysis, then, is to separate its insight about risk from unwarranted implications concerning culpability.

The New York Times story reporting the tragedy of the Ault family presents a case in which the parents of the victim cannot be held liable for causing their daughter's death, even though they are the authors of the events that resulted in it. The story provides an opportunity for comparative testing of the voluntary intervention principle of Hart and Honoré, and the risk theory analysis of Keeton to see which provides the more illuminating account.

In the Palsgraf case, the Court's opinion by Judge Cardozo contains the following statement: "The law of causation, remote or proximate, is thus foreign to the case before us." Few on any court in the United States have been Cardozo's equal as a theorist of the law; yet in spite of his statement, this case has enjoyed the greatest popularity in American law schools as a case presenting the causation issue in torts. It therefore is incumbent on one who reads the case to ask first whether causation is indeed the issue. If the answer accords with the prevailing view, the next questions must be (1) what criteria are invoked in the opinions of the two judges to decide that issue (under whatever rubric they may place it); (2) what principle of causation, if any, can be extracted from the opinions; and (3) what could Judge Cardozo have meant?

Issues of causation raise questions about the antecedents of untoward events that occur. Problems of attempts resemble these issues (though the similarity is often not recognized by theorists). In their own way, attempts also raise questions of what harm is expectable. When there is a criminal attempt but not the completed crime, there has been conduct for which criminal liability is prescribed; but the harm which is also required for the completed crime has not occurred. There has been far less philosophical interest in attempts than in causation, the only question at all widely discussed among philosophers being whether (or why) it is just to punish attempts less severely than completed crimes. But legal theorists have been faced with philosophically rich problems of two sorts. One is the matter of distinguishing an attempt from what is usually called "mere preparation," so that activity far enough advanced for criminal liability may be distinguished from something less than that. The other problem, even more perplexing and offering even greater rewards for the theory of responsibility, is whether the impossibility of the harm occurring (whatever that might mean) is a bar to liability for attempt. Both of these issues, like causation questions, really require judgments about whether the harm of the completed crime is expectable given the conduct engaged in by the accused. Graham Hughes, in the selection entitled "Attempting the Impossible," examines the attempt defense that is based on a claim that the completed crime was impossible. His starting point is the orthodox distinction between a valid defense of legal impossibility and an invalid one of factual impossibility. Leading cases in the literature, both actual and imaginary, are analyzed and compared to extract a better principle, and a dialogue is presented that illustrates the difficulties. Professor Hughes's conclusions are based mainly on rather special considerations of legal policy and have not been included in the selection here. Though such policy considerations may ultimately dictate legal rules that are not pure reflections of principles of responsibility, it is always important first to get those principles as clear as one can, and the portions of the article included here provide much material for that endeavor.

"He is to blame" or "it is his fault" are judgments that often express the point of ascertaining responsibility. There is indeed a common emphatic sense of "he is responsible" that is equivalent to "he is to blame," and the subordinate considerations which lead to that are then obscured by an expression of the ultimate conclusion. In the nonlegal affairs of life we often want to fix blame when something bad has happened, either to fix the stigmata and apply for the remedies that social conventions warrant, or at least to set the record straight for future dealings. In legal contexts, both civil and criminal, fixing blame, while far from the whole matter, is nevertheless of the greatest importance in determining liability. In "Sua Culpa" Joel Feinberg separates and examines the different threads which compose a claim that a harm *is his fault.* The claim is first contrasted with two other fault-imputing expressions, *having a fault* and *being at fault.* One's act is at fault when the harm is one's fault; but there are two other conditions that must be satisfied. The act must be the cause of the harm; and the aspect of it that was faulty must be one of the aspects in virtue of which the act was the cause of the harm. The difficulties of the causal requirement again obtrude themselves, and the author endeavors to define the requirement in the face of them. Criteria for a cause are developed, and the reader may wish to consider what reason there is for an act to meet these criteria in order for blame to be fixed for that act. Finally, the suggestion that "his fault" can be dispensed with as a requirement for tort liability is assessed morally.

Professors Robert E. Keeton and Jeffrey O'Connell are the pioneer theorists and architects of no-fault automobile insurance in the United States, and in "Why Shift Loss?," excerpted from their book *Basic Protection for the Traffic Victim,* they consider reasons that justify shifting loss from the victim to someone else. In doing so, they criticize the two most prominent standing objections to no-fault insurance—that it disregards moral considerations by overlooking blameworthiness, and that it removes the deterrent to careless driving. The reader may wish to consider what moral considerations survive when the burden of liability is in any event placed on an insurance company, and whether there is a conflict between principles of responsibility and principles of justice (including principles supporting a socially desirable wide distribution of risk).

So far, criticism of the fault requirement has questioned whether it is needed in order to do justice. Professor Guido Calabresi carries the attack even further by claiming that it interferes with a fairer system and is a positive source of injustice in tort liability. In the selection from his book *The Cost of Accidents* entitled "The Fairness of the Fault System," the victims and those who injure them are conceived not in a bilateral relation defined by single occasions of injury, but rather in a multilateral web of those who cause and those who suffer harm in a world of accidents. Calabresi's points are not fully developed here, but the reader may wish to spell them out himself and to consider whether (or in what ways) the system the author advocates is more just as a system of accident compensation.

There has also been philosophically important debate about *criminal* liability for negligence, though in this situation it is said by critics that (mere) fault, far from being unnecessary, is not enough. Many theorists in England and America (though not on the Continent) have argued that on grounds of expediency and of justice it is wrong to punish those who did not mean to do harm, or at least were not aware of the harm that might result when they acted. In his essay "Negligence, *Mens Rea* and Criminal Responsibility," H. L. A. Hart makes clear what it is that may be said to justify criminal liability for negligence and shows how common misconceptions in theorizing are responsible for a contrary view. In addition to clarifying the notion of negligence, Professor Hart's discussion advances our understanding of how the criminal law is concerned with conduct when responsibility is at issue.

It may seem paradoxical that punishment for the relatively slight fault of negligence (even gross negligence) has excited more concern among lawyers than has punishment for totally faultless acts. This may be because of the relatively mild punishment and absence of criminal stigma that is usual when the offense is one requiring no fault—a sort of publicly accountable tort that hardly touches the perpetrator's respectability, and does not call for the curtailment of his liberty. Sometimes, however, harsher consequences await the blameless, and then instead of a petty though odious penalty in the interest of public welfare, we have (unless there is good reason for it) a cruel injustice. Liability without fault is most often referred to as "strict liability," and discussions of it in criminal law theory are almost always about when and why it is justified, not whether it ever is. In the selection "Strict Liability," excerpted from Professor Herbert Packer's book *The Limits of the Criminal Sanction*, strict liability is regarded as the preclusion of an excuse of mistake when offered as a defense to a criminal accusation. One must consider carefully whether in the cases discussed the accused is indeed without fault. If he turns out not to be without fault in what he did, there is still the important question whether it is *fair* to impose liability, all things considered. (Lawyers and public officials, as well as philosophers, will also want to ask whether it is prudent as a matter of public policy to do so.)

Liability when harm is not really "his fault" (as "his fault" is explicated in "Sua Culpa") is examined by Joel Feinberg in "Collective Responsibility." Strict liability, both civil and criminal, is explained according to the conventional rationale, and the various ways in which vicarious liability may arise are made clear, as are its proper limits. Collective responsibility is the subject that then occupies the remainder of the essay. Consideration is given first to a form of strict liability deriving from group solidarity. Then there is analysis of the several ways that the fault principles may result in liability for individuals and groups through mediating principles of distribution and collection when the party upon whom liability is imposed would not be liable according to fault principles alone.

One variety of collective responsibility discussed by Feinberg is the responsibility borne by all members of a group who could have and should have acted to save someone in distress but failed to do so. This suggests the more basic problem of when anyone is responsible for failing to act as a "volunteer" (as lawyers put it) or as a "Good Samaritan" (as moralists and laymen would characterize it). On one side, against responsibility, there are purported rights to mind one's own business, if one so chooses, and to avoid any risks—whether of legal liability for an unfortunate outcome, or of harm to oneself in the course of the intervention. In favor of some responsibility, it is argued that indifference to the plight of others in some situations is a willful disregard which is of such immoral proportions that the law must take notice. The argument against responsibility, no matter what, is obviously a losing one in a moral forum, for clearly there are sometimes moral duties of rescue. The issue, then, is whether moral duties ought ever to be recognized as legal duties, the breach of which is grounds for civil or even criminal liability. "Law, Morals, and Rescue" by A. M. Honoré takes up that question. There are subsidiary issues here which the author takes up first: What is required for there to be a moral duty of this sort that is recognized generally in the community? How shall we distinguish between moral duties and moral ideals? When is someone truly a "volunteer" rather than a person who has a duty which the law recognizes on other grounds? What are the limits to be imposed on officious intermeddling so that professed Good Samaritanism does not become an excuse for interference with privacy and self–determination? What claims for compensation may the rescuer assert, and against whom? All these are matters preliminary to the major question that the author then addresses: What policy reasons are there for imposing a legal duty of rescue that at bottom is only the enforcement of a moral duty?

The Good Samaritan may act to rescue someone apparently in distress so that he not only discharges a moral duty, but even more, acts beyond the call of duty as a moral hero. If such a person is then punished as a criminal, we might at first suspect the law has gone mad. But in fact the case of such a moral hero can be a close one, as the New York case of *People v. Young* makes clear. Included here in their entirety are the courts' opinions as well as the dissenting opinions in both the Appellate Division of the Supreme Court and then in the state's highest court, the Court of Appeals. The issues are subtle and challenging, and the reader will be well repaid if he pursues them. As it turned out, the defendant in this case was mistaken about the need for rescue when he saw a youth on the street being forced against his will to accompany two older men. Unknown to the defendant, the two men were detectives making an arrest. His attack upon the man in an attempt to aid the youth resulted in his being charged with criminal assault. As the opinions make clear, no outright justification is possible under New York law, since for that the defendant would have to be bound to protect the one he sought to help (which he was not); or—in a more strictly Good Samaritan vein—would have to have been attempting to prevent an offense against the youth (which was not constituted by the force employed in making a lawful arrest). It is the *mistake* which receives the greatest attention in these opinions. If it is reasonable it is an excuse that should exculpate, so runs the argument on one side. But whether that argument prevails depends on just what intent is legally necessary for the assault, for a mistake has relevance only if the law requires for liability that the thing done by mistake be done intentionally. Does the law, then, require that the accused intentionally do wrong, or only that he do intentionally what happens to be wrong? It seems on all sides to be agreed that the defendant here did the latter but not the former. Disagreement in the opinions is about what the law requires for liability. But those who hold that his mistake exonerates the defendant appear at times to go even further. There is some suggestion that even if the law only requires that he do intentionally what happens to be wrong, the attack is not wrong by virtue of the circumstances; the intimation is that there is a kind of subsidiary justification when a reasonable rescue is made, that it is a worthy endeavor which removes the curse of offensiveness from the otherwise offensive physical contacts. At this point a policy decision is called for, and the interest in safeguarding police from the perils of unwarranted interference is weighed against the countervailing interest of citizens being free to rescue each other from harm.

Concern about justice has so far dominated the discussions of responsibility in a criminal context. It is concern that criminal liability be deserved. But there is another perspective that is radically different, one in which the criminal law appears as an instrument of crime prevention. Convictions, in this view, are for the purpose of being able to subject to remedial treatment those who bring about the socially significant harms that concern the criminal law. Whether a person is responsible or not is then irrelevant (at least when "responsible" means "to blame"). Indeed the very issue of responsibility is a hindrance to the proper functioning of the system of correction that the criminal law serves, for it allows those in need of correction to avoid it by showing that with respect to matters that are significant only for moral judgments they are innocent. Lady Barbara Wootton in the excerpts from her book *Crime and the Criminal Law* advocates such a new perspective and declares that "the concept of responsibility should be allowed to wither away." That concept is attacked in the selection on two fronts. First there is the matter of *mens rea,* a term of art in criminal law theory that lends itself all too readily to gross abuse. Literally it means "culprit" or "guilty" mind, but that tells us nothing about its proper use. As Professor Hart's discussion in "Negligence, *Mens Rea,* and Criminal Responsibility" makes clear, it is a compendious expression characteristically used in denials of such excuses as *mistake* or *accident.* Lady Wootton adopts an interpretation suggested by its literal meaning, however, so that questions of *mens rea* become "questions of motivation," and she then proceeds to criticize the requirement of *mens rea* for criminal liability as undesirable moralism that interferes with the objectives of a forward-looking criminal process. In advocating elimination of the requirement of *mens rea* (to what extent exactly is not clear), she proposes very extensive strict criminal liability. And instead of degrees of culpability according to intention which now separate the more and the less serious forms of each kind of crime, she seems to believe that "the criterion of gravity" of an offense is "the amount of social damage which a crime causes."

Mental abnormality is the second front on which Lady Wootton attacks responsibility. Her discussion points out that unfortunate, even absurd, results may be expected from the way existing defenses of mental abnormality are given effect, and this is especially so in view of present institutional arrangements. Several considerations do indeed argue for reform. One is that there be deprivation of liberty (in whatever form) only when either criminal liability or dangerousness of the person warrants it. Another is that those who are sick (whether criminals or not) be given the care and treatment that humanity requires. Finally, when a person is truly dangerous and without ability to control himself, whether subject to criminal liability for his conduct or not, he is not to be left free to harm others. One may recognize that reform is urgently needed since, as things now stand, these considerations are often not respected. But the elimination from proceedings of concern about whether the accused had capacity to conform his conduct to law may seem to many not only an unnecessary encroachment on justice, but an encouragement of opportunities for violation of rights that are among the most basic a person has. Indeed, the concluding sentence of this selection in which Lady Wootton speaks of "places of safety" for offenders cannot help but sound ominous in view of what has more recently come to be known as "Clockwork Orange" correctional regimes. Further discussion of these matters is to be found in selections in the latter portion of Part Five of this volume.

Professor Hart in "Changing Conceptions of Responsibility" takes up the challenge Lady Wootton has presented. He scrutinizes the consequences of eliminating responsibility from the requirements for criminal conviction, particularly with reference to mental abnormality. Little need be said by way of introduction, for the issue is joined perfectly and the argument pursued with exemplary clarity and order. It does seem desirable, however, to note one point concerning Professor Hart's use here of the troublesome expression *mens rea.* It is a matter of some dispute among theorists whether there is *mens rea* in crimes of negligence, and also whether there can be *mens rea* when there is mental abnormality sufficient to exonerate. The first question is really about what conventions govern the use of a jargon term in criminal law theory. The second question, while it might also be construed that way, is better understood as an inquiry concerning certain matters of fact. As Professor Hart has made abundantly clear in other writings, in its characteristic employment the term is used to preclude excuses claiming that an act was done unintentionally, through assertions that there was *mens rea.* But many persons (though indeed not all) who are legally insane can act fully as intentionally as perfectly normal persons. The relevant abnormality of such a person would, for example, consist of psychotic notions of danger to himself or psychotic misconceptions of the justifiability of the harm he does. It would seem then that while *mens rea* requirements are fully satisfied, there is still a mental abnormality defense available quite independently based on a lack of capacity to choose to do otherwise. In Professor Hart's discussion here, however, this distinction among excuses seems not to be observed.

In "Mental Abnormality as a Criminal Excuse," Hyman Gross has endeavored to make clear the full range of exculpatory claims that look to mental abnormality and to discover what good reasons there are in principle for recognizing them as defenses in a criminal prosecution. Particular attention is given to the defense of insanity in the various versions in which that defense has been developed, and there is an assessment of each version in the light of more general concerns about responsibility as a condition of criminal liability.

The most controversial among the varieties of insanity defense in the United States has been the so-called Durham rule. In 1954, in the case of *Durham v. United States,* the Federal Court of Appeals for the District of Columbia adopted as a new insanity defense for that jurisdiction the rule that an unlawful act that was the product of mental disease or defect does not subject the perpetrator to criminal liability. Such a defense had in essence first been recognized in 1870 in New Hampshire, and two American jurisdictions other than the District of Columbia have also adopted it. In using it, two principal difficulties arise. The more obvious one is how to tell when conduct is the "product" of the abnormal condition. This raises both conceptual issues about just what it takes to be a "product" in the relevant sense, and factual questions about whether what the accused did was or was not a product (in the relevant sense) of his abnormal state. A less obvious but even more basic question is why the product of any mental disease or defect should not be a basis of criminal liability. No hint is given about what grounds there are in considerations of legal policy, justice, humanity, or anything else that might justify an excuse each and every time mental abnormality "produces" the criminal product.

In 1972, the *Durham* rule was overruled in *United States v. Brawner.* The Court's opinion is an ambitious attempt to consider the problems of practice and theory in light of the experience of the intervening years, and to provide instructions for properly implementing the new rule of the Model Penal Code (the ALI rule). The excerpts from the Court's opinion that are included here put the recurring issues in sharp focus. The last portion of these excerpts deals with questions of how culpability may be affected by mental abnormality other than by ways recognized in an insanity defense.

H. G.

J. L. AUSTIN

A Plea for Excuses*

The subject of this paper, *Excuses,* is one not to be treated, but only to be introduced, within such limits. It is, or might be, the name of a whole branch, even a ramiculated branch, of philosophy, or at least of one fashion of philosophy. I shall try, therefore, first to state *what* the subject is, *why* it is worth studying, and *how* it may be studied, all this at a regrettably lofty level: and then I shall illustrate, in more congenial but desultory detail, some of the methods to be used, together with their limitations, and some of the unexpected results to be expected and lessons to be learned. Much, of course, of the amusement, and of the instruction, comes in drawing the coverts of the microglot, in hounding down the minutiae, and to this I can do no more here than incite you. But I owe it to the subject to say, that it has long afforded me what philosophy is so often thought, and made, barren of—the fun of discovery, the pleasures of cooperation, and the satisfaction of reaching agreement.

What, then, is the subject? I am here using the word 'excuses' *for a title,* but it would be unwise to freeze too fast to this one noun and its partner verb: indeed for some time I used to use 'extenuation' instead. Still, on the whole 'excuses' is probably the most central and embracing term in the field, although this includes others of importance —'plea', 'defence', 'justification', and so on. When, then, do we 'excuse' conduct, our own or somebody else's? When are 'excuses' proffered?

In general, the situation is one where someone is *accused* of having done something, or (if that will keep it any cleaner) where someone is *said* to have done something which is bad, wrong, inept, unwelcome, or in some other of the numerous possible ways untoward. Thereupon he, or someone on his behalf, will try to defend his conduct or to get him out of it.

One way of going about this is to admit flatly that he, X, did do that very thing, A, but to argue that it was a good thing, or the right or sensible thing, or a permissible thing to do, either in general or at least in the special circumstances of the occasion. To take this line is to *justify* the action, to give reasons for doing it: not to say, to brazen it out, to glory in it, or the like.

A different way of going about it is to admit that it wasn't a good thing to have done, but to argue that it is not quite fair or correct to say *baldly* 'X did A'. We may say it isn't fair just to say X did it; perhaps he was under somebody's influence, or was nudged. Or, it isn't fair to say baldly he *did* A; it may have been partly accidental, or an unintentional slip. Or, it isn't fair to say he did simply A—he was really doing something quite different and A was only incidental, or he was looking at the whole thing quite differently. Naturally these arguments can be combined or overlap or run into each other.

In the one defence, briefly, we accept responsibility but deny that it was bad; in the other, we admit that it was bad but don't accept full, or even any, responsibility.

By and large, justifications can be kept distinct from excuses, and I shall not be so anxious to talk about them because they have enjoyed more than their fair share of philosophical attention. But the two certainly can be confused, and can *seem* to go very near to each other, even if they do not perhaps actually do so. You dropped the tea-tray: Certainly, but an emotional storm was about to break out: or, Yes, but there was a wasp. In each case the defence, very soundly, insists on a fuller description of the event in its context; but the first is a justification, the second an excuse. Again, if

*From *Aristotelian Society Proceedings,* LVII (1956–57), pp. 1–30. Reprinted by courtesy of the Editor of the Aristotelian Society and Mrs. J. Austin, c 1957, The Aristotelian Society and Mrs. Jean Austin. Footnotes have been renumbered.

the objection is to the use of such a dyslogistic verb as 'murdered', this may be on the ground that the killing was done in battle (justification) or on the ground that it was only accidental if reckless (excuse). It is arguable that we do not use the terms justification and excuse as carefully as we might; a miscellany of even less clear terms, such as 'extenuation', 'palliation', 'mitigation', hovers uneasily between partial justification and partial excuse; and when we plead, say, provocation, there is geniune uncertainty or ambiguity as to what we mean—is he partly responsible, because he roused a violent impulse or passion in me, so that it wasn't truly or merely me acting 'of my own accord' (excuse)? Or is it rather that, he having done me such injury, I was entitled to retaliate (justification)? Such doubts merely make it the more urgent to clear up the usage of these various terms. But that the defences I have for convenience labelled 'justification' and 'excuse' are in principle distinct can scarcely be doubted.

This then is the sort of situation we have to consider under 'excuses'. I will only further point out how very wide a field it covers. We have, of course, to bring in the opposite numbers of excuses—the expressions that *aggravate*, such as 'deliberately', 'on purpose' and so on, if only for the reason that an excuse often takes the form of a rebuttal of one of these. But we have also to bring in a large number of expressions which at first blush look not so much like excuses as like accusations—'clumsiness', 'tactlessness', 'thoughtlessness', and the like. Because it has always to be remembered that few excuses get us out of it *completely:* the average excuse, in a poor situation, gets us only out of the fire into the frying pan—but still, of course, any frying pan in a fire. If I have broken your dish or your romance, maybe the best defence I can find will be clumsiness.

Why, if this is what 'excuses' are, should we trouble to investigate them? It might be thought reason enough that their production has always bulked so large among human activities. But to moral philosophy in particular, a study of them will contribute in special ways, both positively towards the development of a cautious, latter-day version of conduct, and negatively towards the correction of older and hastier theories.

In ethics we study, I suppose, the good and the bad, the right and the wrong, and this must be for the most part in some connexion with conduct or the doing of actions. Yet before we consider what actions are good or bad, right or wrong, it is proper to consider first what is meant by, and what not, and what is included under, and what not, the expression 'doing an action' or 'doing something'. These are expressions still too little examined on their own account and merits, just as the general notion of 'saying something' is still too lightly passed over in logic. There is indeed a vague and comforting idea in the background that, after all, in the last analysis, doing an action must come down to the making of physical movements with parts of the body; but this is about as true as that saying something must, in the last analysis, come down to making movements of the tongue.

The beginning of sense, not to say wisdom, is to realize that 'doing an action', as used in philosophy,[1] is a highly abstract expression—it is a stand-in used in the place of any (or almost any?) verb with a personal subject, in the same sort of way that 'thing' is a stand-in for any (or when we remember, almost any) noun substantive, and 'quality' a stand-in for the adjective. Nobody, to be sure, relies on such dummies quite implicitly quite indefinitely. Yet notoriously it is possible to arrive at, or to derive the idea for, an over-simplified metaphysics from the obsession with 'things' and their 'qualities.' In a similar way, less commonly recognized even in these semisophisticated times, we fall for the myth of the verb. We treat the expression 'doing an action' no longer as a stand-in for a verb with a personal subject, as which it has no doubt some uses, and might have more if the range of verbs were not left unspecified, but as a self-explanatory, ground-level description, one which brings adequately into the open the essential features of everything that comes, by simple inspection, under it. We scarcely notice even the most patent exceptions or difficulties (is to think something, or to say something, or to try to do something, to do an action?), any more than we fret, in the *ivresse des grandes profondeurs,* as to whether flames are things or events. So we come easily to think of our behaviour over any time, and of a life as a whole, as consisting in doing now action A, next action B, then action C, and so on, just as elsewhere we come to think of the world as consisting of this, that and the other substance or material thing, each with its properties. All 'actions' are, as actions (meaning what?), equal, composing a quarrel with striking a match, winning a war with sneezing: worse still, we assimilate them one and all to the supposedly most obvious and easy cases, such as posting letters or moving fingers, just as we assimilate all 'things' to horses or beds.

If we are to continue to use this expression in sober philosophy, we need to ask such questions as: Is to sneeze to do an action? Or is to breathe, or to see, or to checkmate, or each one of countless others? In short, for what range of verbs, as used on what occasions, is 'doing an action' a stand-in? What have they in common, and what do those excluded severally lack? Again we need to ask how we decide what is the correct name for 'the' action that somebody did—and what, indeed, are the rules for the use of 'the' action, 'an' action, 'one' action, a 'part' or 'phase' of an action and the like. Further, we need to realize that even the 'simplest' named actions are not so simple—certainly are not the mere makings of physical movements, and to ask what more, then, comes in (intentions? conventions?) and what does not (motives?), and what is the detail of the complicated internal machinery we use in 'acting'—the receipt of intelligence, the appreciation of the situation, the invocation of principles, the planning, the control of execution and the rest.

In two main ways the study of excuses can throw light on these fundamental matters. First, to examine excuses is to examine cases where there has been some abnormality or failure: and as so often, the abnormal will throw light on the normal, will help us to penetrate the blinding veil of case and obviousness that hides the mechanisms of the natural successful act. It rapidly becomes plain that the breakdowns signalized by the various excuses are of radically different kinds, affecting different parts or stages of the machinery, which the excuses consequently pick out and sort out for us. Further, it emerges that not *every* slip-up occurs in connexion with *everything* that could be called an 'action', that not every excuse is apt with every verb—far indeed from it: and this provides us with one means of introducing some classification into the vast miscellany of 'actions'. If we classify them according to the particular selection of breakdowns to which each is liable, this should assign them their places in some family group or groups of actions,

or in some model of the machinery of acting.

In this sort of way, the philosophical study of conduct can get off to a positive fresh start. But by the way, and more negatively, a number of traditional cruces or mistakes in this field can be resolved or removed. First among these comes the problem of freedom. While it has been the tradition to present this as the 'positive' term requiring elucidation, there is little doubt that to say we acted 'freely' (in the philosopher's use, which is only faintly related to the everyday use) is to say only that we acted *not* unfreely, in one or another of the many heterogeneous ways of so acting (under duress, or what not). Like 'real', 'free' is only used to rule out the suggestion of some or all of its recognized antitheses. As 'truth' is not a name for a characteristic of assertions, so 'freedom' is not a name for a characteristic of actions, but the name of a dimension in which actions are assessed. In examining all the ways in which each action may not be free, that is, the cases in which it will not do to say simply 'X did A', we may hope to dispose of the problem of freedom. Aristotle has often been chidden for talking about excuses or pleas and overlooking 'the real problem'; in my own case, it was when I began to see the injustice of this charge that I first became interested in excuses.

There is much to be said for the view that, philosophical tradition apart, responsibility would be a better candidate for the role here assigned to freedom. If ordinary language is to be our guide, it is to evade responsibility, or full responsibility, that we most often make excuses, and I have used the word myself in this way above. But in fact 'responsibility' too seems not really apt in all cases: I do not exactly evade responsibility when I plead clumsiness or tactlessness, nor, often, when I plead that I only did it unwillingly or reluctantly, and still less if I plead that I had in the circumstances no choice: here I was constrained and have an excuse (or justification), yet may accept responsibility. It may be, then, that at least two key terms, freedom and responsibility, are needed: the relation between them is not clear, and it may be hoped that the investigation of excuses will contribute towards its clarification.[2]

So much, then, for ways in which the study of excuses may throw light on ethics. But there are also reasons why it is an attractive subject methodologically, at least if we are to proceed from 'ordinary language', that is, by examining *what we should say when,* and so why and what we should mean by it. Perhaps this method, at least as *one* philosophical method, scarcely requires justification at present—too evidently, there is gold in them thar hills: more opportune would be a warning about the care and thoroughness needed if it is not to fall into disrepute. I will, however, justify it very briefly.

First, words are our tools, and, as a minimum, we should use clean tools: we should know what we mean and what we do not, and we must forearm ourselves against the traps that language sets us. Secondly, words are not (except in their own little corner) facts or things: we need therefore to prise them off the world, to hold them apart from and against it, so that we can realize their inadequacies and arbitrariness, and can relook at the world without blinkers. Thirdly, and more hopefully, our common stock of words embodies all the distinctions men have found worth drawing, and the connexions they have found worth marking, in the lifetimes of many generations: these surely are likely to be more numerous, more sound, since they have stood up to the long test of the survival of the fittest, and more subtle, at least in all ordinary and reasonably practical matters, than any that you or I are likely to think up in our armchairs of an afternoon—the most favoured alternative method.

In view of the prevalence of the slogan 'ordinary language', and of such names as 'linguistic' or 'analytic' philosophy or 'the analysis of language', one thing needs specially emphasizing to counter misunderstandings. When we examine what we should say when, what words we should use in what situations, we are looking again not *merely* at words (or 'meanings', whatever they may be) but also at the realities we use the words to talk about: we are using a sharpened awareness of words to sharpen our perception of, though not as the final arbiter of, the phenomena. For this reason I think it might be better to use, for this way of doing philosophy, some less misleading name than those given above—for instance, 'linguistic phenomenology', only that is rather a mouthful.

Using, then, such a method, it is plainly preferable to investigate a field where ordinary language is rich and subtle, as it is in the pressingly practical matter of excuses, but certainly is not in the matter, say, of time. At the same time we should prefer a field which is not too much trodden into bogs or tracks by traditional philosophy, for in that case even 'ordinary' language will often have become infected with the jargon of extinct theories, and our own prejudices too, as the upholders or imbibers of theoretical views, will too readily, and often insensibly, engaged. Here too, excuses form an admirable topic; we can discuss at least clumsiness, or absence of mind, or inconsiderateness, even spontaneousness, without remembering what Kant thought, and so progress by degrees even to discussing deliberation without for once remembering Aristotle or self-control without Plato. Granted that our subject is, as already claimed for it, neighbouring, analogous or germane in some way to some notorious centre of philosophical trouble, then, with these two further requirements satisfied, we should be certain of what we are after: a good site for *field work* in philosophy. Here at last we should be able to unfreeze, to loosen up and get going on agreeing about discoveries, however small, and on agreeing about how to reach agreement.[3] How much it is to be wished that similar field work will soon be undertaken in, say, aesthetics; if only we could forget for a while about the beautiful and get down instead to the dainty and the dumpy.

There are, I know, or are supposed to be, snags in 'linguistic' philosophy, which those not very familiar with it find, sometimes not without glee or relief, daunting. But with snags as with nettles, the thing to do is to grasp them—and to climb above them. I will mention two in particular, over which the study of excuses may help to encourage us. The first is the snag of loose (or divergent or alternative) usage; and the second the crux of the last word. Do we all say the same, and only the same, things in the same situations? Don't usages differ? And, Why should what we all ordinarily say be the only or best or final way of putting it? Why should it even be true?

Well, people's usages do vary, and we do talk loosely, and we do say different things apparently indifferently. But first, not nearly as much as one would think. When we come down to cases, it transpires in the very great majority that what we had thought was our wanting to say different things of and in *the same* situation was really not so—we had simply imagined the situation *slightly* differently: which is all too easy to do, because of course no situation (and we are dealing with *imagined* situations) is ever 'completely' described. The more we imagine the situation in detail, with a background of story—and it is worth employing the most idiosyncratic or, sometimes, boring means to stimulate and to discipline our wretched imaginations—the less we find we disagree about what we should say. Nevertheless, *sometimes* we do ultimately disagree: sometimes we must allow a usage to be, though appalling, yet actual; sometimes we should genuinely use either or both of two different descriptions. But why should this daunt us? All that is happening is entirely explicable. If our usages disagree, then you use 'X' where I use 'Y', or more probably (and more intriguingly) your conceptual system is different from mine, though very likely it is at least equally consistent and serviceable: in short, we can find *why* we disagree —you choose to classify in one way, I in another. If the usage is loose, we can understand the temptation that leads to it, and the distinctions that it blurs: if there are 'alternative' descriptions, then the situation can be described or can be 'structured' in two ways, or perhaps it is one where, for current purposes, the two alternatives come down to the same. A disagreement as to what we should say is not to be shied off, but to be pounced upon; for the explanation of it can hardly fail to be illuminating. If we light on an electron that rotates the wrong way, that is a discovery, a portent to be followed up, not a reason for chucking physics; and by the same token, a genuinely loose or eccentric talker is a rare specimen to be prized.

As practice in learning to handle this bogey, in learning the essential *rubrics,* we could scarcely hope for a more promising exercise than the study of excuses. Here, surely, is just the sort of situation where people will say 'almost anything', because they are so flurried, or so anxious to get off. 'It was a mistake', 'It was an accident'—how readily these can *appear* indifferent, and even be used together. Yet, a story or two, and everybody will not merely agree that they are completely different, but even discover for himself what the difference is and what each means.[4]

Then, for the Last Word. Certainly ordinary language has no claim to be the last word, if there is such a thing. It embodies, indeed, something

better than the metaphysics of the Stone Age, namely, as was said, the inherited experience and acumen of many generations of men. But then, that acumen has been concentrated primarily upon the practical business of life. If a distinction works well for practical purposes in ordinary life (no mean feat, for even ordinary life is full of hard cases), then there is sure to be something in it, it will not mark nothing; yet this is likely enough to be not the best way of arranging things if our interests are more extensive or intellectual than the ordinary. And again, that experience has been derived only from the sources available to ordinary men throughout most of civilized history: it has not been fed from the resources of the microscope and its successors. And it must be added too, that superstitition and error and fantasy of all kinds do become incorporated in ordinary language and even sometimes stand up to the survival test (only, when they do, why should we not detect it?). Certainly, then, ordinary language is *not* the last word: in principle it can everywhere be supplemented and improved upon and superseded. Only remember, it *is* the *first* word.[5]

For this problem too the field of excuses is a fruitful one. Here is matter both contentious and practically important for everybody, so that ordinary language is on its toes: yet also, on its back it has long had a bigger flea to bite it, in the shape of the law, and both again have lately attracted the attentions of yet another, and at last a healthily growing, flea, in the shape of psychology. In the law a constant stream of actual cases, more novel and more tortuous than the mere imagination could contrive, are brought up *for decision*— that is, formulae for docketing them must somehow be found. Hence it is necessary first to be careful with, but also to be brutal with, to torture, to fake and to override, ordinary language: we cannot here evade or forget the whole affair. (In ordinary life we dismiss the puzzles that crop up about time, but we cannot do that indefinitely in physics). Psychology likewise produces novel cases, but it also produces new methods for bringing phenomena under observation and study; moreover, unlike the law, it has an unbiased interest in the totality of them and is unpressed for decision. Hence its own special and constant need to supplement, to revise and to supersede the classifications of both ordinary life and the law. We have, then, ample material for practice in learning to handle the bogey of the last word, however it should be handled.

Suppose, then, that we set out to investigate excuses, what are the methods and resources initially available? Our object is to imagine the varieties of situation in which we make excuses, and to examine the expressions used in making them. If we have a lively imagination, together perhaps with an ample experience of dereliction, we shall go far, only we need system: I do not know how many of you keep a list of the kinds of fool you make of yourselves. It is advisable to use systematic aids, of which there would appear to be three at least. I list them here in order of availability to the layman.

First we may use the dictionary—quite a concise one will do, but the use must be *thorough*. Two methods suggest themselves, both a little tedious, but repaying. One is to read the book through, listing all the words that seem relevant; this does not take as long as many suppose. The other is to start with a widish selection of obviously relevant terms, and to consult the dictionary under each; it will be found that, in the explanations of the various meanings of each, a surprising number of other terms occur, which are germane though of course not often synonymous. We then look up each of *these,* bringing in more for our bag from the 'definitions' given in each case; and when we have continued for a little, it will generally be found that the family circle begins to close, until ultimately it is complete and we come only upon repetitions. This method has the advantage of grouping the terms into convenient clusters—but of course a good deal will depend upon the comprehensiveness of our initial selection.

Working the dictionary, it is interesting to find that a high percentage of the terms connected with excuses prove to be *adverbs,* a type of word which has not enjoyed so large a share of the philosophical limelight as the noun, substantive or adjective, and the verb: this is natural because, as was said, the tenor of so many excuses is that I did it but only *in a way,* not just flatly like that —that is, the verb needs modifying. Besides adverbs, however, there are other words of all kinds, including numerous abstract nouns, 'misconception', 'accident', 'purpose', and the like, and a few verbs too, which often hold key positions for the grouping of excuses into classes at a high level

('couldn't help', 'didn't me
or again 'intend', and 'att
with the nouns another neg
is prominent, namely, prep
does it matter considerably
often of several, is being use
stantive, but further the prepositions deserve study on their own account. For the question suggests itself, Why are the nouns in one group governed by 'under', in another by 'on', in yet another by 'by', or 'through' or 'from' or 'for' or 'with', and so on? It will be disappointing if there prove to be no good reasons for such groupings.

Our second source book will naturally be the law. This will provide us with an immense miscellany of untoward cases, and also with a useful list of recognized pleas, together with a good deal of acute analysis of both. No one who tries this resource will long be in doubt, I think, that the common law, and in particular the law of tort, is the richest storehouse; crime and contract contribute some special additions of their own, but tort is altogether more comprehensive and more flexible. But even here, and still more with so old and hardened a branch of the law as crime, much caution is needed with the arguments of counsel and the dicta or decisions of judges: acute though these are, it has always to be remembered that, in legal cases—

(1) there is the overriding requirement that a decision be reached, and a relatively black or white decision—guilty or not guilty—for the plaintiff or for the defendant;

(2) there is the general requirement that the charge or action and the pleadings be brought under one or another of the heads and procedures that have come in the course of history to be accepted by the courts. These, though fairly numerous, are still few and stereotyped in comparison with the accusations and defences of daily life. Moreover contentions of many kinds are beneath the law, as too trivial, or outside it, as too purely moral—for example, inconsiderateness;

(3) there is the general requirement that we argue from and abide by precedents. The value of this in the law is unquestionable, but it can certainly lead to distortions of ordinary beliefs and expressions.

For such reasons as these, obviously closely connected and stemming from the nature and function of the law, practising lawyers and jurists are by no means so careful as they might be to give

nary expressions their ordinary mean-
applications. There is special pleading
evasion, stretching and strait-jacketing, be-
des the invention of technical terms, or technical senses for common terms. Nevertheless, it is
a perpetual and salutary surprise to discover how
much is to be learned from the law; and it is to
be added that if a distinction drawn is a sound
one, even though not yet recognized in law, a
lawyer can be relied upon to take note of it, for
it may be dangerous not to—if he does not, his
opponent may.

Finally, the third source book is psychology,
with which I include such studies as an-
thropology and animal behaviour. Here I speak
with even more trepidation than about the law.
But this at least is clear, that some varieties of
behaviour, some ways of acting or explanations of
the doing of actions, are here noticed and classified which have not been observed or named by
ordinary men and hallowed by ordinary language, though perhaps they often might have
been so if they had been of more practical importance. There is real danger in contempt for the
'jargon' of psychology, at least when it sets out to
supplement, and at least sometimes when it sets
out to supplant, the language of ordinary life.

With these sources, and with the aid of the
imagination, it will go hard if we cannot arrive at
the meanings of large numbers of expressions and
at the understanding and classification of large
numbers of 'actions'. Then we shall comprehend
clearly much that, before, we only made use of
ad hoc. Definition, I would add, explanatory definition, should stand high among our aims: it is
not enough to show how clever we are by showing
how obscure everything is. Clarity, too, I know,
has been said to be not enough; but perhaps it will
be time to go into that when we are within measurable distance of achieving clarity on some
matter.

So much for the cackle. It remains to make a
few remarks, not, I am afraid, in any very coherent order, about the types of significant result to
be obtained and the more general lessons to be
learned from the study of excuses.

1. *No modification without aberration.* When
it is stated that X did A, there is a temptation to
suppose that given some, indeed perhaps *any,*
expression modifying the verb we shall be entitled
to insert either it or its opposite or negation in our
statement: that is, we shall be entitled to ask,
typically, 'Did X do A Mly or not Mly? (for
example, 'Did X murder Y voluntarily or involuntarily?'), and to answer one or the other. Or as
a minimum it is supposed that if X did A there
must be at *least one* modifying expression that we
could, justifiably and informatively, insert with
the verb. In the great majority of cases of the use
of the great majority of verbs ('murder' perhaps
is not one of the majority) such suppositions are
quite unjustified. The natural economy of language dictates that for the *standard* case covered
by any normal verb—not, perhaps, a verb of
omen such as 'murder', but a verb like 'eat' or
'kick' or 'croquet'—no modifying expression is
required or even permissible. Only if we do the
action named in some *special* way or circumstances, different from those in which such an act
is naturally done (and of course both the normal
and the abnormal differ according to what verb in
particular is in question) is a modifying expression called for, or even in order. I sit in my chair,
in the usual way—I am not in a daze or influenced by threats or the like; here, it will not do
to say either that I sat in it intentionally or that
I did not sit in it intentionally,[6] nor yet that I sat
in it automatically or from habit or what you will.
It is bedtime, I am alone, I yawn: but I do not
yawn involuntarily (or voluntarily!), nor yet deliberately. To yawn in any such peculiar way is
just not to just yawn.

2. *Limitation of application.* Expressions modifying verbs, typically adverbs, have limited
ranges of application. That is, given any adverb
of excuse, such as 'unwittingly' or 'spontaneously' or 'impulsively', it will not be found that
it makes good sense to attach it to any and every
verb of 'action' in any and every context: indeed,
it will often apply only to a comparatively narrow
range of such verbs. Something in the lad's up-
turned face appealed to him, he threw a brick at
it—'spontaneously'? The interest then is to discover why some actions can be excused in a particular way but not others, particularly perhaps
the latter.[7] This will largely elucidate the meaning of the excuse, and at the same time will illumi-
nate the characteristics typical of the group of
'actions' it picks out: very often too it will throw
light on some detail of the machinery of 'action'
in general (see 4), or on our standards of accept-

able conduct (see 5). It is specially important in the case of some of the terms most favoured by philosophers or jurists to realize that at least in ordinary speech (disregarding back-seepage of jargon) they are not used so universally or so dichotomistically. For example, take 'voluntarily' and 'involuntarily': we may join the army or make a gift voluntarily, we may hiccough or make a small gesture involuntarily, and the more we consider further actions which we might naturally be said to do in either of these ways, the more circumscribed and unlike each other do the two classes become, until we even doubt whether there is *any* verb with which both adverbs are equally in place. Perhaps there are some such; but at least sometimes when we may think we have found one it is an illusion, an apparent exception that really does prove the rule. I can perhaps 'break a cup' voluntarily, *if* that is done, say, as an act of self-impoverishment: and I can perhaps break another involuntarily, *if*, say, I make an involuntary movement which breaks it. Here, plainly, the two acts described each as 'breaking a cup' are really very different, and the one is similar to acts typical of the 'voluntary' class, the other to acts typical of the 'involuntary' class.

3. *The importance of Negations and Opposites.* 'Voluntarily' and 'involuntarily', then, are not opposed in the obvious sort of way that they are made to be in philosophy or jurisprudence. The 'opposite', or rather 'opposites', of 'voluntarily' might be 'under constraint' of some sort, duress or obligation or influence:[8] the opposite of 'involuntarily' might be 'deliberately' or 'on purpose' or the like. Such divergences in opposites indicate that 'voluntarily' and 'involuntarily', in spite of their apparent connexion, are fish from very different kettles. In general, it will pay us to take nothing for granted or as obvious about negations and opposites. It does not pay to assume that a word must have an opposite, or one opposite, whether it is a 'positive' word like 'wilfully' or a 'negative' word like 'inadvertently'. Rather, we should be asking ourselves such questions as why there is no use for the adverb 'advertently'. For above all it will not do to assume that the 'positive' word must be around to wear the trousers; commonly enough the 'negative' (looking) word marks the (positive) abnormality, while the 'positive' word, *if* it exists, merely serves to rule out the suggestion of that abnormality. It is natural

enough, in view of what was said in (1) above, for the 'positive' word not to be found at all in some cases. I do an act A₁ (say, crush a snail) *inadvertently* if, in the course of executing by means of movements of my bodily parts some other act A₂ (say, in walking down the public path) I fail to exercise such meticulous supervision over the courses of those movements as would have been needed to ensure that they did not bring about the untoward event (here, the impact on the snail).[9] By claiming that A₁ was inadvertent we place it, where we imply it belongs, on this special level, in a class of incidental happenings which must occur in the doing of any physical act. To lift the act out of this class, we need and possess the expression 'not ... inadvertently': 'advertently', if used for this purpose, would suggest that, if the act was not done inadvertently, then it must have been done noticing what I was doing, which is far from necessarily the case (for example, if I did it absent-mindedly), or at least that there is *something* in common to the ways of doing all acts not done inadvertently, which is not the case. Again, there is no use for 'advertently' at the *same* level as 'inadvertently': in passing the butter I do not knock over the cream-jug, though I do (inadvertently) knock over the teacup—yet I do not by-pass the cream-jug *advertently:* for at this level, below supervision in detail, *anything* that we do is, if you like, inadvertent, though we only call it so, and indeed only call it something we have done, if there is something untoward about it.

A further point of interest in studying so-called 'negative' terms is the manner of their formation. Why are the words in one group formed with *un*- or *in*-, those in another with -*less* ('aimless', 'reckless', 'heedless', et cetera), and those in another with *mis*- ('mistake', 'misconception', 'misjudgment', et cetera)? Why carelessly but *in*-attentively? Perhaps care and attention, so often linked, are rather different. Here are remunerative exercises.

4. *The machinery of action.* Not merely do adverbial expressions pick out classes of actions, they also pick out the internal detail of the machinery of doing actions, or the departments into which the business of actions is organized. There is for example the stage at which we have actually to *carry out* some action upon which we embark —perhaps we have to make certain bodily movements or to make a speech. In the course of actu-

ally *doing* these things (getting weaving) we have to pay (some) attention to what we are doing and to take (some) care to guard against (likely) dangers: we may need to use judgment or tact; we must exercise sufficient control over our bodily parts, and so on. Inattention, carelessness, errors of judgment, tactlessness, clumsiness, all these and others are ills (with attendant excuses) which affect one specific stage in the machinery of action, the *executive* stage, the stage where we *muff* it. But there are many other departments in the business too, each of which is to be traced and mapped through its cluster of appropriate verbs and adverbs. Obviously there are departments of intelligence and planning, of decision and resolve, and so on, but I shall mention one in particular, too often overlooked, where troubles and excuses abound. It happens to us, in military life, to be in receipt of excellent intelligence, to be also in self-conscious possession of excellent principles (the five golden rules for winning victories), and yet to hit upon a plan of action which leads to disaster. One way in which this can happen is through failure at the stage of *appreciation* of the situation, that is at the stage where we are required to cast our excellent intelligence into such a form, under such heads and with such weights attached, that our equally excellent principles can be brought to bear on it properly, in a way to yield the right answer.[10] So too in real, or rather civilian, life, in moral or practical affairs, we can know the facts and yet look at them mistakenly or perversely, or not fully realize or appreciate something, or even be under a total misconception. Many expressions of excuse indicate failure at this particularly tricky stage: even thoughtlessness, inconsiderateness, lack of imagination, are perhaps less matters of failure in intelligence or planning than might be supposed, and more matters of failure to appreciate the situation. A course of E. M. Forster and we see things differently: yet perhaps we know no more and are no cleverer.

5. *Standards of the unacceptable.* It is characteristic of excuses to be 'unacceptable': given, I suppose, almost any excuse, there will be cases of such a kind or of such gravity that 'we will not accept' it. It is interesting to detect the standards and codes we thus invoke. The extent of the supervision we exercise over the execution of any act can never be quite unlimited, and usually is

expected to fall within fairly definite limits ('due çare and attention') in the case of acts of some general kind, though of course we set very different limits in different cases. We may plead that we trod on the snail inadvertently: but not on a baby —you ought to look where yŏu are putting your great feet. Of course it *was* (*really*), if you like, inadvertence; but that word constitutes a plea, which is not going to be allowed, because of standards. And if you try it on, you will be subscribing to such dreadful standards that your last state will be worse than your first. Or again, we set different standards, and will accept different excuses, in the case of acts which are rule-governed, like spelling, and which we are expected absolutely to get right, from those we set and accept for less stereotyped actions: a wrong spelling may be a slip, but hardly an accident, a winged beater may be an accident, but hardly a slip.

6. *Combination, dissociation and complication.* A belief in opposites and dichotomies encourages, among other things, a blindness to the combinations and dissociations of adverbs that are possible, even to such obvious facts as that we can act at once on impulse and intentionally, or that we can do an action intentionally yet for all that not deliberately, still less on purpose. We walk along the cliff, and I feel a sudden impulse to push you over, which I promptly do: I acted on impulse, yet I certainly intended to push you over, and may even have devised a little ruse to achieve it: yet even then I did not act deliberately, for I did not (stop to) ask myself whether to do it or not.

It is worth bearing in mind, too, the general rule that we must not expect to find simple labels for complicated cases. If a mistake results in an accident, it will not do to ask whether 'it' was an accident or a mistake, or to demand some briefer description of 'it'. Here the natural economy of language operates: if the words already available for simple cases suffice in combination to describe a complicated case, there will be need for special reasons before a special new word is invented for the complication. Besides, however well-equipped our language, it can never be forearmed against all possible cases that may arise and call for description: fact is richer than diction.

7. *Regina v. Finney.* Often the complexity and difficulty of a case is considerable. I will quote the case of *Regina v. Finney*:[11]

Shrewsbury Assizes. 1874.   12 Cox 625.

Prisoner was indicted for the manslaughter of Thomas Watkins.

The Prisoner was an attendant at a lunatic asylum. Being in charge of a lunatic, who was bathing, he turned on hot water into the bath, and thereby scalded him to death. The facts appeared to be truly set forth in the statement of the prisoner made before the committing magistrate, as follows: 'I had bathed Watkins, and had loosed the bath out. I *intended putting in a clean bath,* and asked Watkins if he would get out. At this time *my attention was drawn* to the next bath by the new attendant, who was asking me a question; and *my attention was taken from the bath* where Watkins was. I put my hand down to turn water on in the bath where Thomas Watkins was. *I did not intend to turn the hot water,* and *I made a mistake in the tap. I did not know what I had done until* I heard Thomas Watkins shout out; and *I did not find my mistake out till* I saw the steam from the water. You cannot get water in this bath when they are drawing water at the other bath; but at other times it shoots out like a water gun when the other baths are not is use. . . .'

(It was proved that the lunatic had such possession of his faculties as would enable him to understand what was said to him, and to get out of the bath.)

A. *Young* (for Prisoner). The death *resulted from accident.* There was no such *culpable negligence* on the part of the prisoner as will support this indictment. A *culpable mistake,* or some degree of *culpable negligence,* causing death, will not support a charge of manslaughter; unless the *negligence* be so gross as to be *reckless.* (*R.* v. *Noakes*).

Lush, J. To render a person liable for *neglect of duty* there must be such a degree of culpability as to amount to *gross negligence* on his part. If you accept the prisoner's own statement, you find no such amount of *negligence* as would come within this definition. It is not every little *trip or mistake* that will make a man so liable. It was the duty of the attendant not to let hot water into the bath while the patient was therein. According to the prisoner's own account, *he did not believe that* he was letting the hot water in while the deceased remained there. The lunatic was, we have heard, a man capable of getting out by himself and of understanding what was said to him. He was told to get out. A new attendant who had come on this day, was at an adjoining bath and he *took off the prisoner's attention.* Now, if the prisoner, knowing that the man was in the bath, had turned on the tap, and turned on the hot instead of the cold water, I should have said there was gross negligence; for he ought to have looked to see. But from his own account he had told the deceased to get out, and *thought he had got out.* If you think that

indicates gross *carelessness,* then you should find the prisoner guilty of manslaughter. But if you think it *inadvertence* not amounting to culpability—that is, what is properly termed an *accident*—then the prisoner is not liable.

Verdict, Not guilty.

In the case there are two morals that I will point:

(i) Both counsel and judge make very free use of a large number of terms of excuse, using several as though they were, and even stating them to be, indifferent or equivalent when they are not, and presenting as alternatives those that are not.

(ii) It is constantly difficult to be sure *what* act it is that counsel or judge is suggesting might be qualified by what expression of excuse.

The learned judge's concluding direction is a paradigm of these faults.[12] Finney, by contrast, stands out as an evident master of the Queen's English. He is explicit as to each of his acts and states, mental and physical: he uses different, and the correct, adverbs in connexion with each: and he makes no attempt to boil down.

8. *Small distinctions, and big too.* It should go without saying that terms of excuse are not equivalent, and that it matters which we use: we need to distinguish inadvertence not merely from (save the mark) such things as mistake and accident, but from such nearer neighbours as, say, aberration and absence of mind. By imagining cases with vividness and fullness we should be able to decide in which precise terms to describe, say, Miss Plimsoll's action in writing, so carefully, 'DAIRY' on her fine new book: We should be able to distinguish between sheer, mere, pure, and simple mistake or inadvertence. Yet unfortunately, at least when in the grip of thought, we fail not merely at these stiffer hurdles. We equate even—I have seen it done—'inadvertently' with 'automatically': as though to say I trod on your toe inadvertently means to say I trod on it automatically. Or we collapse succumbing to temptation into losing control of ourselves—a bad patch, this, for telescoping.[13]

All this is not so much a *lesson* from the study of excuses as the very object of it.

9. *The exact phrase and its place in the sentence.* It is not enough, either, to attend simply to the 'key' word: notice must also be taken of the

full and exact form of the expression used. In considering mistakes, we have to consider seriatim 'by mistake', 'owing to a mistake', 'mistakenly', 'it was a mistake to', 'to make a mistake in or over or about,' 'to be mistaken about', and so on: in considering purpose, we have to consider 'on', 'with the', 'for the', et cetera, besides 'purposeful', 'purposeless', and the like. These varying expressions may function quite differently—and usually do, or why should we burden ourselves with more than one of them?

Care must be taken too to observe the precise position of an adverbial expression in the sentence. This should of course indicate what verb it is being used to modify: but more than that, the position can also affect the *sense* of the expression, that is, the way in which it modifies that verb. Compare, for example:

> a₁ He clumsily trod on the snail.
> a₂ Clumsily he trod on the snail.
> b₁ He trod clumsily on the snail.
> b₂ He trod on the snail clumsily.

Here, in a_1 and a_2, we describe his treading on the creature at all as a piece of clumsiness, incidental, we imply, to his performance of some other action: but with b_1 and b_2 to tread on it is, very likely, his aim or policy, what we criticize is his execution of the feat.[14] Many adverbs, though far from all (not, for example, 'purposely') are used in these two typically different ways.

10. *The style of performance.* With some adverbs the distinction between the two senses referred to in the last paragraph is carried a stage further. 'He ate his soup deliberately' may mean, like 'He deliberately ate his soup', that his eating his soup was a deliberate act, one perhaps that he thought would annoy somebody, as it would more commonly if he deliberately *ate my* soup, and which he decided to do; but it will often mean that he went through the performance of eating his soup in a noteworthy manner or *style*—pause after each mouthful, careful choice of point of entry for the spoon, sucking of moustaches, and so on. That is, it will mean that he ate *with* deliberation rather than *after* deliberation. The style of the performance, show and unhurried, is understandably called 'deliberate' because each movement *has the typical look* of a deliberate act;

but it is scarcely being said that the making of each motion *is* a deliberate act or that he is 'literally' deliberating. This case, then, is more extreme than that of 'clumsily', which does in both uses describe literally a manner of performing.

It is worth watching out for this secondary use when scrutinizing any particular adverbial expression: when it definitely does not exist, the reason is worth inquiring into. Sometimes it is very hard to be sure whether it does exist or does not: it does, one would think, with 'carelessly', it does not with 'inadvertently', but does it or does it not with 'absent-mindedly' or 'aimlessly'? In some cases a word akin to but distinct from the primary adverb is used for this special role of describing a style of performance: we use 'purposefully' in this way, but never 'purposely'.

11. *What modifies what?* The judge in *Regina v. Finney* does not make clear what event is being excused in what way. 'If you think that indicates gross carelessness, then. . . . But if you think it inadvertence not amounting to culpability—that is, what is properly called an accident—then. . . .' Apparently he means that Finney may have *turned on the hot tap* inadvertently:[15] does he mean also that the tap may have been turned accidentally, or rather that *Watkins may have been scalded* and killed accidentally? And was the carelessness in turning the tap or in thinking Watkins had got out? Many disputes as to what excuse we should properly use arise because we will not trouble to state explicitly *what* is being excused.

To do so is all the more vital because it is in principle always open to us, along various lines, to describe or refer to 'what I did' in so many different ways. This is altogether too large a theme to elaborate here. Apart from the more general and obvious problems of the use of 'tendentious' descriptive terms, there are many special problems in the particular case of 'actions'. Should we say, are we saying, that he took her money, or that he robbed her? That he knocked a ball into a hole, or that he sank a putt? That he said 'Done', or that he accepted an offer? How far, that is, are motives, intentions and conventions to be part of the description of actions? And more especially here, what is *an* or *one* or *the* action? For we can generally split up what might be named as one action in several distinct ways, into different *stretches* or *phrases* or *stages*.

Stages have already been mentioned: We can dismantle the machinery of the act, and describe (and excuse) separately the intelligence, the appreciation, the planning, the decision, the execution and so forth. Phases are rather different: we can say that he painted a picture or fought a campaign, or else we can say that first he laid on this stroke of paint and then that, first he fought this action and then that. Stretches are different again: a single term descriptive of what he did may be made to cover either a smaller or a larger stretch of events, those excluded by the narrower description being then called 'consequences' or 'results' or 'effects' or the like of his act. so here we can describe Finney's act *either* as turning on the hot tap, which he did by mistake, with the result that Watkins was scalded, or as scalding Watkins which he did *not* do by mistake.

It is very evident that the problems of excuses and those of the different descriptions of actions are throughout bound up with each other.

12. *Trailing clouds of etymology.* It is these considerations that bring us up so forcibly against some of the most difficult words in the whole story of excuses, such words as 'result', 'effect', and 'consequence', or again as 'intention', 'purpose', and 'motive'. I will mention two points of method which are, experience has convinced me, indispensable aids at these levels.

One is that a word never—well, hardly ever—shakes off its etymology and its formation. In spite of all changes in and extensions of and additions to its meanings and indeed rather pervading and governing these, there will still persist the old idea. In an *accident* something befalls: by *mistake* you take the wrong one: in *error* you stray: when you act *deliberately* you act after weighing it up (*not* after thinking out ways and means). It is worth asking ourselves whether we know the etymology of 'result' or of 'spontaneously', and worth remembering that 'unwillingly' and 'involuntarily' come from very different sources.

And the second point is connected with this. Going back into the history of a word, very often into Latin, we come back pretty commonly to pictures of *models* of how things happen or are done. These models may be fairly sophisticated and recent, as is perhaps the case with 'motive' or 'impulse', but one of the commonest and most primitive types of model is one which is apt to baffle us through its very naturalness and simplicity. We take *some very simple action,* like shoving a stone, usually as done by and viewed by oneself, and use *this,* with the features distinguishable in it, as our model in terms of which to talk about other actions and events: and we continue to do so, scarcely realizing it, even when these other actions are pretty remote and perhaps much more interesting to us in their own right than the acts originally used in constructing the model ever were, and even when the model is really distorting the racts rather than helping us to observe them. In primitive cases we may get to see clearly the differences between, say, 'results', 'effects', and 'consequences', and yet discover that these differences are no longer clear, and the terms themselves no longer of real service to us, in the more complicated cases where we had been bandying them about most freely. A model must be recognized for what it is. 'Causing', I suppose, was a notion taken from a man's own experience of doing simple actions, and by primitive man every event was construed in terms of this model: every event has a cause, that is, every event is an action done by somebody—if not by a man, then by a quasiman, a spirit. When, later, events which are *not* actions are realized to be such, we still say that they must be 'caused', and the word snares us: we are struggling to ascribe to it a new, unanthropomorphic meaning, yet constantly, in searching for its analysis, we unearth and incorporate the lineaments of the ancient model. As happened even to Hume, and consequently to Kant. Examining such a word historically, we may well find that it has been extended to cases that have by now too tenuous a relation to the model case, that it is a source of confusion and superstition.

There is too another danger in words that invoke models, half-forgotten or not. It must be remembered that there is no necessity whatsoever that the various models used in creating our vocabulary, primitive or recent, should all fit together neatly as parts into one single, total model or scheme of, for instance, the doing of actions. It is possible, and indeed highly likely, that our assortment of models will include some, or many, that are overlapping, conflicting, or more generally simply *disparate.*[16]

13. In spite of the wide and acute observation of the phenomena of action embodied in ordinary speech, modern scientists have been able, it seems

to me, to reveal its inadequacy at numerous points, if only because they have had access to more comprehensive data and have studied them with more catholic and dispassionate interest than the ordinary man, or even the lawyer, has had occasion to do. I will conclude with two examples.

Observation of animal behaviour shows that regularly, when an animal is embarked on some recognizable pattern of behaviour but meets in the course of it with an insuperable obstacle, it will betake itself to energetic, but quite unrelated, activity of some wild kind, such as standing on its head. This phenomenon is called 'displacement behaviour' and is well identifiable. If now, in the light of this, we look back at ordinary human life, we see that displacement behaviour bulks quite large in it: yet we have apparently no word, or at least no clear and simple word, for it. If, when thwarted, we stand on our heads or wiggle our toes, then we are not exactly *just* standing on our heads, don't you know, in the ordinary way, yet is there any convenient adverbial expression we can insert to do the trick? 'In desperation'?

Take, again, 'compulsive' behaviour, however exactly psychologists define it, compulsive washing for example. There are of course hints in ordinary speech that we do things in this way—'just feel I have to', 'shouldn't feel comfortable unless I did', and the like: but there is no adverbial expression satisfactorily preempted for it, as 'compulsively' is. This is understandable enough, since compulsive behaviour, like displacement behaviour, is not in general going to be of great practical importance.

Here I leave and commend the subject to you.

NOTES

1. This use has little to do with the more down-to-earth occurrences of 'action' in ordinary speech.

2. Another well-flogged horse in these same stakes is blame. At least two things seem confused together under this term. Sometimes when I blame X for doing A, say for breaking the vase, it is a question simply or mainly of my disapproval of A, breaking the vase, which unquestionably X did: but sometimes it is, rather, a question simply or mainly of how far I think X responsible for A, which unquestionably was bad. Hence if somebody says he blames me for something, I may answer by giving a *justification*, so that he will cease to disapprove of what I did, or else by giving an *excuse*, so that he will cease to hold me, at least entirely and in every way, responsible for doing it.

3. All of which was seen and claimed by Socrates, when he first betook himself to the way of Words.

4. You have a donkey, so have I, and they graze in the same field. The day comes when I conceive a dislike for mine. I go to shoot it, draw a bead on it, fire: the brute falls in its tracks. I inspect the victim, and find to my horror that it is *your* donkey. I appear on your doorstep with the remains and say—what? 'I say, old sport, I'm awfully sorry, et cetera, I've shot your donkey by *accident*? Or '*by mistake*'? Then again, I go to shoot my donkey as before, draw a bead on it, fire—but as I do so, the beasts move, and to my horror yours falls. Again the scene on the doorstep—what do I say? 'By mistake'? Or 'by accident'?

5. And forget, for once and for a while, that other curious question 'Is it true?' May we?

6. Caveat or hedge: of course we can say 'I did *not* sit in it "intentionally" ' as a way simply of repudiating the suggestion that I sat in it intentionally.

7. For we are sometimes not so good at observing what we *can't* say as what we can, yet the first is pretty regularly the more revealing.

8. But remember, when I sign a cheque in the normal way, I do *not* do so *either* 'voluntarily' or 'under constraint'.

9. Or analogously: I do an act A^1 (say, divulge my age, or imply you are a liar), *inadvertently* if, in the course of executing by the use of some medium of communication some other act. A^2 (say, reminiscing about my war service) I fail to exercise such meticulous supervision over the choice and arrangement of the signs as would have been needed to ensure that. . . . It is interesting to note how such adverbs lead parallel lives, one in connexion with physical actions ('doing') and the other in connexion with acts of communication ('saying'), or sometimes also in connexion with acts of 'thinking' ('inadvertently assumed').

10. We know all about how to do quadratics: we know all the needful facts about pipes, cisterns, hours and plumbers: yet we reach the answer '3¾ men'. We have failed to cast our facts correctly into mathematical form.

11. A somewhat distressing favourite in the class that Hart used to conduct with me in the years soon after the war. The italics are mine.

12. Not but what he probably manages to convey his meaning somehow or other. Judges seem to acquire a knack of conveying meaning, and even carrying conviction, through the use of a pithy Anglo-Saxon which sometimes has literally no meaning at all. Wishing to distinguish the case of shooting at a post in the belief that it was an enemy, as *not* an 'attempt', from the case of picking an empty pocket in the belief that money was in it, which *is* an 'attempt', the judge explains that in shooting at the post 'the man is never on the thing at all'.

13. Plato, I suppose, and after him Aristotle, fastened this confusion upon us, as bad in its day and way as the later, grotesque, confusion of moral weakness with weakness of will. I am very partial to ice cream, and a bombe is served divided into segments corresponding one to one with the persons at High Table: I am tempted to help myself to two segments and do so, thus succumbing to temptation and even conceivably (but why necessarily?) going against my principles. But do I lose control of myself? Do I raven, do I snatch the morsels from the dish and wolf them down, impervious to the consternation of my colleagues? Not a bit of it. We often succumb to temptation with calm and even with finesse.

14. As a matter of fact, most of these examples *can* be understood the other way, especially if we allow ourselves inflexions of the voice, or commas, or contexts. a_2 might be a poetic inversion for b_2: b_1, perhaps with commas round the 'clumsily', might be used for a_1: and so on. Still, the two senses are clearly enough distinguishable.

15. What Finney says is different: he says he 'made a mistake in the tap'. This is the basic use of 'mistake', where we simply, and not necessarily accountably, take the wrong one. Finney here attempts to account for his mistake, by saying that his attention was distracted. But suppose the order is 'Right turn' and I turn left: No doubt the sergeant will insinuate that my attention was distracted, or that I cannot distinguish my right from my left—but it was not and I can, this was a simple, pure mistake. As often happens. Neither I nor the sergeant will suggest that there was any accident, or any inadvertence either. If Finney had turned the hot tap inadvertently, then it would have been knocked, say, in reaching for the cold tap: a different story.

16. This is by way of a general warning in philosophy. It seems to be too readily assumed that if we can only discover the true meanings of each of a cluster of key terms, usually historic terms, that we use in some particular field (as, for example, 'right', 'good' and the rest in morals), then it must without question transpire that each will fit into place in some single, interlocking, consistent, conceptual scheme. Not only is there no reason to assume this, but all historical probability is against it, especially in the case of a language derived from such various civilizations as ours is. We may cheerfully use, and with weight, terms which are not so much head-on incompatible as simply disparate, which just do not fit in or even on. Just as we cheerfully subscribe to, or have the grace to be torn between, simply disparate ideals—why *must* there be a conceivable amalgam, the Good Life for Man?

H. L. A. HART

Responsibility*

A wide range of different, though connected, ideas is covered by the expressions 'responsibility', 'responsible', and 'responsible for', as these are standardly used in and out of the law. Though connections exist among these different ideas, they are often very indirect, and it seems appropriate to speak of different *senses* of these expressions. The following simple story of a drunken sea captain who lost his ship at sea can be told in the terminology of responsibility to illustrate, with stylistically horrible clarity, these differences of sense.

'As a captain of the ship, X was responsible for the safety of his passengers and crew. But on his last voyage he got drunk every night and was responsible for the loss of the ship with all aboard. It was rumoured that he was insane, but the doctors considered that he was responsible for his actions. Throughout the voyage he behaved quite irresponsibly, and various incidents in his career showed that he was not a responsible person. He always maintained that the exceptional winter storms were responsible for the loss of the ship, but in the legal proceedings brought against him he was found criminally responsible for his negligent conduct, and in separate civil proceedings he was held legally responsible for the loss of life and property. He is still alive and he is morally responsible for the deaths of many women and children.'

This welter of distinguishable senses of the word 'responsibility' and its grammatical cognates can, I think, be profitably reduced by division and classification. I shall distinguish four heads of classification to which I shall assign the following names:

   (a) Role-Responsibility
   (b) Causal-Responsibility
   (c) Liability-Responsibility
   (d) Capacity-Responsibility.

I hope that in drawing these dividing lines, and in the exposition which follows, I have avoided

*From the *Law Quarterly Review* (1967), Vol. 83. Reprinted by permission of the Editor. This selection was reprinted as the first part of an essay entitled "Postscript: Responsibility and Retribution" in H. L. A. Hart, *Punishment and Responsibility* (New York and Oxford: Oxford University Press, 1968), pp. 211–30.

the arbitrary pedantries of classificatory systematics, and that my divisions pick out and clarify the main, though not all, varieties of responsibility to which reference is constantly made, explicitly or implicitly, by moralists, lawyers, historians, and ordinary men. I relegate to the notes[1] discussion of what unifies these varieties and explains the extension of the terminology of responsibility.

ROLE-RESPONSIBILITY

A sea captain is responsible for the safety of his ship, and that is his responsibility, or one of his responsibilities. A husband is responsible for the maintenance of his wife; parents for the upbringing of their children; a sentry for alerting the guard at the enemy's approach; a clerk for keeping the accounts of his firm. These examples of a person's responsibilities suggest the generalization that, whenever a person occupies a distinctive place or office in a social organization, to which specific duties are attached to provide for the welfare of others or to advance in some specific way the aims or purposes of the organization, he is properly said to be responsible for the performance of these duties, or for doing what is necessary to fulfil them. Such duties are a person's responsibilities. As a guide to this sense of responsibility this generalization is, I think, adequate, but the idea of a distinct role or place or office is, of course, a vague one, and I cannot undertake to make it very precise. Doubts about its extension to marginal cases will always arise. If two friends, out on a mountaineering expedition, agree that the one shall look after the food and the other the maps, then the one is correctly said to be responsible for the food, and the other for the maps, and I would classify this as a case of role-responsibility. Yet such fugitive or temporary assignments with specific duties would not usually be considered by sociologists, who mainly use the word, as an example of a 'role'. So 'role' in my classification is extended to include a task assigned to any person by agreement or otherwise. But it is also important to notice that not all the duties which a man has in virtue of occupying what in a quite strict sense of role is a distinct role, are thought or spoken of as 'responsibilities'. A private soldier has a duty to obey his superior officer and, if commanded by him to form fours or present arms on a given occasion, has a duty

to do so. But to form fours or present arms would scarcely be said to be the private's responsibility; nor would he be said to be responsible for doing it. If on the other hand a soldier was ordered to deliver a message to H.Q. or to conduct prisoners to a base camp, he might well be said to be responsible for doing these things, and these things to be his responsibility. I think, though I confess to not being sure, that what distinguishes those duties of a role which are singled out as responsibilities is that they are duties of a relatively complex or extensive kind, defining a 'sphere of responsibility' requiring care and attention over a protracted period of time, while short-lived duties of a very simple kind, to do or not do some specific act on a particular occasion, are not termed responsibilities. Thus a soldier detailed off to keep the camp clean and tidy for the general's visit of inspection has this as his sphere of responsibility and is responsible for it. But if merely told to remove a piece of paper from the approaching general's path, this would be at most his duty.

A 'responsible person', 'behaving responsibly' (not 'irresponsibly'), require for their elucidation a reference to role-responsibility. A responsible person is one who is disposed to take his duties seriously; to think about them, and to make serious efforts to fulfil them. To behave responsibly is to behave as a man would who took his duties in this serious way. Responsibilities in this sense may be either legal or moral, or fall outside this dichotomy. Thus a man may be morally as well as legally responsible for the maintenance of his wife and children, but a host's responsibility for the comfort of his guests, and a referee's responsibility for the control of the players is neither legal nor moral, unless the word 'moral' is unilluminatingly used simply to exclude legal responsibility.

CAUSAL RESPONSIBILITY

'The long drought was responsible for the famine in India'. In many contexts, as in this one, it is possible to substitute for the expression 'was responsible for' the words 'caused' or 'produced' or some other causal expression in referring to consequences, results, or outcomes. The converse, however, is not always true. Examples of this causal sense of responsibility are legion. 'His neglect was responsible for her distress.' 'The Prime Minister's speech was responsible for the panic.' 'Disraeli was responsible for the defeat of the Government.' 'The icy condition of the road was responsible for the accident.' The past tense of the verb used in this causal sense of the expression 'responsible for' should be noticed. If it is said of a living person, who has in fact caused some disaster, that he *is* responsible for it, this is not, or not merely, an example of causal responsibility, but of what I term 'liability-responsibility'; it asserts his liability on account of the disaster, even though it is also true that he is responsible in that sense *because* he caused the disaster, and that he caused the disaster may be expressed by saying that he was responsible for it. On the other hand, if it is said of a person no longer living that he was responsible for some disaster, this may be either a simple causal statement or a statement of liability-responsibility, or both.

From the above examples it is clear that in this causal sense not only human beings but also their actions or omissions, and things, conditions, and events, may be said to be responsible for outcomes. It is perhaps true that only where an outcome is thought unfortunate or felicitous is its cause commonly spoken of as responsible for it. But this may not reflect any aspect of the meaning of the expression 'responsible for'; it may only reflect the fact that, except in such cases, it may be pointless and hence rare to pick out the causes of events. It is sometimes suggested that, though we may speak of a human being's action as responsible for some outcome in a purely causal sense, we do not speak of a person, as distinct from his actions, as responsible for an outcome, unless he is felt to deserve censure or praise. This is, I think, a mistake. History books are full of examples to the contrary. 'Disraeli was responsible for the defeat of the Government' need not carry even an implication that he was deserving of censure or praise; it may be purely a statement concerned with the contribution made by one human being to an outcome of importance, and be entirely neutral as to its moral or other merits. The contrary view depends, I think, on the failure to appreciate sufficiently the ambiguity of statements of the form 'X *was* responsible for Y' as distinct from 'X *is* responsible for Y' to which I have drawn attention above. The former expression in the case of a person no longer living may be (though it *need* not be) a statement of liability-responsibility.

LEGAL LIABILITY-RESPONSIBILITY

Though it was noted that role-responsibility might take either legal or moral form, it was not found necessary to treat these separately. But in the case of the present topic of liability-responsibility, separate treatment seems advisable. For responsibility seems to have a wider extension in relation to the law than it does in relation to morals, and it is a question to be considered whether this is due merely to the general differences between law and morality, or to some differences in the sense of responsibility involved.

When legal rules require men to act or abstain from action, one who breaks the law is usually liable, according to other legal rules, to punishment for his misdeeds, or to make compensation to persons injured thereby, and very often he is liable to both punishment and enforced compensation. He is thus liable to be 'made to pay' for what he has done in either or both of the senses which the expression 'He'll pay for it' may bear in ordinary usage. But most legal systems go much further than this. A man may be legally punished on account of what his servant has done, even if he in no way caused or instigated or even knew of the servant's action, or knew of the likelihood of his servant so acting. Liability in such circumstances is rare in modern systems of criminal law; but it is common in all systems of civil law for men to be made to pay compensation for injuries caused by others, generally their servants or employees. The law of most countries goes further still. A man may be liable to pay compensation for harm suffered by others, though neither he nor his servants have caused it. This is so, for example, in Anglo-American law when the harm is caused by dangerous things which escape from a man's possession, even if their escape is not due to any act or omission of his or his servants, or if harm is caused to a man's employees by defective machinery whose defective condition he could not have discovered.

It will be observed that the facts referred to in the last paragraph are expressed in terms of 'liability' and not 'responsibility'. In the preceding essay in this volume I ventured the general statement that to say that someone is legally responsible for something often means that under legal rules he is liable to be made either to suffer or to pay compensation in certain eventualities. But I now think that this simple account of liability-responsibility is in need of some considerable modification. Undoubtedly, expressions of the form 'he is legally responsible for Y' (where Y is some action or harm) and 'he is legally liable to be punished or to be made to pay compensation for Y' are very closely connected, and sometimes they are used as if they were identical in meaning. Thus, where one legal writer speaks of 'strict responsibility' and 'vicarious responsibility', another speaks of 'strict liability' and 'vicarious liability'; and even in the work of a single writer the expressions 'vicarious responsibility' and 'vicarious liability' are to be found used without any apparent difference in meaning, implication, or emphasis. Hence, in arguing that it was for the law to determine the mental conditions of responsibility, Fitzjames Stephen claimed that this must be so because 'the meaning of responsibility is liability to punishment'.[2]

But though the abstract expressions 'responsibility' and 'liability' are virtually equivalent in many contexts, the statement that a man is responsible for his actions, or for some act or some harm, is usually not identical in meaning with the statement that he is liable to be punished or to be made to pay compensation for the act or the harm, but is directed to a narrower and more specific issue. It is in this respect that my previous account of liability-responsibility needs qualification.

The question whether a man is or is not legally liable to be punished for some action that he has done opens up the quite general issue whether all of the various requirements for criminal liability have been satisfied, and so will include the question whether the kind of action done, whatever mental element accompanied it, was ever punishable by law. But the question whether he is or is not legally responsible for some action or some harm is usually not concerned with this general issue, but with the narrower issue whether any of a certain range of conditions (mainly, but not exclusively, psychological) are satisfied, it being assumed that all other conditions are satisfied. Because of this difference in scope between questions of liability to punishment and questions of responsibility, it would be somewhat misleading, though not unintelligible, to say of a man who had refused to rescue a baby drowning in a foot of water, that he was not, according to English law, legally responsible for leaving the baby to drown or for the baby's death, if all that is meant is that he was not liable to punishment because refusing aid to those in danger is not generally a crime in English law. Similarly, a book or article entitled 'Criminal Responsibility' would not be expected to contain the whole of the substantive criminal law determining the conditions of liability, but only to be concerned with a specialized range of topics such as mental abnormality, immaturity, *mens rea,* strict and vicarious liability, proximate cause, or other general forms of connection between acts and harm sufficient for liability. These are the specialized topics which are, in general, thought and spoken of as 'criteria' of responsibility. They may be divided into three classes: (i) mental or psychological conditions; (ii) causal or other forms of connection between act and harm; (iii) personal relationships rendering one man liable to be punished or to pay for the acts of another. Each of these three classes requires some separate discussion.

(i) *Mental or psychological criteria of responsibility.* In the criminal law the most frequent issue raised by questions of responsibility, as distinct from the wider question of liability, is whether or not an accused person satisfied some mental or psychological conditions required for liability, or whether liability was strict or absolute, so that the usual mental or psychological conditions were not required. It is, however, important to notice that these psychological conditions are of two sorts, of which the first is far more closely associated with the use of the word responsibility than the second. On the one hand, the law of most countries requires that the person liable to be punished should at the time of his crime have had the capacity to understand what he is required by law to do or not to do, to deliberate and to decide what to do, and to control his conduct in the light of such decisions. Normal adults are generally assumed to have these capacities, but they may be lacking where there is mental disorder or immaturity, and the possession of these normal capacities is very often signified by the expression 'responsible for his actions'. This is the fourth sense of responsibility which I discuss below under the heading of 'Capacity-Responsibility'. On the other hand, except where responsibility is strict, the law may excuse from punishment persons of normal capacity if, on particular occasions where their outward conduct fits the definition of the crime, some element of intention or knowledge, or some other of the familiar constituents of *mens rea,* was absent, so that the particular action done was defective, though the agent had the normal capacity of understanding and control. Continental codes usually make a firm distinction between these two main types of psychological conditions: Questions concerning general capacity are described as matters of responsibility or 'imputability', whereas questions concerning the presence or absence of knowledge or intention on particular occasions are not described as matters of 'imputability', but are referred to the topic of 'fault' (*schuld, faute, dolo,* et cetera).

English law and English legal writers do not mark quite so firmly this contrast between general capacity and the knowledge or intention accompanying a particular action; for the expression *mens rea* is now often used to cover all the variety of psychological conditions required for liability by the law, so that both the person who is excused from punishment because of lack of intention or some ordinary accident or mistake on a particular occasion and the person held not to be criminally responsible on account of immaturity or insanity are said not to have the requisite *mens rea.* Yet the distinction thus blurred by the extensive use of the expression *mens rea* between a persistent incapacity and a particular defective action is indirectly marked in terms of responsibility in most Anglo-American legal writing, in the following way. When a person is said to be not responsible for a particular act or crime, or when (as in the formulation of the M'Naghten Rules and s. 2 of the Homicide Act, 1957) he is said not to be responsible for his 'acts and omissions in doing' some action on a particular occasion, the reason for saying this is usually some mental abnormality or disorder. I have not succeeded in finding cases where a normal person, merely lacking some ordinary element of knowledge or intention on a particular occasion, is said for that reason not to be responsible for that particular action, even though he is for that reason not liable to punishment. But though there is this tendency in statements of liability-responsibility to confine the use of the expression 'responsible' and 'not responsible' to questions of mental abnormality or general incapacity, yet all the psychological conditions of liability are to be

found discussed by legal writers under such headings as 'Criminal Responsibility' or 'Principles of Criminal Responsibility'. Accordingly I classify them here as criteria of responsibility. I do so with a clear conscience, since little is to be gained in clarity by a rigid division which the contemporary use of the expression *mens rea* often ignores.

The situation is, however, complicated by a further feature of English legal and non-legal usage. The phrase 'responsible for his actions' is, as I have observed, frequently used to refer to the capacity-responsibility of the normal person, and, so used, refers to one of the major criteria of liability-responsibility. It is so used in s. 2 of the Homicide Act 1957, which speaks of a person's mental 'responsibility' for his actions being *impaired,* and in the rubric to the section, which speaks of persons 'suffering from diminished responsibility'. In this sense the expression is the name or description of a psychological condition. But the expression is also used to signify liability-responsibility itself, that is, liability to punishment so far as such liability depends on psychological conditions, and is so used when the law is said to 'relieve insane persons of responsibility for their actions'. It was probably also so used in the form of verdict returned in cases of successful pleas of insanity under English law until this was altered by the Insanity Act 1964: the verdict was 'guilty but insane so as not to be responsible according to law for his actions'.

(ii) *Causal or other forms of connection with harm.* Questions of legal liability-responsibility are not limited in their scope to psychological conditions of either of the two sorts distinguished above. Such questions are also (though more frequently in the law of tort than in the criminal law) concerned with the issue whether some form of connection between a person's act and some harmful outcome is sufficient according to law to make him liable; so if a person is accused of murder the question whether he was or was not legally responsible for the death may be intended to raise the issue whether the death was too remote a consequence of his acts for them to count as its cause. If the law, as frequently in tort, is not that the defendant's action should have caused the harm, but that there be some other form of connection or relationship between the defendant and the harm, for example, that it should have been caused by some dangerous thing escaping from the defendant's land, this connection or relationship is a condition of civil responsibility for harm, and, where it holds, the defendant is said to be legally responsible for the harm. No doubt such questions of connection with harm are also frequently phrased in terms of liability.

(iii) *Relationship with the agent.* Normally in criminal law the minimum condition required for liability for punishment is that the person to be punished should himself have done what the law forbids, at least so far as outward conduct is concerned; even if liability is 'strict', it is not enough to render him liable for punishment that someone else should have done it. This is often expressed in the terminology of responsibility (though here, too, 'liability' is frequently used instead of 'responsibility') by saying that, generally, vicarious responsibility is not known to the criminal law. But there are exceptional cases; an innkeeper is liable to punishment if his servants, without his knowledge and against his orders, sell liquor on his premises after hours. In this case he is vicariously responsible for the sale, and of course, in the civil law of tort there are many situations in which a master or employer is liable to pay compensation for the torts of his servant or employee, and is said to be vicariously responsible.

It appears, therefore, that there are diverse types of criteria of legal liability-responsibility: The most prominent consist of certain mental elements, but there are also causal or other connections between a person and harm, or the presence of some relationship, such as that of master and servant, between different persons. It is natural to ask why these very diverse conditions are singled out as criteria of responsibility, and so are within the scope of questions about responsibility, as distinct from the wider question concerning liability for punishment. I think that the following somewhat Cartesian figure may explain this fact. If we conceive of a person as an embodied mind and will, we may draw a distinction between two questions concerning the conditions of liability and punishment. The first question is what general types of outer conduct *(actus reus)* or what sorts of harm are required for liability? The second question is how closely connected with such conduct or such harm must the embodied mind or will of an individual person be to render him liable to punishment? Or, as some would put it, to what extent must the embodied

mind or will be the author of the conduct or the harm in order to render him liable? Is it enough that the person made the appropriate bodily movements? Or is it required that he did so when possessed of a certain capacity of control and with a certain knowledge or intention? Or that he caused the harm or stood in some other relationship to it, or to the actual doer of the deed? The legal rules, or parts of legal rules, that answer these various questions define the various forms of connection which are adequate for liability, and these constitute conditions of legal responsibility which form only a part of the total conditions of liability for punishment, which also include the definitions of the *actus reus* of the various crimes.

We may therefore summarize this long discussion of legal liability-responsibility by saying that, though in certain general contexts legal responsibility and legal liability have the same meaning, to say that a man is legally responsible for some act or harm is to state that his connection with the act or harm is sufficient according to law for liability. Because responsibility and liability are distinguishable in this way, it will make sense to say that because a person is legally responsible for some action he is liable to be punished for it.

LEGAL LIABILITY-RESPONSIBILITY AND MORAL BLAME

My previous account of legal liability-responsibility, in which I claimed that in one important sense to say that a person is legally responsible meant that he was legally liable for punishment or could be made to pay compensation, has been criticized on two scores. Since these criticisms apply equally to the above amended version of my original account, in which I distinguish the general issue of liability from the narrower issue of responsibility, I shall consider these criticisms here. The first criticism, made by Mr. A. W. B. Simpson,[3] insists on the strong connection between statements of legal responsibility and moral judgment, and claims that even lawyers tend to confine statements that a person is legally responsible for something to cases where he is considered morally blameworthy, and, where this is not so, tend to use the expression 'liability' rather than 'responsibility'. But, though moral blame and legal responsibility may be connected in some ways, it is surely not in this simple way.

Against any such view not only is there the frequent use already mentioned of the expressions 'strict responsibility' and 'vicarious responsibility', which are obviously independent of moral blameworthiness, but there is the more important fact that we can, and frequently do, intelligibly debate the question whether a mentally disordered or very young person who has been held legally responsible for a crime is morally blameworthy. The coincidence of legal responsibility with moral blameworthiness may be a laudable ideal, but it is not a necessary truth nor even an accomplished fact.

The suggestion that the statement that a man is responsible generally means that he is blameworthy and not that he is liable to punishment is said to be supported by the fact that it is possible to cite, without redundancy, the fact that a person is responsible as a ground or reason for saying that he is liable to punishment. But, if the various kinds or senses of responsibility are distinguished, it is plain that there are many explanations of this last mentioned fact, which are quite independent of any essential connection between legal responsibility and moral blameworthiness. Thus cases where the statement that the man is responsible constitutes a reason for saying that he is liable to punishment may be cases of role-responsibility (the master is legally responsible for the safety of his ship, therefore he is liable to punishment if he loses it) or capacity-responsibility (he was responsible for his actions therefore he is liable to punishment for his crimes); or they may even be statements of liability-responsibility, since such statements refer to part only of the conditions of liability and may therefore be given, without redundancy, as a reason for liability to punishment. In any case this criticism may be turned against the suggestion that responsibility is to be equated with moral blameworthiness; for plainly the statement that someone is responsible may be given as part of the reason for saying that he is morally blameworthy.

LIABILITY-RESPONSIBILITY FOR PARTICULAR ACTIONS

An independent objection is the following, made by Mr. George Pitcher.[4] The wide extension I have claimed for the notion of liability-responsibility permits us to say not only that a man is legally responsible in this sense for the consequences of his action, but also for his action or actions. According to Mr. Pitcher 'this is an improper way of talking', though common amongst philosophers. Mr. Pitcher is concerned primarily with moral, not legal, responsibility, but even in a moral context it is plain that there is a very well established use of the expression 'responsible for his actions' to refer to capacity-responsibility for which Mr. Pitcher makes no allowance. As far as the law is concerned, many examples may be cited from both sides of the Atlantic where a person may be said to be responsible for his actions, or for his act, or for his crime, or for his conduct. Mr. Pitcher gives, as a reason for saying that it is improper to speak of a man being responsible for his own actions, the fact that a man does not produce or cause his own actions. But this argument would prove far too much. It would rule out as improper not only the expression 'responsible for his actions', but also our saying that a man was responsible vicariously or otherwise for harmful outcomes which he had not caused, which is a perfectly well established legal usage.

None the less, there are elements of truth in Mr. Pitcher's objection. First, it seems to be the case that even where a man is said to be legally responsible for what he has done, it is rare to find this expressed by a phrase conjoining the verb of action with the expression 'responsible for'. Hence, 'he is legally responsible for killing her' is not usually found, whereas 'he is legally responsible for her death' is common, as are the expressions 'legally responsible for his act (in killing her)'; 'legally responsible for his crime'; or, as in the official formulation of the M'Naghten Rules, 'responsible for his actions or omissions in doing or being a party to the killing'. These common expressions in which a noun, not a verb, follows the phrase 'responsible for' are grammatically similar to statements of causal responsibility, and the tendency to use the same form no doubt shows how strongly the overtones of causal responsibility influence the terminology ordinarily used to make statements of liability-responsibility. There is, however, also in support of Mr. Pitcher's view, the point already cited that, even in legal writing, where a person is said to be responsible for his act or his conduct, the relevant mental element is usually the question of insanity or immaturity, so that the ground in such cases for the assertion that the person is responsible or is not responsible for his act is the presence or absence of 'responsibility for actions' in the sense of capacity-responsibility, and not merely the presence or absence of knowledge or intention in relation to the particular act.

MORAL LIABILITY-RESPONSIBILITY

How far can the account given above of legal liability-responsibility be applied *mutatis mutandis* to moral responsibility? The *mutanda* seem to be the following: 'deserving blame' or 'blame-worthy' will have to be substituted for 'liable to punishment', and 'morally bound to make amends or pay compensation' for 'liable to be made to pay compensation'. Then the moral counterpart to the account given of legal liability-responsibility would be the following: To say that a person is morally responsible for something he has done or for some harmful outcome of his own or others' conduct, is to say that he is morally blameworthy, or morally obliged to make amends for the harm, so far as this depends on certain conditions. These conditions relate to the character or extent of a man's control over his own conduct, or to the causal or other connection between his action and harmful occurrences, or to his relationship with the person who actually did the harm.

In general, such an account of the meaning of 'morally responsible' seems correct, and the striking differences between legal and moral responsibility are due to substantive differences between the content of legal and moral rules and principles rather than to any variation in meaning of responsibility when conjoined with the word 'moral' rather than 'legal'. Thus, both in the legal and the moral case, the criteria of responsibility seem to be restricted to the psychological elements involved in the control of conduct, to causal or other connections between acts and harm, and to the relationships with the actual doer of misdeeds. The interesting differences between legal and moral responsibility arise from the differences in the particular criteria falling under these general heads. Thus a system of criminal law may make responsibility strict, or even absolute, not even exempting very young children or the grossly insane from punishment; or it may vicariously punish one man for what another has done, even though the former had no control of

the latter; or it may punish an individual or make him compensate another for harm which he neither intended nor could have foreseen as likely to arise from his conduct. We may condemn such a legal system which extends strict or vicarious responsibility in these ways as barbarous or unjust, but there are no conceptual barriers to be overcome in speaking of such a system as a legal system, though it is certainly arguable that we should not speak of 'punishment' where liability is vicarious or strict. In the moral case, however, greater conceptual barriers exist: The hypothesis that we might hold individuals morally blameworthy for doing things which they could not have avoided doing, or for things done by others over whom they had no control, conflicts with too many of the central features of the idea of morality to be treated merely as speculation about a rare or inferior kind of moral system. It may be an exaggeration to say that there could not logically be such a morality or that blame administered according to principles of strict or vicarious responsibility, even in a minority of cases, could not logically be moral blame; none the less, admission of such a system as a morality would require a profound modification in our present concept of morality, and there is no similar requirement in the case of law.

Some of the most familiar contexts in which the expression 'responsibility' appears confirm these general parallels between legal and moral liability-responsibility. Thus in the famous question 'Is moral responsibility compatible with determinism?' the expression 'moral responsibility' is apt just because the bogey raised by determinism specifically relates to the usual criteria of responsibility; for it opens the question whether, if 'determinism' were true, the capacities of human beings to control their conduct would still exist or could be regarded as adequate to justify moral blame.

In less abstract or philosophical contexts, where there is a present question of blaming someone for some particular act, the assertion or denial that a person is morally responsible for his actions is common. But this expression is as ambiguous in the moral as in the legal case: It is most frequently used to refer to what I have termed 'capacity-responsibility', which is the most important criterion of moral liability-responsibility; but in some contexts it may also refer to moral liability-responsibility itself. Perhaps the most frequent use in moral contexts of the expression 'responsible for' is in cases where persons are said to be morally responsible for the outcomes or results of morally wrong conduct, although Mr. Pitcher's claim that men are never said in ordinary usage to be responsible for their actions is, as I have attempted to demonstrate above with counter-examples, an exaggerated claim.

CAPACITY-RESPONSIBILITY

In most contexts, as I have already stressed, the expression 'he is responsible for his actions' is used to assert that a person has certain normal capacities. These constitute the most important criteria of moral liability-responsibility, though it is characteristic of most legal systems that they have given only a partial or tardy recognition to all these capacities as general criteria of legal responsibility. The capacities in question are those of understanding, reasoning, and control of conduct: the ability to understand what conduct legal rules or morality require, to deliberate and reach decisions concerning these requirements, and to conform to decisions when made. Because 'responsible for his actions' in this sense refers not to a legal status but to certain complex psychological characteristics of persons, a person's responsibility for his actions may intelligibly be said to be 'diminished' or 'impaired' as well as altogether absent, and persons may be said to be 'suffering from diminished responsibility' much as a wounded man may be said to be suffering from a diminished capacity to control the movements of his limbs.

No doubt the most frequent occasions for asserting or denying that a person is 'responsible for his actions' are cases where questions of blame or punishment for particular actions are in issue. But, as with other expressions used to denote criteria of responsibility, this one also may be used where no particular question of blame or punishment is in issue, and it is then used simply to describe a person's psychological condition. Hence it may be said purely by way of description of some harmless inmate of a mental institution, even though there is no present question of his misconduct, that he is a person who is not responsible for his actions. No doubt if there were no social practice of blaming and punishing people for their misdeeds, and excusing them from punishment because they lack the normal capacities of understanding and control, we should lack this shorthand description for describing their condition which we now derive from these social practices. In that case we should have to describe the condition of the inmate directly, by saying that he could not understand what people told him to do, or could not reason about it, or come to, or adhere to any decisions about his conduct.

Legal systems left to themselves may be very niggardly in their admission of the relevance of liability to legal punishment of the several capacities, possession of which are necessary to render a man morally responsible for his actions. So much is evident from the history sketched in the preceding chapter of the painfully slow emancipation of English criminal law from the narrow, cognitive criteria of responsibility formulated in the M'Naghten Rules. Though some Continental legal systems have been willing to confront squarely the question whether the accused 'lacked the ability to recognize the wrongness of his conduct and to act in accordance with that recognition,'[5] such an issue, if taken seriously, raises formidable difficulties of proof, especially before juries. For this reason I think that, instead of a close determination of such questions of capacity, the apparently coarser-grained technique of exempting persons from liability to punishment if they fall into certain recognized categories of mental disorder is likely to be increasingly used. Such exemption by general category is a technique long known to English law; for in the case of very young children it has made no attempt to determine, as a condition of liability, the question whether on account of their immaturity they could have understood what the law required and could have conformed to its requirements, or whether their responsibility on account of their immaturity was 'substantially impaired', but exempts them from liability for punishment if under a specified age. It seems likely that exemption by medical category rather than by individualized findings of absent or diminished capacity will be found more likely to lead in practice to satisfactory results, in spite of the difficulties pointed out in the last essay in the discussion of s. 60 of the Mental Health Act, 1959.

Though a legal system may fail to incorporate in its rules any psychological criteria of responsibility, and so may apply its sanction to those who are not morally blameworthy, it is none the less dependent for its efficacy on the possession by a sufficient number of those whose conduct it seeks to control of the capacities of understanding and control of conduct which constitute capacity-responsibility. For if a large proportion of those concerned could not understand what the law required them to do or could not form and keep a decision to obey, no legal system could come into existence or continue to exist. The general possession of such capacities is therefore a condition of the *efficacy* of law, even though it is not made a condition of liability to legal sanctions. The same condition of efficacy attaches to all attempts to regulate or control human conduct by forms of *communication:* such as orders, commands, the invocation of moral or other rules or principles, arguments, and advice.

'The notion of prevention through the medium of the mind assumes mental ability adequate to restraint'. This was clearly seen by Bentham and by Austin, who perhaps influenced the seventh report of the Criminal Law Commissioners of 1833 containing this sentence. But they overstressed the point; for they wrongly assumed that this condition of efficacy must also be incorporated in legal rules as a condition of liability. This mistaken assumption is to be found not only in the explanation of the doctrine of *mens rea* given in Bentham's and Austin's works, but is explicit in the Commissioners' statement preceding the sentence quoted above that 'the object of penal law being the prevention of wrong, the principle does not extend to mere involuntary acts or even to harmful consequences the result of inevitable accident'. The case of morality is however different in precisely this respect: the possession by those to whom its injunctions are addressed of 'mental ability adequate to restraint' (capacity-responsibility) has there a double status and importance. It is not only a condition of the efficacy of morality; but a system or practice which did not regard the possession of these capacities as a necessary condition of liability, and so treated blame as appropriate even in the case of those who lacked them, would not, as morality is at present understood, be a morality.

NOTES

1. The author's discussion of this appears at pp. 264–65 of *Punishment and Responsibility* [editors].
2. *A History of The Criminal Law,* Vol. II, p. 183.
3. In a review of 'Changing Conceptions & Responsibility', in *Crim. L. R.* (1966) 124.
4. In 'Hart on Action and Responsibility', *The Philosophical Review* (1960), p. 266.
5. German Criminal Code, Art. 51.

H. L. A. HART AND
A. M. HONORÉ

Causation and Responsibility*

I. RESPONSIBILITY IN LAW AND MORALS

. . . In the moral judgments of ordinary life, we have occasion to blame people because they have caused harm to others, and also, if less frequently, to insist that morally they are bound to compensate those to whom they have caused harm. These are the moral analogues of more precise legal conceptions; for, in all legal systems, liability to be punished or to make compensation frequently depends on whether actions (or omissions) have caused harm. Moral blame is not of course confined to such cases of causing harm. We blame a man who cheats or lies or breaks promises, even if one one has suffered in the particular case: This has its legal counterpart in the punishment of abortive attempts to commit crimes, and of offences constituted by the unlawful possession of certain kinds of weapons, drugs, or materials, for example, for counterfeiting currency. When the occurrence of harm is an essential part of the ground for blame the connection of the person blamed with the harm may take any of the forms of causal connection we have examined. His action may have initiated a series of physical events dependent on each other and culminating in injury to persons or property, as in wounding and killing. These simple forms are the paradigms for the lawyer's talk of harm 'directly' caused. But we blame people also for harm which arises from or is the consequence of their neglect of common precautions; we do this even if harm would not have come about without the intervention of an-other human being deliberately exploiting the opportunities provided by neglect. The main legal analogue here is liability for 'negligence'. The wish of many lawyers to talk in this branch of the law of harm being 'within the risk' rather than 'caused by' the negligent conduct manifests appreciation of the fact that a different form of relationship is involved in saying that harm is the consequence, on the one hand, of an explosion and, on the other, of a failure to lock the door by which a thief has entered. Again, we blame people for the harm which we say is the consequence of their influence over others, either exerted by nonrational means or in one of the ways we have designated 'interpersonal transactions'. To such grounds for responsibility there correspond many important legal conceptions: The instigation of crimes ('commanding' or 'procuring') constitutes an important ground of criminal responsibility and the concepts of enticement and of inducement (by threats or misrepresentation) are an element in many civil wrongs as well as in criminal offences.

The law, however, especially in matters of compensation, goes far beyond these causal grounds for responsibility in such doctrines as the vicarious responsibility of a master for his servant's civil wrongs and that of the responsibility of an occupier of property for injuries suffered by passersby from defects of which the occupier had no knowledge and which he had no opportunity to repair. There is a recognition, perhaps diminishing, of this noncausal ground of responsibility outside the law; responsibility is sometimes admitted by one person or group of persons, even if no precaution has been neglected by them, for harm done by persons related to them in a special way, either by family ties or as members of the

*From *Causation in the Law* by H. L. A. Hart and A. M. Honoré (Oxford: The Oxford University Press, 1959), pp. 59–78, © 1959 Oxford University Press. Reprinted by permission of The Clarendon Press, Oxford. Footnotes have been renumbered.

same social or political association. Responsibility may be simply 'placed' by moral opinion on one person for what others do. The simplest case of such vicarious moral responsibility is that of a parent for damage done by a child; its more complex (and more debatable) form is the moral responsibility of one generation of a nation to make compensation for their predecessors' wrong, such as the Germans admitted in payment of compensation to Israel.

At this point it is necessary to issue a *caveat* about the meaning of the expression 'responsible' if only to avoid prejudicing a question about the character of *legal* determinations of causal connection with which we shall be much concerned in later chapters. Usually in discussion of the law and occasionally in morals, to say that someone is responsible for some harm means that in accordance with legal rules or moral principles it is at least permissible, if not mandatory, to blame or punish or exact compensation from him. In this use[1] the expression 'responsible for' does not refer to a factual connection between the person held responsible and the harm but simply to his liability under the rules to be blamed, punished, or made to pay. The expressions 'answerable for' or 'liable for' are practically synonymous with 're-sponsible for' in *this* use, in which there is no implication that the person held responsible actually *did* or *caused* the harm. In this sense a master is (in English law) responsible for the damage done by his servants acting within the scope of their authority and a parent (in French and German law) for that done by his children; it is in this sense that a guarantor or surety is responsible for the debts or the good behaviour of other persons. Very often, however, especially in discussion of morals, to say that someone is responsible for some harm is to assert (*inter alia*) that he *did* the harm or *caused* it though such a statement is perhaps rarely confined to this for it usually also carries with it the implication that it is at least permissible to blame or punish. This double use of the expression no doubt arises from the important fact that doing or causing harm constitutes not only the most usual but the primary type of ground for holding persons responsible in the first sense. We still speak of inanimate or natural causes such as storms, floods, germs, or the failure of electricity supply as 'responsible for' disasters; this mode of expression, now taken only to

mean that they caused the disasters, no doubt originated in the belief that all that happens is the work of spirits when it is not that of men. Its survival in the modern world is perhaps some testimony to the primacy of causal connection as an element in responsibility and to the intimate connection between the two notions.

We shall consider later an apparent paradox which interprets in a different way the relationship between cause and responsibility. Much modern thought on causation in the law rests on the contention that the statement that someone has caused harm either means no more than that the harm would not have happened without ('but for') his action or where (as in normal legal usage and in all ordinary speech), it apparently means more than this, it is a disguised way of asserting the 'normative' judgment that he is responsible in the first sense, that is, that it is proper or just to blame or punish him or make him pay. On this view to say that a person caused harm is not really, though ostensibly it is, to give a *ground or reason* for holding him responsible in the first sense; for we are only in a position to say that he has caused harm when we have decided that he is responsible. Pending consideration of the theories of legal causation which exploit this point of view we shall use the expression 'responsible for' only in the first of the two ways explained, that is, without any implication as to the type of factual connection between the person held responsible and the harm; and we shall provisionally, though without prejudicing the issue, treat statements that a person caused harm as one sort of nontautologous ground or reason for saying that he is responsible in this sense.

If we may provisionally take what in ordinary life we say and do at its face value, it seems that there coexist in ordinary thought, apart from the law though mirrored in it, several different types of connection between a person's action and eventual harm which render him responsible for it; and in both law and morals the various forms of causal connection between act or omission and harm are the most obvious and least disputable reasons for holding anyone responsible. Yet, in order to understand the extent to which the causal notions of ordinary thought are used in the law, we must bear in mind the many factors which must differentiate moral from legal responsibility in spite of their partial correspondence:

the law is not only not bound to follow the moral patterns of attribution of responsibility but, even when it does, it must take into account, in a way which the private moral judgment need not and does not, the general social consequences which are attached to its judgments of responsibility; for they are of a gravity quite different from those attached to moral censure. The use of the legal sanctions of imprisonment, or enforced monetary compensation against individuals, has such formidable repercussions on the general life of society that the fact that individuals have a type of connection with harm which is adequate for moral censure or claims for compensation is only *one* of the factors which the law most consider, in defining the kinds of connection between actions and harm for which it will hold individuals legally responsible. Always to follow the private moral judgment here would be far too expensive for the law: not only in the crude sense that it would entail a vast machinery of courts and officials, but in the more important sense that it would inhibit or discourage too many other valuable activities of society. To limit the *types* of harm which the law will recognize is not enough; even if the types of harm are limited it would still be too much for any society to punish or exact compensation from individuals whenever their connection with harm of such types would justify moral censure. Conversely, social needs may require that compensation should be paid and even (though less obviously) that punishment be inflicted where no such connection between the person held responsible and the harm exists.

So causing harm of a legally recognized sort or being connected with such harm in any of the ways that justify moral blame, though vitally important and perhaps basic in a legal system, is not and should not be either always necessary or always sufficient for legal responsibility. All legal systems in response either to tradition or to social needs both extend responsibility and cut it off in ways which diverge from the simpler principles of moral blame. In England a man is not guilty of murder if the victim of his attack does not die within a year and day. In New York a person who negligently starts a fire is liable to pay only for the first of several houses which it destroys. These limitations imposed by legal policy are *prima facie* distinguishable from limitations due to the frequent requirement of legal rules that responsibility be limited to harm caused by wrongdoing. Yet a whole school of thought maintains that this distinction does not exist or is not worth drawing.

Apart from this, morality can properly leave certain things vague into which a legal system must attempt to import some degree of precision. Outside the law nothing requires us, when we find the case too complex or too strange, to say whether any and, if so, which of the morally significant types of connection between a person's action and harm exists; we can simply say the case is too difficult for us to pass judgment, at least where moral condemnation of others is concerned. No doubt we evade less easily our questions about our own connection with harm, and the great novelists have often described, sometimes in language very like the lawyers, how the conscience may be still tortured by uncertainties as to the *character* of a part in the production of harm, even when all the facts are known.[2] The fact that there is no precise system of punishments or rewards for common sense to administer, and so there are no 'forms of action' or 'pleadings' to define precise heads of responsibility for harm, means that the principles which guide common-sense attributions of responsibility give precise answers only in relatively simple types of case.

II. TRACING CONSEQUENCES

'To consequences no limit can be set': 'Every event which would not have happened if an earlier event had not happened is the consequence of that earlier event.' These two propositions are not equivalent in meaning and are not equally or in the same way at variance with ordinary thought. They have, however, both been urged sometimes in the same breath by the legal theorist[3] and the philosopher: They are indeed sometimes said by lawyers to be 'the philosophical doctrine' of causation. It is perhaps not difficult even for the layman to accept the first proposition as a truth about certain physical events; an explosion may cause a flash of light which will be propagated as far as the outer nebulae; its effects or consequences continue indefinitely. It is, however, a different matter to accept the view that whenever a man is murdered with a gun his death was the consequence of (still less an 'effect' of or 'caused by') the manufacture of the bullet. The first tells a perhaps unfamiliar tale about unfamiliar events;

the second introduces an unfamiliar, though, of course, a possible way of speaking about familiar events. It is not that this unrestricted use of 'consequence' is unintelligible or never found; it is indeed used to refer to bizarre or fortuitous connections or coincidences: but the point is that the various causal notions employed for the purposes of explanation, attribution of responsibility or the assessment of contributions to the course of history carry with them implicit limits which are similar in these different employments.

It is, then, the second proposition, defining consequence in terms of 'necessary condition', with which theorists are really concerned. This proposition is the corollary of the view that, if we look into the past of any given event, there is an infinite number of events, each of which is a necessary condition of the given event and so, as much as any other, is its cause. This is the 'cone'[4] of causation, so-called because, since any event has a number of simultaneous conditions, the series fans out as we go back in time. The justification, indeed only partial, for calling this 'the philosophical doctrine' of causation is that it resembles Mill's doctrine that 'we have no right to give the name of cause to one of the conditions exclusive of the others of them'. It differs from Mill's view in taking the essence of causation to be 'necessary condition' and not 'the sum total'[5] of the sufficient conditions of an event.

Legal theorists have developed this account of cause and consequence to show what is 'factual', 'objective', or 'scientific' in these notions: this they call 'cause in fact' and it is usually stressed as a preliminary to the doctrine that any more restricted application of these terms in the law represents nothing in the facts or in the meaning of causation, but expresses fluctuating legal policy or sentiments of what is just or convenient. Moral philosophers have insisted in somewhat similar terms that the consequences of human action are 'infinite': this they have urged as an objection against the utilitarian doctrine that the rightness of a morally right action depends on whether its consequences are better than those of any alternative action in the circumstances. 'We should have to trace as far as possible the consequences not only for the persons affected directly but also for those indirectly affected and to these no limit can be set.'[6] Hence, so the argument runs, we cannot either inductively establish the utilitarian doctrine that right acts are 'optimific' or use it in particular cases to discover what is right. Yet, however vulnerable at other points utilitarianism may be as an account of moral judgment, this objection seems to rest on a mistake as to the sense of 'consequence'. The utilitarian assertion that the rightness of an action depends on its consequences is not the same as the assertion that it depends on all those later occurrences which would not have happened had the action not been done, to which indeed 'no limit can be set'. It is important to see that the issue here is not the linguistic one whether the word 'consequence' would be understood if used in this way. The point is that, though we could, we do not think in this way in tracing connections between human actions and events. Instead, whenever we are concerned with such connections, whether for the purpose of explaining a puzzling occurrence, assessing responsibility, or giving an intelligible historical narrative, we employ a set of concepts restricting in various ways what counts as a consequence. These restrictions colour *all* our thinking in causal terms; when we find them in the law we are not finding something invented by or peculiar to the law, though of course it is for the law to say when and how far it will use them and, where they are vague, to supplement them.

No short account can be given of the limits thus placed on 'consequences' because these limits vary, intelligibly, with the variety of causal connection asserted. Thus we may be tempted by the generalization that consequences must always be something intended or foreseen or at least foreseeable with ordinary care: but counter-examples spring up from many types of context where causal statements are made. If smoking is shown to cause lung cancer, this discovery will permit us to describe past as well as future cases of cancer as the effect or consequence of smoking even though no one foresaw or had reasonable grounds to suspect this in the past. What is common and commonly appreciated and hence foreseeable certainly controls the scope of consequences in certain varieties of causal statement but not in all. Again the voluntary intervention of a second person very often constitutes the limit. If a guest sits down with a table laid with knife and fork and plunges the knife into his hostess's breast, her death is not in any context thought of as caused by, or the effect or result of the waiter's action in laying the table; nor would it be linked with this action as its consequence for any of the purposes, explanatory or attributive, for which we employ causal notions. Yet as we have seen there are many other types of case where a voluntary action or the harm it does are naturally attributed to some prior neglect of precaution as its consequence. Finally, we may think that a simple answer is already supplied by Hume and Mill's doctrine that causal connection rests on general laws asserting regular connection; yet, even in the type of case to which this important doctrine applies, reference to it alone will not solve our problem. For we often trace a causal connection between an antecedent and a consequent which themselves very rarely go together: we do this when the case can be broken down into intermediate stages, which themselves exemplify different generalizations, as when we find that the fall of a tile was the cause of someone's death, rare though this be. Here our problem reappears in the form of the question: When can generalizations be combined in this way?

We shall examine first the central type of case where the problem is of this last-mentioned form. Here the gist of the causal connection lies in the general connection with each other of the successive stages; and is not dependent on the special notions of one person providing another with reasons or exceptional opportunities for actions. This form of causal connection may exist between actions and events, and between purely physical events, and it is in such cases that the words 'cause' and 'causing' used of the antecedent action or event have their most obvious application. It is convenient to refer to cases of the first type where the consequence is harm as cases of 'causing harm', and to refer to cases where harm is the consequence of one person providing another with reasons or opportunities for doing harm as cases of 'inducing', 'advising', or 'occasioning' harmful acts. In cases of the first type a voluntary act, or a conjunction of events amounting to a coincidence, operates as a limit in the sense that events subsequent to these are not attributed to the antecedent action or event as its consequence even though they would not have happened without it. Often such a limiting action or coincidence is thought of and described as 'intervening': and lawyers speak of them as 'superseding' or 'extra-neous' causes 'breaking the chain of causation'. To see what these metaphors rest on (and in part obscure) and how such factors operate as a limit we shall consider the detail of three simple cases.

(i) A forest fire breaks out, and later investigation shows that shortly before the outbreak A had flung away a lighted cigarette into the bracken at the edge of the forest, the bracken caught fire, a light breeze got up, and fanned the flames in the direction of the forest. If, on discovering these facts, we hesitate before saying that A's action caused the forest fire this would be to consider the alternative hypothesis that in spite of appearances the fire only succeeded A's action in point of time, that the bracken flickered out harmlessly and the forest fire was caused by something else. To dispose of this it may be necessary to examine in further detail the process of events between the ignition of the bracken and the outbreak of fire in the forest and to show that these exemplified certain types of continuous change. If this is shown, there is no longer any room for doubt: A's action *was* the cause of the fire, whether he intended it or not. This seems and is the simplest of cases. Yet it is important to notice that even in applying our general knowledge to a case as simple as this, indeed in regarding it as simple, we make an implicit use of a distinction between types of factor which constitute a limit in tracing consequences and those which we regard as mere circumstances 'through' which we trace them. For the breeze which sprang up after A dropped the cigarette, and without which the fire would not have spread to the forest, was not only subsequent to his action but entirely independent of it: It was, however, a common recurrent feature of the environment, and, as such, it is thought of not as an 'intervening' force but as merely part of the circumstances in which the cause 'operates'. The decision so to regard it is implicitly taken when we combine our knowledge of the successive stages of the process and assert the connection.

It is easy here to be misled by the natural metaphor of a causal 'chain', which may lead us to think that the causal process consists of a series of single events each of which is dependent upon (would not have occurred without) its predecessor in the 'chain' and so is dependent upon the initiating action or event. In truth in any causal process we have at each phase not single events but complex sets of conditions, and among these conditions are some which are not only subsequent to, but independent of, the initiating action or event. Some of these independent conditions such as the evening breeze in the example chosen, we classify as mere conditions in or on which the cause operates; others we speak of as 'interventions' or 'causes'. To decide how such independent elements shall be classified is also to decide how we shall combine our knowledge of the different general connections which the successive stages exemplify, and it is important to see that nothing *in* this knowledge itself can resolve this point. We may have to go to science for the relevant general knowledge before we can assert with proper confidence that A's action did cause the fire, but science, though it tells us that an air current was required, is silent on the difference between a current in the form of an evening breeze and one produced by someone who deliberately fanned the flames as they were flickering out in the bracken. Yet an air current in this form is not a 'condition' or 'mere circumstance' through which we can trace the consequence; its presence would force us to revise the assertion that A caused the fire. Conversely if science helped us to identify as a necessary factor in producing the fire some condition or element of which we had previously been totally ignorant, for example the persistence of oxygen, this would leave our original judgment undisturbed if this factor were a common or pervasive feature of the environment or of the thing in question. There is thus indeed an important sense in which it is true that the distinction between cause and conditions is not a 'scientific' one. It is not determined by laws or generalizations concerning connections between events.

When we have assembled all our knowledge of the factors involved in the fire, the residual question which we then confront (the attributive question) may be typified as follows: Here is A's action, here is the fire. Can the fire be attributed to A's action as its consequence given that there is also this third factor (the breeze or B's intervention) without which the fire would not have happened? It is plain that, both in raising questions of this kind and in answering them, ordinary thought is powerfully influenced by the analogy between the straightforward cases of causal attribution (where the elements required for the production of harm in addition to the initiating action are all 'normal' conditions) and even simpler cases of responsibility which we do not ordinarily describe in causal language at all but by the simple transitive verbs of action. These are the cases of the direct manipulation of objects involving changes in them or their position: cases where we say 'He pushed it', 'He broke it,' 'He bent it.' The cases which we do confidently describe in causal language ('The fire was caused by his carelessness,' 'He caused a fire') are cases where no other human action or abnormal occurrence is required for the production of the effect, but only normal conditions. Such cases appear as mere long range or less direct versions or extensions of the most obvious and fundamental case of all for the attribution of responsibility: the case where we can simply say 'He did it.' Conversely in attaching importance to thus causing harm as a distinct ground of responsibility and in taking certain kinds of factor (whether human interventions or abnormal occurrences), without which the initiating action would not have led to harm, to preclude the description of the case in simple causal terms, common sense is affected by the fact that here, because of the manner in which the harm eventuates, the outcome cannot be represented as a mere extension of the initiating action; the analogy with the fundamental case for responsibility ('He did it') has broken down.

When we understand the power exerted over our ordinary thought by the conception that causing harm is a mere extension of the primary case of doing harm, the interrelated metaphors which seem natural to lawyers and laymen, in describing various aspects of causal connection, fall into place and we can discuss their factual basis. The persistent notion that some kinds of event required in addition to the initiating action for the production of harm 'break the chain of causation' is intelligible, if we remember that though such events actually complete the *explanation* of the harm (and so *make* rather than *break* the causal explanation) they do, unlike mere normal conditions, break the *analogy* with cases of simple actions. The same analogy accounts for the description of these factors as 'new actions' (*novus actus*) or 'new causes', 'superseding', 'extraneous', 'intervening forces': and for the description of the initiating action when 'the chain of causation' is broken as 'no longer operative', 'having worn out', *functus officio.*[7] So too when the 'chain' is held not to be 'broken' the initiating action is said to be still 'potent',[8] 'continuing', 'contributing', 'operative', and the mere conditions held insufficient to break the chain are 'part of the background',[9] 'circumstances in which the cause operates',[10] 'the stage set', 'part of the history'.

(ii) A throws a lighted cigarette into the bracken which catches fire. B, just as the flames are about to flicker out, deliberately pours petrol on them. The fire spreads and burns down the forest. A's action, whether or not he intended the forest fire, was not the cause of the fire: B's was.

The voluntary intervention of a second human agent, as in this case, is a paradigm among those factors which preclude the assimilation in causal judgments of the first agent's connection with the eventual harm to the case of simple direct manipulation. Such an intervention displaces the prior action's title to be called the cause and, in the persistent metaphors found in the law, it 'reduces' the earlier action and its immediate effects to the level of 'mere circumstances' or 'part of the history.' B in this case was not an 'instrument' through which A worked or a victim of the circumstances A has created. He has, on the contrary, freely exploited the circumstances and brought about the fire without the cooperation of any further agent or any chance coincidence. Compared with this the claim of A's action to be ranked the cause of the fire fails. That this and not the moral appraisal of the two actions is the point of comparison seems clear. If A and B both intended to set the forest on fire, and this destruction is accepted as something wrong or wicked, their moral wickedness, judged by the criterion of intention, is the same. Yet the causal judgment differentiates between them. If their moral guilt is judged by the outcome, this judgment though it would differentiate between them cannot be the source of the causal judgment; for it presupposes it. The difference just is that B has caused the harm and A has not. Again, if we appraise these actions as good or bad from different points of view, this leaves the causal judgments unchanged. A may be a soldier of one side anxious to burn down the enemy's hideout: B may be an enemy soldier who has decided that his side is too iniquitous to defend. Whatever is the moral judgment passed on these actions by different speakers it would remain true that A had not caused the fire and B had.

There are, as we have said, situations in which a voluntary action would not be thought of as an intervention precluding causal connection in this way. These are the cases discussed further below where an opportunity commonly exploited for harmful actions is negligently provided, or one person intentionally provides another with a certain type of reason for wrongdoing. Except in such cases a voluntary intervention is a limit past which consequences are not traced. By contrast, actions which in any of a variety of different ways are less than fully voluntary are assimilated to the means by which or the circumstances in which the earlier action brings about the consequences. Such actions are not the outcome of an informed choice made without pressure from others, and the different ways in which human action may fall short in this respect range from defective muscular control, through lack of consciousness or knowledge, to the vaguer notions of duress and of predicaments, created by the first agent for the second, in which there is no 'fair' choice.

In considering examples of such actions and their bearing on causal judgments there are three dangers to avoid. It would be folly to think that in tracing connections through such actions instead of regarding them, like voluntary interventions, as a limit, ordinary thought has clearly separated out their nonvoluntary aspect from others by which they are often accompanied. Thus even in the crude case where A lets off a gun (intentionally or not) and startles B, so that he makes an involuntary movement of his arm which breaks a glass, the commonness of such a reaction as much as its compulsive character may influence the judgment that A's action was the cause of the damage.

Secondly we must not impute to ordinary thought all the fine discriminations that could be made and in fact are to be found in a legal system, or an equal willingness to supply answers to complex questions in causal terms. Where there is no precise system of punishment, compensation or reward to administer, ordinary men will not often have faced such questions as whether the injuries suffered by a motorist who collides with another in swerving to avoid a child are consequences attributable to the neglect of the child's parents in allowing it to wander on to the road. Such questions courts have to answer and in such cases common judgments provide only a general, though still an important indication of what are the relevant factors.

Thirdly, though very frequently nonvoluntary actions are assimilated to mere conditions or means by which the first agent brings about the consequences, the assimilation is never quite complete. This is manifested by the general avoidance of many causal locutions which are appropriate when the consequences are traced (as in the first case) through purely physical events. Thus even in the case in which the second agent's rôle is hardly an 'action' at all, for example, where A hits B, who staggers against a glass window and breaks it, we should say that A's blow made B stagger and break the glass, rather than that A's blow caused the glass to break, though in any explanatory or attributive context the case would be *summarized* by saying that A's action was the cause of the *damage* or that A had caused it.

In the last two cases where B's movements are involuntary in the sense that they are not part of any action which he chose or intended to do, their connection with A's action would be described by saying that A's blow *made* B stagger or *caused* him to stagger or that the noise of A's shot *made* him jump or *caused* him to jump. This would be true, whether A intended or expected B to react in this way or not, and the naturalness of treating A's action as the cause of the ultimate damage is due to the causal character of this part of the process involving B's action. The same is however true where B's actions are not involuntary movements but A is considered to have made or caused B to do them by less crude means. This is the case if, for example, A uses treats or exploits his authority over B to make B do something, for example, knock down a door. At least where A's threats are of serious harm, or B's act was unquestionably within A's authority to order, he too has made or forced or (in formal quasi-legal parlance) 'caused' B to act.

Outside the area of such cases, where B's will would be either said not to be involved at all, or to be overborne by A, are cases where A's act creates a predicament for B *narrowing* the area of choice so that he has either to inflict some harm on himself or others, or sacrifice some important interest or duty. Such cases resemble coercion in

that A narrows the area of B's choice but differ from it in that this predicament need not be intentionally created. A sets a house on fire (intentionally or unintentionally): B to save himself has to jump from a height involving certain injury, or to save a child rushes in and is seriously burned. Here of course B's movements are not involuntary; the 'necessity' of his action is here of a different order. His action is the outcome of a choice between two evils forced on him by A's action. In such cases, when B's injuries are thought of as the consequence of the fire, the implicit judgment is made that his action was the lesser of two evils and in this sense a 'reasonable' one which he was obliged to make to avoid the greater evil. This is often paradoxically, though understandably, described by saying that here the agent 'had no choice' but to do what he did. Such judgments involve a comparison of the importance of the respective interests sacrificed and preserved, and the final assertion that A's action was the cause of the injuries rests on evaluations about which men may differ.

Finally, ground for treating some harm which would not have occurred without B's action as the consequence of A's action may be that B acted in ignorance of, or under a mistake as to some feature of, the situation created by A. Poisoning offers perhaps the simplest example of the bearing on causal judgments of actions which are less than voluntary in this Aristotelian sense. If A intending B's death deliberately poisons B's food and B, knowing this, deliberately takes the poison and dies, A has not caused B's death: if however B does not know the food to be poisoned, eats it and dies A has caused his death, even if he put the poison in unwittingly. Of course only the roughest judgments are passed in causal terms in such cases outside law courts, where fine degrees of 'appreciation' or reckless shutting of the eyes, may have to be discriminated from 'full knowledge'. Yet, rough as these are, they indicate clearly enough the controlling principles.

Though in the foregoing cases A's initiating action might often be described as 'the cause' of the ultimate harm, this linguistic fact is of subordinate importance to the fact that, for whatever purpose, explanatory, descriptive or evaluative, consequences of an action are traced, discriminations are made (except in the cases discussed later) between free voluntary interventions and less than voluntary reactions to the first action or the circumstances created by it.

(iii) The analogy with single simple actions which guides the tracing of consequences may be broken by certain kinds of conjunctions of physical events. A hits B who falls to the ground stunned and bruised by the blow; at that moment a tree crashes to the ground and kills B. A has certainly caused B's bruises but not his death: for though the fall of the tree was, like the evening breeze, in our earlier example, independent of and subsequent to the initiating action, it would be differentiated from the breeze in any description in causal terms of the connection of B's death with A's action. It is to be noticed that this is not a matter which turns on the intention with which A struck B. Even if A hit B inadvertently or accidentally his blow would still be the cause of B's bruises: he would have caused them though unintentionally. Conversely even if A had intended his blow to kill, this would have been an attempt to kill but still not the cause of B's death. On this legal and ordinary judgments would be found to agree; and most legal systems would distinguish for the purposes of punishment an attempt with a fatal upshot, issuing by such chance or anomalous events, from 'causing death' —the terms in which the offences of murder and manslaughter are usually defined.

Similarly the causal description of the case does not turn on the moral appraisal of A's action or the wish to punish it. A may be a robber and a murderer and B a saint guarding the place A hoped to plunder. Or B may be a murderer and A a hero who has forced his way into B's retreat. In both cases the causal judgment is the same. A had caused the minor injuries but not B's death, though he tried to kill him. A may indeed be praised or blamed but not for causing B's death. However intimate the connection between causation and responsibility, it does not determine causal judgments in this simple way. Nor does the causal judgment turn on a refusal to attribute grave consequences to actions which normally have less serious results. Had A's blow killed B outright and the tree, falling on his body, merely smashed his watch we should still treat the coincidental character of the fall of the tree as determining the form of causal statement. We should then recognize A's blow as the cause of B's death but not of the breaking of the watch.

The connection between A's action and B's death in the first case would naturally be described in the language of *coincidence*. 'It was a coincidence: it just happened that, at the very moment when A knocked B down, a tree crashed at the very place where he fell and killed him.' The common legal metaphor would describe the fall of the tree as an 'extraneous' cause. This, however, is dangerously misleading, as an analysis of the notion of coincidence will show. It suggests merely an event which is subsequent to and independent of some other contingency, and of course the fall of the tree has both these features in relation to A's blow. Yet in these respects the fall of the tree does not differ from the evening breeze in the earlier case where we found no difficulty in tracing causal connection. The full elucidation of the notion of a coincidence is a complex matter for, though it is very important as a limit in tracing consequences, causal questions are not the only ones to which the notion is relevant. The following are its most general characteristics. We speak of a coincidence whenever (1) the conjunction of two or more events in certain spatial or temporal relations is very unlikely by ordinary standards and (2) is for some reason significant or important, provided (3) that they occur without human contrivance and (4) are independent of each other. It is therefore a coincidence if two persons known to each other in London meet without design in Paris on their way to separate independently chosen destinations; or if two persons living in different places independently decide to write a book on the same subject. The first is a coincidence of time and place ('It just happened that we were at the same place at the same time'), and the second a coincidence of time only ('It just happened that they both decided to write on the subject at the same time').

Use of this general notion is made in the special case when the conjunction of two or more events occurs in temporal and/or spatial relationships which are significant, because, as our general knowledge of causal processes shows, this conjunction is required for the production of some given further event. In the language of Mill's idealized model, they form a necessary part of a complex set of jointly sufficient conditions. In the present case the fall of the tree just as B was struck down within its range satisfies the four criteria for a coincidence which we have enumerated. First, though neither event was of a very rare or exceptional kind, their conjunction would be rated very unlikely judged by the standards of ordinary experience. Secondly, this conjunction was causally significant for it was a necessary part of the process terminating in B's death. Thirdly, this conjunction was not consciously designed by A; had he known of the impending fall of the tree and hit B with the intention that he should fall within its range B's death would not have been the result of any coincidence. A would certainly have caused it. The common-sense principle that a contrived conjunction cannot be a coincidence is the element of truth in the legal maxim (too broadly stated even for legal purposes) that an intended consequence cannot be too 'remote'. Fourthly, each member of the conjunction in this case was independent of the other; whereas if B had fallen against the tree with an impact sufficient to bring it down on him, this sequence of physical events, though freakish in its way, would not be a coincidence and in most contexts of ordinary life, as in the law, the course of events would be summarized by saying that in this case, unlike that of the coincidence, A's act was the cause of B's death, since each stage is the effect of the preceding stage. Thus, the blow forced the victim against the tree, the effect of this was to make the tree fall and the fall of the tree killed the victim.

One further criterion in addition to these four must be satisfied if a conjunction of events is to rank as a coincidence and as a limit when the consequences of the action are traced. This further criterion again shows the strength of the influence which the analogy with the case of the simple manipulation of things exerts over thought in causal terms. An abnormal *condition* existing at the time of a human intervention is distinguished both by ordinary thought and, with a striking consistency, by most legal systems from an abnormal event or conjunction of events subsequent to that intervention; the former, unlike the latter, are not ranked as coincidences or 'extraneous' causes when the consequences of the intervention come to be traced. Thus A innocently gives B a tap over the head of a normally quite harmless character, but because B is then suffering from some rare disease the tap has, as we say, 'fatal results'. In this case A has caused B's death though unintentionally. The scope of the principle which thus distinguishes contempo-

raneous abnormal conditions from subsequent events is unclear; but at least where a human being initiates some physical change in a thing, animal, or person, abnormal physical states of the object affected, existing at the time, are ranked as part of the circumstances in which the cause 'operates'. In the familiar controlling imagery these are part of 'the stage already set' before the 'intervention'.

Judgments about coincidences, though we often agree in making them, depend on two related ways on issues incapable of precise formulation. One of these is patent, the other latent but equally important. Just how unlikely must a conjunction be to rank as a coincidence, and in the light of what knowledge is likelihood to be assessed? The only answer is: 'very unlikely in the light of the knowledge available to ordinary men.' It is of course the indeterminacies of such standards, implicit in causal judgments, that make them inveterately disputable, and call for the exercise of discretion or choice by courts. The second and latent indeterminacy of these judgments depends on the fact that the things or events which they relate do not have pinned to them some uniquely correct description always to be used in assessing likelihood. It is an important pervasive feature of all our empirical judgments that there is a constant possibility of more or less specific description of any event or thing with which they are concerned. The tree might be described not simply as 'a tree' but as a 'rotten tree' or as a 'fir tree' or a 'tree sixty feet tall'. So too its fall might be described not as a 'fall' but as a fall of a specified distance at a specified velocity. The likelihood of conjunctions framed in these different terms would be differently assessed. The criteria of appropriate description like the standard of likelihood are supplied by consideration of common knowledge. Even if the scientist knew the tree to be rotten and could have predicted its fall with accuracy, this would not change the judgment that its fall at the time when B was struck down within its range was a coincidence; nor would it make the description 'rotten tree' appropriate for the assessment of the chances involved in this judgment. There are other controls over the choice of description derived from the degree of specificity of our interests in the final outcome of the causal process. We are concerned with the fall of an object sufficient to cause 'death' by impact and the precise force or direction which may account for the detail of the wounds is irrelevant here.

OPPORTUNITIES AND REASONS

Opportunities. The discrimination of voluntary interventions as a limit is no longer made when the case, owing to the commonness or appreciable risk of such harmful intervention, can be brought within the scope of the notion of providing an opportunity, known to be commonly exploited for doing harm. Here the limiting principles are different. When A leaves the house unlocked the range of consequences to be attributed to this neglect, as in any other case where precautions are omitted, depends primarily on the way in which such opportunities are commonly exploited. An alternative formulation of this idea is that a subsequent intervention would fall within the scope of consequences if the likelihood of its occurring is one of the reasons for holding A's omission to be negligent.

It is on these lines that we would distinguish between the entry of a thief and of a murderer; the opportunity provided is believed to be sufficiently commonly exploited by thieves to make it usual and often morally or legally obligatory not to provide it. Here, in attributing consequences to prior actions, causal judgments are directly controlled by the notion of the risk created by them. Neglect of such precautions is both unusual and reprehensible. For these reasons it would be hard to separate the two ways in which such neglect deviates from the 'norm'. Despite this, no simple identification can be made of the notion of responsibility with the causal connection which is a ground for it. This is so because the provision of an opportunity commonly taken by others is ranked as the cause of the outcome independently of the wish to praise or blame. The causal judgment may be made simply to assess a contribution to some outcome. Thus, whether we think well or ill of the use made of railways, we would still claim that the greater mobility of the population in the nineteenth century was a consequence of their introduction.

It is obvious that the question whether any given intervention is a sufficiently common exploitation of the opportunity provided to come within the risk is again a matter on which judgments may differ though they often agree. The courts, and perhaps ordinary thought also, often describe those that are sufficiently common as 'natural' consequences of the neglect. They have in these terms discriminated the entry of a thief from the entry of a man who burnt the house down, and refused to treat the destruction of the house as a 'natural' consequence of the neglect. . . .[11]

Reasons. In certain varieties of interpersonal transactions, unlike the case of coercion, the second action is quite voluntary. A may not threaten B but may bribe or advise or persuade him to do something. Here, A does not 'cause' or 'make' B do anything: the strongest words we should use are perhaps that he 'induced' or 'procured' B's act. Yet the law and moral principles alike may treat one person as responsible for the harm which another free agent has done 'in consequence' of the advice or the inducements which the first has offered. In such cases the limits concern the range of those actions done by B which are to rank as the consequence of A's words or deeds. In general this question depends on A's intentions or on the 'plan of action' he puts before B. If A advises or bribes B to break in and steal from an empty house and B does so, he acts in consequence of A's advice or bribe. If he deliberately burns down the house this would not be treated as the consequence of A's bribe or advice, legally or otherwise, though it may in some sense be true that the burning would not have taken place without the advice or bribe. Nice questions may arise, which the courts have to settle, where B diverges from the detail of the plan of action put before him by A.

NOTES

1. Cf. *O.E.D. sub tit.* Responsible: Answerable, Accountable (*to* another *for* something); liable to be called to account 'being responsible to the King for what might happen to us', 1662.

2. See the following passage from *The Golden Bowl* by Henry James. (Mrs. Assingham whose uncertain self-accusation is described here, had, on the eve of the Prince's marriage, encouraged him to resume an old friendship with Charlotte Stant. The relationship which developed came to threaten the marriage with disaster.) 'She had stood for the previous hour in a merciless glare, beaten upon, stared out of countenance, it fairly seemed to her, by intimations of her mistake. For what she was most immediately feeling was that she had in the past been active for these people to ends that were now bearing fruit and that might yet bear a greater crop. She but brooded at first in her corner of the carriage: it was like burying her exposed face, a face too helplessly exposed in the

cool lap of the common indifference ... a world mercifully unconscious and unreproachful. It wouldn't like the world she had just left know sooner or later what she had done or would know it only if the final consequence should be some quite overwhelming publicity. ... The sense of seeing was strong in her, but she clutched at the comfort of not being sure of what she saw. Not to know what it would represent on a longer view was a help in turn to not making out that her hands were embrued; since if she had stood in the position of a producing cause she should surely be less vague about what she had produced. This, further, in its way, was a step toward reflecting that when one's connection with any matter was too indirect to be traced, it might be described also as too slight to be deplored' (*The Golden Bowl*, Book 3, chap. 3). We are much indebted to Mrs. H. M. Warnock for this quotation.

3.   Lawson, *Negligence in the Civil Law*, p. 53.
4.   Glanville Williams, *Joint Torts and Contributory Negligence*, p. 239.
5.   Mill, Book III, chap. v, s. 2.
6.   Ross, *The Right and the Good*, p. 36.
7.   *Davies v. Swan Motor Co.*, [1947] 2 K.B. 291, 318.
8.   *Minister of Pensions v. Chennell*, [1947] K.B. 250, 256. Lord Wright (1950), 13 *Mod. L.R.* 3.
9.   *Norris v. William Moss & Son Ltd.*, [1954] 1 W.L.R. 46, 351.
10.   *Minister of Pensions v. Chennell*, [1947] K.B. 250, 256.
11.   *Bellows v. Worcester Storage Co.* (1937), 297 Mass 188, 7 N.E. 2d 588.

R O B E R T   E.   K E E T O N

The Basic Rule of Legal Cause in Negligence Cases*

DIVERSE FORMULATIONS OF THE RISK RULE

STATEMENT AND ILLUSTRATION OF THREE FORMULATIONS

The defendant, proprietor of a restaurant, placed a large, unlabeled can of rat poison beside cans of flour on a shelf near a stove in a restaurant kitchen. The victim, while in the kitchen making a delivery to the restaurant, was killed by an explosion of the poison. Assume that the defendant's handling of the rat poison was negligent because of the risk that someone would be poisoned but that defendant had no reason to know of the risk that the poison would explode if left in a hot place. Is the defendant liable for the death of the victim?[1]

This question illustrates the central problem of scope of liability for negligence. The problem is commonly subdivided into issues associated with, first, the foreseeability of any kind of harm to the

*Reprinted from *Legal Cause in the Law of Torts* by Robert E. Keeton, Copyright © 1963 by the Ohio State University Press, by permission of the author and the publisher.

victim who, in fact, was harmed and, second, the foreseeability of the particular harm or kind of harm that occurred.

The predominant theme in judicial utterances on the scope of liability in negligence cases is expressed in a proposition that, for convenience, will be referred to as the Risk Rule. This rule, quite commonly expressed in substance both in charges to the jury and in appellate opinions, is as follows:

A negligent actor is legally responsible for that harm, and only that harm, of which *negligence* is a cause in fact.

Some explanatory comments are in order. First, this rule is addressed not only to matters uniformly classified as problems of legal cause but also to other matters sometimes classified as problems of duty. Comments directed specifically to this choice of terminology are reserved for the second and third chapters.[2]

Other explanatory comments that seem necessary at the outset are concerned with the meaning of the words "actor" and "negligence." "Actor" is used here to signify the person whose "conduct" is being judged, whether plaintiff or defendant, and whether charged with acting negligently or with negligently failing to act. "Conduct" is used in a sense that includes both "acting" and "failing to act." "Negligence," in the context of this rule, must be understood in a more precise sense than merely "the negligent actor's conduct." This statement of the Risk Rule makes no sense unless interpreted as meaning that the actor's *conduct* during the period of his negligence may be a cause of harm of which his *negligence* is not a cause. For example, in the case of the explosive rat poison, it is not enough to ask whether the defendant's conduct in placing the poison where he did was a cause of the death of the victim. We should, as well, ask whether the defendant's negligence was a cause of the death. As a means of arriving at a satisfactory answer to that question, it will be useful to consider another.

What was that aspect of the conduct of the defendant that caused it to be characterized as negligence? Placing rat poison on a shelf may or may not be negligence. The negligence here consisted of placing the poison where it was likely to be mistaken for something intended for human consumption. This description says nothing about the proximity of the shelf to heat. That circumstance is omitted because of the assumption that the defendant had no reason to know of the explosive character of the poison; in such a situation it would not have been negligent to put the poison in a place that happened to be near heat, provided it was not a place where the poison was likely to be mistaken as something intended for human consumption. Thus, the defendant's *negligence* (his placing the poison where it was likely to be mistaken for something intended for human consumption) was not a *sine qua non* of the harm. For present purposes I draw no distinction between the several expressions "but-for cause," "necessary antecedent," and "*sine qua non.*"[3] That is, I am speaking simply of the concept that it cannot be said that the harm of death from explosion would not have occurred but for defendant's placing the poison where it was likely to be mistaken for something intended for human consumption. Defendant's negligence was not in this sense a but-for cause, or a necessary anteced-

ent, or a *sine qua non* of the death. But his conduct (placing the poison near heat) was, at least in a qualified sense, a *sine qua non*.

The qualification is concerned with the hypothetical character of the assertion. That is, the assertion that the harm would not have occurred but for the defendant's conduct is a hypothetical assertion the accuracy of which is not subject to demonstration. For example, how are we to know that, had the poison been placed elsewhere than near a hot stove, it would not have been exploded by some other source of heat that might have happened to be applied to the poison while the victim was present? Also, imbedded in the hypothetical assertion of what would not have happened are ambiguities in the meaning of "conduct" and "harm." Does "conduct" refer to placing the poison in the exact spot where it was placed? If so, might it not be said that the conduct was not a *sine qua non* since death at the same time and place might have occurred if the poison had been placed near a hot radiator rather than the stove? Does "the harm" refer merely to death of the victim, or to the time, place, and manner of death in all their detail, or to something between these extremes? In some instances, the ambiguity and hypothetical character of the assertion will present serious difficulty.[4] But, in the case of the explosive rat poison, we can readily understand and accept, in at least a rough sense, the assertion that the defendant's conduct was a *sine qua non* of the harm because there appears to have been no substantial possibility either that the harm in all its details would have occurred or that something generally resembling it would have occurred in the absence of defendant's conduct of placing the rat poison near heat. Also, no doubt, we can agree that if defendant's negligence is defined in the limited sense of that quality of his conduct consisting of his placing the poison where it was likely to be mistaken for something intended for human consumption, his negligence was not a *sine qua non*.

There is yet another difficulty, however, in the assertion that one aspect of his conduct was a cause of harm and another aspect of the same conduct, the same single action of putting down a can of poison, was not a cause of the harm. It is more normal, perhaps, to think of the conduct as indivisible and to reject the suggestion that the negligent aspect can be separated from other aspects for an inquiry into causal relation. Perhaps it will be helpful in this respect to think of negligence as the creation of unreasonable risks[5] and, rather than thinking of harm itself as the focus of the concept of risk, to think of a risk as a set of forces and conditions and circumstances that might foreseeably bring about harm.[6] No special point is made here regarding the choice among the terms "force," "condition," and "circumstance" to convey the intended idea, though the word "circumstance" seems the most congenial to the separation of aspects of a single state of affairs. Negligence, then, consists of creating a set of unduly risky forces or conditions or circumstances, and the negligence is a *sine qua non* of subsequent harm only if some force or condition or circumstance within this set is a *sine qua non*. In the case of the rat poison, the negligence consisted of creating a force or condition or circumstance of having a poisonous substance where it might be mistaken as something intended for human consumption. That circumstance was not a cause of the harm, though the coexisting circumstance of having an explosive substance near heat was a cause.

This focus upon the negligent aspect of conduct as the meaning of the unqualified word "negligence" in the statement of the Risk Rule presented above suggests a second, perhaps less ambiguous, formulation of exactly the same meaning:

A negligent actor is legally responsible for that harm, and only that harm, of which the *negligent aspect of his conduct* is a cause in fact.

In many cases it is less easy than in the case of the explosive rat poison to extract the negligent aspect from the total conduct. To meet this difficulty, still another formulation of the Risk Rule is helpful. A moment ago, we were thinking of risk with a focus upon the forces or conditions or circumstances that might produce harm. Shift the focus now to the harm that might be produced. With this focus, in order to find that the negligence (that is, the negligent aspect of the conduct) bears a causal relation to the harm, we must find that the harm that came about was one of the things that was risked. Another way of expressing the same idea is to say that the harm must be a result within the scope of at least one

of the risks on the basis of which the actor is found to be negligent. Thus the Risk Rule of legal cause as stated in the first and second formulations above may be restated in a third formulation without change of meaning:

A negligent actor is legally responsible for the harm, and only the harm, that not only (1) is caused in fact by his conduct but also (2) is a result within the scope of the risks by reason of which the actor is found to be negligent.

In the case of the explosive rat poison, injury by explosion was not a result within the scope of the risks by reason of which the defendant was found to be negligent, though injury by poisoning would have been.

The third formulation of the rule is often expressed in the statement that the actor is responsible only for "results within the risk." Among those who remain constantly alert to its meaning, there is no objection to use of such a shorthand expression. But this cryptic phrase is apt to be misleading to the unsophisticated because it does not designate the point of view from which the composite of risks is defined. The concept of "risk" and the cognate concept of "probability" are founded on prediction from some selected point of view. But they do not necessarily imply any particular point of view, such as that of a reasonable man in the position of the actor. Thus, results that in the wisdom of hindsight are said to have been "probable" may yet have been beyond the scope of those risks by reason of which the actor's conduct is found to have been negligence. Also, such concepts as "risk," "probability," and "foreseeability" imply a point of view involving a degree of ignorance about the factors at work in a situation. To one who knows all, a future event is not "probable" or merely "foreseeable" but either certain to occur or certain not to occur. When we say a result was "probable" as a matter of hindsight, we are using a point of view that is neither that of a reasonable person in the actor's position nor that of an omniscient observer after the fact. It is a point of view based on foresight in the face of incomplete knowledge, but with greater knowledge or greater mental capacity than that of the actor or that of the standard man in the actor's circumstances. As used in the Risk Rule, on the other hand, "risk" implies a standard based on foresight from the point of view of the standard man in the actor's circumstances at the time of the conduct that is being judged.

As we examine the policy foundation of the Risk Rule, reasons will appear for using, in relation to problems of legal cause, this standard of foresight that is also used in determining whether the actor was negligent. But, first, we digress for further explanation of the use of three formulations of the Risk Rule.

WHY THREE FORMULATIONS?

The first formulation of the Risk Rule tracks language found in many jury charges today, as well as in appellate opinions, though supplemented usually by elaborations upon the theme and occasionally by qualifications. The third formulation tracks the rationale of exponents of what has come to be known as the risk theory of legal cause, and of Professor Seavey in particular.[7] Professors Harper and James also recommended an inquiry in terms generally consistent with the rationale expressed in the third formulation,[8] though they appear less happy than Professor Seavey with adherence to the limitation on scope of liability implicit in accepting this as the basic rule of legal cause. They also observed that in essence this is the same inquiry as the question whether there is causal relation "between *that aspect of the defendant's conduct which is wrongful* and the injury."[9] Thus, the second formulation offered here is supported by their analysis. This formulation is offered as a transitional bond between the first and the third, in the belief that the intended substance of these different expressions is the same. Candor requires disclosure that Professor Seavey dislikes both the first and the second formulations because of a concern, as I understand him, that they are more likely to mislead than to clarify. His disfavor is firm, though expressed in the warmhearted spirit that has characterized his rigorous intellectual assaults upon the ideas of generations of students, colleagues, and judges. At the risk of suffering an intermeddler's unhappy fate, I persist in offering the second formulation and in marshaling the three together in the hope of improving relations between adherents of two ways of thought that I believe to be compatibly directed toward the same goal.

THE RISK RULE AS A RULE OF CAUSATION

Perhaps a secondary benefit of this focus on three formulations of one rule is to expose rather persuasive evidence that the Risk Rule is indeed a rule of causation in a cause-in-fact sense. There are various deviations from the Risk Rule—some toward greater liability, some toward less—that are founded in notions beyond causation. But the predominant theme represented by the Risk Rule is a theme of causation. It concerns cause-in-fact relation between the negligent aspect of the conduct and the harm.

This conclusion is supported by only a few of the multitude of authors on legal cause—among them Professor Carpenter,[10] and, more recently, Professors Harper and James.[11] Even these three appear not willing to carry the separation of aspects of the conduct as far as is suggested here. The following passage from Harper and James is relevant:

> But there are cases where causal relation exists between defendant's fault and the injury, yet where liability will not be imposed. Thus in Gorris v. Scott, L.R. 9 Ex. 125 (1874), defendants' wrongful failure to have pens for cattle on shipboard was the cause in fact of their being washed overboard in a heavy sea. There was no liability, however, since the statutory requirement was designed to protect the cattle only from perils from contagious disease, a hazard which was not encountered and from which their loss did not result. See Carpenter, Workable Rules for Determining Proximate Cause, 20 Calif. L. Rev. 396, 408 (1932).[12]

The claim of negligence in *Gorris* v. *Scott* was violation of orders issued pursuant to the Contagious Diseases (Animals) Act of 1869, the violation being failure to provide battens or foot-holds for the animals and failure to provide pens not larger than 9 by 15 feet each. Under the analysis suggested in this chapter, the negligent aspect of the conduct was not the circumstance that absence of such pens and foot-holds placed the cattle in position to be washed overboard. No doubt, reluctance to declare that there is no causal connection between the the negligent aspect of the conduct and the result in these circumstances arises from the difficulty of imagining facts in which compliance with the required safeguards against disease would not also protect the cattle against being washed overboard. The case is thus unlike that of the speeding automobile that strikes a child who could not have been avoided by a driver proceeding at a reasonable speed; in that situation, speed causes the automobile to be at the scene at the critical time, but we can imagine the defendant's starting sooner and arriving in time to strike the child though he drives at a reasonable speed throughout the journey. Perhaps the converse point of view is also relevant, however. That is, perhaps we should consider not only whether situations can be imagined in which the required safeguard would have been ineffectual to prevent the particular kind of harm of which plaintiff is complaining but also whether situations can be imagined in which despite absence of the required safeguards the plaintiff would have been fully protected against this kind of harm. This is not to say that a required safeguard is intended to be an exclusive safeguard against the dangers to which it is directed. But this point of view does suggest that, when we treat one circumstance (that absence of pens placed the cattle in position to be washed overboard) as an aspect of the conduct separate from another circumstance (that absence of pens placed the cattle in position to be subject to an increased risk of contagious disease), we are no more attempting to separate inseparable aspects of a single faulty course of conduct than in the converse situation illustrated by the case of excessive speed. Pursuing this line of thought, we may observe that it would have been possible in *Gorris v. Scott* to have larger pens and no footholds and yet have the cattle protected against the risk of being washed overboard. In any event, the negligence was concerned with the circumstance that absence of the required safeguards increased the risks of disease, including the risk that affected cattle would communicate the disease widely among animals not separated into small groups by use of small enclosures. It was not concerned with the circumstance that the cattle were in position to be washed overboard. Thus, there was no causal relation between the negligent aspect of the conduct and the harm.

Possibly some passages in the recent broad study of causation by a distinguished pair of English scholars, Hart and Honoré, can also be fairly interpreted as supporting the assertion that the Risk Rule is concerned with causal relation between the negligent aspect of conduct and the harm of which plaintiff complains.[13] Yet, elsewhere they may be thought to be saying that foreseeability is a policy factor, that causal principles are policy neutral, and that use of foreseeability as a test for scope of liability is a departure from use of causal criteria.[14] They argue that the foreseeability test breaks down, especially in cases of what they call "ulterior" harm (e.g., harm following a foreseeable impact on an unforeseeably thin skull), and that causal criteria must be used instead.[15] Perhaps these several passages can be reconciled on the basis that Hart and Honoré mean not to declare that the foreseeability test is unconcerned with causal relation between the negligent aspect of the conduct and the harm but only that in some situations, especially those of "ulterior" harm, the scope of liability is fixed by a test of causal relation between conduct and harm rather than between negligent aspect of conduct and harm. If this reading of their book is proper, then the views of Hart and Honoré tend to support the assertion that the three separate formulations of the Risk Rule are in essence expressions of one idea and that this idea is concerned with cause-in-fact relation between the negligent aspect of the conduct and the harm.

To the contrary, other writers, probably a majority, have insisted that doctrines of legal cause generally, and the result-within-the-risk formulation in particular, are based on policy considerations having nothing to do with cause in fact.[16] The insight produced by a focus upon the relation between the negligent aspect of conduct and the ensuing harm is nevertheless persuasive. The persistence of courts in dealing with this problem under the rubric of causation is perhaps more than evidence of a judicial instinct for right results; perhaps it is also evidence that on occasion judicial perception surpasses that of the majority of reflective critics. This accolade to the courts is not intended to imply a preference for the first or the second formulation of the Risk Rule over the third. It does, however, express a conviction that the first and second formulations offer added illumination on the problem though the third is generally the more manageable in difficult applications. Inevitably, different formulations are likely to produce different nuances and connotations. Since all three formulations are expressions of a single theme, it will often be an aid to deliberate and rational choice to examine the implications of the Risk Rule from the several points of view of all three formulations.

THE POLICY FOUNDATION OF THE RISK RULE

SCOPE OF LIABILITY COMMENSURATE WITH THE BASIS OF LIABILITY

The policy foundation of the Risk Rule can be summarized in this way: The factors determining that the actor is liable for unintended harm caused by his conduct should also determine the scope of his liability. There is surely an interest of public policy in formulating rules that do not impose crushing liability.[17] Since the unintended consequences of one's conduct go on indefinitely, some limit of responsibility is a practical necessity. The theory of the Risk Rule is that the scope of liability should be commensurate with the basis of liability. "Prima facie at least, the reasons for creating liability should limit it."[18]

Opponents of the Risk Rule have argued that in applying the risk concept first to the issue of liability and again to the issue of scope of liability a court gives the defendant an unwarranted advantage by applying twice a restrictive test of foreseeability of harm.[19] The argument is not persuasive. In the first place, the test is expansive rather than restrictive if we start with the assumption that the burden is on the plaintiff to prove some good reason for entering a loss-shifting judgment. That is, when the test for negligence is found to have been fulfilled, liability is expanded in the sense of establishment of an obligation not previously acknowledged. Only if we make a comparison with an assumed state of broader liability, or if we start with the assumption that there is a burden on the defendant to prove nonliability, can we think of an application of the test of foreseeability of harm as restrictive rather than expansive. This is true whether it be applied to the liability issue alone, to the scope of liability issue as well, or to the combination as a unit. In the second place, separating the issues of liability and scope of liability is simply a means of organizing thought. There is no more reason for characterizing the process as a double application of a standard, either restrictive or expansive, when the issues are separated than when they are merged into one issue of liability for how much

—none, all, or something between. This double-advantage argument is a conclusion derived from the premise that the scope of liability *should be* governed by a separate test. The opposing premise on which the Risk Rule is founded—the premise that the scope of liability should be limited by the factors accounting for liability—has been described as the view that there is only one question in negligence cases, not two.[20]

RELATION TO THE PRINCIPLE THAT LIABILITY IS BASED ON FAULT

The policy argument underlying use of the Risk Rule in negligence cases is a corollary of the foundation of tort law on fault. Generally one is not liable for an unintended harm caused by his nonnegligent conduct. If negligence in one respect were to make the actor liable for all unintended harms to follow, the legal consequences would be disproportionate to the fault. For example, suppose the defendant's negligence consisted of his transporting dynamite in an unmarked truck, otherwise carefully operated, and the only harm caused was injury to one who, without negligence, fainted, fell into the path of the truck, and was run down. Defendant was negligent with respect to risks of explosion but not with respect to risks of an injury of the kind that occurred. The policy judgment underlying the Risk Rule is that with respect to the kind of injury that occurred, the defendant was not at fault.

It may be argued that, as between a negligent defendant and a nonnegligent plaintiff, a loss of which defendant's conduct was a cause in fact ought to be imposed upon the defendant irrespective of whether it was a kind of loss within the risks by reason of which his conduct is characterized as negligence. But if it is relevant to take into account defendant's fault with respect to a risk different from any that would include the harm plaintiff has suffered, then would it not also be relevant to take into account his other faults as well? And would it not seem equally relevant to consider plaintiff's shortcomings? Shall we fix legal responsibility by deciding who is the better and who the worse person? An affirmative answer might involve us, and quickly too, in the morality of run-of-the-ranch TV drama, where the good guys always win.

If we reject this standard of judgment, then so long as liability is to be based on fault, should we not limit the scope of legal responsibility to those consequences with respect to which the actor was negligent—to those consequences of which the negligent aspect of his conduct was a cause? An affirmative answer implies, in relation to the hypothetical case of the transportation of explosives, that legal responsibility should be limited to damages caused by explosion or by conduct responsive to the explosion risk, rather than being extended to injuries that would have occurred even if the driver had used warning signs or had transported no explosives, while acting in other respects exactly as he did.

The policy foundation for the Risk Rule, though applicable more broadly to all problems of results outside the risk, is seen in its most persuasive context in relation to *persons outside the risk*. In this context Judge Learned Hand expressed the philosophy of the rule in an opinion that is especially illuminating on matters of legal cause. After noting that there are in tort law some instances of strict liability, he said:

But so long as it is an element of imposed liability that the wrongdoer shall in some degree disregard the sufferer's interests, it can only be an anomaly, and indeed vindictive, to make him responsible to those whose interests he has not disregarded.[21]

Perhaps this is as forcefully as one can fairly state the policy justification for the Risk Rule. Indeed, it is easy to exaggerate the weight of this argument as brought to bear upon one of those close cases about which dispute is likely. In the first place, this policy argument is essentially one of blameworthiness, resting distinctly on moral judgment. The twilight zones of disputed legal judgment are also zones of disputed moral judgment, not alone in the minds of judges, but as well in the views of the community at large.[22] Uncertainty is increased by the multiplicity of influences that bear on judgments of blameworthiness. Moreover, even aside from this element of uncertainty about which way underlying moral justifications point for a particular case in the twilight zone, the very fact that the policy is one based on a moral judgment exerts a restraint upon its influence, because we are less content today with moral justifications for our legal rules than with political, economic, and social justifications. It is characteristic of our time to be discomfited about the imposition of our moral judgments on others, especially judgments concerning individual rather than group morality.

One may disagree with the policy argument underlying the Risk Rule, or he may believe that it has been too widely influential, or he may believe that we should now move beyond the Risk Rule in sympathetic conformity with a trend away from liability based on fault and toward strict liability. But to believe that the Risk Rule is without rational, policy foundation is to misunderstand, and to deny the existence of that foundation because of aversion to its moralizing quality is to misrepresent. Its force may be doubtful in a range of close cases; and, like most policy arguments, it falls short of providing a firm guide to decision in close cases. But demonstration of these uncertainties on the fringe leaves the hard core of the policy argument intact. This hard core continues to serve as the basic theme of decisions on legal cause.

NOTES

1. Cf. Larrimore v. American Nat'l Ins. Co., 184 Okla. 614, 89 P.2d 340 (1939). This hypothetical variation upon the facts of that case is chosen for the purpose of eliminating possible grounds of decision other than those to which attention is directed here.

2. The author's reference is to his discussion of the *Palsgraf* case—Eds.

3. Challenges to some of the common assumptions about these expressions appear in Hart & Honoré, Causation in the Law 19 n.1, 84 n.2, 103–22 (1959); and in Becht & Miller, The Test of Factual Causation in Negligence and Strict Liability Cases 13–21 (1961). See also Williams, *Causation in the Law*, 1961 Camb. L. J. 62, 63–79, for comments evoked by the Hart & Honoré book.

4. See, *e.g.*, Hart & Honoré, Causation in the Law 95–96 (1959); 2 Harper & James, Torts 1138 (1956). Compare Becht & Miller, The Test of Factual Causation in Negligence and Strict Liability Cases 21–25 (1961), discussing the hypothetical character of any assertion that an omission was a cause of a subsequent occurrence. Their discussion is addressed to what might be thought of as the converse of the problem referred to here. Here the issue is, Would the same thing have happened if the actor had not engaged in the conduct (whether described as an act, an omission, or a combination) alleged to be negligent? The issue they discuss is, Would the same thing have happened if the actor had done a particular thing he omitted doing? Both inquiries are hypothetical.

5. In the context of this discussion of legal cause, the plural, "risks," is chosen in preference to the more commonly used singular form as a means of avoiding the confusion that the risk within which the result falls must be such that, standing alone, it would make the conduct unreasonable. A composite of substantial, foreseeable risks is weighed against utility in judging whether the conduct is unreasonable.

6. Cf. P. Keeton, *Negligence, Duty, and Causation in Texas,* 16 Texas L. Rev. 1, 11–12 (1937). Though the idea expressed in the text above was suggested to me by the cited passage, the subsequent development in that article of the meaning of "force" (*id.* at 12–14) indicates that its author might not regard the present idea as one of the legitimate progeny of his teaching.

7. E.g., see Seavey, Cogitations on Torts 31–36 (1954); Seavey *Principles of Torts,* 56 Harv. L. Rev. 72, 90–93 (1942); Seavey, *Mr. Justice Cardozo and the Law of Torts,* 39 Colum. L.·Rev. 20, 29–39; 52 Harv. L. Rev. 372, 381–91; 48 Yale L.J. 390, 399–409 (1939). For expressions of generally compatible points of view from the other side of the Atlantic, see Goodhart, *Liability and Compensation,* 76 L.Q. Rev. 567 (1960) and Williams, *The Risk Principle,* 77 L.Q. Rev. 179 (1961).

8. 2 Harper & James, Torts 1138 (1956).

9. *Ibid.* (emphasis in original).

10. Carpenter, *Workable Rules for Determining Proximate Cause,* 20 Calif. L. Rev. 229, 231, 408–19 (1932).

11. 2 Harper & James, Torts 1138 (1956). Perhaps some degree of support for this thesis can be found in the analysis of Becht and Miller, which, for the purpose of inquiries into "factual causation," distinguishes between conduct and the "negligent segment" of it. See Becht & Miller, The Test of Causation in Negligence and Strict Liability Cases 25–28 (1961). But both the explanation of their distinction and the applications of it in their book indicate that it is a physical, rather than a qualitative, distinction. That is, a segment of conduct is an act or an omission among the many acts and omissions that make up the conduct, rather than an unreasonably risky quality of either the total conduct or some part of it. Thus, their distinction is not directed to the question whether the Risk Rule concerns cause-in-fact relation between the harm and the negligent *aspect* of conduct, as that concept is developed here. Moreover, in some situations where their thesis produces a finding of causal relation between the negligent *segment* of the conduct and the harm (and either supports liability or else explains nonliability on the "policy" ground that the harm is not within the type against which the rule of conduct is directed), the present thesis produces a finding of no causal relation between the negligent *aspect* of the conduct and the harm. *E.g.,* they find that the negligent segment of a plaintiff's conduct in sitting on an unsafe wall was a cause of the injury he suffered when the wall was knocked down by a careless motorist whose conduct would have caused the same injuries if the wall had been safe. See *id.* at 182–84, where they criticize the view of Hart and Honoré that the plaintiff's negligence in this situation was causally irrelevant. Under the thesis presented here, as under the thesis of Hart and Honoré apparently, the plaintiff's negligence consisted of placing himself where he was likely to be injured by the collapse of the wall, either without an external impact or under an external impact insufficient to cause the collapse of a safe wall. This aspect of his conduct was not a *sine qua non* of the injury he suffered.

12. 2 Harper & James, Torts 1138 n. 15 (1956).

13. Hart & Honoré, Causation in the Law 110–12, 192–93 (1959).

14. See, *e.g., id.* at 231–38, 259, and 266.

15. See *id.* at 259.

16. E.g., Green, *The Causal Relation Issue in Negligence Law,* 60 Mich. L. Rev. 543, 576 (1962) ("the *only cause issue* is the connection between the defendant's conduct and the victim's injury"; the issue of causal relation should be unloaded of other considerations [emphasis in the original]); Prosser, Torts 252, 258, 266 (2d ed. 1955), (proximate cause "is nearly always a matter of various considerations of policy which have nothing to do with the fact of causation"; the problem of scope of liability for unforeseeable consequences "is in no way one of causation, and it does not arise until causation has been established"; the problem of intervening causes is one of policy, not causation); Restatement, Torts § 433, Reason for Changes (1948 Supp.), (Legal cause consists of two elements: 'the substantial factor' element deals with causation in fact"; the second element is concerned with whether there is a rule of law restricting "liability for harm occurring in the particular manner" at issue, and "deals with a legal policy relieving the actor of liability for harm he has, as a matter of fact, caused"; "[i]t is completely faulty analysis" to confuse "the question of policy with the question of fact"). Insistence that the result-within-the-risk problem is not one of causation is found even among advocates of the principle expressed in the several formulations of the Risk Rule. For example, Professor Goodhart declares: "But consequences cannot 'flow' from negligence. Consequences 'flow' from an act or an omission." Goodhart, *Liability for the Consequences of a "Negligent Act,"* in Cambridge Legal Essays 101, 105–6 (1926), reprinted in Goodhart, Essays in Jurisprudence and the Common Law 110, 114 (1931). See also Foster, Grant & Green, *The Risk Theory and Proximate Cause—A Comparative Study,* 32 Neb. L. Rev. 72, 79–80 (1952) (advocating the risk theory and the "relational" quality of negligence, but declaring that "proximate cause often has little if anything to do with causation in fact, except that no issue of proximate cause arises unless actual causation is present," and observing of a typical case that if defendant is held not liable "it is not because its fault was not a cause of the disaster").

17. Cf. 2 Harper & James, Torts 1132–33 (1956).

18. Seavey, *Mr. Justice Cardozo and the Law of Torts,* 39 Colum. L. Rev. 20, 34; 52 Harv. L. Rev. 372, 386; 48 Yale L. J. 390, 404 (1939).

19. E. g., Smith, *Legal Cause in Actions of Tort,* 25 Harv. L. Rev. 103, 223, 245 (1912). Cf. Green, *Foreseeability in Negligence Law,* 61 Colum. L. Rev. 1401, 1408 (1961), noting that there are numerous devices for controlling decisions of both liability and damages, and asserting that "the foreseeability formula" need not "reach beyond the negligence issue" into the area of other limitations on scope of liability.

20. See Pound, *Causation,* 67 Yale L. J. 1, 10 (1957), referring to Pollock's view. Pollock stated the question as one "whether the accepted test of liability for negligence in the first instance is or not also the proper measure of liability for the consequences of proved or admitted default." Pollock, *Liability for Consequences,* 38 L.Q. Rev. 165 (1922).

21. Sinram v. Pennsylvania R.R., 61 F.2d 767, 770 (2d Cir. 1932).

22. Cf. Morris, *Proximate Cause in Minnesota,* 34 Minn L. Rev. 185, 207 (1950).

THE AMBIGUOUS SUICIDE CASE

N.Y. Times, February 7, 1968: "Phoenix, Ariz., Feb. 6 (AP)—Linda Marie Ault killed herself, policemen said today, rather than make her dog Beauty pay for her night with a married man.

" 'I killed her. I killed her. It's just like I killed her myself,' a detective quoted her grief-stricken father as saying.

" 'I handed her the gun. I didn't think she would do anything like that.'

"The 21-year-old Arizona State University coed died in a hospital yesterday of a gunshot wound in the head.

"The police quoted her parents, Mr. and Mrs Joseph Ault, as giving this account:

"Linda failed to return home from a dance in Tempe Friday night. On Saturday she admitted she had spent the night with an Air Force lieutenant.

"The Aults decided on a punishment that would 'wake Linda up.' They ordered her to shoot the dog she had owned about two years.

"On Sunday, the Aults and Linda took the dog into the desert near their home. They had the girl dig a shallow grave. Then Mrs. Ault grasped the dog between her hands, and Mr. Ault gave his daughter a .22-caliber pistol and told her to shoot the dog.

"Instead, the girl put the pistol to her right temple and shot herself.

"The police said there were no charges that could be filed against the parents except possibly cruelty to animals."

PALSGRAF v. THE LONG ISLAND RAILROAD CO.

New York Court of Appeals, 1928*

CARDOZO, Ch. J. Plaintiff was standing on a platform of defendant's railroad after buying a ticket to go to Rockaway Beach. A train stopped at the station, bound for another place. Two men ran forward to catch it. One of the men reached the platform of the car without mishap, though the train was already moving. The other man, carrying a package, jumped aboard the car, but seemed unsteady as if about to fall. A guard on the car, who had held the door open, reached forward to help him in, and another guard on the platform pushed him from behind. In this act, the package was dislodged, and fell upon the rails. It was a package of small size, about fifteen inches long, and was covered by a newspaper. In fact it contained fireworks, but there was nothing in its appearance to give notice of its contents. The fireworks when they fell exploded. The shock of the explosion threw down some scales at the other end of the platform, many feet away. The scales struck the plaintiff, causing injuries for which she sues.

The conduct of the defendant's guard, if a wrong in its relation to the holder of the package, was not a wrong in its relation to the plaintiff, standing far away.

*248 N.Y. 339 (1928).

Relatively to her it was not negligence at all. Nothing in the situation gave notice that the falling package had in it the potency of peril to persons thus removed. Negligence is not actionable unless it involves the invasion of a legally protected interest, the violation of a right. "Proof of negligence in the air, so to speak, will not do."* "Negligence is the absence of care, according to the circumstances."* The plaintiff as she stood upon the platform of the station might claim to be protected against intentional invasion of her bodily security. Such invasion is not charged. She might claim to be protected against unintentional invasion by conduct involving in the thought of reasonable men an unreasonable hazard that such invasion would ensue. These, from the point of view of the law, were the bounds of her immunity, with perhaps some rare exceptions, survivals for the most part of ancient forms of liability, where conduct is held to be at the peril of the actor (*Sullivan* v. *Dunham,* 161 N.Y. 290). If no hazard was apparent to the eye of ordinary vigilance, an act innocent and harmless, at least to outward seeming, with reference to her, did not take to itself the quality of a tort because it happened to be a wrong, though apparently not one involving the risk of bodily insecurity, with reference to some one else. "In every instance, before negligence can be predicated of a given act, back of the act must be sought and found a duty to the individual complaining, the observance of which would have averted or avoided the injury."* "The ideas of negligence and duty are strictly correlative."* (Bowen, L. J., in *Thomas* v. *Quartermaine,* 18 Q. B. D. 685, 694). The plaintiff sues in her own right for a wrong personal to her, and not as the vicarious beneficiary of a breach of duty to another.

A different conclusion will involve us, and swiftly too, in a maze of contradictions. A guard stumbles over a package which has been left upon a platform. It seems to be a bundle of newspapers. It turns out to be a can of dynamite. To the eye of ordinary vigilance, the bundle is abandoned waste, which may be kicked or trod on with impunity. Is a passenger at the other end of the platform protected by the law against the unsuspected hazard concealed beneath the waste? If not, is the result to be any different, so far as the distant passenger is concerned, when the guard stumbles over a valise which a truckman or a porter has left upon the walk? The passenger far away, if the victim of a wrong at all, has a cause of action, not derivative, but original and primary. His claim to be protected against invasion of his bodily security is neither greater nor less because the act resulting in the invasion is a wrong to another far removed. In this case, the rights that are said to have been violated, the interests said to have

been invaded, are not even of the same order. The man was not injured in his person nor even put in danger. The purpose of the act, as well as its effect, was to make his person safe. If there was a wrong to him at all, which may very well be doubted, it was a wrong to a property interest only, the safety of his package. Out of this wrong to property, which threatened injury to nothing else, there has passed, we are told, to the plaintiff by derivation or succession a right of action for the invasion of an interest of another order, the right to bodily security. The diversity of interests emphasizes the futility of the effort to build the plaintiff's right upon the basis of a wrong to some one else. The gain is one of emphasis, for a like result would follow if the interests were the same. Even then, the orbit of the danger as disclosed to the eye of reasonable vigilance would be the orbit of the duty. One who jostles one's neighbor in a crowd does not invade the rights of others standing at the outer fringe when the unintended contact casts a bomb upon the ground. The wrongdoer, as to them is the man who carries the bomb, not the one who explodes it without suspicion of the danger. Life will have to be made over, and human nature transformed, before prevision so extravagant can be accepted as the norm of conduct, the customary standard to which behavior must conform.

The argument for the plaintiff is built upon the shifting meanings of such words as "wrong" and "wrongful," and shares their instability. What the plaintiff must show is "a wrong" to herself, *i. e.,* a violation of her own right, and not merely a wrong to some one else, nor conduct "wrongful" because unsocial, but not "a wrong" to any one. We are told that one who drives at reckless speed through a crowded city street is guilty of a negligent act and, therefore, of a wrongful one irrespective of the consequences. Negligent the act is, and wrongful in the sense that it is unsocial, but wrongful and unsocial in relation to other travelers, only because the eye of vigilance perceives the risk of damage. If the same act were to be committed on a speedway or a race course, it would lose its wrongful quality. The risk reasonably to be perceived defines the duty to be obeyed, and risk imports relation; it is risk to another or to others within the range of apprehension (Seavey, Negligence, Subjective or Objective, 41 H. L. Rv. 6; *Boronkay* v. *Robinson & Carpenter,* 247 N.Y. 365). This does not mean, of course, that one who launches a destructive force is always relieved of liability if the force, though known to be destructive, pursues an unexpected path. It was not necessary that the defendant should have had notice of the particular method in which an accident would occur, if the possibility of an accident was clear to the ordinarily prudent eye" (*Munsey* v. *Webb,* 231 U.S. 150, 156; *Condran* v. *Park & Tilford,* 213 N.Y. 341, 345; *Robert* v. *U.S.E.F.*

*Citations omitted [Ed.].

Corp., 240 N.Y. 474, 477). Some acts, such as shooting, are so imminently dangerous to any one who may come within reach of the missile, however unexpectedly, as to impose a duty of prevision not far from that of an insurer. Even today, and much oftener in earlier stages of the law, one acts sometimes at one's peril.* Under this head, it may be, fall certain cases of what is known as transferred intent, an act willfully dangerous to A resulting by misadventure in injury to B.* These cases aside, wrong is defined in terms of the natural or probable, at least when unintentional.* The range of reasonable apprehension is at times a question for the court, and at times, if varying inferences are possible, a question for the jury. Here, by concession, there was nothing in the situation to suggest to the most cautious mind that the parcel wrapped in newspaper would spread wreckage through the station. If the guard had thrown it down knowingly and willfully, he would not have threatened the plaintiff's safety, so far as appearances could warn him. His conduct would not have involved, even then, an unreasonable probability of invasion of her bodily security. Liability can be no greater where the act is inadvertent.

Negligence, like risk, is thus a term of relation. Negligence in the abstract, apart from things related, is surely not a tort, if indeed it is understandable at all.* Negligence is not a tort unless it results in the commission of a wrong, and the commission of a wrong imports the violation of a right, in this case, we are told, the right to be protected against interference with one's bodily security. But bodily security is protected, not against all forms of interference or aggression, but only against some. One who seeks redress at law does not make out a cause of action by showing without more that there has been damage to his person. If the harm was not willful, he must show that the act as to him had possibilities of danger so many and apparent as to entitle him to be protected against the doing of it though the harm was unintended. Affront to personality is still the keynote of the wrong. Confirmation of this view will be found in the history and development of the action on the case. Negligence as a basis of civil liability was unknown to mediaeval law.* For damage to the person, the sole remedy was trespass, and trespass did not lie in the absence of aggression, and that direct and personal.* Liability for other damage, as where a servant without orders from the master does or omits something to the damage of another, is a plant of later growth.* When it emerged out of the legal soil, it was thought of as a variant of trespass, an offshoot of the parent stock. This appears in the form of action, which was known as trespass on the case.* The victim does not sue derivatively, or by right of subrogation, to vindicate an interest invaded in the person of another. Thus to view his cause of action is to ignore the fundamental difference between tort and crime.* He sues for breach of a duty owing to himself.

The law of causation, remote or proximate, is thus foreign to the case before us. The question of liability is always anterior to the question of the measure of the consequences that go with liability. If there is no tort to be redressed, there is no occasion to consider what damage might be recovered if there were a finding of a tort. We may assume, without deciding, that negligence, not at large or in the abstract, but in relation to the plaintiff, would entail liability for any and all consequences, however novel or extraordinary.* There is room for argument that a distinction is to be drawn according to the diversity of interests invaded by the act, as where conduct negligent in that it threatens an insignificant invasion of an interest in property results in an unforeseeable invasion of an interest of another order, as *e. g.,* one of bodily security. Perhaps other distinctions may be necessary. We do not go into the question now. The consequences to be followed must first be rooted in a wrong.

The judgment of the Appellate Division and that of the Trial Term should be reversed, and the complaint dismissed, with costs in all courts.

ANDREWS, J. (dissenting). Assisting a passenger to board a train, the defendant's servant negligently knocked a package from his arms. It fell between the platform and the cars. Of its contents the servant knew and could know nothing. A violent explosion followed. The concussion broke some scales standing a considerable distance away. In falling they injured the plaintiff, an intending passenger.

Upon these facts may she recover the damages she has suffered in an action brought against the master? The result we shall reach depends upon our theory as to the nature of negligence. Is it a relative concept—the breach of some duty owing to a particular person or to particular persons? Or where there is an act which unreasonably threatens the safety of others, is the doer liable for all its proximate consequences, even where they result in injury to one who would generally be thought to be outside the radius of danger? This is not a mere dispute as to words. We might not believe that to the average mind the dropping of the bundle would seem to involve the probability of harm to the plaintiff standing many feet away whatever might be the case as to the owner or to one so near as to be likely to be struck by its fall. If, however, we adopt the second hypothesis we have to inquire only as to the relation between cause and effect. We deal in terms of proximate cause, not of negligence.

Negligence may be defined roughly as an act or omission which unreasonably does or may affect the

*Citations omitted [Eds.]

rights of others, or which unreasonably fails to protect oneself from the dangers resulting from such acts. Here I confine myself to the first branch of the definition. Nor do I comment on the word "unreasonable." For present purposes it sufficiently describes that average of conduct that society requires of its members.

There must be both the act or the omission, and the right. It is the act itself, not the intent of the actor, that is important.* In criminal law both the intent and the result are to be considered. Intent again is material in tort actions, where punitive damages are sought, dependent on actual malice—not on merely reckless conduct. But here neither insanity nor infancy lessens responsibility.

As has been said, except in cases of contributory negligence, there must be rights which are or may be affected. Often though injury has occurred, no rights of him who suffers have been touched. A licensee or trespasser upon my land has no claim to affirmative care on my part that the land be made safe.* Where a railroad is required to fence its tracks against cattle, no man's rights are injured should he wander upon the road because such fence is absent.* An unborn child may not demand immunity from personal harm.*

But we are told that "there is no negligence unless there is in the particular case a legal duty to take care, and this duty must be one which is owed to the plaintiff himself and not merely to others."* This, I think too narrow a conception. Where there is the unreasonable act, and some right that may be affected there is negligence whether damage does or does not result. That is immaterial. Should we drive down Broadway at a reckless speed, we are negligent whether we strike an approaching car or miss it by an inch. The act itself is wrongful. It is a wrong not only to those who happen to be within the radius of danger but to all who might have been there—a wrong to the public at large. Such is the language of the street. Such the language of the courts when speaking of contributory negligence. Such again and again their language in speaking of the duty of some defendant and discussing proximate cause in cases where such a discussion is wholly irrelevant on any other theory.* As was said by Mr. Justice HOLMES many years ago, "the measure of the defendant's duty in determining whether a wrong has been committed is one thing, the measure of liability when a wrong has been committed is another."* Due care is a duty imposed on each one of us to protect society from unnecessary danger, not to protect A, B or C alone.

It may well be that there is no such thing as negligence in the abstract. "Proof of negligence in the air, so to speak, will not do." In an empty world negligence would not exist. It does involve a relationship between man and his fellows. But not merely a relationship between man and those whom he might reasonably expect his act would injure. Rather, a relationship between him and those whom he does in fact injure. If his act has a tendency to harm some one, it harms him a mile away as surely as it does those on the scene. We now permit children to recover for the negligent killing of the father. It was never prevented on the theory that no duty was owing to them. A husband may be compensated for the loss of his wife's services. To say that the wrongdoer was negligent as to the husband as well as to the wife is merely an attempt to fit facts to theory. An insurance company paying a fire loss recovers its payment of the negligent incendiary. We speak of subrogation—of suing in the right of the insured. Behind the cloud of words is the fact they hide, that the act, wrongful as to the insured, has also injured the company. Even if it be true that the fault of father, wife or insured will prevent recovery, it is because we consider the original negligence not the proximate cause of the injury.*

In the well-known *Polemis Case* (1921, 3 K. B. 560), SCRUTTON, L. J., said that the dropping of a plank was negligent for it might injure "workman or cargo or ship." Because of either possibility the owner of the vessel was to be made good for his loss. The act being wrongful the doer was liable for its proximate results. Criticized and explained as this statement may have been, I think it states the law as it should be and as it is.*

The proposition is this. Every one owes to the world at large the duty of refraining from those acts that may unreasonably threaten the safety of others. Such an act occurs. Not only is he wronged to whom harm might reasonably be expected to result, but he also who is in fact injured, even if he be outside what would generally be thought the danger zone. There needs be duty due the one complaining but this is not a duty to a particular individual because as to him harm might be expected. Harm to some one being the natural result of the act, not only that one alone, but all those in fact injured may complain. We have never, I think, held otherwise. Indeed in the *Di Caprio* case we said that a breach of a general ordinance defining the degree of care to be exercised in one's calling is evidence of negligence as to every one. We did not limit this statement to those who might be expected to be exposed to danger. Unreasonable risk being taken, its consequences are not confined to those who might probably be hurt.

If this be so, we do not have a plaintiff suing by "derivation or succession." Her action is original and primary. Her claim is for a breach of duty to herself—not that she is subrogated to any right of action of the owner of the parcel or of a passenger standing at the scene of the explosion.

*Citations omitted [Eds.].

The right to recover damages rests on additional considerations. The plaintiff's rights must be injured, and this injury must be caused by the negligence. We build a dam, but are negligent as to its foundations. Breaking, it injures property down stream. We are not liable if all this happened because of some reason other than the insecure foundation. But when injuries do result from our unlawful act we are liable for the consequences. It does not matter that they are unusual, unexpected, unforeseen and unforeseeable. But there is one limitation. The damages must be so connected with the negligence that the latter may be said to be the proximate cause of the former.

These two words have never been given an inclusive definition. What is a cause in a legal sense, still more what is a proximate cause, depend in each case upon many considerations, as does the existence of negligence itself. Any philosophical doctrine of causation does not help us. A boy throws a stone into a pond. The ripples spread. The water level rises. The history of that pond is altered to all eternity. It will be altered by other causes also. Yet it will be forever the resultant of all causes combined. Each one will have an influence. How great only omniscience can say. You may speak of a chain, or if you please, a net. An analogy is of little aid. Each cause brings about future events. Without each the future would not be the same. Each is proximate in the sense it is essential. But that is not what we mean by the word. Nor on the other hand do we mean sole cause. There is no such thing.

Should analogy be thought helpful, however, I prefer that of a stream. The spring, starting on its journey, is joined by tributary after tributary. The river, reaching the ocean, comes from a hundred sources. No man may say whence any drop of water is derived. Yet for a time distinction may be possible. Into the clear creek, brown swamp water flows from the left. Later, from the right comes water stained by its clay bed. The three may remain for a space, sharply divided. But at last, inevitably no trace of separation remains. They are so commingled that all distinction is lost.

As we have said, we cannot trace the effect of an act to the end, if end there is. Again, however, we may trace it part of the way. A murder at Serajevo may be the necessary antecedent to an assassination in London twenty years hence. An overturned lantern may burn all Chicago. We may follow the fire from the shed to the last building. We rightly say the fire started by the lantern caused its destruction.

A cause, but not the proximate cause. What we do mean by the word "proximate" is, that because of convenience, of public policy, of a rough sense of justice, the law arbitrarily declines to trace a series of events beyond a certain point. This is not logic, it is practical politics. Take our rule as to fires. Sparks from my burning haystack set on fire my house and my neighbor's. I may recover from a negligent railroad. He may not. Yet the wrongful act as directly harmed the one as the other. We may regret that the line was drawn just where it was, but drawn somewhere it had to be. We said the act of the railroad was not the proximate cause of our neighbor's fire. Cause it surely was. The words we used were simply indicative of our notions of public policy. Other courts think differently. But somewhere they reach the point where they cannot say the stream comes from any one source.

Take the illustration given in an unpublished manuscript by a distinguished and helpful writer on the law of torts. A chauffeur negligently collides with another car which is filled with dynamite, although he could not know it. An explosion follows. A, walking on the sidewalk nearby, is killed. B, sitting in a window of a building opposite, is cut by flying glass. C, likewise sitting in a window a block away, is similarly injured. And a further illustration. A nursemaid, ten blocks away, startled by the noise, involuntarily drops a baby from her arms to the walk. We are told that C may not recover while A may. As to B it is a question for court or jury. We will all agree that the baby might not. Because, we are again told, the chauffeur had no reason to believe his conduct involved any risk of injuring either C or the baby. As to them he was not negligent.

But the chauffeur, being negligent in risking the collision, his belief that the scope of the harm he might do would be limited is immaterial. His act unreasonably jeopardized the safety of any one who might be affected by it. C's injury and that of the baby were directly traceable to the collision. Without that, the injury would not have happened. C had the right to sit in his office, secure from such dangers. The baby was entitled to use the sidewalk with reasonable safety.

The true theory is, it seems to me, that the injury to C, if in truth he is to be denied recovery, and the injury to the baby is that their several injuries were not the proximate result of the negligence. And here not what the chauffeur had reason to believe would be the result of his conduct, but what the prudent would foresee, may have a bearing. May have some bearing, for the problem of proximate cause is not to be solved by any one consideration.

It is all a question of expediency. There are no fixed rules to govern our judgment. There are simply matters of which we may take account. We have in a somewhat different connection spoken of "the stream of events." We have asked whether that stream was deflected— whether it was forced into new and unexpected channels.* This is rather rhetoric than law. There is in truth little to guide us other than common sense.

*Citations omitted [Eds.].

There are some hints that may help us. The proximate cause, involved as it may be with many other causes, must be, at the least, something without which the event would not happen. The court must ask itself whether there was a natural and continuous sequence between cause and effect. Was the one a substantial factor in producing the other? Was there a direct connection between them, without too many intervening causes? Is the effect of cause on result not too attentuated? Is the cause likely, in the usual judgment of mankind, to produce the result? Or by the exercise of prudent foresight could the result be foreseen? Is the result too remote from the cause, and here we consider remoteness in time and space,* where we passed upon the construction of a contract—but something was also said on this subject. Clearly we must so consider, for the greater the distance either in time or space, the more surely do other causes intervene to affect the result. When a lantern is overturned the firing of a shed is a fairly direct consequence. Many things contribute to the spread of the conflagration—the force of the wind, the direction and width of streets, the character of intervening structures, other factors. We draw an uncertain and wavering line, but draw it we must as best we can.

Once again, it is all a question of fair judgment, always keeping in mind the fact that we endeavor to make a rule in each case that will be practical and in keeping with the general understanding of mankind.

Here another question must be answered. In the case supposed it is said, and said correctly, that the chauffeur is liable for the direct effect of the explosion although he had no reason to suppose it would follow a collision. "The fact that the injury occurred in a different manner than that which might have been expected does not prevent the chauffeur's negligence from being in law the cause of the injury." But the natural results of a negligent act—the results which a prudent man would or should foresee—do have a bearing upon the decision as to proximate cause. We have said so repeatedly. What should be foreseen? No human foresight would suggest that a collision itself might injure one a block away. On the contrary, given an explosion, such a possibility might be reasonably expected. I think the direct connection, the foresight of which the courts speak, assumes prevision of the explosion, for the immediate results of which, at least, the chauffeur is responsible.

*Citations omitted [Eds.].

It may be said this is unjust. Why? In fairness he should make good every injury flowing from his negligence. Not because of tenderness toward him we say he need not answer for all that follows his wrong. We look back to the catastrophe, the fire kindled by the spark, or the explosion. We trace the consequences—not indefinitely, but to a certian point. And to aid us in fixing that point we ask what might ordinarily be expected to follow the fire or the explosion.

This last suggestion is the factor which must determine the case before us. The act upon which defendant's liability rests is knocking an apparently harmless package onto the platform. The act was negligent. For its proximate consequences the defendant is liable. If its contents were broken, to the owner; if it fell upon and crushed a passenger's foot, then to him. If it exploded and injured one in the immediate vicinity, to him also as to A in the illustration. Mrs. Palsgraf was standing some distance away. How far cannot be told from the record—apparently twenty-five or thirty feet. Perhaps less. Except for the explosion, she would not have been injured. We are told by the appellant in his brief "it cannot be denied that the explosion was the direct cause of the plaintiff's injuries." So it was a substantial factor in producing the result—there was here a natural and continuous sequence—direct connection. The only intervening cause was that instead of blowing her to the ground the concussion smashed the weighing machine which in turn fell upon her. There was no remoteness in time, little in space. And surely, given such an explosion as here it needed no great foresight to predict that the natural result would be to injure one on the platform at no greater distance from its scene than was the plaintiff. Just how no one might be able to predict. Whether by flying fragments, by broken glass, by wreckage of machines or structures no one could say. But injury in some form was most probable.

Under these circumstances I cannot say as a matter of law that the plaintiff's injuries were not the proximate result of the negligence. That is all we have before us. The court refused to so charge. No request was made to submit the matter to the jury as a question of fact, even would that have been proper upon the record before us.

The judgment appealed from should be affirmed, with costs.

POUND, LEHMAN and KELLOGG, JJ., concur with CARDOZO, Ch. J.; ANDREWS, J., dissents in opinion in which CRANE and O'BRIEN, JJ., concur.

Judgment reversed, etc.

GRAHAM HUGHES

Attempting the Impossible*

The relevance on a charge of criminal attempt of the impossibility of the accused's attaining his objective has for some time been a subject of sharp dispute among jurists of the criminal law, although it has not received a great deal of attention in the courts. That teachers of criminal law and writers in the field should devote time and energy to this question is perfectly proper, for it is an important question in a number of ways. It raises very basic interrogatories concerning the aims and purposes of the criminal law; it compels us to focus attention on concepts such as "intention" and "purpose," an analysis of which is indispensable to criminal law scholarship; and it provides an excellent opportunity for reflecting on the pervasive and difficult distinction between mistake of fact and mistake of law. For these reasons the problem is a splendid set-piece which exhibits in a short space some of the most difficult issues of criminal law analysis. Before offering any new comment it will be necessary to sketch the apparent state of the law and the divergent opinions of the commentators.

I

It has long been agreed that impossibility is not a general defense to a charge of attempt.[1] But it is just as generally agreed that in some circumstances impossibility may be a defense, and we are therefore faced initially with the task of discriminating between two senses of the concept of impossibility. This has been done conventionally by distinguishing between legal impossibility and factual impossibility.[2]

Legal impossibility describes a situation in which the objective of the accused (an admittedly ambiguous phrase to which we shall return later) does not constitute an offense known to the law, even though the accused may mistakenly believe the law to be other than it is. Mistake of law may not generally excuse, but neither can it in itself be a sufficient ground for indictment. So an American on a visit to England might quite reasonably have the mistaken belief that fornication is a crime in England since it is one in the American jurisdiction in which he resides. Such a mistaken belief clearly cannot subject him to prosecution for a nonexistent crime of committing the sexual act, and it would be a strange notion to talk of a prosecution for attempting to commit a crime which is not on the statute book. How after all could the indictment be drafted, unless we recognized the existence of a general offense of doing what one mistakenly believed to be a crime? It will be noticed that the argument here does not essentially depend on the concept of attempt in the usual sense of that word, for it is not necessarily a case of trying and failing. The inappropriateness of convicting such a person remains whether he has committed sexual intercourse or only attempted it. The reason for not convicting him has nothing to do with the failure of the enterprise, but rather with the absence of any prohibition of the conduct whether completed or not.

Factual impossibility, by contrast, is thought of as a situation in which the objective of the accused, if achieved, would amount to an offense known to the law, but where the achievement is frustrated by some circumstance such as the inadequacy of the instrument, the intervention of some third person, or the misapprehension of some material matter by the accused. Picking the empty pocket is a classic example of this; others would be attempting to open a safe with instruments which turn out to be inadequate for the job,

*From Graham Hughes, "One Further Footnote on Attempting the Impossible," *New York University Law Review,* Vol. 42, No. 6 (1967); pp. 1005–1020. Reprinted by permission of the author and the publisher.

or shooting a bullet into the head of a dummy which is arranged in a bed in which the intended victim habitually sleeps, the accused believing that he was shooting into the head of his victim. Here there is thought to be no barrier to conviction if the acts done go beyond mere preparation and are accompanied by the accused's intention to achieve the objective which, if achieved, would constitute an offense known to the law. Here, unlike the case of legal impossibility, we are dealing with the failure of an endeavor which, if successful, would have amounted to a known offense.

This distinction between legal and factual impossibility has been crystallized in the famous hypotheticals concerning Lady Eldon and her, by now surely bedraggled, French lace.

Lady Eldon, when traveling with her husband on the Continent, bought what she supposed to be a quantity of French lace, which she hid, concealing it from Lord Eldon in one of the pockets of the coach. The package was brought to light by a customs officer at Dover. The lace turned out to be an English manufactured article of little value and, of course, not subject to duty. Lady Eldon had bought it at a price vastly above its value, believing it to be genuine, intending to smuggle it into England.[3]

The majority opinion among the writers is that Lady Eldon might properly be convicted of an attempt to smuggle dutiable lace into England, the facts being treated as amounting to an attempt to commit an offense known to the law and being thus diagnosed as factual rather than legal impossibility.[4]

The contrast with legal impossibility is underlined by the variation on the Lady Eldon hypothetical devised by Professors Paulsen and Kadish.

Suppose the lace which Lady Eldon had purchased was in fact the expensive French lace she meant to buy. The customs officer at Dover brings it to light. He then says to Lady Eldon: "Lucky for you you returned to England today rather than yesterday. I just received word this morning that the Government has removed French lace from the duty list." Could Lady Eldon be held for attempt to smuggle in these circumstances?[5]

The answer must be negative, for there is no offense known to the law which can be said to be Lady Eldon's objective. (It will be suggested later

that this is very questionable, but at this point I am interested only in expounding the current orthodox view.) It is true that Lady Eldon had an intent to do what she believed to be criminal, but the law can only concern itself with intents that go to objectives which as a matter of fact have been declared to be criminal objectives by the law of the land. "Criminal intent" in this connection must be taken to mean an intent to do that which is a crime, and not that which the party thinks is a crime. A broader view would involve the law in punishment for thoughts unexpressed in significant behavior. If a man does his best to kill a victim who fortunately survives, we do not punish him for murder. He gets the benefit of the lucky circumstance, quite undesired by him, that the victim survived. Similarly Lady Eldon must get the benefit of the lucky circumstance, quite unknown to her, that the duty on French lace had been repealed.

This distinction between legal and factual impossibility now seems to be the dominant orthodox position. It has been reinforced by an opinion of the United States Court of Military Appeals in 1962, where a majority of the court restored a conviction of the defendants for attempted rape although the victim, unknown to the accused, was dead at the time of the assault.[6] There is some disagreement about the use of the labels "legal" and "factual" impossibility, but there is no doubt that the way in which the distinction has been set out above represents majority opinion.

But many dissident voices have been raised from time to time both in the courts and in academic commentaries. Some of the major dissents from current orthodoxy in this area will now be examined, in the hope of assessing the sense and utility of the principal distinction between legal and factual impossibility. It will be suggested that though there is some validity and cogency in some of the criticisms that have been made, there has not yet been any full articulation or exploration of the most important weaknesses and difficulties that attend the prevalent doctrine.

A leading case which obtrudes irritatingly in defiance of majority opinion is the 1906 decision of the New York Court of Appeals in *People v. Jaffe*.[7] The accused had been charged with receiving stolen goods. The evidence disclosed that though the accused believed the goods to have a stolen character at the time of his receipt, they had in fact by that time lost such a character since, between the original theft and the receipt, the true owner had re-acquired possession. The defendant was convicted of an attempt to receive stolen goods, and this conviction was affirmed by the appellate division. In quashing the conviction, the court of appeals offered the following analysis:

[I]t is important to bear in mind precisely what it was that the defendant attempted to do. He simply made an effort to purchase certain specific pieces of cloth. He believed the cloth to be stolen property, but it was not such in fact. The purchase, therefore, if it had been completely effected, could not constitute the crime of receiving stolen property. . . .

[T]he act, which it was doubtless the intent of the defendant to commit, would not have been a crime if it had been consummated. . . .

. . . .

If all which an accused person intends to do would if done constitute no crime, it cannot be a crime to attempt to do with the same purpose a part of the thing intended.[8]

The critics of *Jaffe* have not found much difficulty in demolishing the analysis contained in this passage. It has been pointed out that the *Jaffe* court's statement that "the act, which it was doubtless the intent of the defendant to commit would not have been a crime if it had been consummated" is very questionable and turns upon a choice of what is relevant in establishing what his intention was.[9] It certainly seems no defiance of ordinary language to say that Jaffe intended to receive stolen goods, for, in speaking of a person's intention, we frequently incorporate his mistaken view of a situation, since belief and intent cannot be neatly separated. So, if I am sitting in a plane flying from New York to Los Angeles, which I mistakenly think is flying to London—my desired destination—it would be a perfectly reasonable statement to say that, at least until the mistake is pointed out to me, it was my intention to reach London on that plane. The rejection of *Jaffe,* so Professor Glanville Williams contends, is not only supported by such a view of intent but also by the policy underlying the law of attempts. Jaffe, in this way of looking at the facts, intended to commit an offense known to the law, so this is not a case of legal impossibility.[10] Where the prosecution can discharge its burden of proof by

showing beyond a reasonable doubt that an accused had such an intent, expressed in a sufficient overt act, then in terms of the prohibitions of the criminal law such a person is socially dangerous and deserves punishment.

This certainly has a superficial appearance of being an adequate demolition of the *Jaffe* opinion. Later I shall suggest that there are arguments in favor of the outcome in the *Jaffe* case which are not so easily met by the conventional refutation of the opinion.

Another well known judicial calling in question of the majority view is to be found in the English case of *Rex v. Osborn.*[11] The accused was charged with the statutory offense of attempting to administer a noxious thing to a woman, in that he had given to a pregnant woman some pills with the belief that they would induce an abortion. At the trial the questions were raised of whether the pills were in fact an effective abortifacient and, if not, whether the accused mistakenly believed them to be effective. In directing the jury on the latter question, Mr. Justice Rowlatt said:

[S]uppose it was innoxious but he thought it was noxious. . . . [I]f he does not begin to do the very thing, however morally culpable he may be, he does not attempt. . . . It is well known that the impossibility of the thing does not prevent an attempt being made. If you try to burst open the very best kind of steel safe with a wholly insufficient instrument, . . . still you are guilty of the attempt although you never could have completed it, because you are at it, you are at the very thing and trying to do it. . . . But . . . where the man is never on the thing itself at all—it is not a question of the impossibility—he is not on the job although he thinks he is; if he fires a gun at a stump of a tree thinking it is his enemy and his enemy is miles away, and there is nobody in the field at all, he is not near enough to the job to attempt it; he has not begun it; he has done it all under a misapprehension. . . . [I]f the thing was not noxious though he thought it was, he did not attempt to administer a noxious thing by administering the innoxious thing. . . .

[T]he real question . . . is whether it was noxious.[12]

This "on the job" test, as Glanville Williams has styled it,[13] is clearly difficult of application in its invitation to distinguish between doing a thing with inadequate means and not doing a thing at all. In the first place, as put by Mr. Justice Rowlatt, it comes close to a demand that the "victim" of the crime at least be physically present, but this is clearly an unnecessary condition in many situations. If I plant a bomb in my victim's house set to explode at night when he is asleep, am I not guilty of attempted murder because he does not sleep at home that night? There may be thought to be a difference between such a case and shooting at the stump of a tree believing it to be a man, in that when I put a bomb in the house I am quite overtly, and apart from any question of mistake, planting a lethal device in a place where a person habitually sleeps. This may indeed be a significant difference but it has nothing to do with the actual presence of the victim or the question of inadequate means. At the risk of being facetious, one might ask whether the impotent man who makes a sexual attack on a woman should be thought of, in the context of rape, as attempting to attain his objective with inadequate means or as never being on the job at all. (The conventional mistake test is not so easy here either. Should it depend on whether he mistakenly believed himself to be potent or had a mere, as it were, *spes successionis?*) As Glanville Williams points out, it has been held that to administer an inadequate dose of poison under the mistaken belief that the dose is lethal is generally treated as attempted murder. Should it make a difference if the mistake is more radical in that the accused mistakes water for poison?[14] Or what if the intended victim is already dead, unknown to the accused? Here again conviction is generally thought to be possible, as in the recent court martial case of *United States v. Thomas,*[15] though this was a case of rape and not murder. The distinction between inadequate means and not being on the job is much too imprecise to be of help as an explanation of such cases. While a proper uneasiness lies behind Mr. Justice Rowlatt's remarks in *Osborn,* his formulation of it was very defective and therefore fairly easily disposed of by the champions of the current position.

In the academic literature, several forceful dissenting opinions have been expressed, notably by Professor Keedy and Professor Perkins in the United States and by Professor Smith in England. Professor Keedy writes:

The first requisite of a criminal attempt is the intent to commit a specific crime. . . .

Intent as used in this connection must be distin-

guished from motive, desire, and expectation. If C by reason of his hatred of A plans to kill him, but mistaking B for A shoots B, his motive, desire and expectation are to Kill A but his intent is to kill B. If a married man forcibly has intercourse with a woman whom he believes to be his wife's twin sister, but who in fact is his wife, he is not guilty of rape because his intent was to have intercourse with the woman he attacked, who was in fact his wife. If A takes an umbrella which he believes to belong to B, but which is in fact his own, he does not have the intent to steal, his intent being to take the umbrella he grasps in his hand, which is his own umbrella. If a man mistaking a dummy in female dress for a woman, tries to ravish it he does not have the intent to commit rape since the ravishment of an inanimate object cannot be rape. If a man mistakes a stump for his enemy and shoots at it, notwithstanding his desire and expectation to shoot his enemy, his intent is to shoot the object aimed at, which is the stump.[16]

In a similar vein Professor Perkins distinguishes between "primary" and "secondary" intent to argue for an absence of liability in this type of case.[17] Such distinctions might be acceptable if they fulfilled the requirements of being intelligible, workable, and compliant with sensible policy justifications. They are in essence once more an invitation to confine the concept of an intent to the circumstances which in fact exist and to dub the accused's mistaken view of the situation as being a matter of "motive" or "secondary intent." Such an invitation must at the least be supported by argument before we can accept it, for it certainly is not supported by the conventions of ordinary language, which would not in the least be strained by saying, for example, that a man who forcibly has intercourse with his wife believing her to be her own twin sister intends to commit rape. Professors Keedy and Perkins offer no reasons founded either in morality or policy why we should depart from such ordinary usage. If a man forcibly has intercourse with his wife's sister, mistakenly believing her to be his wife, he may have an excuse in that there is an absence of mens rea, that is, he did not intent to rape a woman other than his wife. But if he believed the woman to be his wife's sister when in fact she was his wife, then lack of intent is a strange ground for refusing to convict him. If we come to the conclusion that a conviction is for some reason unjustified here, lack of intent is surely not the appropriate justification.

Professors Paulsen and Kadish raise an interesting hypothetical calculated to expose an alleged anomaly raised by the orthodox analysis:

Consider the following case. Two friends, Mr. Fact and Mr. Law, go hunting in the morning of October 15 in the fields of the state of Dakota, whose law makes it a misdemeanor to hunt any time other than from October 1 to November 30. Both kill deer on the first day out, October 15. Mr. Fact, however, was under the erroneous belief that the date was September 15; and Mr. Law was under the erroneous belief that the hunting season was confined to the month of November, as it was the previous year. Under the Lady Eldon formulation Mr. Fact could be convicted of an attempt to hunt out of season; but Mr. Law could not be. We fail to see how any rational system of criminal law could justify convicting one and acquitting the other on so fragile and unpersuasive a distinction that one was suffering under a mistake of fact, and the other under a mistake of law. Certainly if the ultimate test is the dangerousness of the actor (that is, readiness to violate the law), as Lady Eldon would have it, no distinction is warranted—Mr. Law has indicated himself to be no less "dangerous" than Mr. Fact.[18]

This doubt about the way in which the conventional position works out has in principle already been answered when it was pointed out earlier that the only intents which it is proper for the law to notice are those which relate to behavior or consequences which as a matter of fact have been declared criminal. But it is true that an uneasiness remains about the conviction of Mr. Fact and the acquittal of Mr. Law, if that should be the stipulated outcome of the hypothetical. This uneasiness is difficult to dispel within the confines of the orthodox position. Perhaps the defenders of orthodoxy could point to the comparatively innocuous character of the crime in question. The concept of attempt is in practice seldom invoked outside crimes of some gravity, and in England the better opinion seems to be that it relates only to indictable offenses and that a charge of attempting to commit a summary offense will not lie.[19] A second comment might relate to the regulatory nature of the offense in question and what might be a relative indifference about the dates on which hunting is permitted as long as it is only permitted for a portion of the year. Given such a relative indifference and the concomitant somewhat arbitrary selection of permitted and forbidden periods, Mr. Fact and Mr. Law certainly

appear to differ little in their dangerousness. The lesson of this is perhaps that as either a matter of law or prosecutorial discretion, it is better to confine prosecutions for attempts to offenses of some gravity.

A fresh attack on the legal impossibility-factual impossibility division has been made by an English criminal lawyer, Professor J. C. Smith.[20] Professor Smith introduces a distinction between those who have failed in their purpose (perhaps because of inadequate means) and those who have succeeded in their purpose which turns out not to be a completed crime at all. The former, he suggests, may properly be convicted but not the latter, for in the second group of cases the activities of the defendants "do not look like attempts." "One reason [why they do not look like attempts] appears to be that, while there was a failure of *intention* in each of these cases, D succeeded in his *purpose*. Purpose and intention may be the same thing, but they are by no means necessarily so; and attempt, as we have seen, is essentially concerned with purpose."[21]

Professor Smith has certainly got hold of a perceptible difference here between two kinds of cases, but the conclusion he bases upon it is questionable. He is correct in drawing our attention to the circumstance that in some of these cases the defendant is thwarted because of his mistake (for example, finding a pocket empty), while in others his mistake does not seem to detract in any substantial sense from the successful outcome of his project (for example, buying at a very low price goods that one wishes to acquire, believing them to be stolen when in fact they are not). But it is not easy to see how this could be a workable test nor why it should be thought to be very relevant. As Professor Williams has pointed out, the test would involve us in a very curious inquiry into whether the defendant felt himself to be disappointed or not.[22] It may be that for special reasons it is important to the defendant that the goods he is receiving should be stolen quite apart from the low price he is paying. Are we to convict him only if their stolen character was an important part of his motivation and acquit him if he was indifferent to this although he believed them to be stolen? The difficulty of the test is apparent in the way in which Smith himself classifies some of the cases he examines. Thus he seems to regard *Jaffe* as a case where the defendant succeeded in his purpose, but he regards *Regina v. Hensler*[23] as one where the defendant failed to achieve his purpose.[24] In *Hensler,* the defendant made a false representation in a begging letter; the recipient of the letter, aware that the representation was false, nevertheless sent the money. If Jaffe did not really care whether the goods were stolen as long as he got them at a low price, it seems equally likely that Hensler cared little about whether his representation was believed or not as long as he got the money.

Professor Smith does not assert that failure is an essential element in the concept of attempt, but he does argue that where the defendant succeeds in his purpose and that successful venture turns out to be no complete crime, then a conviction for attempt is improper. Glanville Williams comments: "Consider the situation where D takes his own umbrella, mistakenly thinking that he is stealing P's. Professor Smith assumes that this is not attempted larceny, because D has achieved his purpose. But has he? Since his purpose was to steal, he evidently intended to enrich himself by the acquisition of an umbrella, and this he has not succeeded in doing."[25]

In the umbrella controversy, Professor Smith seems to have refined his position somewhat in his later writings. He now offers two versions of the umbrella hypothetical:

D finds an umbrella left in his house after a party. He hides it, intending to steal it. It has been left by P and there is a note inside it saying that it is a present to D. D is not guilty of an attempt.

D sees P, a celebrity, put his umbrella in a stand at D's club. D resolves to steal it. When no one is looking, he goes to the stand and takes the umbrella in the place where P's was. But, someone has moved the umbrella and D has taken his own. He is guilty of an attempt.[26]

Presumably the conclusion is thought to differ in the two examples because in the first D has achieved his objective or purpose of acquiring an umbrella that was not his own and in the circumstances this turns out to be no completed crime, while in the second D has failed in his purpose of acquiring an umbrella not his own, a purpose which if achieved would in the circumstances have constituted a completed crime. There are certainly real differences in the two hypotheticals. In the first only one umbrella is involved; in the second there are two umbrellas, and D does not get the particular umbrella he intended to get. In the first example D might be said to be proceeding under ignorance of the exercise of a legal power by P, while in the second D is ignorant of or mistaken about the physical location of a particular umbrella at a particular time. We may wish to decide on further reflection that these are indeed significant differences, but the point to be made now is that they are not happily expressed in Professor Smith's emphasis on the notion of purpose as the relevant issue. It may well be that in the first example D is not at all interested in acquiring an umbrella for himself but only in doing P an injury. He may mean to destroy the umbrella. If such were the case, it would make no sense to say that D has succeeded in his objective or purpose. He has failed just as much as in the second hypothetical. But can we then say that D is to be convicted if his motive was to injure P but acquitted if his motive was the acquisition of someone else's umbrella? The fundamental weakness in Professor Smith's formulation is that, although he steers away from the word, his test really turns on an inquiry into the motive of the accused which, for evident and excellent reasons, is generally dismissed in the criminal law as being irrelevant to culpability, though it may be relevant to severity of punishment.

II

From the above it can be seen that there has been a constant current of unease about the dominant juristic position with regard to attempting the impossible. The real difficulties with the orthodox view have not been fully articulated. In this connection it is first necessary to demonstrate the full complexity of the orthodox position by tracking down the rather fine distinctions that it forces one to draw. An attempt will now be made to do this, by conducting a running dialogue about ways of applying the legal impossibility-factual impossibility distinction. A good starting point will be the second Lady Eldon hypothetical and we will cast A in the role of the defender of orthodoxy and B as the gadfly:

A. "The correctness of the contention that Lady Eldon must be acquitted in the second French lace hypothetical is demonstrated by the impossibility of drafting an acceptable indictment. To speak of 'attempting to import a dutiable article, to wit French lace' will not do because French lace simply is not a dutiable article."

B. "That may be so but then you must admit that it is equally difficult to argue for the propriety of convicting Jaffe whom it seems you want to convict. For how could the indictment speak of 'attempting to receive certain stolen goods, to wit certain rolls of cloth' when in fact the cloth simply was not stolen at the time of the receipt?[27] And this would apply also to the hypothetical of attempting to steal an umbrella which turns out to be one's own. For what would the indictment say? 'Attempting to take an umbrella the property of ? ? ?' It was the property of the defendant all the time and the indictment simply would not on its face allege an essential ingredient of the crime of larceny as set out in the general definitions of larceny, that the article should be the property of another."

A. "In *Jaffe* I think the answer would be this. The completed crime of receiving requires knowledge that the goods are stolen. In a crime of attempting to receive, why should it not be enough to allege in the indictment that the accused believed the goods to be stolen?[28] After all everyone seems to agree that it is proper to convict a person of attempting to pick an empty pocket and yet in such a case there is also no specific property of another which can be named in the indictment. Again, in the umbrella case, why should the indictment not say that the accused took an umbrella which he believed to be the property of another? The attempt notion in such a case does not consist in the failure to take an umbrella at all but in the failure to take the umbrella of another."

B. "But if you want to put it that way, I don't see now why you want to argue for the acquittal of Lady Eldon in the second French lace case. Can't you say that the complete crime there consists of failing to pay duty on a dutiable article, and Lady Eldon did believe the article to be dutiable? So, according to the position you now seem to be adopting, we could draft an indictment for Lady Eldon that would allege her attempt to import an article that she believed to be dutiable, to wit French lace. This seems to go back on the proposition with which you began."

A. "I think that to answer the point you have just made the argument will have to become rather subtle. It depends, I think, on exactly what

the actus reus of the offense is under the wording of the statute. If the offense in Lady Eldon's case were phrased in terms of 'importing a dutiable article,' I agree that at first sight it seems difficult to distinguish the Lady Eldon case from *Jaffe*. But we have to look further and inquire how the concept of 'dutiable article' is amplified in the law. We shall probably find that there is a schedule (amended from time to time) of articles on which varying customs duties must be paid and that there is then a general criminal provision which makes it an offense to import any article named in the schedule without paying the duty. The concept of 'stolen goods' is rather different. It is not amplified by a detailed catalogue or listing of individual items of merchandise but is amplified rather by reference to a generic description contained in other rules of law. Thus the statute might say that for the purposes of the crime of receiving, the term "stolen goods" shall mean any goods acquired in a way that constitutes one of the offenses of larceny, embezzlement, or obtaining by false pretenses. Now Jaffe was not under any mistake about the general circumstances in which according to law goods are stolen. But Lady Eldon was under a mistake about the legal amplification of the notion of a dutiable article. And that is why it is proper to convict Jaffe but not Lady Eldon."

B. "It sounds to me as if you are making everything turn on a distinction between a mistake of fact and a mistake of law. That distinction has always been an obscure one to make in theory and practice, and it seems to present particular difficulties in this area. Let me give you a few hypotheticals around the facts of *Jaffe* to see how you would deal with them. It seems from what you have just said that you look upon a conviction as proper in *Jaffe* by taking the view that Jaffe made a mistake of fact. He was not mistaken about the legal definition of circumstances in which goods are stolen but only ignorant of the factual circumstance that the goods had come back into the control of the true owner or the police acting as the owner's agents. So his mistake was not about what makes goods stolen goods but about whether the particular goods had those qualities at that time. Suppose then that D receives goods from X which X has obtained from Y by false promises which X never intended to perform. Suppose further that in the particular jurisdiction, obtaining goods in this way by making false promises *de futuro* is not a crime, but that D, not being a good scholar of the criminal law, believed that X's mode of obtaining the goods amounted to a crime. Would you have to say that D should be acquitted since he is making a mistake of law? And let me give you a second hypothetical, closer to the facts of *Jaffe*. Suppose that Jaffe did know that the goods which had been initially stolen had come back fleetingly into the control of the true owner. Jaffe believed that this contact was insufficient in law to restore the possession of the owner and therefore concluded that the goods were still stolen. His view of the law is wrong, and it is held that the goods had come back into the possession of the owner and were therefore not stolen goods at the time of D's receipt. That looks to me like a mistake of law, so I imagine that you would have to say that Jaffe should be acquitted."

A. "Certainly that conclusion would be correct in your first hypothetical. We can't convict people for attempting to receive stolen goods when the goods never were stolen, even under the circumstances as the accused believed them to be. Your variation on *Jaffe* is a bit different because the goods were initially stolen there, but again I think the conclusion is correct that we cannot convict because here too the elements of the actus reus of the completed crime are present neither in fact nor in the mind of the accused. After all a full statement of the concept of stolen goods in law would require one not only to state that the goods were acquired in circumstances amounting to theft, but also to state the negative condition, that circumstances had not occurred after the theft which would amount to recaption by the owner. Jaffe in the case of that name was mistaken about whether such circumstances had occurred and was thus making a mistake of fact about the actus reus. But the defendant in your hypothetical is well aware of the circumstances that have occurred but is mistaken about their legal import. He therefore should be acquitted. Curiously here the usual position is reversed, for we are saying that mistake of fact will not be a defense while mistake of law will be. The apparent paradox of saying that is of course really quite sensible since the mistake is an inculpating one and not an exculpating one in the sense that, but for proof of the mistake, there would be no other demonstration of liability."

B. "Aren't you now admitting that the line between guilt and innocence here is a very obscure one? It seems to me that in practice it would be enormously difficult to prove what kind of mistake the defendant had made. Let me inflict one or two more hypotheticals on you. Suppose someone in an eccentric whim builds a small office building which looks exactly like a dwelling-house. D comes along at night and believing it to be a dwelling-house breaks and enters with intent to steal. He is clearly guilty of some degree of the offense of burglary. But what if the jurisdiction confines first-degree burglary to breaking and entering dwelling-houses? Is D guilty of an attempt to commit burglary in the first degree? To convict him under your approach, I suppose, we would have to show that his mistake related to the existence of one of those elements which in law go to make up the concept of a dwelling-house—that somebody habitually slept there *animo revertendi,* and otherwise treated it as a home, etcetera. If he thought that first-degree burglary covered office buildings as well as dwelling-houses, he could not be convicted; at least not for that reason alone, unless he also believed this structure to be a dwelling-house."

A. "I think that analysis is quite correct."

B. "Well, suppose D comes along in the night and finds a converted bus or railroad coach in which a family is living. He breaks and enters with intent to steal. Let us assume that in this jurisdiction the courts have held that such a structure is not a dwelling-house if it remains in a readily mobile condition, but may be classified as a dwelling-house if it has lost its mobility by becoming attached to the realty. Do you really want to say that D is guilty of attempted burglary in the first degree if he thought the structure was embedded in concrete when in fact it had wheels, but not guilty if he knew very well that it had wheels but believed that the law on first degree burglary included such structures?"

A. "Yes, indeed, and I can't see what is objectionable about saying that. After all the burden of proof here is on the prosecution. If they want to get a conviction, they will have to prove beyond a reasonable doubt that the kind of mistake D was making was such that if his mistaken belief had been true all the elements of the actus reus would have been present. It may well be that in the kind of ingenious hypothetical you are constructing such proof would be very difficult to furnish. But in that case there probably will be no prosecution on such a count, which no doubt explains the dearth of cases of this kind in the reports. But I must still insist that where the prosecution is able to make such proof then a conviction would be perfectly proper."

B. "I think the position with which you began has now become rather tortuously convoluted."

A. "I would prefer to say I have refined it."

NOTES

1. The English courts held in 1892 that the accused could be convicted of attempting to pick an empty pocket, Regina v. Ring, 17 Cox Crim. Cas. 491 (1892), and had earlier held that the accused could be convicted of attempting to obtain money by false pretenses even though the recipient of his "begging" letter well knew the pretense to be false. Regina v. Hensler, 11 Cox Crim. Cas. 570 (1870). In 1897, Mr. Justice Holmes, then of the Massachusetts court, was firmly of the opinion that impossibility was not a general defense. Commonwealth v. Kennedy, 170 Mass. 18, 48 N.E. 770 (1897). For a good review of the American cases, see United States v. Thomas, 13 U.S.C.M.A. 278, 32 C.M.R. 278 (1962).

2. The leading exponents of this view are, perhaps, Glanville Williams and Jerome Hall. See G. Williams, Criminal Law: The General Part 633-37 (2d ed. 1961) [hereinafter Williams]; J. Hall, General Principles of Criminal Law 586 (2d ed. 1960).

3. 1 F. Wharton, Criminal Law 304 n.9 (12th ed. 1932).

4. Id.; see Sayre, Criminal Attempts, 41 Harv. L. Rev. 821, 852 (1928).

5. M. Paulsen & S. Kadish, Criminal Law and Its Processes 484 (1962).

6. United States v. Thomas, 13 U.S.C.M.A. 278, 32 C.M.R. 278 (1962).

7. 185 N.Y. 497, 78 N.E. 169 (1906).

8. Id. at 500-01, 78 N.E. at 169-70.

9. Williams 650.

10. Id.

11. 84 J.P. 63 (1919).

12. Id. at 63-64.

13. Williams 638.

14. Williams thinks not. Id. at 643-44.

15. 13 U.S.C.M.A. 278, 32 C.M.R. 278 (1962).

16. Keedy, Criminal Attempts at Common Law, 102 U. Pa. L. Rev. 464, 466-67 (1954).

17. Perkins, Criminal Attempts and Related Problems, 2 U.C.L.A.L. Rev. 319, 330-32 (1955).

18. M. Paulsen & S. Kadish, supra note 5, at 485-86.

19. Williams 614.

20. Smith, Two Problems in Criminal Attempts Re-Examined, [1962] Crim. L. Rev. 212.

21. Id. Criminal Attempts, at 217.

22. Williams, Criminal Attempts—A Reply, [1962] Crim. L. Rev. 300.

23. 11 Cox Crim. Cas. 570 (1870).

24. Smith, Criminal Attempts, supra note 20, at 215.

25. Williams, Criminal Attempts, supra note 22, at 301.

26. J. C. Smith & B. Hogan, Criminal Law 157-58 (1965).

27. This difficulty of drafting the indictment in such cases is raised by Smith, Criminal Attempts, supra note 20, at 218.

28. This point is convincingly made by Williams. Williams 650-51.

JOEL FEINBERG

Sua Culpa*

I

It is common enough for philosophers to analyze moral judgments and for philosophers—usually other philosophers—to analyze causal judg-

*From *Doing and Deserving: Essays in the Theory of Responsibility* (Princeton, N.J.: Princeton University Press, 1970), pp. 187–221. Copyright © 1970 by Princeton University Press. Reprinted by permission of the Princeton University Press.

ments. But statements to the effect that a given harm is some assignable person's fault, having both moral and causal components, import the complexities of judgments of the other two kinds. They are, therefore, especially challenging. Yet they are rarely considered by analytical philosophers. This neglect is to be regretted, because "his fault" judgments (as I shall call them) are important and ubiquitous in ordinary life. Historians employ them to assign blame for wars and depressions; politicians, sportswriters, and litigants use them to assign blame for losses. The disagreements they occasion are among the most common and intensely disputed in all "ethical discourse."

It may seem that most of those who quibble and quarrel about "his fault" are either children or lawyers; and even lawyers, therefore, can seem childish when they are preoccupied with the question. But investigators, editorialists, and executives must assign blame for failures and thereby judge the faults of their fellows. (Indeed, their inquiries and debates are most childish when they do *not* carefully consider fault and instead go scapegoat-hunting.) My assumption in what follows is that the faults that concern non-lawyers, both children and adults, are faults in the same sense of the word as those that concern the lawyer, that the concept of "his fault" is imported into the law from the world of everyday affairs. On the other hand, "proximate cause" (to pick just one of a thousand examples) is a technical term of law invented by lawyers to do a special legal job and subject to continual refashioning in the interests of greater efficiency in the performance of its assigned legal task. To explain this term to a layman is precisely to explain what *lawyers* do with it; if it should ever happen that a child, or a sportswriter, or an historian should use the expression, that fact would be of no relevance to its proper analysis. But to explain the concept of "his fault," we must give an account that explains what both lawyers and laymen do with it and how it is possible for each to understand and to communicate with the other by means of it.

An equivalent way of saying that some result is a man's fault is to say that he is to *blame* for it. Precisely the same thing can also be said in the language of *responsibility.* Of course, to be responsible for something (after the fact) may also mean that one did it, or caused it, or now stands answerable, or accountable, or liable to unfavorable responses from others for it. One can be responsible for a result in all those senses without being to blame for it. One can be held liable for a result either because it is one's fault or for some quite different kind of reason; and one can be to blame for an occurrence and yet escape all liability for it. Still, when one is to blame for harm, one can properly be said to be "responsible for it *re-*

ally"; that is, there is a sense of "responsible for" that simply means "chargeable to one as one's fault." One of the commonest uses of the expression "*morally* responsible for" is for being responsible for something in this sense. (Another is for chargeability to a fault of a distinctively moral kind. Still another is for being *liable* to responses of a distinctively moral kind.)

II

The word "fault" occurs in three distinct idioms. We can say of a man that he *has a fault,* or that he is (or was) *at fault,* or that he is "to blame" for a given harm, which is to say that the harm is (or was) *his fault.* In this essay I shall be directly concerned only with the last of these idioms, except to make some necessary preliminary remarks about the other two.

TO HAVE A FAULT

A fault is a shortcoming, that is, a failure to conform to some norm or standard. Originally, perhaps, the word "fault" gave emphasis to failures through deficiency; but now any sort of failure to "measure up" is a fault, and we find no paradox in "falling short through excess." Not all defective human properties are faults. Evanescent qualities are hardly around long enough to qualify. To be a fault, a defective property must be sufficiently durable, visible, and potent to tell us something interesting about its possessor. A fault can be a durable manifestation almost constantly before the eye; but, more typically, human faults are latencies that manifest themselves only under special circumstances. Flaws of character are tendencies to act or feel in subpar ways, which, as tendencies, are *characteristic* of their possessor, that is, genuinely representative of him. Moreover, faults, like virtues, are commonly understood as comparative notions. An irascible man, for example, is not merely one who can become angry, for on that interpretation we may all be considered irascible. Rather, he is one who is more prone than most to become angry, either in the sense that he becomes angry on occasions when most men would not or in the sense that he gets angrier than most men on those occasions when most men would be angry. Equally commonly, however, we interpret a tendency-fault as a failure to satisfy not merely a statistical norm, but a norm of propriety; an irascible man has a tendency to get angry on occasions when he *ought* not to. And even when the implied norm is a statistical one, the fault predicate does more than describe neutrally. A fault word always expresses derogation.

The concept of fault has a close relation to that of harm, but it would be an overstatement to claim that all human faults create the risk of harm. David Hume was closer to the mark when he divided faults into four categories: those that cause displeasure or harm to self or others. Immediate displeasure, however, is only one of the diverse negative reactions that, quite apart from harmfulness, can be the sign of a fault. I would also include, for example, offense, wounded feelings, disaffection, aversion, disgust, shock, annoyance, and "uneasy sensations"—reactions either of the faulty self or of others. If we use the word "offensiveness" to cover the provoking of this whole class of negative responses, and if we assume that everything that is offensive to self, in this broad sense, is likely also to be offensive to others, we can summarize Hume's view by saying that it is either harmfulness or social offensiveness that makes some characteristics faults. Hume notwithstanding, there are some (though perhaps not many) faults that neither harm nor offend but simply fail to benefit, such as unimaginativeness and various minor intellectual flaws. We can modify Hume's account of the offensive faults further, perhaps in a way Hume would not have welcomed, by adding that it is not the mere *de facto* tendency of a trait to offend that renders it a fault. Normally when we attach the fault label to personal characteristics—that is, when we speak as moralists expressing our own judgments, and not merely as sociologists describing the prevailing sentiments of our communities—we are not simply predicting that the characteristics will offend; we are instead (or also) endorsing offense as an appropriate reaction to them. Most of those faults that do not harm, we think, are traits that naturally, or properly, or understandably offend (in the widest sense of "offend").

Often we speak as if a man's fault can enter into causal relations with various outcomes external to him. These assertions, when sensible, must be taken as elliptical forms of more complex statements. To say that a man's faulty disposition, his carelessness or greed, caused some harm is to say that the man's action or omission that did the causing was of the type that he characteristically does (or would do) in circumstances of the kind that in fact were present, or that the act or omission was of the sort he has a predominant tendency to do in circumstances of that kind. (He may, of course, also have a countertendency to restrain himself by an act of will, or the like.) To cite a man's character flaw as a cause of a harm, in short, is to *ascribe* the cause to an act or omission and then to *classify* that act or omission in a certain way—as characteristic of the actor. (It is just the sort of thing he *would* do, as we say.) It is also, finally, to *judge* the manifested characteristic as substandard and thereby to derogate it.

One can be *at fault* on a given occasion, however, even though one does not act in a characteristic way. Even very careful men sometimes slip up; even the most talented make mistakes; even the very calm sometimes lose their tempers. When these uncharacteristic failures cause harm, it is correct to say that a *faulty aspect* of some act or omission did the causing, but incorrect to ascribe the cause to some faulty characteristic of the actor, for that would be to imply, contrary to the hypothesis, that he is a generally careless, irascible, or inept person. This is the kind of faulty doing (as opposed to "faulty being") that could happen, as we say, to anyone; but in the long run it will be done more often to those who have serious character faults than by those who do not.

"Being at fault," even in one's perfectly voluntary and representative conduct, is in a sense partly a matter of luck. No one has complete control over what circumstances he finds himself in—whether, for example, he lives in times of war or peace, prosperity or depression, under democratic or autocratic government, in sickness or health, and so on. Consequently, a man may, by luck merely, escape those circumstances that would actualize some dreadful latency in him of which he is wholly unaware. It may even be true of *most* of us virtuous persons that we are to some small degree, at least, "lucky" in this sense. (We do not, however, normally refer to the mere absence of very bad luck as "good luck.") Not only can one *have a fault*; and "luckily" escape *being at fault* in one's actions (on analogy with the hemophiliac who never in fact gets cut); one can also have a small fault (that is, a disposition very difficult to actualize) and unluckily stumble into those very rare circumstances that can actualize it. (The latter is "bad luck" in a proper sense.) Both of these possibilities—the luckily unactualized and the unluckily actualized latencies—follow from the analysis of faults as dispositions and, if that analysis is correct, should be sufficient at least to temper anyone's self-righteousness about the faulty actions of others.

TO BE AT FAULT

When a man is "at fault" on a given occasion, the fault characterizes his action itself and not necessarily the actor, except as he was during the performance of the action. There is no necessary relation between this kind of fault and general dispositions of the actor—though, for all we know, every faultily undertaken or executed action *may* exemplify extremely complicated dispositions. When we say that a man is at fault, we usually mean only to refer to occurrent defects of acts or omissions, and only derivatively to the *actor's* flaw as the doer of the defective deed. Such judgments are at best presumptive evidence about the man's general character. An act can be faulty even when not characteristic of the actor, and the actor may be properly "to blame" for it anyway; for if the action is faulty and it is also *his* action (characteristic or not), then he must answer for it. The faultiness of an action always reflects *some* discredit upon its doer, providing the doing is voluntary.

One standard legal classification divides all ways of being at fault into three categories: intentional wrongdoing, recklessness, and negligence. The traditional legal test of intentional doing has been a disjunctive one: There is intentional wrongdoing if either one acts with a wrongful conscious objective or one knowingly produces a forbidden result even incidentally as a kind of side-effect of his effort to achieve his objective. When the occurrence of the forbidden or undesirable side-effect is not certain, but nevertheless there is a known substantial likelihood of its coming about as an incidental byproduct of one's action, its subsequent production cannot be called "intentional" or "knowing" but verges into *recklessness*. What is known in recklessness is the existence of a *risk*. When the actor knowingly runs the risk, when he is willing to gamble with his own interests or the interests of others, then,

providing the risk itself is unreasonable, his act is reckless.[1]

One can hardly escape the impression that what is called "negligence" in the law is simply the miscellaneous class of faulty actions that are not intentional (done purposely or knowingly) or reckless; that in this classification of faults, once wrongful intentions and reckless quasi-intentions have been mentioned, "negligence" stands for everything else. This would leave a class of faults, however, that is *too* wide and miscellaneous. Humorlessness (to take just one example) is a kind of fault that is not intentional; yet we would hardly accuse a man of being "negligent" in failing to be amused or to show amusement at what is truly amusing. The point, I think, is that inappropriate failures to be amused are not the sorts of faults likely to cause *harm*. There is no great risk in a blank stare or a suppressed giggle. Negligence is the name of a heterogeneous class of acts and omissions that are unreasonably *dangerous*. Creation of risk is absolutely essential to the concept, and so is fault. But the fault is not merely conjoined coincidentally to the risk; rather, the fault consists in creating the risk, however unintentionally. When one knowingly creates an unreasonable risk to self or others, one is reckless; when one unknowingly but faultily creates such a risk, one is negligent.

There are a large number of ways of "unintentionally but faultily" creating an unreasonable risk. One can consciously weigh the risk but misassess it, either because of hasty or otherwise insufficient scrutiny (rashness), or through willful blindness to the magnitude of the risk, or through the conscientious exercise of inherently bad judgment. Or one can unintentionally create an unreasonable risk by failing altogether to attend either to what one is doing (the manner of execution) or to the very possibility that harmful consequences might ensue. In the former case, best called *carelessness* or *clumsiness* (in execution), one creates a risk precisely in virtue of not paying sufficient attention to what one is doing; in the latter case, which we can call *heedlessness* (in the very undertaking of the action), the risk is already there in the objective circumstances, but unperceived or mindlessly ignored.

There are still other faults that can render a given act or omission, unknown to its doer, unreasonably dangerous. Overly attentive drivers with the strongest scruples and the best intentions can drive as negligently as inattentive drivers and, indeed, a good deal more negligently than experienced drivers of strong and reliable habits who rely on those habits while daydreaming, their car being operated in effect by a kind of psychic "automatic pilot." Timidity, excitability, organic awkwardness, and slow reflexes can create unreasonable risks too, even when accompanied by attentive and conscientious advertence; and so can normal virtues like gallantry when conjoined with inexperience or poor judgment. (Imagine stopping one's car and waving a pretty pedestrian across the street right into the path of a speeding car passing on the right, unseen because momentarily in the "blind spot" of one's rear view mirror.) Almost any defect of conduct, except the likes of humorlessness, can be the *basis* of negligence, that is, the fault in virtue of which a given act or omission becomes, unknown to its actor, unreasonably dangerous. "Negligence" in the present sense is the name of a category of faulty acts. The negligence of any particular act or kind of act in the general category is always a consequential fault, a fault supervenient upon a fault of another kind that leads to an unreasonable risk in the circumstances.

It is worth emphasizing that this analysis applies to *legal negligence* only, which is negligence in a quite special sense. In ordinary nontechnical discourse, the word "negligence" is often a rough synonym for "carelessness" and as such refers to only one of the numerous possible faults that can, in a given set of circumstances, be the faulty basis of negligent conduct in the legal sense.

III

We come now to the main business at hand: the analysis of the concept of "his fault." It should be clear at the outset that, in order for a given harm to be someone's fault, he must have been somehow "at fault" in what he did or omitted to do, and also that there must have been some sort of causal connection between his action or omission and the harm. It is equally obvious that neither of these conditions by itself can be sufficient. Thus a motorist may be at fault in driving with an expired license or in exceeding the speed limit by five miles per hour, but unless his faulty act is a cause of the collision that ensues, the accident can hardly be his fault. Fault without causally deter-

mining action, then, is not sufficient. Similarly, causation without fault is not sufficient for the caused harm to be the causer's fault. It is no logical contradiction to say that a person's action caused the harm yet the harm was not his fault.

THE TRICONDITIONAL ANALYSIS

It is natural at this point to conclude that a harm is "his fault" if and only if (1) he was at fault in acting (or omitting) and (2) his faulty act (or omission) caused the harm. This analysis, however, is incomplete, being still vulnerable to counterexamples of faulty actions causing harm that is nevertheless not the actor's fault. Suppose that A is unlicensed to drive an automobile but drives anyway, thereby "being at fault." The appearance of him driving in an (otherwise) faultless manner causes an edgy horse to panic and throw his rider. His faultily undertaken act caused a harm that cannot be imputed to him because the respect in which his act was faulty was causally irrelevant to the production of the harm. (When we come to give a causal explanation of the harm, we will not mention the fact that the driver had no license in his pocket. *That* is not what scared the horse.) This example suggests that a further condition is required to complete the analysis: (3) the aspect of the act that was faulty was also one of the aspects in virtue of which the act was a cause of the harm.

The third condition in the analysis is especially important when the fault in question falls under the general heading of negligence. Robert Keeton in effect devotes most of a book to commentary on a hypothetical example which illustrates this point:

The defendant, proprietor of a restaurant, placed a large unlabelled can of rat poison beside cans of flour on a shelf near a stove in a restaurant kitchen. The victim, while in the kitchen making a delivery to the restaurant, was killed by an explosion of the poison. Assume that the defendant's handling of the rat poison was negligent because of the risk that someone would be poisoned but that the defendant had no reason to know of the risk that the poison would explode if left in a hot place.[2]

The defendant's action, in Keeton's example, was faulty, and it was also the cause of the victim's death; but, on the analysis I have suggested, the death was nevertheless not his fault. The defendant's conduct was negligent because it created a risk of *poisoning,* but the harm it caused was not within the ambit of *that* risk. The risk of *explosion* was not negligently created. Hence the aspect of the act in virtue of which it was faulty was not the cause of the harm. Keeton puts the point more exactly: the harm was not "a result within the scope of the risks by reason of which the actor is found to be negligent."[3] Keeton's concern is with a theory of liability for negligence, not with an analysis of the nontechnical concept of "his fault"; but, liability aside, the analysis I have given entails that the death, in Keeton's example, was *not* the defendant's fault.

We can refer to this account as "the triconditional analysis" and to its three conditions as (in order) "the fault condition," "the causal condition" (that the act was a cause of the harm), and "the causal relevance condition" (that the faulty aspect of the act was its causal link to the harm). I shall conclude that the triconditional analysis goes a long way toward providing a correct account of the commonsense notion of "his fault" and that its three conditions are indeed necessary to such an account even if, in the end, they must be formulated much more carefully and even supplemented by other conditions in an inevitably more complicated analysis. The remainder of this section discusses difficulties for the analysis as it stands which, I think, it can survive (at least after some tinkering, modifying, and disclaiming). One of these difficulties stems from a heterogeneous group of examples of persons who, on our analysis, would be blamed for harms that are clearly not their fault. I try to sidestep these counterexamples by affixing a restriction to the fault condition and making corresponding adjustments in the formulation of the relevance condition. The other difficulties directly concern the causal condition and the relevance condition. Both of these can involve us quickly in some fundamental philosophical problems.

RESTRICTIONS ON THE FAULT CONDITION

There are some exceptional cases (but readily accessible to the philosophical imagination) in which a person who is clearly not to blame for a given harm nevertheless is the sole person who satisfies the conditions of the tripartite analysis.

These cases, therefore, constitute counterexamples to that analysis if it is taken to state not only necessary but sufficient conditions for blame. Nicholas Sturgeon has suggested an especially ingenious case:

A has made a large bet that no infractions of the law will occur at a certain place in a certain period of time; but *B,* at that place and time, opens a pack of cigarettes and fails to destroy the federal tax seal thereby breaking the law. *A,* seeing *B's* omission, is so frustrated that he suffers a fatal heart attack on the spot. (To simplify matters, we may suppose that no one has any reason to suppose *A* is endangering his health by gambling in this way.)[4]

Clearly, *A's* death is not *B's* fault. Yet (1) *B* was at fault in acting contrary to law; (2) his faulty act frustrated *A,* causing the heart attack; and (3) the aspects of *B's* act (omission) that were faulty (the illegality of his omission to destroy the tax stamps) were also among the aspects of it in virtue of which there was a causal connection between it and the harm. A similar example is provided by John Taurek:

C is so programmed (by hypnosis, perhaps *C* is a clever robot, whatever) that if *A* lies in answering *B's* question, *C* will harm *D. B* asks *A* her age and she lies. *C* harms *D. A's* action seems to be a causal factor in the production of harm to *D,* and just in virtue of his faulty aspect. Yet who would hold that *D's* harm was *A's* fault?[5]

Perhaps it is possible to add further conditions to the analysis to obviate this kind of counterexample, but a more likely remedy would be to restrict the kinds of faults that can be elements of "his fault" judgments. Sometimes a man can be said to be at fault in acting (or omitting to act) precisely because his action or omission will offend or fail to benefit himself or others, or because it is a violation of faith (even a *harmless* instance of promise-breaking, such as a secret breaking of faith to a person now dead), or simply and precisely because it breaks an authoritative legal rule. Most intentional wrongdoing, on the other hand, and all recklessness and negligence are instances of being at fault for another (perhaps additional) reason—either because "they make a certain kind of harm or injury inevitable, or because they create an unreasonable risk of a certain kind of harm."[6] We can attempt to avoid counterexamples of the sort Sturgeon and Taurek suggested by tampering with the first condition (the fault condition). We can say now (of course, only tentatively and not without misgiving) that, for the purpose of this analysis, the way of being at fault required by the fault condition is to be understood as the harm-threatening way, not the nonbenefiting, offense-threatening, harmless faith-breaking, or law-violating ways. The fault condition then can be reformulated as follows (in words suggested by Sturgeon): a given harm is A's fault only if (1) A was at fault in acting or omitting to act and "the faultiness of his act or omission consisted, at least in part, in the creation of either a certainty or an unreasonable risk of harm. . . ."[7] Now the faulty smoker in Sturgeon's example and the liar in Taurek's example are no longer "at fault" in the requisite way, and the revised analysis no longer pins the blame for coincidental harms on them. To open a cigarette package in an overly fastidious fashion is not to endanger unduly the health of others; nor is lying about one's age (except in very special contexts) to threaten others with harm.

In the light of this new restriction on the fault condition, we can formulate the causal relevance condition in an alternative way, along the lines suggested by Keeton's account of harm caused by negligence. We can now say that the (harm-threatening) "faulty aspect" of an act is a cause of subsequent harm when the risk or certainty of harm in virtue of which the act was at fault was a risk or certainty of "just the sort of harm that was in fact caused,"[8] and not harm of some other sort. The resultant harm, in other words, must be within the scope of the risk (or certainty) in virtue of which the act is properly characterized as faulty. This is more than a mere explication of the original way of putting the third condition. It is a definite modification designed to rule out cases of *coincidence* where the faulty aspect of an act, even when it is of the harm-threatening sort, may be causally linked to a subsequent harm via such adventitious conditions as standing wagers and programmed robots. Under the revised formulation, the very same considerations involved in the explanation of *why* the act is faulty are also involved, essentially and sufficiently, in the explanation of *how* the harm was caused.

We have not even considered, of course, the crucial question of how reasonable risks are to be distinguished from unreasonable ones; and there are still other problems resulting from the fact that a "sort of harm" (crucial phrase) can be described in either more or less full and determinate ways. These problems, like several other closely related ones, are too complicated to be tackled here.

FAULT AND CAUSE: DEPENDENT AND INDEPENDENT DETERMINATIONS

Can we tell whether an act caused a given harm independently of knowing whether the actor was at fault in acting? The answer seems to be that we can determine the causal question independently of the fault question in some cases but not in others. Part of our problem is to explain his variation. Consider first some examples. A blaster takes every reasonable precaution, and yet by a wildly improbable fluke his explosion of dynamite sends a disjarred rock flying through the window of a distant isolated cabin. He was not at fault, but whether he was or not, we are able to say independently that his setting off the blast was the cause of the broken window. Similarly, the motorist in our earlier example, by driving (whether with or without fault is immaterial to this point) along a rarely traveled stretch of country road, caused a nervous horse to bolt. That is, it was his activity as he conducted it then and there, with its attendant noise and dust, that caused the horse to bolt; and we can know this independently of any determination of fault.

Examples provided by J. L. Mackie and William Dray, however, seem to cut the other way. Mackie[9] describes an episode in which a motorcyclist exceeded a speed limit and was chased by a policeman, also on a motorcycle, at speeds up to seventy miles per hour. An absentminded pedestrian stepped off a bus into the policeman's path and was killed instantly. The newspapers for the next few days were full of debates over the questions of whose conduct was the "real cause" of the death, debates that seemed to center on the question of whose conduct was the least *reasonable* intrusion into the normal course of events. To express an opinion at all on the causal question seemed to be to take a stand, plain and simple, about the *propriety* of pursuits by police in heavily populated areas.

Dray discusses a hypothetical debate between two historians who argue "whether it was Hitler's invasion of Poland or Chamberlain's pledge to defend it which caused the outbreak of the Second World War." The question they *must* be taken to be trying to settle, he avers, is "who was to blame." "The point," he says, "is not that we cannot hold an agent responsible for a certain happening unless his action can be said to have caused it. It is rather that, unless we are prepared to hold the agent responsible for what happened, we cannot say that his action *was* the cause."[10] Mackie comes to a similar conclusion, embracing what he calls a "curious inversion of utilitarianism," namely, that one often cannot tell whether a given harm is a causal consequence of a given act without first deciding whether the actor was *at fault* in acting the way he did.

To clarify the relations between cause and fault, it will be necessary to disgress briefly and remind ourselves of certain features of causal judgments as they are made in ordinary life. That one condition is causally necessary or, in a given context, sufficient for the occurrence of a given event is normally a question simply for empirical investigation and the application of a scientific theory. Normally, however, there will be a plurality of distinguishable causal conditions (often called "causal factors") for any given event, and the aim of a causal inquiry will be to single out one[11] of these to be denominated "the cause" of the event in question.[12] A judgment that cites one of the numerous eligible causal conditions for an event as "the cause" I call a *causal citation*. The eligibility of an event or state as a causal factor is determined empirically via the application of inductive criteria.[13] On the other hand, the citation of one of the eligible candidates as "the cause" is normally made, as we shall see, via the application of what Dray calls "pragmatic criteria." In Dray's convenient phrase, the inductive inquiry establishes the "importance of a condition to the event," whereas the causal citation indicates its "importance to the inquirer."

The point of a causal citation is to single out one of the certified causal candidates that is especially *interesting* to us, given our various practical purposes and cognitive concerns. These purposes and concerns provide a convenient way of classifying the "contexts of inquiry" in which causal citations are made. The primary division is between explanatory and nonexplanatory contexts. The occasion for an explanatory citation is one in which there is intellectual puzzlement of a quite specific kind. A suprising or unusual event has occurred which is a deviation from what is understood to be the normal course of things. A teetotaler is drunk, or an alcoholic sober; a punctual man is tardy, or a dilatory man early; it rains in the dry season, or it fails to rain in the wet season. Sometimes the breach of routine is disappointing, and we wish to know what went wrong this time. But sometimes the surprise is pleasant or, more commonly, simply stimulating to one's curiosity. We ask what caused the surprising event and expect an explanation that will cite a factor normally present but absent this time, or normally absent but present this time, that made the difference. The occasion for explanation is a breach of routine; the explanatory judgment cites another deviation from routine to correlate with it.

Very often one of the causal conditions for a given upshot is a faulty human action. Human failings tend to be more "interesting" factors than events of other kinds, even for purely explanatory purposes; but it is important to notice that this need not always be the case. Faulty human actions usually do *not* fall within the normal course of events, so that a dereliction of duty, for example, when it is a causally necessary condition for some puzzling breach of routine, being itself a departure from the normal course of things, is a prime candidate for causal citation. But when the faulty conduct of Flavius is constant and unrelieved and known to be such to Titus, it will not relieve Titus's perplexity over how a given unhappy event came about simply to cite Flavius's habitual negligence or customary dereliction of duty as "the cause." What Titus wishes to know is what new intrusive event made the difference *this* time; and it won't help *him* to mention a causal factor that has always been present even on those occasions when no unhappy result ensued.

Not all causal explanations by any means employ causal citations. Especially when we are puzzled about the "normal course of events" itself and wish explanations for standardly recurring regularities (Why do the tides come in? Why do released objects fall? Why do flowers bloom in the spring?), mere brief citations will not do. In such cases we require long stories involving the descriptions of diverse states of affairs and the invocation of various laws of nature. Similarly, not all causal citations are explanatory. Sometimes there is no gap in a person's understanding of how a given interesting event came about, and yet he may seek nevertheless to learn its "real" or "most important" cause. Nonexplanatory citations are those made for some purpose other than the desire simply to put one's curiosity to rest. Most frequently they cite the causal factor that is of a kind that is easiest to manipulate or control. Engineers and other practical men may be concerned to eliminate events of the kind that occasioned the inquiry if they are harmful or to produce more of them if they are beneficial. In either case, when they seek "the cause," they seek the causal factor that has a handle on it (in Collingwood's phrase) that they can get hold of and manipulate. Another of our practical purposes in making causal citations is to *fix the blame,* a purpose which introduces considerations not present when all the leading causal factors are things other than human actions (as they often are in agricultural, medical, or engineering inquiries). Insects, viruses, and mechanical stresses and strains are often "blamed" for harms, but the word "blame" in these uses, of course, has a metaphorical sense.

In summary, causal citations can be divided into those made from explanatory and those made from nonexplanatory standpoints, and the latter group into those made from the "engineering" and those made from the "blaming" standpoints. Explanatory citations single out abnormal interferences with the normal course of events or hitherto unknown missing links in a person's understanding. They are designed simply to remove puzzlement by citing the causal factor that can shed the most light. Hence we can refer to the criterion of selection in explanatory contexts (for short) as *the lantern criterion.* Causal citations made from the "engineering standpoint" are made with a view to facilitating control over future events by citing the most efficiently and economically manipulable causal factor. The criterion for selection in engineering contexts can thus be called (for short) *the handle criterion.* The point of causal citations in purely blaming

contexts is simply to pin the label of blame on the appropriate causal factor for further notice and practical use. These judgments cite a causal factor that is a human act or omission "stained" (as an ancient figure of speech would have it) with fault. The criterion in blaming contexts can be called (for short) *the stain criterion.* When we look for "the cause," then, we may be looking for the causal factor that has either a lantern, a handle, or a stain on it.

Purely blaming citations can be interpreted in two different ways. On the first model, to say that a person's act was the cause of the harm is precisely equivalent to saying that he is to blame for the harm, that is, that the harm is his fault. The causal inquiry undertaken from the purely blaming perspective, according to this view, is one and the same as the inquiry into the question of who was to blame or of whose fault it was. On this model, then, causal citation is not a condition for the fixing of blame; it is, rather, precisely the same thing. It is simply a fact of usage, which the examples of Dray and Mackie illustrate, that questions of blame often get posed and answered in wholly causal language. Historians, for example, are said by Dray often to "use expressions like 'was responsible for' [or 'was to blame for'] when they want to put into other words conclusions which they would also be prepared to frame in causal language."[14]

On the second model of interpretation, which is also sometimes *a propos,* the truth of the causal citation "His act was the cause of the harm" is only one of the *conditions* for the judgment that "The harm was his fault." Here we separate cause and fault before bringing them together again in a "his fault" judgment, insisting that the harm was his fault *only if* his action caused it. The causal inquiry, so conceived, is undertaken for the sake of the blame inquiry, but its results are established independently.

Now how do we establish a causal citation on the first model (or, what is the same thing, a "his fault" citation on the second)? Again, we have two alternatives: Either we can hold that the person (or his act) was *the cause* of the harm (meaning that he was to blame for it) only if his act was a genuine causal factor in the production of the harm; or we can require that his act be *the cause* of the harm, and not merely a "causal factor." But then we must find a way of avoiding a vitiating circularity. If we mean "the cause" as selected by *the stain criterion,* we have made a full circle; for, on this first model, our *original inquiry* is aimed at citing the cause by a stain criterion, and now we say that the achievement of this goal is a condition of itself. Clearly, if we are going to insist that his act be "the cause" as a condition of its being "the cause for purposes of fixing blame," we have to mean that it must be the cause *as determined by either the lantern or the handle criteria.* A quick examination of cases will show that this is just what we do mean.

When a man sets off a charge of dynamite and the earth shifts, dust rises, and rocks fly, the blasting is conspicuously the cause of these results by the lantern criterion (since it is the abnormal intervention) and equally clearly by the handle criterion (since it is part of the handiest causal recipe for producing results of precisely that kind). We can know, therefore, that the blasting caused the results by these commonsense criteria before we know anything at all about fault. Then we can go on to say, without circularity, that one or another of these causal criteria must be satisfied if those of the results that are harmful are to be charged to the blaster as his fault, but that further conditions of faultiness must also be satisfied.

Should we say that being "the cause" by the other commonsense criteria is *always* a necessary condition of being the cause by the stain criterion? I think this specification would prove to be artificially restrictive, for we sometimes (though perhaps not often) wish to ascribe blame whether or not the blamed action satisfies the lantern and handle criteria, and even in some instances where (allowing for the usual relativity of context) it appears not to. Suppose *A,* an impressive adult figure, offers a cigarette to *B,* an impressionable teenager. *A* is *B's* original attractive model of a smoker and also one who deliberately seduces him into the habit. Much later, after thirty years of continuous heavy smoking, *B* begins to suffer from lung cancer. Neither the lantern nor the handle criteria in most contexts are likely to lead one to cite *A's* earlier act as the cause of *B's* cancer, for *A's* act is not conspicuously "the cause" of the harm by these criteria (as the blasting was, in the earlier example). Yet we may wish to say that *A's* seduction of *B* was the cause of his eventual cancer for purposes of fixing blame or as a mode of expressing that blame. Such a

judgment may not be morally felicitous, but it can be made without committing some sort of conceptual solecism.

The best way of avoiding both circularity and artificial restriction of expression in our account of blame-fixing citations is to require not that the blamed action be citable as "the cause" (by *any* criteria), but only that it be a genuine causal factor, in the circumstances that obtained, and then to add fault and relevance conditions to the analysis. Most of the time, perhaps, being "the cause" by the lantern or handle criteria will also be required; but being a *causal factor merely* will be required always.

THE CAUSAL RELEVANCE CONDITION: IS IT ALWAYS NECESSARY?

Does the analysis of commonsense "his fault" judgments really require a causal relevance condition? Many people, I suspect, are prepared to make "his fault" judgments in particular cases even when they know that a causal relevance condition has not been satisfied; and many puzzling cases are such as to make even most of us hesitate about the matter. Consider, for example, the case of the calamitous soup-spilling at Lady Mary's formal dinner party. Sir John Stuffgut so liked his first and second bowls of soup that he demanded a third just as Lady Mary was prepared to announce with pride to the hungry and restless guests the arrival of the next course. Sir John's tone was so gruff and peremptory that Lady Mary quite lost her composure. She lifted the heavy tureen with shaking arms and, in attempting to pass it to her intemperate guest, spilled it unceremoniously in the lap of the Reverend Mr. Straightlace. Now both Sir John and Lady Mary were at fault in this episode. Sir John was thoughtless, gluttonous, and, especially, *rude* in demanding another bowl in an unsettling tone of voice. Lady Mary was (perhaps forgivably) negligent in the way she executed her action, and, besides she should have known that the tureen was too heavy for her to lift. Furthermore, both Lady Mary's faulty action and Sir John's faulty action were necessary conditions for the ensuing harm. Assuming that we must fix the blame for what happened, whose fault, should we say, was the harm?

Most of us would be inclined to single out Sir John's rudeness as "the cause" for purposes of blaming, partly because it was the most striking deviation from routine, perhaps, but mainly because, of the causal factors with stains on them, his action was the most at fault. Moreover, his action was a causal factor in the production of the harm precisely in virtue of that aspect which was faulty, namely, its unsettling rudeness, which created an unreasonable risk of upsetting the hostess, the very result that in fact ensued. Thus the causal relevance condition is satisfied in this example.

Suppose, however, that the facts had been somewhat different. Sir John, at just the wrong moment (as before), requested his third bowl, but in a quiet and gentle manner, and in a soft and mellifluous tone of voice, perfectly designed to calm its auditor. Sir John this time was not being rude, though he was still at fault in succumbing to his excessive appetites and indulging them in an unseemly public way to the inconvenience of others. In short, his primary fault in this new example was not rudeness, but plain gluttony; and (as before), but for his act which was at fault, the harm would not have occurred. Likewise (as before) the clumsiness of Lady Mary was a causal factor in the absence of which the harm would not have resulted. This case differs from the earlier one in that the causal relevance condition is not satisfied, for gluttony normally creates a risk to the glutton's own health and comfort, not to the interests of others. Unlike rudeness, it is a primary self-regarding fault. Thus that aspect of Sir John's request for more soup that was faulty was an irrelevant accompaniment of the aspects that contributed to the accident. Hence we could conclude that, although Sir John was *at fault* in what he did, the resulting harm was not *his fault.* [15]

It would be sanguine, however, to expect everybody to agree with this judgment. Mr. Straightlace, for example, might be altogether indisposed to let Sir John escape the blame so easily. He and others might prefer to reject the causal relevance condition out of hand as too restrictive and urge instead that the blame always be placed on the person *most at fault,* whether the fault is causally relevant or not, providing his faulty action was a genuine causal factor. This alternative would enable one to pin the blame on Sir John in both versions of the soup-spilling story. It does not commend itself to the intuitive understanding in

a quiet reflective hour, however, and seems to me to have no other merit than that of letting the indignation and vindictiveness occasioned by harm have a respectable outlet in our moral judgments. If we really want to keep Sir John on the hook, *we do not have to say* that the harm was "really his fault" and thereby abuse a useful and reasonably precise concept. Rather, if we are vindictively inclined, we can say that to impose liability on a person to enforced compensation or other harsh treatment for some harm does not always require that the harm be his fault. This would be the moral equivalent of a departure from what is called "the fault principle" in the law of torts. It is an attempt to do justice to our spontaneous feelings, without confusing our concepts, and has the merits at least of openness and honesty.

Disinterested parties might reject causal relevance as a condition for being to blame in a skeptical way, offering as an alternative to it a radical contextual relativism. One might profess genuine bafflement when asked whose fault was the second soup-spilling, on the grounds that the question cannot be answered until it is known for what purpose it is asked. Is the person singled out for blame the one to be punished, forced to make compensation, expected to apologize? What is the point of narrowly pinning blame? We could, after all, simply tell the narrative as accurately as possible and decline to say whose fault, on balance, the harm was, although that evasive tactic might not be open to, say, an insurance investigator. The point, according to this skeptical theory, is that, after all the facts are in, we are still not committed by "the very logic of the everyday concept" to saying anything at all about whose fault it was. The blame-fixing decision is still logically open and will be determined in part by our practical purposes in raising the question. This skeptical theory, however, strikes me as a combined insight and *non sequitur.* The insight is that we are not *forced* to pinpoint blame unless some practical question like liability hinges on it and that is often the better part of wisdom to decline to do so when one can. But it does not follow from the fact that "his fault" judgments can sometimes be avoided that it is logically open to us to make them in any way we wish when we do make them. I hold, therefore, to the conclusion that, in fixing the blame for harm, we are restricted by our very concepts to the person(s) whose faulty act was a causal factor in the production of the harm in virtue of its causally relevant faulty aspect.

There often is room for discretion in the making of "his fault" judgments, but it comes at a different place and is subject to strict limitations. The person whose fault the harm is said to be *must* satisfy the conditions of the triconditional analysis (and perhaps others as well); but when more than one person is so qualified, the judgment-maker may sometimes choose between them on "pragmatic grounds," letting some of them off the hook. When this discretion is proper, the three conditions of our analysis must be honored as necessary, but they are no longer taken to be sufficient. Suppose one thousand persons satisfy the three conditions of our analysis in respect to harm *X,* and they acted independently (not in concert) over a period of many years. To say simply that the harm is (all) *their* fault, or part his, and part his, and part his, and so on, would be to defeat altogether the usual point of a "his fault" judgment, namely, to fix more narrowly, to single out, to focus upon. When fixings of blame become too diffuse, they can no longer perform this function. They might still, of course, be *true,* but just not very useful. It is not exactly false to say of the first soup-spilling example that it was the fault of *both* Lady Mary and Sir John; but "practical purposes" may dictate instead that we ignore minor or expectable faults and confer all the blame on the chief culprit. At any rate, if it is given that we must, for some practical purpose, single out a wrongdoer more narrowly, then we have discretion to choose among those (but only those) who satisfy the necessary conditions of the tripartite analysis.[16]

FAULT AND TORT LIABILITY

Suppose we accept the revised triconditional analysis of "his fault" but jettison the causal relevance condition as a requisite for tort *liability,* so that we can get the likes of Sir John on the hook after all, even though we admit he is not *to blame* for the harm. The prime consequence of dropping the causal relevance condition is to downgrade the role of causation as a ground for liability and to increase the importance of simply being at fault. If causal relevance is not required, it would seem that being at fault is the one centrally im-

portant necessary condition for liability, and indeed so important as to render the causal condition itself a mere dispensable formality. To upgrade the fault condition to that extent is most likely to seem reasonable when the fault is disproportionately greater than the harm it occasions. Imagine a heinously faulty act that is a necessary causal condition for a relatively minor harm. Suppose that *A,* a matricidal fiend, in the cruelest way possible sets himself to shoot his mother dead just as *B,* the lady across the street, is fondling a delicate and fragile art object. The sound of the revolver shot startles *B,* causing her to drop the art object which shatters beyond repair. Is its loss *A's* fault? Let us assume (for the sake of the argument) that the murderous act was at fault in at least two ways: (1) it created a certainty of death or severe injury to the actor's mother (the primary way it was at fault); and (2), in making a loud report, it created an unreasonable risk to (among other things) the art objects of neighbors. Thus, in virtue of (2), *A* is at fault in the manner required for his being to blame for breaking the neighbor's glass vase. His act caused the breaking and did so in virtue of its faulty aspect (2); hence it was his fault. But even if he had (thoughtfully) used a silencer on the gun, and nevertheless the very slight noise caused by his act had startled a supernervous vase-fondling neighbor, causing the dropping and breaking, we might find it proper to charge him for the damage *even though the loss was not his fault.* (The "faulty aspect" of his act—its heinousness—was causally irrelevant to that loss.) It is precisely this kind of case where common sense seems most at home without the causal relevance condition; for no question of "fairness" to the faulty one is likely to trouble us when his fault is so great. Any number of minor harms of which his act was a necessary condition can be charged to his moral bill without disturbing us—at least so long as we remain "spontaneous" and unreflective.

It is another matter, however, when the harm is disproportionately greater than the fault, when a mere slap causes an unsuspected hemophiliac to bleed to death, or a clumsy slip on the sidewalk leads one to bump an "old soldier with an egg shell skull," causing his death. Hart and Honoré suggest that even here commonsense considerations can help justify abandonment, in some cases at least, of the causal relevance condition by mitigating its apparent harshness:

The apparent unfairness of holding a defendant liable for a loss much greater than he could foresee to some extent diappears when we consider that a defendant is often negligent without suffering punishment or having to pay compensation. I may drive at an excessive speed a hundred times before the one occasion on which my speeding causes harm. The justice of holding me liable, should the harm on that occasion turn out to be extraordinarily grave, must be judged in the light of the hundred other occasions on which, without deserving such luck, I have incurred no liability.[17]

This argument is reminiscent of the Augustinian theory of salvation. We are all sinners; therefore, no one really deserves to be saved. Hence if anyone at all is saved, it can only be through God's supererogatory grace. The others are (relatively) unlucky; but, being undeserving sinners, they can have no just complaint. All of us are negligent, goes the parallel argument; so none of us really deserves to escape liability for great harm. That majority of us who do escape are lucky, but the others who fall into liability in excess of their fault on the occasion have no just complaint, since they have accumulated enough fault on other occasions to redress the disproportion.

If justice truly requires (as the Hart-Honoré argument suggests) that blame and liability be properly apportioned to *all* a person's faults as accumulated in the long run, causal linkage to harm aside, why not go all the way in this direction and drop the "causal factor" condition altogether in the interest of Aristotelian "due proportion" and fairness? To say that we are all negligent is to say that on other occasions, at least, we have all created unreasonable risk of harms, sometimes great harms of one kind or another, to other persons. Even in circumstances where excessive harm actually results, we may have created other risks of a different kind to other individuals, risks which luckily failed to eventuate in harm. Robert Keeton foresees the consequences for the law of torts of taking all such faults seriously in the assignment of liability for particular harms:

... if it is relevant to take into account defendant's fault with respect to a risk different from any that would include the harm plaintiff has suffered, then would it not also be relevant to take into account his other faults as well? And would it not seem equally relevant to consider plaintiff's shortcomings? Shall we fix legal responsibility by deciding who is the better and who the worse person? An affirmative answer might involve us, and quickly too, in the morality of run-of-the-ranch TV drama, where the good guys always win.[18]

In effect Keeton challenges those who would drop the causal relevance condition to explain why they would maintain any causal condition at all. If the existence of fault of one kind or another, on one occasion or another, is the controlling consideration, why do we not simply tally up merits and demerits and distribute our collective compensation expenses in proportion to each person's moral score?

Why not indeed? This is not an unthinkable alternative system. We could, in principle, begin with the notion of a "compensable harm" as one caused by fault. (Other harms could be paid for out of tax funds or voluntary insurance.) Then we could estimate the total cost of compensable harms throughout the country for a one-year period. We would have to acquire funds equal to that amount by assigning demerits throughout the year to persons discovered to be "at fault" in appropriate ways in their conduct. Those who fail to clear their sidewalks of ice and snow within a reasonable period after the finish of a storm would be given so many demerits per square foot of pavement. Those convicted of traffic offenses would be assigned demerits on a graduated scale corresponding to the seriousness (as compounded out of unreasonableness and dangerousness) of their offense. Then, at the end of the year, the total cost of compensable harms would be divided by the total number of assigned demerits to yield the dollar value per demerit. and each person would be fined the dollar equivalent of the sum of his demerits. These fines would all go into a central fund used to compensate all victims of faulty accidents and crimes. Such a system would impose on some persons penalties disproportionately greater than the harm they actually caused; others would pay less than the harm they caused; but as far as is practically possible, everyone would be fined in exact proportion to the unreasonable risks he created (as well as certain and deliberate harms) to others.[19]

The system just described could be called a system of "liability without *contributory* fault," since it bypasses a causation requirement. It is a system of liability based on fault simply, whether or not the fault contributes to harm. It thus differs sharply from the traditional system of liability based in part upon what is called *the fault principle,* which requires that accidental losses be borne by the party whose fault the accident was. This is liability based on "his fault" ascriptions, rather than "at fault" imputations. In contrast, the principle underlying a system of liability based on fault without causation might well be called the *retributive theory of torts.* It surely deserves this name drawn from the criminal law more than the so-called fault principle does since it bases liability *entirely* upon fault purged of all extraneous and fortuitous elements. To be sure, what is called retributivism in the criminal law[20] is a principle that would base (criminal) liability entirely on *moral* fault, and most retributivists would oppose punishing nonmoral faults, including much negligence, as ardently as they would oppose punishing the wholly faultless. A retributive principle of reparation *could* take this very moralistic form. As we have seen, legal negligence is always supervenient upon a fault of some other kind, sometimes "moral" (callousness, inconsiderateness, self-centeredness), sometimes not (timidity, excitability, awkwardness). A moralistic principle would issue demerits to negligence only when it is supervenient upon a fault judged to be a *moral* failing. In a sense, the more inclusive version of the theory is more "moralistic" still, since it treats even nonmoral failings as essentially deserving of penalty, that is, just *as if* they were moral failings. We can safely avoid these complications here.

One way to understand the retributive theory of torts is to relate it to, or derive it from, a general moral theory that bears the name of retributivism. In treating of this more general theory, it is very important to distinguish a strong from a weak version, for failure to do so has muddled discussions of retributivism in criminal law and would very likely do the same in discussion of principles of tort liability. According to the strong version of the general retributive principle, *all* evil or, more generally still, all *fault* deserves its comeuppance; it is an end in itself, quite apart from other consequences, that all

wrongdoers (or faulty doers) be made to suffer some penalty, handicap, or forfeiture as a requital for their wrongdoing. Similarly, it is an end in itself, morally fitting and proper irrespective of other consequences, that the meritorious be rewarded with the means to happiness. Thus the best conceivable world would be that in which the virtuous (or faultless) flourish, the wicked (or, more generally, the faulty) suffer, and those in between perfect virtue and perfect wickedness enjoy happiness or suffer unhappiness in exact proportion to their virtuous and faulty conduct. Both a world in which everyone suffers regardless of moral condition and a world in which everyone flourishes regardless of moral condition would be intrinsically inferior morally to a world in which all and only the good flourish and all and only the bad suffer. If everyone without exception is a miserable sinner, then it is intrinsically better that everybody suffer than that everybody, or even anybody, be happy. There may be intrinsic goods other than the just apportionment of reward and penalty to the virtuous and the faulty respectively; but insofar as a state of affairs deviates from such apportionment, it is intrinsically defective.

Note that this way of putting retributivism makes it apply only to apportionments of a noncomparative kind, where to give to one is not necessarily to take from another and where to take from one is not necessarily to give to another. It is not, therefore, a principle of distributive justice, telling us in the abstract how all pies are to be cut up or how all necessary burdens are to be divided. Indeed, for some situations it would decree that no one get any pie, and in others that no one should suffer any burdens. It is concerned with deserving good or deserving ill, not with deserving one's fair share relative to others. To be sure, the world in which the good suffer and the evil are happy it calls a moral abomination, but not because of the conditions of the parties relative to one another, but rather because the condition of each party is the opposite of what *he* deserves, quite independently of the condition of the others. A world in which every person is equally a sinner and equally very happy would also be moral abomination, on this view, even though it involves no social inequality.

The weaker version of general retributivism, on

the other hand, is essentially a comparative principle, applying to situations in which it is given that someone or other must do without, make a sacrifice, or forfeit his interest. The principle simply asserts the moral priority, *ceteris paribus,* of the innocent party. Put most pithily, it is the principle that *fault forfeits first,* if forfeit there must be. If someone must suffer, it is better, *ceteris paribus,* that it be the faulty than the meritorious. This weaker version of retributivism, which permeates the law, especially the criminal law, has strong support in common sense. It commonly governs the distribution of that special kind of benefit called "the benefit of the doubt," so that, where there is doubt, for example, about the deterrent efficacy of a particular mode of punishment for a certain class of crimes, the benefit of that doubt is given to potential victims instead of convicted criminals.

I find the weaker version of retributivism much more plausible intuitively than the stronger, though even it is limited—for example, by the values of intimacy and friendship. (If I negligently spill your coffee cup at lunch, will you insist that I pay for a new cup, or will you prefer to demonstrate how much more important my friendship is to you than the forfeiture of a dime?) The weaker principle allows us to say, if we wish, though it does not require us to say, that universal happiness, if it were possible, would be intrinsically better than happiness for the good only, with the wicked all miserable. (Indeed, what would wickedness come to if its usually negative effect on the happiness of others was universally mitigated or nullified?) The weak principle also permits but does not require us to say that, even though it is better that the faulty forfeit first where there is no alternative to *someone's* forfeiting, it is better still that some other alternative be found.

Now let us return to our tort principles. What is called the "fault principle" (or, better, the "his fault" principle) does not derive from, and indeed is not even compatible with, the strong version of general retributivism. As we have seen, the causal component of "his fault" ascriptions introduces a fortuitous element, repugnant to pure retributivism. People who are very much at fault may luckily avoid causing proportionate harm, and unlucky persons may cause harm in excess of their minor faults. In the former case, little or no

harm may be a person's fault even though he is greatly at fault; hence his liability, based on "his fault," will not be the burden he deserves, and the moral universe will be out of joint. In the latter case, unhappily coexistent circumstances may step up the normal magnitude of harm resulting from a minor fault, and again the defendant's liability will not do proper justice to his actual fault.

The tort principle that is called for by strong retributivism is that which I have called "the retributive theory of torts." Being at fault gets its proper comeuppance from this principle, whether or not it leads directly to harm; and the element of luck— except for luck in escaping detection— is largely eliminated. Hence fault suffers its due penalty, and if that is an end in itself, as strong retributivism maintains, then the retributive theory of torts is well recommended indeed. But the lack of intuitive persuasiveness of the general theory, I think, diminishes the plausibility of its offshoot in torts. Weak retributivism, which is generally more plausible, in my opinion, than its strong counterpart, does not uniquely favor either the retributive theory of torts or the "his fault" principle. Except in straightforwardly comparative contexts where the necessity of forfeiture is given, it takes no stand whatever about principles of tort liability. If *A* and *B* are involved in an accident causing a loss to *B* only, which is wholly *A's* fault, and it is given that either *A* or *B* must pay for the loss, no other source of compensation being available, then the weak principle says that *A* should be made to pay, or rather (put even more weakly in virtue of the *ceteris paribus* clause) it holds that, insofar as the loss was *A's* fault, that is a good and relevant reason why *A* should pay and, in the absence of other relevant considerations, a sufficient reason. In short, if someone has got to be hurt in this affair, let it be the wrongdoer (other things being equal). But where there is no necessity that the burden of payment be restricted to the two parties involved, weak retributivism has no application and, indeed, is quite compatible with a whole range of nonfault principles.

One final point remains to be made. If we hold that we are all more or less equally sinners in respect to a certain area of conduct or a certain type of fault—if, for example, we are all as likely, more or less, to be erring defendants as wronged plaintiffs in driving accident suits—then the principle of strong retributivism itself would call for the jettisoning of the "his fault" principle in that area of activity. If fault is distributed equally, the "his fault" principle, in distributing liability *unequally* among a group, will cause a lack of correspondence between fault and penalty. On the assumption of equal distribution of fault, the use of the "his fault" principle would lead to *less* correspondence, *less* exact proportioning of penalty to fault, even than various principles of social insurance that have the effect of spreading the losses as widely as possible among a whole community of persons presumed to be equally faulty. But then these schemes of nonfault liability are supported by strong reasons of their own, principles both of justice and economy,[21] and hardly need this bit of surprising added support from the principle of strong retributivism.

NOTES

1. I intend here no more than what is in the Model Penal Code definition: "A person acts recklessly with respect to a material element of an offense when he consciously disregards a substantial and unjustifiable risk that the material element exists or will result from his conduct. . . . Recklessness involves conscious risk creation."

2. *Legal Cause in the Law of Torts* (Columbus: Ohio State University Press, 1963), 3. The facts in Keeton's fictitious case are closely similar to those in the actual case of *Larrimore v. American Nat. Ins. Co.,* 184 Okl. 614 (1930).

3. *Ibid.,* 10 and *passim.*

4. The example is from a very helpful letter sent to me by Professor Sturgeon after I read an earlier version of this paper at Cornell in May 1969.

5. The example is just one of many in an extremely thorough criticism of an earlier version of this paper made by Professor Taurek, who was my official commentator at the Chapel Hill Colloquium in Philosophy, Oct. 17–19, 1969.

6. Sturgeon, letter, note 4.

7. *Ibid.*

8. *Ibid.*

9. "Responsibility and Language," *Australasian Journal of Philosophy, 33* (1955), 145.

10. *Laws and Explanation in History* (London: Oxford University Press, 1957), 100.

11. In unusual cases, two or three.

12. The distinction in common sense between a "causal factor" and "the cause" corresponds roughly—very roughly—to the technical legal distinction between "cause in fact" and "proximate cause."

13. A causal factor is an earlier necessary condition in at least the weaker sense of "necessary condition," *viz.,* a member of a set of jointly sufficient conditions whose presence was necessary to the sufficiency of the set; but it need not be necessary in the stronger sense, *viz.,* a necessary element in every set of conditions that would be jointly sufficient, as oxygen is necessary to every instance of combustion. Not all prior necessary conditions, of course, are genuine causal factors. Analytic connections ("But for his having been born, the accident would not have happened") are ruled out, and so are "incidental connections" (earlier speeding bringing one to a given point just at the moment a tree falls on the road). Unlike necessary conditions connected in a merely incidental way to results, causal factors are "necessary elements in a set of conditions generally connected through intermediate stages with it." See H. L. A. Hart and A. M. Honoré, *Causation in the Law* (Oxford: Clarendon Press, 1959), 114. See also Keeton, *Legal Cause,* footnote 2, 62.

14. Dray, *Laws and Explanation in History,* footnote 10, 99–100.

15. Perhaps a better example to illustrate this condition would be the following: Sir John is not a glutton. He has requested only one bowl of soup, but it is spilled by the hostess. But Sir John is at fault in agreeing to have even one bowl passed his way, since he knows, or ought to know, that this kind of soup always gives him indigestion, insomnia, allergic reactions, and hiccups. It is not only imprudent for him to taste it; it is also inconsiderate to his wife, who is usually kept awake all night by his restlessness. When his wife is kept awake after this party, *that* is his fault; but when the hostess spills the soup (which she should not have had to pass his way in the first place), that is *not* his fault.

16. If it is given that a particular "his fault" judgment on a particular occasion must single out one or a small number to be assigned the blame, then the concept of "his fault" can perhaps be understood to limit discretion by providing two additional necessary conditions to the triconditional analysis: (4) there is no other person to whom conditions (1)–(3) apply who was substantially more at fault than the present assignee(s); and (5) there is no other person to whom conditions (1)–(3) apply whose act was a more striking deviation from routine, or of a kind patently more manipulable, or otherwise a more "direct" or "substantial" cause. In the first soup-spilling example, Lady Mary satisfies conditions (1)–(3), but certainly not condition (4) and possibly not condition (5).

17. Hart and Honoré, *Causation in the Law,* footnote 13, 243.

18. Keeton, *Legal Cause in the Law of Torts,* footnote 2, 21.

19. This is not quite true of the system as described in the text, for a man's penalty in that system is determined in part by the number of demerits others incur and the total amount of compensable harm caused, both factors over which he has no control. Thus a man who accumulates one hundred demerits in 1970 might pay a smaller fine than he does in 1971 when he accumulates only seventy five. Instead of assigning demerits, therefore, the system would have to impose penalties directly, according to a fixed and invariant retributive scale. These funds could then go into a pool to compensate victims; and if, in a given year, they prove to be insufficient, they could be supplemented, say, by tax funds instead of stepped-up fines; for, on a purely retributive theory, there is one "fitting" penalty for a given degree of fault, and that uniquely correct quantum should be independent of the fluctuations of the marketplace.

20. "Retributivism" has served as the name of the large number of distinct theories of the grounds for justifiable punishment having little in common except that they are all nonutilitarian. The theories referred to in the text are those that hold that a certain degree of pain or deprivation is *deserved* by, or matches, fits, or suits, a certain magnitude of evil, quite apart from consequences. The emphasis is on fitness or proportion; and often the theorists invokes aesthetic analogies. Cf. the definitions of A. C. Ewing in *The Morality of Punishment* (London: Kegan Paul, Trench, Trubner & Co.,

1929), 13, and John Rawls, "Two Concepts of Rules," *The Philosophical Review,* 64 (1955), 4–5. G. E. Morre's "theory of organic unities" also suggests this kind of retributivism. But there are many other theories that have borne the retributive label which I do not refer to here—e.g., Hegel's theory of annulment; theories of punishment as putting the universe back in joint, or wiping clean the criminal's slate, or paying a debt to society, or expiating a sin, or expressing social denunciation, or demonstrating to the criminal the logical consequences of the universalization of his maxim, or satisfying the natural instinct for vengeance, or preventing the criminal from prospering while his victim suffers, or restoring a moral equilibrium between the "burdens" of conformity to law as against the "benefits" of disobedience; and even the "logical truism" of A. M. Quinton (*Analysis,* 14 [1954]).

21. E.g., the *benefit principle* (of commutative justice) that accidental losses should be borne according to the degree to which people benefit from an enterprise or form of activity; the *deep pocket principle* (of distributive justice) that the burden of accidental losses should be borne by those most able to pay in direct proportion to that ability; the *spread-it-out principle* that the cost of accidental losses should be spread as widely as possible "both interpersonally and intertemporally"; the *safety* or *loss-diminution principle* that the method of distributing losses that leads to the smallest net amount of loss to be distributed is the best one.

ROBERT E. KEETON and JEFFREY O'CONNELL

Why Shift Loss?*

Tort law is in one sense public law. It concerns public interest, its impact extends into the lives of all people in the community, and it reflects as faithfully as any branch of law—and more pervasively than most—fundamental assumptions of the social order it serves. Yet in another sense, tort law is distinctly private law. It focuses on private interests, and it concerns the rights and duties of private individuals toward each other. This two-party, plaintiff-defendant focus of tort law contrasts, for example, with labor law and business regulatory law, in which a special focus upon the public interest occurs through the involvement of governmental agencies such as the National Labor Relations Board and the Federal Trade Commission.

The question whether a money judgment should be awarded can be approached from the point of view of the public interest in the effect of awards generally. We shall consider that perspective in due course.[1] First we shall consider reasons for awards through a more limited focus on the reasons for shifting loss from one party to another. This approach emphasizes a comparison of the conduct and circumstances of a plaintiff and defendant in a particular case. What reasons for shifting loss between a plaintiff and a defendant might serve as guiding principles for an automobile claims system? What arguments, beyond simply a need for compensation, might be advanced for a decision that a defendant pay money damages to a plaintiff injured in a traffic accident?

1. FAULT

Fault is the justification most often given for shifting loss in automobile cases. Liability in such cases is ordinarily dependent upon proof of negli-

*See Keeton and O'Connell, *Basic Protection for the Traffic Victim: A Blueprint for Reforming Automobile Insurance* (Boston: Little, Brown and Company, 1966), pp. 243–50. Reprinted by permission of the authors and the publisher. Footnotes have been renumbered.

gence of the defendant or someone for whose conduct he is accountable. A prima facie case of liability is ordinarily subject to defeat by proof of contributory negligence of the plaintiff or someone for whose conduct he is accountable. Thus it has been a commonly accepted principle that the loss is to be shifted from one who has innocently suffered it to another whose fault has caused it. Disagreement emerges, however, about the meaning of fault and the effect that should be given to different degrees of fault. Two questions about the principles of basing awards on fault point up this disagreement.

1. *Subjective or objective standards.* Should the minimum fault required for liability be conduct that is morally blameworthy, or is it enough that the conduct violates some objective standard of judgment that one cannot always be blamed for failing to meet? For example, should it be enough to impose liability that an elderly driver doing his best simply failed to respond as a younger and more nearly "normal" driver would have responded? Or must the elderly driver be personally culpable—for example, because he knew his responses were too slow for driving but drove anyway?

In the early development of the common law, in the view of many historians, objective standards of judgment regarding the causation of injury were preferred over standards that subjectively evaluated the culpability of an individual defendant in the light of his personal traits and the circumstances in which he acted.[2] According to one view of the matter, this penchant for objective standards continued even during the nineteenth century,[3] when the influence of personal culpability as a factor in tort law was most apparent. In twentieth century negligence law, increased reliance plainly has been placed on objective standards that impose liability on some whose conduct does not deserve moral censure. One might justify this use of objective standards on the basis of practicalities of administration.[4] It is after all much simpler to administer a hard-and-fast objective rule applicable to everyone in the same way than a rule subject to all the vicissitudes—both physical and psychological—of infinitely variable human beings. In addition, objective rules need not often in fact punish those who are not morally blameworthy since an objec-

tive standard, which is based on a norm, can be designed to approximate the capabilities of most.

Current use of objective standards cannot be justified, however, on the ground that in most cases only the morally blameworthy are punished. Some applications of modern negligence law quite regularly, rather than only occasionally, produce findings of negligence against defendants whom we would be unwilling to censure as morally blameworthy. A striking example of this is the liability of a mentally incompetent adult for harm caused by conduct falling below the standard of ordinary prudence. Whether such liability would be imposed was still a sharply disputed issue when the first two volumes of the *Restatement of Torts* were published in 1934.[5] Today it is clear that a mentally incompetent adult can be held liable for harm he causes accidentally and nonculpably.[6] A second instance in which negligence law deviates from a basis in moral fault was established at an earlier date. The standard of ordinary prudence has traditionally been applied to the adult below normal capacity but not so far below as to be considered incompetent. While disputes were being waged about the liability of the mentally incompetent, the liability of the barely competent for failure to measure up to ordinary prudence, in motoring cases as well as others, was generally accepted without question. These two examples, along with the widespread use of objective standards generally, demonstrate that tort law, including that segment of it applied in automobile cases, has by no means adhered rigidly to a principle of basing awards on moral fault.

b. *Contributory fault.* A second area of disagreement about basing awards on fault concerns the effect given to contributory fault. The common law rule is clear: Contributory fault is a complete bar to recovery. Latter-day developments working toward apportionment of damages on the basis of respective degrees of fault are commonly regarded as dubious departures from fault principles. The most obvious of these developments is the doctrine of comparative negligence. If, for instance, the defendant's fault is determined to be twice as great as that of the plaintiff, the plaintiff under this doctrine recovers two thirds of his losses and bears the remainder himself. A less obvious example of apportionment is an improper but prevalent practice of juries and some judges in states where contributory negligence is by law a complete bar to recovery. They often find for the plaintiff, despite strong evidence of contributory negligence, and then scale down the damages below the actual loss. Such developments toward apportionment, however, are arguably more consistent with the notion of basing awards on fault than is the doctrine that contributory negligence is a complete bar. They tend toward distributing the loss according to fault rather than placing all the loss on one of two negligent parties. One can consistently embrace such rules of apportionment while adhering tenaciously to fault as the central theme of his favored system.

Despite such disagreements, the principle of basing awards on fault was long so generally accepted as the essence of justice in tort cases that little was to be gained by asking why. Perhaps the only real justification for this principle is that most people believe fairness requires one who causes harm intentionally or carelessly to pay for it. It is important to note, however, that few automobile cases raise issues of intentional tort. Thus the consensus that it is fair to base awards on fault has been virtually a consensus on the desirability of basing awards on negligence. Negligence law, however, has never adhered rigidly to a principle of awards based on fault in the sense of morally blameworthy conduct. Moreover, further inroads upon the role of fault in automobile law have occurred in recent times, particularly as a consequence of the increasing use of liability insurance.

Thus, though "fault" is the explanation most frequently given for shifting losses in automobile cases, this explanation is acceptable only if it is understood that the word is used in a technical sense that does not imply culpability. Despite frequent statements that our lawmaking institutions are committed to a "fault" principle, it has become increasingly clear that culpability has by no means been an exclusive guide in formulating rules for automobile cases.

2. PUNISHMENT AND DETERRENCE

Closely related to fault as a reason for shifting loss are objectives associated with punishment—retribution, reformation, and deterrence. Retribution connotes an avenging condemnation that contributes to keeping the peace by appeasing the victim and reducing the likelihood that he or another acting on his behalf will resort to self-help. This is an objective of little significance in automobile cases. Reformation is concerned with improving the qualities of the individual whose substandard conduct has singled him out for attention. It is an objective of tort law in automobile cases only insofar as the deterrent effects of judgments of liability or denials of recovery work this result.

One way of serving the objective of deterrence is to award punitive damages. Such awards are common in cases of intentional torts and also are given occasionally in instances of risky conduct that is especially blameworthy though falling short of supporting a claim for intentional injury. Thus, in many jurisdictions punitive damages are allowed in cases involving injuries caused by the reckless conduct of the defendant—including reckless driving. In practice, however, the automobile cases in which punitive damages are awarded are relatively few.

Compensatory damages, as well as punitive damages, may have a deterrent effect by imposing economic burdens upon negligent drivers. Similarly, barring an injured person's claim because of his contributory negligence imposes an economic burden on him; the deterrent effect of this doctrine upon drivers as potential victims is, however, countered by withdrawal of the threat of liability to other victims who are also negligent. Deterrence is also served to some extent by the psychological and educational effect of adjudications of fault. Placing the stamp of fault on identifiable aspects of a driver's conduct is likely to influence significantly his future conduct, and that of others as well, if knowledge and understanding of the adjudication is spread through the community. To be effective in this way, however, the standard of adjudication must be one that can be understood and applied by drivers generally. Adjudications cannot serve to educate drivers about dangerous driving practices and to deter them from such conduct unless it is made clear exactly what practices are being condemned. Moreover, the condemned practices must be ones that a driver can avoid if he tries. In fact, however, the meaning of the negligence standard for particular fact situations in traffic cases is uncertain, and there has been a continuing tendency to brand as negligent more and more conduct that is neither avoidable nor morally culpable. These factors sharply reduce the educational and psychological effect of adjudications of negligence, which might otherwise deter dangerous driving. Under these circumstances, the deterrent effect of adjudications of negligence is a matter of speculation. It is our belief that the effect is rather limited and that the objective of deterrence has played a relatively small role in shaping rules of automobile tort law.

At first thought it might seem anomalous that deterrence has played such a minor role in automobile law, especially in view of the great number of motor vehicle accidents and the obvious desirability of reducing this toll. This circumstance, however, is easily explained. In the first place, deterrence looks more to the public interest in the effect of awards than to the private interest of parties to particular cases, and focusing on the contest between two parties after the accident tends to bring private interests rather than public interests into the foreground.[7] A second, more significant reason for the limited role deterrence has played in shaping automobile law is doubt about the effectiveness of personal liability, or the threat of personal liability, as a deterrent influence on drivers. Some observers have taken the view that most accidents are products of personal traits that cannot be controlled by threat of personal liability.[8] In addition, whatever the percentage of accidents attributable to accident-prone individuals may be, many other accidents, involving only normal drivers, are caused by circumstances that cannot be altered by deterrent influences on the driver. This is a consequence of rapidly changing traffic conditions and the quick responses that driving entails. Finally, it seems clear that the deterrent effect of possible liability is minimal compared to other deterrent influences such as fear of injury to oneself and fear of criminal sanctions. A driver who is not deterred from dangerous driving by such possibilities is not likely to be deterred by the added threat of liability for harm resulting to someone else.

3. BEARING AND DISTRIBUTING RISK

As we have seen, neither fault nor deterrence is a wholly adequate answer to the question: Why shift loss? What other answer is there? Implicit in relatively recent writings is the suggestion that the decision to award or deny compensation might be made to turn on one's capacity to bear or distribute the risks of loss. This suggestion takes a wide variety of forms.

Few, if any, advocates of the view that risk-bearing capacity should affect liability would suggest focusing sharply on a comparison between the two parties to a particular case, asking: Which of these two individuals is better able to bear the loss? If that question were asked, one apparent basis for selecting the party better able to bear the loss would be that the wealthier should be chosen. The trouble with this criterion, of course, is that it offends us to hold a man liable for no other reason than his wealth or "deep pocket." This is "one law for the rich and one for the poor," though with a reverse twist in that it favors the latter.

A more appealing variant of the notion that liability should be based on capacity to bear or distribute risk de-emphasizes such capacity of the plaintiff and the defendant considered individually. Instead, this more sophisticated view compares two classes of persons, one including the defendant and the other the plaintiff. This view centers attention, first, on the capacity of a group of similarly circumstanced individuals, engaging in the type of risky activity responsible for a loss, to distribute the risk among themselves and, second, on the fairness of requiring that each bear a share of the losses caused by such activity. This approach can serve, for example, to justify the liability without negligence imposed on those engaged in blasting or other especially dangerous activities. Those persons as a class are better able than victims as a class to make provision for distributing and bearing losses either by purchasing insurance or by self-insuring. This is not to say, of course, that an individual victim will never be better able than an individual dynamiter to provide for distributing and bearing losses. Nonetheless, the generality remains true for the two classes of persons.

This focus on classes and distribution is the only form in which a principle of awards based on capacity to bear or distribute risk is likely to gain acceptance in the foreseeable future. In this form the principle has in fact made very considerable headway already. It is particularly significant that tort liability insurance distributes losses of a prescribed type among the members of a large class of persons whose conduct creates risks of such losses. Thus, to recognize the legitimacy of tort liability insurance is implicitly to approve this principle of distributing losses among a class. The extent to which this principle is operative in present automobile claims systems becomes apparent with awareness of the large number of injured persons who are now compensated by tort liability insurance.

NOTES

1. See pp. 248–249, 259–272 in Keeton and O'Connell, *Basic Protection for the Traffic Victim.*
2. See 3 Holdsworth, A History of English Law 375 (5th

ed. 1942); Plucknett, A Concise History of the Common Law 409–411 (2d ed. 1936) (reporting this view and challenging at least its more extreme expressions).
3. Holmes, The Common Law 107–111 (1881). See generally 2 Howe, Justice Oliver Wendell Holmes, The Proving Years 1870–1882, at 184–194 (1963).
4. Cf. Holmes, *supra* at 111.
5. Restatement of Torts § 283, caveat (1934).
6. Id. § 283 (Supp. 1948); 2 Restatement of Torts Second § 283B (1965).
7. See pp. 243–244 in Keeton and O'Connell, *Basic Protection for the Traffic Victim.*
8. See James & Dickinson, Accident Proneness and Accident Law, 63 Harv. L. Rev. 769, 779–789 (1950). Messrs. James and Dickinson believe, however, that large units such as trucking concerns are in a better position than the individual driver to reduce accidents. Threatening such units with liability will have a deterrent effect. Id. at 780.

GUIDO CALABRESI

The Fairness of the Fault System*

There is no doubt that some possible justifications for the fault system can be found in rather undifferentiated notions of justice. It strikes critic and community as unfair if a person injured by someone who has violated a moral code is not compensated, or if someone who violates a moral code and is hurt is compensated at the expense of an innocent party. It also strikes us as unfair if acts that we deem wrong and immoral go unpunished, quite apart from any issue of compensation of the possible victims of such acts. Such sentiments are often said to be the principal mainstays of the fault system.

From the critic's point of view, though these sentiments are valid they do not in reality support the fault system. They would only do so if the

*From *The Cost of Accidents* (New Haven: Yale University Press, 1970), pp. 301–08. Copyright © 1970 by Yale University. Reprinted by permission of the publisher. Footnotes have been renumbered.

choice society faced was which of two or more parties directly involved in each accident should ultimately bear its costs. Then it would be true that if an injured party were not compensated by his faulty injurer, he would go uncompensated. It would also be true that any compensation of a faulty victim would in many cases have to come from the pocket of an innocent party. Such results would, of course, violate the critic's sense of justice. Similarly, it would seem unfair if in the absence of a fault system wrongdoers went unpunished. But to say that to avoid such results we must use the fault system is patent nonsense based on a simplistic bilateral view of the accident problem.

In reality, we live in a multilateral world with a whole population of injurers and victims. The degree of wrongdoing and the amount of damages vary throughout the population. In such a world, the question need not be whether it seems fair for an individual injurer to compensate an individual victim; in our society it can be how much all injurers should pay, in relation to their individual wrongdoing, into a fund to compensate all victims in relation to their injuries and *their* wrongdoing. It is difficult to see why payments based on how faulty a particular injurer is in relation to *all* injurers would not seem fairer than payments depending only on his fault in relation to his victim's fault and to injuries suffered by that particular victim.[1] It is equally difficult to see why recoveries by a victim should depend on how his conduct compares with that of the individual who injured him, rather than how it compares with that of all individuals involved in accidents. Certainly the broader comparison is much more consistent with how we treat wrongdoing in areas other than accident law. Indeed, one could go even further and suggest that the fortuity of involvement in an accident is not a fair manner of determining payments. Would it not seem fairer for compensation of relatively worthy victims to come from a fund made up of payments by all who are at fault that is, who violate society's code) according to their faultiness, whether they are involved in an accident or not? This may not be feasible. But if it were, would it not be more just?[2]

The moment one accepts the notion that justice does not require that an individual injurer compensate his individual victim—and the allowance of insurance for faulty parties is clear indication that this notion is accepted—and the moment one realizes that wrongdoers can be punished for wrongful acts quite apart from whether they must compensate victims, it becomes very hard to see how the fault system can be supported on grounds of justice. Nevertheless, in a world that has abandoned the necessity of a one-to-one relationship between injurer and victim, attempts to support fault on grounds of justice have been made. They usually take the form of suggesting that individual determinations of fault in each accident situation result in the creation of actuarial insurance categories which reflect the risk of faulty conduct being undertaken by its members. This, it is argued, amounts to the same thing as making the least worthy pay for accident costs in relation to their blameworthiness.[3] Passing over the question of whether the fault system with all its defects actually gives rise to such fair insurance categories, one must still ask whether the

categories it creates are the best possible ones in this sense, and whether the fault system is the best way of creating these categories.

I shall not spend much time on these questions; they have been answered earlier. Where conduct can be defined as undesirable with sufficient precision, the best way to make those who engage in it pay (and the way that is most consistent with other areas of law) is to assess them directly and individually—through noninsurable fines if they can be caught regardless of accidents, and through noninsurable tort fines if they cannot. Where conduct cannot be defined with sufficient precision before an accident (if it makes sense to speak of fault at all in this area), our moral imperatives can be worked into actuarial categories—that is, we can charge different groups different amounts in relation to the relative desirability or blameworthiness of the activities in which they are engaged—and more efficiently and effectively through means other than the case-by-case adversary determinations of fault. What I said before still holds: Unless one considers the purpose of creating fair insurance categories to be not the deterrence of wrongful acts, nor the deterrence of accident costs, nor even the deterrence of both, but rather the deterrence of those accidents in which wrongful acts are involved, the insurance categories the fault system creates cannot be thought of as required by fairness.

It may be argued, however, that I have been too quick to suggest that our sense of justice does not require payments by each individual injurer to his victim on the basis of their relative faultiness and the injuries that resulted. Logic is all very well, and it may affect the critic's sense of justice, it may be said, but the community's sense of justice depends on other things. People may require a one-to-one world of payment and compensation even if logic and economics make it unnecessary and even, in some sense, unjust. And it is not enough to point out what ought to satisfy the public's sense of justice if people simply do not view it that way. I would argue, however, that as a practical matter our society is quite ready to abandon the view that justice requires individual injurers to pay their victims on the basis of fault and that moreover, wherever an adequate alternative has been presented, people have tended to prefer it to the traditional fault system.[4]

One need only look at the general acceptance of workmen's compensation and at jury verdicts that seem to ignore negligence on the plaintiff's part and lack of negligence on the defendant's to get some sense of this.[5] Similarly, the general acceptance of insurance strongly suggests that we do not worry too much about whether the individual faulty party pays his victim, so long as the victim is paid. Of course, we have not yet reached a point where we are willing lightheartedly to compensate a victim who is *really* faulty (that is, "wanton and willful"), though we do—with some misgivings—generally allow insurance against liability for wanton and willful misconduct, which is close to the same thing. The source of our misgivings is that we sometimes fear that noninsurable fines proportionate to the wrongdoing and adequate to achieve deterrence will not in fact be placed on wanton and willful wrongdoers. If they were, we would not be troubled by the fact that liability beyond such fines could be insured against. Analogously, were a wanton and willful victim jailed or made to pay a noninsurable fine that was in some way commensurate with his wrongdoing and with the specific deterrence we wished to obtain, we would hardly be troubled if the excess of the damages to him (and inevitably to his family) were compensated, so long as it did not appear that the burden ultimately fell on individual innocent parties. (Such punishment would be totally in keeping with what was needed to destroy a one-to-one, victim-injurer combat right in criminal law.)

I think one can fairly conclude that the traditional defense of the fault system based on the notion that justice requires that the costs of a particular accident be divided according to the relative faultiness of the parties involved has been given more importance in scholarly writings than it deserves. The critic and the public have been concerned, and rightly so, that burdens should not rest heavily on the relatively innocent while the relatively guilty go unpunished. But both the logical and practical indications are that this concern does not necessitate the fault system. It requires only that all parties involved in similar accidents divide all the injury costs according to a scale of relative guilt.

We could go further and perhaps do still better by fining wrongdoers, whether or not an accident occurs, to help pay for compensation of those who are injured, and even by taxing activities and people according to the likelihood of their involvement in accidents in which their conduct would be deemed blameworthy. The burden, whether called fine, tax, or insurance, would depend on the general wrongdoing or undesirability of the activity, not on the fortuity of an accident occurring to the particular parties. Once again, therefore, we return to the fact that the issue does not simply involve two parties to an accident, but involves, instead how we establish insurance categories fairly and how we punish individual wrongdoers justly and effectively. And the fault system cannot deal with that issue as well as a system that mixes noninsurable fines and limitations on undesirable activities with market deterrence in a way that is consistent with our spreading demands.

The basic difficulty with supporting the fault system on grounds of justice can be stated simply. Our sense of justice is made up of history and tradition, but it is also highly dependent on consistency within a moral context. While the fault system may be consistent with our moral history in blaming the relatively guilty party in any given accident situation, it leads to results that are totally inconsistent with other existing penalties because it imposes a burden that is substantially unrelated to wrongdoing or to penalties inflicted on similar wrongdoing in other areas of law. It also leads to results that are totally inconsistent with what occurs in many situations within accident law. Workmen's compensation is the prime example of this inconsistency, but the fact that the fault system allows insurance, and therefore in practice allows faulty injurers to spread the burden more easily than faulty victims, is an equally good instance. Indeed, these basic inconsistencies are additional reasons for the fault system's current instability, since even if the fault system meets some requirements of our sense of justice, its inconsistencies violate still more pressing requirements of that goal.

In the end, justice will support the fault system only if there is no sensible alternative system presented, only if the choice is solely between crushing one relatively wrongful and one relatively innocent party. It will not support the fault system in a world where faulty or undesirable acts, activities, and actors (whether victims or injurers) can be penalized according to their unde-sirability, and injured parties can be compensated according to their injury. I do not suggest for a moment by this that compensation should pre-dominate over deterrence, general or specific. I only suggest that the moral aims of our society, and even our undifferentiated sense of justice, can be better met through systems that concentrate on the deterrence and compensation we want than through an archaic system of liability that presumes an organization of society in which the best that can be done is to treat each accident instance as a universe unto itself.

The fault system may have arisen in a world where one injurer and one victim were the most that society could handle adequately, and in such a world it probably was a fairly good mixed sys-tem. It did a good job of meeting our combination of goals: general and specific deterrence, spread-ing, justice, and even efficiency.[6] But even assum-ing that such was the world in which the fault system grew, it is not today's world. Today acci-dents must be viewed not as incidental events linking one victim with one injurer, but as a more general societal problem. That is why the fault system has become totally inadequate for *any* of our mixed goals, even justice. It has become so inadequate, in fact, that other mixed systems can improve our record as far as *each* of these goals is concerned, even though at their extremes some of the goals are inconsistent with one another.

NOTES

1. This comparison assumes at least a comparative negli-gence system and therefore gives the devil more than his due by considering the fault system as though it were modified in ways that would make it fairer than the present all-or-nothing system.

2. Once again, this would not rule out making a differen-tiation between wrongdoing that resulted in serious harm and wrongdoing that did not, where the fact of serious harm could be taken to be an indication that the injurer was particularly faulty. It should be obvious, however, that in gauging faulti-ness the fact of serious harm is at most one of many factors. See generally supra notes 22, Chapter 6 and 5, Chapter II.

3. Compare and contrast Blum and Kalven, *Public Law Perspectives,* at 14, 66–67. Even if the fault system could be viewed as creating optimal insurance categories for injurers, it does not even pretend to do so for victims.

4. Whether prople say they prefer fault may depend on what question is put to them, of course. When asked: "It has been suggested, when there is an accident involving two cars, that each driver be paid damages by his own insurance com-pany without trying to determine if one driver was at fault. Does that sound like a good idea or a poor idea to you?" only 34% of those questioned in a Minnesota poll said the sugges-tion sounded like a good idea. "Minnesotans Reject Premises of Keeton-O'Connell Plan," 9 *For the Defense* 65 (November 1968).

5. See, e.g., Wilkerson v. McCarthy, 336 U.S. 53 (1949) and the Utah Supreme Court opinion it reversed, 112 Utah 300, 187 P.2d 188 (1947). Said Mr. Justice Jackson in dissent: "I am not unaware that even in this opinion the Court contin-ues to pay lip service to the doctrine that liability in these cases is to be based only upon fault,. But its standard of fault is such in this case as to indicate that the principle is without much practical meaning." 336 U.S. at 76. It is, of course, often difficult to say whether public acceptance of a new approach such as workmen's compensation precedes or results from its institution.

6. If there are only the two parties to choose from, fault can be defended as a fair mixture of such relevant consider-ations as allotting costs to the activities causing them, spread-ing, and providing a just standard of foreseeability. Even in their earliest days juries may well have tempered, somewhat clumsily, the worst evils of fault by modifying the verdict called for under the premises of fault if it resulted in extreme visible hardship or social dislocation. Also, Holmes' argument that efficiency dictates letting costs lie where they fall in the absence of fault may make sense when only the two "in-volved" parties are considered.

An interesting view of the historical development of the law of torts is presented in Jorgensen, "The Decline and Fall of the Law of Torts," soon to be published in the *American Journal of Comparative Law.*

H. L. A. HART

Negligence, Mens Rea and Criminal Responsibility*

'I didn't *mean* to do it: I just didn't think.' 'But you should have thought.' Such an exchange, perhaps over the fragments of a broken vase destroyed by some careless action, is not uncommon; and most people would think that, in ordinary circumstances, such a rejection of 'I didn't think' as an excuse is quite justified. No doubt many of us have our moments of scepticism about both the justice and the efficacy of the whole business of blaming and punishment; but, if we are going in for the business at all, it does not appear unduly harsh, or a sign of archaic of unenlightened conceptions of responsibility, to include gross, unthinking carelessness among the things for which we blame and punish. This does not seem like the 'strict liability' which has acquired such odium among Anglo-American lawyers. There seems a world of difference between punishing people for the harm they unintentionally but carelessly cause, and punishing them for the harm which no exercise of reasonable care on their part could have avoided.

So 'I just didn't think' is not in ordinary life, in ordinary circumstances, an excuse; nonetheless it has its place in the rough assessments which we make, outside the law, of the gravity of different offences which cause the same harm. To break your Ming china, deliberately or intentionally, is worse than to knock it over while waltzing wildly round the room and not thinking of what might get knocked over. Hence, showing that the damage was not intentional, but the upshot of thoughtlessness or carelessness, has its relevance as a mitigating factor affecting the quantum of blame or punishment.

*From *Oxford Essays in Jurisprudence*, ed. by A. G. Guest (Oxford: Oxford University Press, 1961), pp. 29–49, © 1961 Oxford University Press. Reprinted by permission of The Clarendon Press, Oxford. Reprinted in *Punishment and Responsibility: Essays in the Philosophy of Law* (New York and Oxford: Oxford University Press, 1968), pp. 136–57.

1. THE CRIMINAL LAW

These rough discriminations of ordinary life are worked out with more precision in the criminal law, and most modern writers would agree with the following distinctions and terminology. 'Inadvertent negligence' is to be discriminated not only from deliberately and intentionally doing harm but also from 'recklessness', that is, wittingly flying in the face of a substantial, unjustified risk, or the conscious creation of such a risk. The force of the word 'inadvertent' is to emphasize the exclusion both of intention to do harm and of the appreciation of the risk; most writers after stressing this point, then use 'negligence' simply for inadvertent negligence.[1] Further, within the sphere of inadvertent negligence, different degrees are discriminated: 'gross negligence' is usually said to be required for criminal liability in contrast with something less ('ordinary' or 'civil' negligence) which is enough for civil liability.

In Anglo-American law there are a number of statutory offences in which negligence, in the sense of a failure to take reasonable precautions against harm, unaccompanied either by intention to do harm or an appreciation of the risk of harm, is made punishable. In England, the Road Traffic Act, 1960, affords the best known illustration: Under section 10 driving without due care and attention is a summary offence even though no harm ensues. In other jurisdictions, criminal codes often contain quite general provisions penalizing those who 'negligently hurt' or cause bodily harm by negligence.[2] With due respect to one English authority, Dr. Turner (whose views are examined in detail below), the common law as distinct from statute also admits a few crimes,[3] including manslaughter, which can be committed by inadvertent negligence if the negligence is sufficiently 'gross'.[4] It is, however, the case that a number of English and American writers on criminal law feel uneasy about different aspects of negligence. Dr. Glanville Williams[5] thinks that its punishment cannot be justified on either a retributive or a deterrent basis. Professor Jerome Hall[6], who thinks that moral culpability is the basis of criminal responsibility and that punishment should be confined to 'intentional or reckless doing of a morally wrong act', disputes both the efficacy and justice of the punishment of negligence.

In this essay I shall consider a far more thoroughgoing form of scepticism. It is to be found in Dr. Turner's famous essay *The Mental Element in Crimes at Common Law.*[7] There he makes three claims; first, that negligence has no place in the Common Law as a basis of criminal responsibility, and so none in the law of manslaughter; secondly, the idea of degrees of negligence and so of gross negligence is nonsensical; thirdly (and most important), that to detach criminal responsibility from what he terms 'foresight of consequences', in order to admit negligence as a sufficient basis of such responsibility is necessarily to revert to a system of 'absolute' or strict liability in which no 'subjective element' is required.

Dr. Turner's essay has of course been very influential; he has reaffirmed the substance of its doctrines in his editions of both Kenny[8] and Russell.[9] This, however, is not my reason for submitting his essay to a fresh scrutiny so long after its publication. My reason is that his arguments have a general interest and importance quite independent of his conclusions about the place of negligence in the common law. I shall argue that they rest on a mistaken conception both of the way in which mental or 'subjective' elements are involved in human action, and of the reasons why we attach the great importance which we do to the principle that liability to criminal punishment should be conditional on the presence of a mental element. These misconceptions have not been sufficiently examined: yet they are I think widely shared and much encouraged by our traditional legal ways of talking about the relevance of the mind to responsibility. Dr. Turner's arguments are singularly clear and uncompromising; even if I am right in thinking them mistaken, his mistakes are illuminating ones. So much cannot always be said for the truths uttered by other men.

Before we reach the substance of the matter one tiresome question of nomenclature must be got out of the way. This concerns the meaning of the phrase '*mens rea*'. Dr. Turner, as we shall see, confines this expression to a combination of two elements, one of which is the element required if the accused's conduct is to be 'voluntary,' the other is 'foresight' of the consequences of conduct. Dr. Glanville Williams, although he deprecates the imposition of criminal punishment for negligence, does not describe it or (apparently) think of it, as Dr. Turner does, as a form of 'strict' or 'absolute' liability; nonetheless, though not including it under the expression 'strict liability', he excludes it from the scope of the term '*mens rea*', which he confines to intention and recklessness. Judicial pronouncements, though no very careful ones, can be cited on either side.[10]

There is, I think, much to be said in mid-twentieth century in favour of extending the notion of '*mens*' beyond the 'cognitive' element of knowledge or foresight, so as to include the capacities and powers of normal persons to think about and control their conduct: I would therefore certainly follow Stephen and others and include negligence in '*mens rea*' because, as I shall argue later, it is essentially a failure to exercise such capacities. But this question of nomenclature is not important so long as it is seen for what it is, and not allowed either to obscure or prejudge the issue of substance. For the substantial issue is not whether negligence should be called '*mens rea*'; the issue is whether it is true that to admit negligence as a basis of criminal responsibility is *eo ipso* to eliminate from the conditions of criminal responsibility the subjective element which, according to modern conceptions of justice, the law should require. Is its admission tantamount to that 'strict' liability which we now generally hold odious and tolerate with reluctance?

2. VOLUNTARY CONDUCT AND FORESIGHT OF CONSEQUENCES

According to Dr. Turner, the subjective element required for responsibility for common law crimes consists of two distinct items specified in the second and third of three general rules which he formulates.

'Rule I—It must be proved that the conduct of the accused person caused the *actus reus.*

Rule II—It must be proved that this conduct was *voluntary*.

Rule III—It must be proved that the accused person *realised at the time* that his conduct would, or might *produce results of a certain kind,* in other words that he must have foreseen that certain consequences were likely to follow on his acts or omissions. The extent to which this foresight of the consequences must have extended is fixed by law and differs in the case of each specific crime. . . .'[11]

We shall be mainly concerned with Rule III—as is Dr. Turner's essay. But something must be said about the stipulation in Rule II that the accused's 'conduct' must be 'voluntary'. Dr. Turner himself considers that the truth contained in his Rule III has been obscured because the mental element requried to make conduct voluntary has not been discriminated as a separate item in *mens rea*. I, on the other hand, harbour the suspicion that a failure on Dr. Turner's part to explore properly what is involved in the notion of 'voluntary conduct' is responsible for much that seems to me mistaken in his further argument.

Certainly it is not easy to extract either from this essay or from Dr. Turner's editions of Kenny or Russell what is meant by 'conduct', and what the mental element is which makes conduct 'voluntary'. At first sight Dr. Turner's doctrine on this matter looks very like the old simple Austinian[12] theory that what we normally speak of and think of as actions (killing, hitting, et cetera) must be divided into two parts (*a*) the 'act' or initiating movement of the actor's body or (in more extreme versions) a muscular contraction, (*b*) the consequences of the 'act'; so that an 'act' is voluntary when and only when it is caused by a 'volition' which is a desire for the movement (or muscular contraction). But such an identification of Dr. Turner's 'conduct' with the Austinian 'act' (or movement of the body), and the mental element which makes it voluntary, with the Austinian volition or desire for movement, is precluded by two things. First, Dr. Turner says conduct includes not only physical acts but omissions. Secondly, though 'conduct' is always something less than the *actus reus* which is its 'result' (for example killing in murder) it is by no means confined by him as 'act' is by Austin to the mere initiating movement of the actor's body. Dr. Turner tells us that 'by definition *conduct, as*

such, cannot be criminal'.[13] He also explains that 'conduct is of course itself a series of deeds, each of which is the result of those which have come before it; but at some stage in this series a position of affairs may be brought into existence which the governing power in the state regards as so harmful as to call for repression by the criminal law. It is this point of selection by the law, this designation of an event as an *actus reus,* which for the purposes of our jurisprudence marks the distinction between *conduct* and *deed.*'[14]

About the mental element required to make conduct voluntary, Dr. Turner tells us[15] only that it is a 'mental attitude to [his] conduct' (as distinct from the consequences of conduct) and that if conduct is to be voluntary 'it is essential that the conduct should have been the result of the exercise of the will'. He does however give us examples of involuntary conduct in a list not meant to be exhaustive: 'For example, if *B* holds a weapon and *A,* against *B*'s will, seizes his hand and the weapon, and therewith stabs *C;* and possibly an act done under hypnotic suggestion or when sleep-walking or by pure accident. In certain cases of insanity, infancy and drunkenness the same defence may be successfully raised.'[16]

This account of voluntary conduct presents many difficulties. What is it for conduct to be 'the result of the exercise of the will'? Must the actor desire or will only the initiating movement of his body or the whole course of 'conduct' short of the point when it becomes an *actus reus?* And how does this account of the distinction between the course of conduct and the *actus reus* which is said to be its 'result' apply to omissions? The examples given suggest that Dr. Turner is here grossly hampered by traces of the old psychology of 'act' and 'volition', and no satisfactory account of what it is which makes 'conduct' voluntary or involuntary, capable of covering both acts and omissions can be given in his terminology of 'states of mind', or 'mental attitude'. What is required (as a minimum) is the notion of a general *ability* or *capacity* to control bodily movements, which is usually present but may be absent or impaired.

But even if we waive these difficulties, Dr. Turner's twofold account of *mens rea* in terms of 'voluntary conduct' and 'foresight of consequences' is at points plainly inadequate. It does not fit certain quite straightforward, familiar, cases where criminal responsibility is excluded because of the lack of the appropriate subjective element. Thus it does not, as it stands, accommodate the case of mistake; for a mistaken belief sufficient to exclude liability need not necessarily relate to *consequences;* it may relate to *circumstances* in which the action is done, or to the character or identity of the thing or person affected. Of course, Dr. Turner in his edition of Kenny, under the title of 'Mistake as a Defence at Common Law', discusses well-known cases of mistake such as *Levett's case,*[17] where the innocent victim was killed in mistake for a burglar, and says (in a footnote) that the subjective element in such cases relates to the agent's belief in the facts upon which he takes action.[18] He does not think this calls for a modification in his two-limbed general theory of *mens rea;* instead he adopts the view that such mistakes, since they do not relate to consequences, negative an element in the *actus reus* but do not negative *mens rea.* Besides this curious treatment of mistake, there is also the group of defences which Dr. Turner discusses in the same work under the heading of Compulsion,[19] which include marital coercion and duress *per minas.* Here, as the author rightly says, English law is 'both meagre and vague'; nonetheless, confidence in his general definition as an exhaustive account of *mens rea,* has led him into a curious explanation of the theoretical basis of the relevance to responsibility of such matters of coercion or duress. He cites first an example of compulsion in the case of 'a powerful man who, seizing the hand of one much weaker than himself and overcoming his resistance by sheer strength, forces the hand to strike someone else'.[20] Of this case he says, 'the defence . . . must be that the mental element of volition is absent— the accused, in other words, pleads that his conduct was not voluntary'[21] and to explain this he refers back to the earlier account of voluntary conduct which we have discussed. The author then says that compulsion can take other forms than physical force,[22] and he proceeds to discuss under this head obedience to orders, marital coercion, duress, and necessity. It is, however, clear that such defences as coercion or duress (where they are admitted) lie quite outside the ambit of the definition of voluntary *conduct* given by Dr. Turner: they are not just different instances of *movement* which is not voluntary because, like

the case of physical compulsion or that of epilepsy cited earlier, the agent has no control over his bodily movements. Defences like duress or coercion refer not to involuntary *movements,* but, as Austin[23] himself emphasized, to other, quite different ways in which an *action* may fail to be voluntary; here the *action* may not be the outcome of the agent's free choice, though the *movements* of the body are not in any way involuntary.

So far, my objection is that Dr. Turner's formulation of the subjective element in terms of the two elements of voluntary conduct and foresight of consequences leads to a mis-assimilation of different cases; as if the difference between an action under duress and involuntary *conduct* lay merely in the kind of compulsion used. But in fact the definition of *mens rea* in terms of voluntary conduct *plus* foresight of consequences, leads Dr. Turner to great incoherence in the division of the ingredients of a crime between *mens rea* and *actus reus.* Thus in discussing the well-known case of *R.* v. *Prince*[24] (where the accused was found guilty of the statutory offence of taking a girl under 16 out of the possession of her father notwithstanding that he believed on reasonable grounds that she was over 16) Dr. Turner examines the argument that the word 'knowingly' might have been read into the section creating the offence (in which case the offence would not have been committed by the prisoner) and says "this change would merely not affect the *mens rea* of the accused person, but it would add another necessary fact to the *actus reus,* namely the offender's knowledge of the girl's age'.[25] But there is nothing to support[26] this startling view that where knowledge is required as an ingredient of an offence this may be part of the *actus reus,* not of the *mens rea,* except the author's definition of *mens rea* exclusively in terms of the two elements of 'voluntary conduct' and foresight of consequences'. If knowledge (the constituent *par excellence* of *mens rea*) may be counted as part of the *actus reus,* it seems quite senseless to insist on any distinction at all between the *actus reus* and the *mens rea,* or to develop a doctrine of criminal responsibility in terms of this distinction.

3. NEGLIGENCE AND INADVERTENCE

So far it is plain that, quite apart from its exclusion of negligence, the account of the subjective element required for criminal responsibility in terms of the two elements 'voluntary conduct' and 'foresight of consequences' is, at certain points, inadequate. Dr. Turner's arguments against the inclusion of negligence must now be examined. They are most clearly presented by him in connection with manslaughter. Of this, Dr. Turner says[27] 'a man, to be guilty of manslaughter, must have had in his mind the idea of bodily harm to someone'. On this view, what is known to English law as 'manslaughter by negligence' is misdescribed by the words; and Dr. Turner expressly says that judges in trying cases of manslaughter should avoid all reference to 'negligence' and so far as *mens rea* is concerned should direct the jury to two questions:

(i) Whether the accused's conduct was voluntary;
(ii) Whether at the time he either intended to inflict on someone a physical harm, or foresaw the possibility of inflicting a physical harm and took the risk of it.[28]

To treat these cases otherwise would, it is suggested, be to eliminate the element of *mens rea* as an element in criminal liability and to return to the old rule of strict or absolute liability.

In developing his argument Dr. Turner roundly asserts that negligence is a state of mind. It is 'the state of mind of a man who pursues a course of conduct *without adverting at all* to the consequences'.[29] Dr. Turner admits that this state of mind may be 'blameworthy'[30] and ground *civil* liability. Here it is important to pause and note that if anything is 'blameworthy', it is not the 'state of mind' but the agent's failure to inform himself of the facts and so *getting into* this 'state of mind'. But, says Dr. Turner, 'negligence, in its proper meaning of inadvertence cannot at Common Law amount to *mens rea*',[31] for 'no one could reasonably contend that a man, in a fit of inadvertence, could make himself guilty of the following crimes, "arson", "burglary", "larceny," "rape," "robbery" ...'.[32] This of course is quite true; but proves nothing at all, until it is independently shown that to act negligently is the same as to act in 'a fit of inadvertence'. Precisely the same comment applies to the use made by Dr. Turner of many cases[33] where the judges have insisted that for criminal responsibility 'mere inadvertence' is not enough.

It is of course most important at this point to realize that the issue here is *not* merely a verbal one which the dictionary might settle. Much

more is at stake; for Dr. Turner is really attempting by the use of his definitions to establish his general doctrine that if a man is to be held criminally responsible he must 'have in his mind the idea of bodily harm to someone', by suggesting that the only alternative to this is the quite repugnant doctrine that a man may be criminally liable for mere inadvertence when, through no failure of his to which the criminal law could attach importance, his mind is a mere blank. This alternative indeed would threaten to eliminate the doctrine of *mens rea*. But we must not be stampeded into the belief that we are faced with this dilemma. For there are not just two alternatives; we can perfectly well both deny that a 'mere inadvertence' and also deny that he is only responsible if 'he has an idea in his mind of harm to someone'. Thus, to take the familiar example, a workman who is mending a roof in a busy town starts to throw down into the street building materials without first bothering to take the elementary precaution of looking to see that no one is passing at the time. We are surely not forced to choose, as Dr. Turner's argument suggests, between two alternatives: (1) Did he have the idea of harm in his mind? (2) Did he merely act in a fit of inadvertence? Why should we not say that he has been grossly negligent because he has failed, though not deliberately, to take the most elementary of the precautions that the law requires him to take in order to avoid harm to others?

At this point, a careful consideration is needed of the differences between the meaning of expressions like 'inadvertently' and 'while his mind was a blank' on the one hand, and 'negligently' on the other. In ordinary English, and also in lawyers' English, when harm has resulted from someone's negligence, if we say of that person that he has acted negligently we are not thereby *merely* describing the frame of mind in which he acted. 'He negligently broke a saucer' is not the same *kind* of expression as 'He inadvertently broke a saucer'. The point of the adverb 'inadvertently' *is* merely to inform us of the agent's psychological state, whereas if we say 'He broke it negligently' we are not merely adding to this an element of blame or reproach, but something quite specific, to wit, we are referring to the fact that the agent failed to comply with a standard of conduct with which any ordinary reasonable man *could* and *would* have complied: a standard requiring him to take precautions against harm. The word 'negligently', both in legal and in nonlegal contexts, makes an essential reference to an omission to do what is thus required: It is not a flatly descriptive psychological expression like 'his mind was a blank'.

By contrast, if we say of an agent 'He acted inadvertently', this contains no implications that the agent fell below any standard of conduct. Indeed it is most often proffered as an excuse. 'X hit Smith inadvertently' means that X, in the course of doing some other action (for example, sweeping the floor) through failing to attend to his bodily movements (for example, his attention being distracted) and, more strongly, not foreseeing the consequences, hit Smith.

There is of course a *connection,* and an important one, between inadvertence and negligence, and it is this. Very often if we are to comply with a rule or standard requiring us to take precautions against harm we must, before we act, acquire certain information: We must examine or *advert* to the situation and its possible dangers (for example, see if the gun we are playing with is loaded) and watch our bodily movements (handle the gun carefully if it is loaded). But this connection far from identifying the concepts of negligence and inadvertence shows them to be different. *Through* our negligence in not examining the situation before acting or in attending to it as we act, we may fail to realise the possibly harmful consequences of what we are doing and as to these our mind is in a sense a 'blank'; but the negligence does not, of course, consist in this blank state of mind but in our failure to take precautions against harm by examining the situation. Crudely put, 'negligence' is not the name of 'a state of mind' while 'inadvertence' is.

We must now confront the claim made by Dr. Turner that there is an absurdity in stipulating that a special (gross) degree of negligence is required. 'There can be no different degrees of inadvertence as indicating a state of mind. The man's mind is a blank as to the consequences in question; his realization of their possibility is nothing and there are no different degrees of nothing'.[34] This *reductio ad absurdum* of the notion of gross negligence depends entirely on the view that negligence is merely a name for a state of mind consisting in the absence of foresight of consequences. Surely we should require some-

thing more to persuade us to drop notions so firmly embedded, not only in the law, but in common speech, as 'very negligent', 'gross carelessness', a 'minor form of negligence'. Negligence is gross if the precautions to be taken against harm are very simple, such as persons who are but poorly endowed with physical and mental capacities can easily take.[35] So, in the workman's case, it was gross negligence not to look and see before throwing off the slates; perhaps it was somewhat less gross (because it required more exertion and thought) to have failed to shout a warning for those not yet in view; it was less gross still to have failed to have put up some warning notice in the street below.

4. NEGLIGENCE AND NORMAL CAPACITIES

At the root of Dr. Turner's arguments there lie, I think, certain unexamined assumptions as to what the mind is and why its 'states' are relevant to responsibility. Dr. Turner obviously thinks that unless a man 'has in his mind the idea of harm to someone' it is not only bad law, but morally objectionable, as a recourse to strict or absolute liability, to punish him. But here we should ask why, in or out of law courts, we should attach this crucial importance to foresight of consequences, to the 'having of an idea in the mind of harm to someone'. On what theory of responsibility is it that the presence of this particular item of mental furniture is taken to be something which makes it perfectly satisfactory to hold that the agent is responsible for what he did? And why should we necessarily conclude that in its absence an agent cannot be decently held responsible? I suspect, in Dr. Turner's doctrine, a form of the ancient belief that possession of knowledge of consequences is a sufficient and necessary condition of the capacity for self-control, so that if the agent knows the consequences of his action we are bound to say 'he could have helped it'; and, by parity of reasoning, if he does not know the consequences of his action, even though he failed to examine or think about the situation before acting, we are bound to say that he could not have helped it.

Neither of these views is acceptable. The first is not only incompatible with what large numbers of scientists and lawyers and plain men now believe about the capacity of human beings for self-control. But it is also true that there is nothing to compel us to say 'He could not have helped it' in *all* cases where a man omits to think about or examine the situation in which he acts and harm results which he has not foreseen. Sometimes we do say this and should say it; this is so when we have evidence, from the personal history of the agent or other sources, that his memory or other faculties were defective, or that he could not distinguish a dangerous situation from a harmless one, or where we know that repeated instructions and punishment have been of no avail. From such evidence we may conclude that he was unable to attend to, or examine the situation, or to assess its risks; often we find this so in the case of a child or a lunatic. We should wish to distinguish from such cases the case of a signalman whose duty it is to signal a train, if the evidence clearly shows that he has the normal capacities of memory and observation and intelligence. He may say after the disaster, 'Yes, I went off to play a game of cards. I just didn't stop to think about the 10.15 when I was asked to play'. Why, in such a case, should we say 'He could not help it—because his mind was a blank as to the consequences'? The kind of evidence we have to go upon in distinguishing those omissions to attend to, or examine, or think about the situation, and to assess its risks before acting, which we treat as culpable, from those omissions (for example, on the part of infants or mentally deficient persons) for which we do not hold the agent responsible, is not different from the evidence we have to use whenever we say of anybody who has failed to do something 'He could not have done it' or 'He could have done it'. The evidence in such cases relates to the general capacities of the agent; it is drawn, not only from the facts of the instant case, but from many sources, such as his previous behaviour, the known effect upon him of instruction or punishment, et cetera. Only a theory that mental operations like attending to, or thinking about, or examining a situation are somehow 'either there or not there', and so utterly outside our control, can lead to the theory that we are *never* responsible if, like the signalman who forgets to pull the signal, we fail to think or remember. And this theory of the uncontrollable character of mental operations would, of course, be fatal to responsibility for even the most cold-blooded, deliberate action performed by an agent with the maximum 'foresight'. For just as the signalman, inspired by Dr. Turner's argument, might say 'My mind was a blank' or 'I just forgot' or 'I just didn't think, I could not help not thinking' so the cold-blooded murderer might say 'I just decided to kill; I couldn't help deciding'. In the latter case we do not normally allow this plea because we know from the general history of the agent, and others like him, that he could have acted differently. This general evidence is what is relevant to the question of responsibility, not the mere presence or absence of foresight. We should have doubts, which now find legal expression in the category of diminished responsibility, even in the case of deliberate murder, if it were shown that in spite of every warning and every danger and without a comprehensible motive the agent had deliberately and repeatedly planned and committed murder. After all, a hundred times a day persons are blamed outside the law courts for not being more careful, for being inattentive and not stopping to think; in particular cases, their history or mental or physical examination may show that they could not have done what they omitted to do. In such cases they are not responsible; but *if* anyone is *ever* responsible for *anything*, there is no general reason why men should not be responsible for such omissions to think, or to consider the situation and its dangers before acting.

5. SUBJECTIVE AND OBJECTIVE

Excessive distrust of negligence and excessive confidence in the respectability of 'foresight of harm' or 'having the thought of harm in the mind' as a ground of responsibility have their roots in a common misunderstanding. Both oversimplify the character of the subjective element required in those whom we punish, if it is to be morally tolerable, according to common notions of justice, to punish them. The reason why, according to modern ideas, strict liability is odious, and appears as a sacrifice of a valued principle which we should make, if at all, only for some overriding social good, is not merely because it amounts, as it does, to punishing those who did not at the time of acting 'have in their minds' the elements of foresight or desire for muscular movement. These psychological elements are not *in themselves* crucial though they are important as aspects of responsibility. What is crucial is that those whom we punish should have had, when they acted, the normal capacities, physical and mental, for doing what the law requires and abstaining from what it forbids, and a fair opportunity to exercise these capacities. Where these capacities and opportunities are absent, as they are in different ways in the varied cases of accident, mistake, paralysis, reflex action, coercion, insanity, et cetera, the moral protest is that it is morally wrong to punish because 'he could not have helped it' or 'he could not have done otherwise' or 'he had no real choice'. But, as we have seen, there is no reason (unless we are to reject the whole business of responsibility and punishment) *always* to make this protest when someone who 'just didn't think' is punished for carelessness. For in some cases at least we may say 'he could have thought about what he was doing' with just as much rational confidence as one can say of any intentional wrongdoing 'he could have done otherwise'.

Of course, the law compromises with competing values over this matter of the subjective element in responsibility as it does over other matters. All legal systems temper their respect for the principle that persons should not be punished if they could not have done otherwise, that is, had neither the capacity nor a fair opportunity to act otherwise. Sometimes this is done in deference to genuine practical difficulties of proof; sometimes it represents an obstinate refusal to recognize that human beings may not be able to control their conduct though they know what they are doing. Difficulties of proof may lead one system to limit consideration of the subjective element to the question whether a person acted intentionally and had volitional control of his muscular movements; other systems may let the inquiry go further and, in relation to some offences, consider whether the accused had, owing to some external cause, lost the power of such control, or whether his capacity to control was 'diminished' by mental abnormality or disease. In these last cases, exemplified in 'provocation' and 'diminished responsibility', if we punish at all we punish *less,* on the footing that, though the accused's capacity for self-control was not absent its exercise was a matter of abnormal difficulty. He is punished in effect for a failure to exercise control; and this is also involved when punishment for negligence is morally justifiable.

The most important compromise which legal systems make over the subjective element consists in its adoption of what has been unhappily termed the 'objective standard'. This may lead to an individual being treated for the purposes of conviction and punishment as if he possessed capacities for control of his conduct which he did not possess, but which an ordinary or reasonable man possesses and would have exercised. The expression 'objective' and its partner 'subjective' are unhappy because, as far as negligence is concerned, they obscure the real issue. We may be tempted to say with Dr. Turner that just because the negligent man does not have 'the thought of harm in his mind', to hold him responsible for negligence is *necessarily* to adopt an objective standard and to abandon the 'subjective' element in responsibility. It then becomes vital to distinguish this (mistaken) thesis from the position brought about by the use of objective standards in the application of laws which make negligence criminally punishable. For, when negligence is made criminally punishable, this itself leaves open the question: whether, before we punish, both or only the first of the following two questions must be answered affirmatively:

(i) Did the accused fail to take those precautions which any reasonable man with normal capacities would in the circumstances have taken?

(ii) Could the accused, given his mental and physical capacities, have taken those precautions?

One use of the dangerous expressions 'objective' and 'subjective' is to make the distinction between these two questions; given the ambiguities of those expressions, this distinction would have been more happily expressed by the expressions 'invariant' standard of care, and 'individualised conditions of liability'. It may well be that, even if the 'standard of care' is pitched very low so that individuals are held liable only if they fail to take very elementary precautions against harm, there will still be some unfortunate individuals who, through lack of intelligence, powers of concentration or memory, or through clumsiness, could not attain even this low standard. If our conditions of liability are invariant and not flexible, that is, if they are not adjusted to the capacities of the accused, then some individuals will be held liable for negligence though they could not have helped their failure to comply with the standard. In *such* cases, indeed, criminal responsibility will be made independent of any 'subjective element', since the accused could not have conformed to the required standard. But this result is nothing to do with negligence being taken as a basis for criminal liability; precisely the same result will be reached if, in considering whether a person acted intentionally, we were to attribute to him foresight of consequences which a reasonable man would have foreseen but which he did not. 'Absolute liability' results, not from the admission of the principle that one who has been grossly negligent is criminally responsible for the consequent harm even if 'he had no idea in his mind of harm to anyone', but from the refusal in the application of this principle to consider the capacities of an individual who has fallen below the standard of care.

It is of course quite arguable that no legal system could afford to individualize the conditions of liability so far as to discover and excuse all those who could not attain the average or reasonable man's standard. It may, in practice, be impossible to do more than excuse those who suffer from gross forms of incapacity, to wit, infants, or the insane, or those afflicted with recognizably inadequate powers of control over their movements, or who are clearly unable to detect, or extricate themselves, from situations in which their disability may work harm. Some confusion is, however, engendered by certain inappropriate ways of describing these excusable cases, which we are tempted to use in a system which, like our own, defines negligence in terms of what the reasonable man would do. We may find ourselves asking whether the infant, the insane, or those suffering from paralysis did all that a reasonable man would *in the circumstances* do, taking 'circumstances' (most queerly) to include personal qualities like being an infant, insane or paralyzed. This paradoxical approach leads to many difficulties. To avoid them we need to hold apart the primary question (1) What *would* the reasonable man with ordinary capacities have done in these circumstances? from the second question (2), *Could* the accused with *his* capacities have done that? Reference to such factors as lunacy or disease would be made in answering only the second of these questions. This simple, and surely realistic, approach avoids difficulties which the notion of individualizing the standard of care has presented for certain writers; for these difficulties are usually created by the mistaken assumption that the only way of allowing for individual incapacities is to treat them as part of the 'circumstances' in which the reasonable man is supposed to be acting. Thus Dr. Glanville Williams said that if 'regard must be had to the make-up and circumstances of the particular offender, one would seem on a determinist view of conduct to be pushed to the conclusion that there is no standard of conduct at all. For if every characteristic of the individual is taken into account, including his heredity the conclusion is that he could not help doing as he did.'[36]

But 'determinism' presents no special difficulty here. The question is whether the individual had the capacity (inherited or not) to act otherwise than he did, and 'determinism' has no relevance to the case of one who is accused of negligence which it does not have to one accused of intentionally killing. Dr. Williams supports his arguments by discussion of the case of a motorist whom a blow or illness has rendered incapable of driving properly. His conclusion, tentatively expressed, is that if the blow or illness occurred long ago or in infancy he should not be excused, but if it occurred shortly before the driving in respect of which he is charged he should. Only thus, it seems to him, can any standard of conduct be preserved.[37] But there seems no need to make this extraordinary distinction. Again, the first question which we should ask is: What *would* a reasonable driver with normal capacities have done? The second question is whether or not the accused driver had at the time he drove the normal capacity of control (either in the actual conduct of the vehicle in driving or in the decision to engage in driving). If he was incapable, the date recent or otherwise of the causal origin of the incapacity is surely beside the point, except that if it was of long standing, this would suggest that he knew of it and was negligent in driving with that knowledge.

Equally obscure to me are the reasons given by Dr. Williams for doubting the efficacy of punishment for negligence. He asks, 'Even if a person admits that he occasionally makes a negligent mistake, how, in the nature of things, can punishment for inadvertence serve to deter?[38] But if this question is meant as an argument, it rests on the old, mistaken identification of the 'subjective element' involved in negligence with 'a blank mind', whereas it is in fact a failure to exercise the capacity to advert to, and to think about and control, conduct and its risks. Surely we have plenty of empirical evidence to show that, as Professor Wechsler has said, 'punishment supplies men with an additional motive to take care before acting, to use their faculties, and to draw upon their experience.'[39] Again there is no difficulty here peculiar to negligence, though of course we can doubt the efficacy of any punishment to deter any kind of offence.

I should add (out of abundant caution) that I have not been concerned here to advocate punishing negligence, though perhaps better acquaintance with motoring offences would convert me into a passionate advocate. My concern has been to show only that the belief that criminal responsiblity for negligence is a form of strict or absolute liability, rests on a confused conception of the 'subjective element' and its relation to responsibility.

NOTES

1. This terminology is used by Glanville Williams, *Criminal Law, The General Part* (2nd edn.), Ch. III, p. 100 et seq., and also by the American Law Institute Draft Model Penal Code s. 2.0.2 (Tentative Draft 4, p. 26 and Comment, ibid., pp. 126–7). So, too, Cross and Jones, *Introduction to Criminal Law* (5th edn.). pp. 42–45.

2. See for these and other cases Glanville Williams op. cit., p. 120 n. 22.

3. Other common law crimes commonly cited are non-repair of a highway and public nuisance. Besides these there are controversial cases including certain forms of murder (*R. v. Ward*(1956) 1 Q.B. 351, Cross and Jones, op. cit., pp. 48–52 and *D. P. P.* v. *Smith* (1961), A.C. 290. These cases some writers consider as authorities for the proposition that criminal negligence is sufficient malice for the crime of murder. There are, however, reasons for doubting this interpretation of these cases.

4. See Cross and Jones, *Introduction to Criminal Law*, pp. 152–5. The American Law Institute accepts this view of the English law of manslaughter (Tentative Draft 9, p. 50) but advocates treatment of negligent homicide as an offence of lower degree than manslaughter. Glanville Williams, *Criminal Law*, p. 106 (s. 39) after stating that manslaughter can be committed by inadvertent negligence 'for the accused need not have foreseen the likelihood of *death*' says that the 'ordinary formulations' leave in doubt the question whether foresight of some bodily harm (not necessarily serious injury or death) is required for manslaughter. He describes (op. cit., p. 108) as 'not altogether satisfactory' the cases usually taken to establish that no such foresight is required viz. *Burdee* (1916), 86 L. J. K. B. 871, 12 Cr. App. Rep. 153; *Pittwood* (1902), 19 T. L. R. 37; *Benge* (1865), 4 F. & F. 504; *John Jones* (1874), 12 Cox 628. Of *Bateman* (1925), 28 Cox 33; 19 Cr. App. Rep. 8 he says 'it may be questioned whether this does not extend the law of manslaughter too widely' and thinks in spite of *Andrews* v. *D. P. P.* (1937), A.C. 576 that the issue is still open for the House of Lords. (op. cit., pp. 107, 110).

5. *Criminal Law*, pp. 122–3.

6. *Principles of Criminal Law*, pp. 366–7, and *43 C. L. R.*, p. 775. Professor Herbert Wechsler (Reporter in the A. L. I. Draft Model Penal Code) rejects this criticism and holds that punishment for conduct which inadvertently creates improper risks 'supplies men with an additional motive to take care before acting, to use their faculties and to draw on their experience in gauging the potentialities of contemplated con-

duct', Tentative Draft 4, pp. 126–7, and Tentative Draft 9, pp. 52–53.

7. *The Modern Approach to Criminal Law* (1945), p. 195.

8. Kenny's *Outlines of Criminal Law* (19th edn.), pp. 37–40.

9. Russell on Crime (12 edn.), pp. 43–44, 52, 62–66.

10. See Glanville Williams, *Criminal Law*, p. 102, n. 8. Examples on each side are Shearman J. in *Allard* v. *Selfridge*, (1925) 1 K. B. 129, at p. 137. ('The true translation of that phrase is criminal intention, or an intention to do the act which is made penal by statute or by the common law') and Fry L. J. in *Lee* v. *Dangar, Grant & Co.*, (1892) 2 Q. B. 337, at p. 350. 'A criminal mind or that negligence which is itself criminal'. See also for a more discursive statement *R. v. Bateman* (1925), 19 Cr. App. Rep. 8 *per* Hewart C. J.

11. *The Modern Approach to Criminal Law* (1945), p. 199.

12. Austin, *Lectures on Jurisprudence* (5th edn.), Lecture XVIII.

13. *Modern Approach to Criminal Law,* p. 240.

14. Ibid., p. 239.

15. Kenny (19th edn.), p. 30.

16. *The Modern Approach to Criminal Law* (1945), p. 204. See the further examples suggested in Kenny (19th edn.), p. 29: viz., when harm 'results from a man's movements in an epileptic seizure, or while suffering from St. Vitus's Dance'.

17. (1638), Cro. Car. 538.

18. Kenny, *Outlines of Criminal Law,* (19th edn.), p. 58 n. 3.

19. Ibid., p. 66.

20. Kenny, *Outlines of Criminal Law.*

21. Ibid.

22. Ibid.

23. Lectures on Jurisprudence, p. 417. Notes to Lecture XVIII, 'Voluntary—Double Meaning of the word Voluntary'.

24. (1875), L. R. 2 C. C. R. 154.

25. In 'The Mental Element in Crimes at Common Law': *The Modern Approach to Criminal Law* (1945), op. 219.

26. There is plain authority against it: see *R. v. Tolson* (1889), 23 Q.B.D. 168 *per* Stephen J. 'The mental element of most crimes is marked by one of the words "maliciously", "fraudulently", "negligently", or "knowingly".'

27. *The Modern Approach to Criminal Law* (1945), p. 228.

28. Ibid., p. 231.

29. Ibid., p. 207.

30. Ibid., p. 208.

31. Ibid., p. 209.

32. Ibid.

33. E.g., *R. v. Finney* (1874), 12 Cox 625. See also *R. v. Bateman, Andrews* v. *D. P. P.,* and others discussed op. cit., pp. 216–17.

34. *The Modern Approach to Criminal Law,* p. 211.

35. 'It is such a degree of negligence as exludes the loosest degree of care' quoted by Hewart C. J. in *R.* v. *Bateman* (1925), 19 Cr. App. Rep. 8.

36. *Criminal Law: The General Part* (1st edn.), p. 82. In the second edition (p. 101) this passage is replaced by the following: 'But if the notional person by whom the defendant is judged is invested with every characteristic of the defendant, the standard disappears. For, in that case, the notional person would have acted in the same way as the defendant acted."

37. op. cit. (1st edn.), p. 84. This passage is omitted from the second edition.

38. op. cit. (2nd edn.), p. 123.

39. loc. cit. *supra* p. 138, 6.

HERBERT PACKER

Strict Liability*

When we leave the area of the dilemmatic choice, which comprises what is technically known as the law of justification and excuse, "mistake" becomes the operational signal for invoking a vast range of excuses. Indeed, the idea of mistake underlies the whole question of *mens rea* or the mental element, with the dubious exception of the insanity defense (which, as I shall argue subsequently, is most usefully viewed as something other than a problem of *mens rea*). When we say that a person, whose conduct in other respects fits the definition of a criminal offense, lacked the requisite *mens rea*, what we mean is that he made a mistake about some matter of fact or value that constitutes a material element of the offense.

A few examples will show that the question of mistake pervades the entire criminal law. Arthur is charged with homicide and claims that he thought the man he shot at was really a deer. Barry is charged with stealing a raincoat that he claims he thought was really abandoned property. Charlie is charged with possessing heroin; he says he thought the white powder in the packet was talcum powder. Dan is charged with bigamy; he says that he thought his first wife had divorced him. Evan is charged with statutory rape; he claims the girl told him she was over the age of consent. Frank is charged with selling adulterated drugs; he says that so far as he knew the drugs conformed to requirements. George is charged with failing to file his income tax return; he says he didn't know about the income tax. Harry is charged with carrying a concealed weapon; he claims he didn't know it was against the law to do so.

*Reprinted from *The Limits of the Criminal Sanction* by Herbert L. Packer, with the permission of the publishers, Stanford University Press. © 1968 by Herbert L. Packer. This section of Chapter Six appears at pp. 121–31. Footnotes have been renumbered.

Under existing law Arthur, Barry, and probably Charlie will be listened to. That is, the trier of fact will decide whether each of them really did make the mistake he claims to have made. If it is believed that he did and (ordinarily) if the mistake is thought to be "reasonable," no crime has been committed. As recently as fifteen years ago Dan's mistake was simply ignored; however, he might be excused in some jurisdictions today if his claim is believed. Evan is probably out of luck, although there is a developing trend in his favor. Frank, George, and Harry might just as well save their breath; their exulpatory claim of mistake will not be listened to.

If all this seems confusing and arbitrary, that is only because it is confusing and arbitrary. Traditional criminal law has fallen into the deliberate, and on occasion inadvertent, use of strict liability or liability without fault. For our purposes strict liability can be defined as the refusal to pay attention to a claim of mistake. In a behavioral-utilitarian view of the criminal law there is, as we have seen, good reason to ignore the defense of mistake. But if the preventive goal of criminal law is to be limited by the negative implication of the retributive position, as we have concluded it should, then mistakes must be considered and, if found relevant and believable, accepted as excuses.

The story of how traditional law slipped into an easy reliance on strict liability, to the detriment of its essential doctrinal content, need not concern us here. However, it may be instructive to consider one famous case in which the Supreme Court of the United States contributed to the erosion of *mens rea*, because it shows that important values may be sacrificed as easily through inadvertence as through design. The narrow issue in *United States* v. *Dotterweich*[1] was whether the president of a company that shipped misbranded or adulterated products in interstate commerce was a "person" who had done so under the Food, Drug, and Cosmetic Act, notwithstanding the fact that he had nothing to do with the shipment. Buffalo Pharmacal Company, a drug wholesaler, purchased drugs from manufacturers, repackaged them under its own label, and shipped them on order to physicians. Dotterweich and the company were prosecuted for two interstate shipments alleged to be adulterated or misbranded. The first consisted of a cascara compound that conformed to specifications but whose label included reference to an ingredient that had, a short time before, been dropped from the National Formulary. One infers that the old labels were still being used. The other shipment was of digitalis tablets that were less potent than their label indicated. The company did not manufacture these tablets, but merely repackaged them under its own label. So far as appears, there was no way short of conducting a chemical analysis of the tablets for their seller to know that they were not what their label declared them to be. The jury found Dotterweich guilty but for "some unexplainable reason" disagreed as to the company's guilt. Dotterweich was sentenced to pay a fine and to "probation for 60 days." Under the statute he could have been sentenced to a year's imprisonment. The court of appeals reversed, on the ground that the statute should not be read as applying to an individual agent of the principal (here the company), since only the principal was in a position to exculpate itself by obtaining a guaranty of nonadulteration from its supplier. Since there appeared to be no statutory basis for distinguishing between a high corporate agent, like Dotterweich, who might have obtained such a guaranty, and a shipping clerk or other menial employee who might have actually made the forbidden shipment and who would not necessarily be covered by the statutory provision protecting people who obtained a guaranty, a divided court of appeals concluded that Dotterweich's conviction could not stand.[2]

It will be noticed that the answer to the question whether this was indeed a "forbidden shipment" was dealt with rather cursorily. The court of appeals held merely that "intention to violate the statute" was not an element of the offense. The shipments in question were illegal under the statute, and that was that. Whether Dotterweich (or anyone else) had failed to take reasonable precautions was not put to the jury. Negligence as a possible mode of culpability was overlooked.

The court of appeals opinion had at least the merit of keeping separate two questions that it would confound analysis to blur: first, whether whoever was responsible for the shipment could be held criminally liable, notwithstanding the absence of culpability on his part (the issue of "strict liability"); and second, whether Dotterweich could be held criminally liable, notwithstanding his own lack of connection with the shipment (the issue of "vicarious liability"). It is obvious that the second issue is dependent on the first; if no one committed a crime, there was no crime for which Dotterweich could have been held vicariously liable. The underlying issue was whether the statute imposed strict liability.

The opinion for the Court, by Mr. Justice Frankfurter, did not make the essential distinction between the issues of strict and vicarious liability. It is not paraphrasing unfairly to say that the Court held that since the liability was strict it was also vicarious. But the premise that the Act dispensed with *mens rea* and imposed strictly liability was assumed rather than examined:

The prosecution to which Dotterweich was subjected is based on a now familiar type of legislation whereby penalties serve as effective means of regulation. Such legislation dispenses with the conventional requirement for criminal conduct—awareness of some wrongdoing. In the interest of the larger good it puts the burden of acting at hazard upon a person otherwise innocent but standing in responsible relations to a public danger. *United States* v. *Balint,* 258 U.S. 250. And so it is clear that shipments like those now in issue are "punished by the statute if the article is misbranded [or adulterated], and that the article may be misbranded [or adulterated] without any conscious fraud at all. It was natural enough to throw this risk on shippers with regard to the identity of their wares. . . ."[3]

It is well to note that this offhand passage is precisely all that the opinion had to say on the *mens rea* issue, despite the fact that this was the first time the Supreme Court had before it the construction of the mental element in this important federal criminal statute. It is also well to note the primitive and rigid view of *mens rea* that the quoted passage reflects. "Conscious fraud" and "awareness of some wrongdoing" are impossibly high standards, the opinion seems to say, and that leaves only strict liability. Did the company or its responsible agents behave recklessly or negligently with respect to the possibility that these shipments were not up to standard? Perhaps it was inexcusably careless not to have destroyed the old cascara labels and prepared new ones. Perhaps not. But could not the lower courts have been told that this question should be submitted to the jury? The case posed an obvious opportunity for framing a more discriminating set of standards for the mental element, but the opportunity was forgone.

Next, let us consider the areas in which the minimal doctrinal content of the criminal law has been eroded. There are four categories to be considered in determining how responsive the traditional common law has been to the notion of *mens rea.* These may be characterized as:

(1) Basic offenses dispensing in whole or in part with *mens rea.*
(2) Negligence as a mode of culpability.
(3) The barrier of *ignorantia legis.*
(4) Public welfare offenses.

Basic Offenses. The usual examples are sexual offenses, notably "statutory rape" and bigamy. These are universally regarded, in their traditional manifestations, as examples of strict liability in the criminal law. They serve as the basis for an assertion that might otherwise seem surprising, that there is no adequate operational distinction between offenses that dispense entirely with *mens rea* and offenses that dispense with *mens rea* only partially, or with respect to only one material element of the offense. Indeed, there is no such thing as a "strict liability" offense except as a partial rather than a complete discarding of *mens rea,* for there is always some element of any offense with respect to which a mental element is attached. In both the statutory rape and bigamy situations, it is the exclusion of *mens rea* with respect to the "circumstance" element of the offense that results in the imposition of strict liability: in the case of statutory rape, the circumstance that the girl is under the age of consent; in the case of bigamy, the circumstance that one or both of the parties is not legally free to remarry. Although there is an encouraging trend of contrary decisions in the bigamy field, it probably remains the majority rule in this country that a good-faith belief that one is legally free to remarry is not a defense to a charge of bigamy. Indeed, this view apparently has constitutional sanction. In the area of statutory rape, the strength of the traditional strict liability view has not been appreciably diminished.

These examples are familiar ones. It might perhaps be thought that they represent rather unusual exceptions to a generally pervasive principle of applicability of *mens rea.* Actually, the contrary is true. Two conspicuous examples arise in the area of homicide. Both the felony-murder and the misdemeanor-manslaughter rules, insofar as they have independent force and are not simply instances of the more general operation of homicide doctrines, reflect the imposition of strict liability as to the homicidal result. If a robber is automatically to be held for the death of an accomplice who is shot by their intended victim, or if a person commits a battery that leads to the unforeseen and reasonably unforeseeable result of the victim's death, liability for the homicide rests upon the refusal to consider *mens rea* as to the result.

The standard rejoinder to the argument that strict liability is being imposed in such a situation is that habitually given in the sex-offense cases. It comes down to the assertion that, since the underlying conduct is "wrongful," the actor must take all the consequences of that conduct, whether or not he foresaw or desired them. But it begs the question to assert that one who has intercourse with an underage girl, even though he is ignorant of her age, is to be held for statutory rape because his underlying conduct is "wrongful." The question is whether he should be held for an offense to whose elements he did not advert as well as for an offense to whose elements he did advert. The fact that various limitations have been worked out to prevent some of the most absurd consequences of rigid adherence to this "at peril" notion should not distract attention from its incompatibility with the spirit of *mens rea.*

NEGLIGENCE

If a man purposely or recklessly brings about a forbidden harm, we have no hesitation in saying that he had the requisite *mens rea* with respect to his conduct. But if he negligently brings about the forbidden harm, a different problem is presented.

Negligence is not readily transformable into a state of mind. It is, by definition, the absence of a state of mind. Negligence is, in short, an extension rather than an example of the idea of *mens rea* in the traditional sense.

There are those who argue that negligence as a mode of culpability has no place in the criminal law, because the threat of punishment for causing harms inadvertently must be either inefficacious or unjust or both.[4] Whatever the merits of this philosophic position, it is plain that negligence has a very strong foothold in the criminal law. It finds its most explicit formulation in the statutes penalizing negligent homicide in the driving of an automobile. But its hold on the criminal law is far more pervasive than this. Negligence suffices as a mode of culpability whenever the question asked with respect to the actor's perception is not whether he knew but whether he should have known. In the case of homicide, the difference between negligent inadvertence to the risk of death and conscious advertence to that risk is, very roughly speaking, the dividing line between manslaughter and murder. But beyond this, murder itself is sometimes treated as an offense that may be committed negligently, either by applying an external standard to the actor's perception of the risk or by applying an external standard to his perception of the basis for some excuse, such as self-defense. To the extent that we subject persons to liability for this most serious of offenses on the basis of an external standard, we are retreating very far from a doctrinal purist's stance. But even if murder by negligence is rejected as anomalous, we must face the challenge that negligence as a mode of culpability cannot be reconciled with the principle of *mens rea*.

It has been suggested that negligence has closer affinities with strict liability than it has with those modes of culpability that reflect subjective awareness on the part of the actor.[5] However, there are important differences between a legislative determination that all instances of a certain kind of conduct are unacceptable and a jury's determination that a particular instance of such conduct falls below a previously established community standard. The decisive difference is that the legislature cannot and does not foresee the infinite variation of circumstance that may affect the jury's view of a particular case. If there is an issue of fault for the jury to adjudicate, the line between subjective and objective fault—between "he knew" and "he should have known"—is a very shadowy one. Often, a judgment that "he knew" will simply reflect an inference from "he should have known." Conversely, a judgment that "he should have known" may contain the further unarticulated statement: "and we think he probably did know but we aren't sure enough to say so." There simply isn't a definite line between imputations of subjective awareness and those of objective fault: They are points on a continuum. The jury's opportunity to make an individualized determination of fault may focus indifferently upon one or the other. Putting the issue in this light, it seems plausible for the criminal law to employ a negligence standard on occasion, although not as a matter of course, without being charged with having abandoned the substance of *mens rea*. To put it another way, it seems to me proper to view negligence as an extension of rather than a departure from the values associated with the *mens rea* concept.

IGNORANTIA LEGIS

The principle that ignorance of the law is no excuse is deeply embedded in our criminal law. If the criminal law faithfully reflected prevalent community standards of minimally acceptable conduct, there would be no difficulty in reconciling the principle *ignorantia legis* with the requirements of *mens rea*. Yet, the proliferation of minor sumptuary and regulatory offenses, many of them penalizing conduct under circumstances in which the fact of illegality can scarcely be known to a first offender, creates a sharp problem. Sometimes a legislature specifies that awareness of the law's requirement is a necessary ingredient of guilt. More often it does not. Courts rarely remedy the deficiency by fashioning a doctrine that distinguishes sensibly between innocent and guilty conduct in contravention of an esoteric legal proscription.

It has been suggested by the framers of the Model Penal Code that a limited defense should be available to persons accused of crime if they can show a good-faith belief that their conduct does not legally constitute an offense, owing to lack of publication or reasonable availability of the enactment.[6] It is not entirely clear how broad this defense is meant to be. I should like to read it as establishing a negligence standard for the defense of ignorance or mistake of law. If read (or expanded) in this way, the proposal would go a long way toward resolving the *ignorantia legis* paradox. If we assume that an actor is unblameworthy in failing to know that his conduct violates a particular enactment (a condition that will ordinarily obtain only if either he or the enactment is a stranger to prevailing standards in the relevant community), then criminal punishment is objectionable for precisely those reasons that obtain in respect to strict liability.

PUBLIC WELFARE OFFENSES

Ever since Francis B. Sayre gave the phrase currency, this category of offenses has been treated by commentators as the main "exception" to the principle of *mens rea* and by courts as a convenient pigeonhole for any crime construed to dispense with *mens rea.* Perhaps the principal significance of the public welfare offenses lies in their open flouting of *mens rea,* as opposed to the more covert erosions that have gone on in the main body of the criminal law. Despite the enormous body of judge-made law that affirms dispensing with the mental element in violations of food and drug regulations, liquor regulations, traffic rules, and the like, few courts have explicitly considered and avowed the propriety of applying distinctively "criminal" sanctions to minor infractions. On the contrary, these offenses have been treated as something different from traditional criminal law, as a kind of hybrid category to which the odium and hence the safeguards of the criminal process do not attach. However limited in application the departure from *mens rea* may be in this category of offenses, it cannot be doubted that acceptance of this departure has been a powerful brake on the development of a general theory of *mens rea* in the criminal law.

This discussion of the "exceptions" to *mens rea* is intended to suggest that in every one of the cases enumerated at the beginning of this section

the defense of "mistake" should be entertained and, if found warranted by the facts, accepted. This conclusion follows, however, only if what we are confronted with is a case in which the criminal sanction is fully appropriate. Here we are touching on a major thesis of this book, namely, that the criminal sanction should not be applied to trivial infractions such as minor traffic offenses, to cite perhaps the most conspicuous example of current misuse. The culpability issue highlights this point. Treating every kind of conduct that the legislature unthinkingly labels as criminal with the full doctrinal apparatus of culpability would place an intolerable burden on the courts. Yet our principles compel us to entertain *mens rea* defenses whenever the consequences of a criminal conviction are severe, whenever we are using the full force of the criminal sanction. A line must be drawn that does not depend simply upon the fortuitous use of the label "criminal." Labels aside, the combination of stigma and loss of liberty involved in a conditional or absolute sentence of imprisonment sets that sanction apart from anything else the law imposes. When the law permits that degree of severity, the defendant should be entitled to litigate the issue of culpability by raising the kinds of defenses we have been considering. If the burden on the courts is thought to be too great, a less severe sanction than imprisonment should be the maximum provided for. The legislature ought not to be allowed to have it both ways.

NOTES

1. 320 U.S. 277 (1943).
2. United States v. Buffalo Pharmacal Co., 131 F. 2d 500 (2d Cir. 1942).
3. 320 U.S. at 280–81.
4. E.g., Jerome Hall, *General Principles of Criminal Law,* 2d ed. (Indianapolis, 1960), pp. 135–41.
5. Richard Wasserstrom, *Strict Liability in Criminal Law,* 12 Stan. L. Rev. 731, 741–45 (1960).
6. American Law Institute, MODEL PENAL CODE § 2.04 (3), and Comment, pp. 138–39 (Tent. Draft No. 4, 1955).

JOEL FEINBERG

Collective Responsibility*

When we state that a person is responsible for some harm, we sometimes mean to ascribe to him *liability* to certain responsive attitudes, judgments, or actions. Some responsive actions require authority; of these some are punitive, and others force compensation of a harmed victim. In the typical case of individual liability to unfavorable responses from others, three preconditions must be satisfied. First, it must be true that the responsible individual did the harmful thing in question, or at least that his action or omission made a substantial causal contribution to it. Second, the causally contributory conduct must have been in some way *faulty*. Finally, if the harmful outcome was truly "his fault," the requisite causal connection must have been directly between the faulty aspect of his conduct and the outcome. It is not sufficient to have caused harm *and* to have been at fault if the fault was irrelevant to the causing. We can use the expression "contributory fault" to refer compendiously to these three conditions. Thus, in the standard case of responsibility for harm, there can be no liability without contributory fault.

Certain familiar deviations from the standard case, however, give rise to confusion and misgiving. All primitive legal systems, and our own common law until about the fifteenth century, abound with examples of liability without contributory fault. For three centuries or so these examples were gradually eliminated from the common law, but they have returned in somewhat different form, often via statutes, in the last century, to the great alarm of many critics. Some of this alarm, I think, is justified; but there is little ground for fearing a recrudescence of primitive tribalism. Much legal liability without fault rests on very solid rationales, which are quite another thing than primitive supersition. The cases I have in mind can be discussed under three headings.

STRICT LIABILITY

What is called "strict liability" in the law is simply any liability for which the contributory fault condition is weakened or absent. This is the most general category; vicarious and collective liability are among its more interesting subspecies. For the most part, contractual liability has always tended to be "strict." Since this is liability that one imposes on oneself voluntarily, there is rarely any doubt expressed about its propriety. And no doubt can be expressed about its utility. Manufacturers brag about their warrantees and unconditional guarantees; and private bargainers quite often find it to their mutual advantage when one promises that, "if anything goes wrong, I'll bear the loss, no matter whose fault it is." In the law of torts, certain classes of persons are put on warning that, if they engage in certain ultra-hazardous activities, then they must be prepared to compensate any innocent parties who may incidentally be harmed, no matter how carefully and faultlessly the activities are carried out. There is always a risk of harm to others when one starts fires even on his own land, or keeps wild animals, or engages in blasting with high explosives. The law, of course, permits such activities, but it assigns the risk in advance to those who engage in them. This may seem to be a hard arrangement, since even if a construction company, for example, takes every reasonable precaution before dynamiting, it nevertheless can be found liable, if through some freakish chance a person at a great distance is injured by a flying rock set in motion by the blast, and can be forced to compensate the injured party for his losses. That the company

*From the *Journal of Philosophy,* Vol. LXV No. 21, (November 7, 1968), pp. 674–88. Reprinted by permission of the publisher. Reprinted in *Doing and Deserving: Essays in the Theory of Responsibility* (Princeton, N.J.: Princeton University Press, 1970) pp. 222–51.

was faultlessly careful in its operations is no defense. Still, this rule is by no means an arbitrary harassment, and its rigors are easily mitigated. The prospective responsibility imposed on blasters by law applies even to events beyond their control, but, *knowing this in advance* (an all-important consideration), they will be more careful than ever; and, further, they can guard against disastrous expenses by adjusting their prices and figuring compensation costs among their normal business expenses.

Strict liability in the criminal law is much less likely to accord with reasonable standards of justice than in contracts and torts; but even penalties and punishments may, in certain circumstances, dispense with the requirement of fault, provided that prior assignments of risks are clear and that some degree of prior control is possible. Perhaps the best known strict liability statutes in the criminal law are those creating "public welfare offenses." Here the rationale for disregarding actual fault is similar, in part, to that supporting strict liability for ultra-hazardous activities in torts. All milk producers, for example, are put on notice by one statute that, if any of their marketed product is found to be adulterated, they will be subject to stiff penalty. The producers have the power and authority to regulate their own facilities, procedures, and employees. The law in effect tells them that, since there is such a paramount public interest in pure foods, they must give the public an unconditional guarantee of the purity of their product. If the guarantee fails, no questions will be asked about fault; the fine will be imposed automatically. Then it will be up to the company to exercise its control by locating and eliminating the fault. If this arrangement seems unfair, the company can be reminded that the risk is well known and is in fact the price producers pay for the privilege of serving the public for their own profit—a price they presumably have been quite willing to pay. Moreover, it really does protect the public by providing incentive to vigilant safety measures; and the penalties, in any case, are only fines. No perfectly innocent persons are sent to prison.

When criminal punishment involving imprisonment is involved, the case for strict liability, of course, is much weaker; but even here, in certain circumstances, the conviction of the "faultless" can sometimes be supported. Among serious crimes for which faultless ignorance ("reasonable mistake") is no excuse, the most celebrated example is the old English offense of taking an unmarried girl, under sixteen, from the possession of her father (for illicit purposes) without his consent. The rationale here, apparently, was that the harm done is so serious, and the opportunity and temptation so great, that any philanderer should be put on warning that, even if he has very good reason to believe his prey to be a thirty-year-old woman, he and he alone assumes the risk that she may be only fifteen—and a serious risk it is! The policy underlying the law was that philandery is a socially undesirable activity which it is the business of the law to discourage, but not the kind of moral offense that can properly (or practically) be prohibited absolutely. Hence young men are permitted to engage in it, but at their own peril. Understanding in advance where the risks lie, they will presumably be far more careful than they might otherwise be. The law here gives young sports a sporting chance. If they gamble and lose, even with the best of odds, they can blame no one but themselves. So interpreted, strict liability seems a relatively libertarian and humane means of social control.

In all the examples of plausibly just strict liability, the liable party must have had some control over his own destiny—some choice whether to take the risk assigned him by the law and some power to diminish the risk by his own care. When liability may be imposed even without such control, however, then it can "fall from the sky," like a plague, and land senselessly on complete strangers. Strict liability, when rational, is never totally unconditional or random.

VICARIOUS LIABILITY

Much, but by no means all, strict liability is also vicarious liability. There can be strict liability when *no one* is at fault, or where the question of contributory fault cannot be settled. There is vicarious liability, on the other hand, when the contributory fault, or some element of it, is properly ascribed to one party (or group of parties), but the liability is ascribed to a different party (or parties). In such cases we say that the latter party is responsible for the harmful consequences of a faulty action or omission of the former party. The person who did or caused the harm is not the one who is called upon to answer for it.

One familiar and surely unobjectionable type of vicarious liability is that which derives from the process of *authorization*. One party, called a "principal," authorizes another party, called the "agent," to act, within a certain range, for him. "He that acteth for another," wrote Hobbes, is said to bear his person, or act in his name."[1] Acting in another's name is quite another thing than merely acting in his interests (also called "acting for him") or merely substituting for him, as an understudy, for example, replaces an indisposed actor (also called "acting in place of him"). An agent acts "for" or "in place of" his principal in a different sense. The agent is often given the right to act, speak, sign contracts, make appointments, or the like, and these acts are as binding on the principal as if he had done them himself. The relation of authorization, as Hanna Pitkin points out,[2] is lopsided: The rights go to the agent, and the responsibilities to the principal.

The relation of authorization can take two very different forms, depending on the degree of discretion granted to the agent, and there is a continuum of combinations between the extremes. On the one hand, there is the agent who is the mere "mouthpiece" of his principal. He is a "tool" in much the same sense as is a typewriter or telephone: He simply transmits the instructions of his principal. Thus messengers, delegates, spokesmen, typists, and amanuenses are sometimes called agents. Miss Pitkin points out that such persons are often called "mere agents," or (I might add) "bound agents" as opposed to "free agents."[3] The principal acts *through* his agent much as he might act through some mechanical medium. On the other hand, an agent may be some sort of expert hired to exercise his professional judgment on behalf of, and in the name of, the principal. He may be given, within some limited area of expertise, complete independence to act as he deems best, binding his principal to all the beneficial or detrimental consequences. This is the role played by trustees and some other investment managers, some lawyers, buyers, and ghost-writers. At the extreme of "free agency" is the Hobbesian sovereign; for each of his subjects has in effect authorized in advance *all* of his "actions and judgments . . . in the same manner, as if they were his own."[4]

It is often said that the very actions of agents themselves, and not merely their normative consequences, are directly ascribable to their principals, through "a kind of fiction";[5] but this, I submit, is a dangerously misleading way of talking. If A has B's power of attorney, he may have the right to sign B's signature; and if he signs it on a contract or a check, the pecuniary consequences may be exactly as they would be had B himself signed his name. The results are *as if B* had himself acted; but it is nevertheless true that *he* did not act—A acted for him. Even the Old Testament, which finds nothing objectionable in the vicarious criminal liability of children for the sins of their fathers, balks at the doctrine of literally transferred agency and causality. In Deuteronomy 24:16, Jeremiah and Ezekiel repeat that, if the fathers had eaten sour grapes, the children's teeth would not be set on edge (though if the fathers had *stolen* the grapes, the children, perhaps, would be punishable).

Another form of vicarious liability derives from the relation between superior and subordinate in hierarchical institutions, of which military organizations are perhaps the clearest model. At the lowest rank persons have no authority to command others and are responsible only for their own performances. Officers of the higher ranks have greater authority—that is, the right to command larger numbers of persons and make them "tools"—and correspondingly greater answerability for failures. A superior's failure may be the fault of some of his subordinates, but he must nevertheless answer for it to *his* superiors. Subordinates, on the other hand, are not liable for the foolish or wicked commands of their superiors, since they are not "to reason why" but just to obey. In a way, a military hierarchy, then, can be viewed as a system of unidirectional vicarious liability. Something like it often exists in a less clear-cut form outside of military organizations. A recent press dispatch, for example, reports that there will no longer be automatic promotions of teachers in the Detroit public high schools and that teachers and principals will be held responsible for the academic performance of their students. Thus if students do poorly, their teachers will be "punished," and if they do well, their teachers will be rewarded. This liability is not entirely vicarious, of course, since there is presumably some causal connection between the teacher's performance and the student's; but it can approach pure vicarious liability when classes of students differ widely in ability. Its point, I think, is an interesting one, namely, to bolster the motivation of the *teachers*. (The students presumably do not care enough about the welfare of their teachers to be affected directly by the arrangement). In this respect, it is the very opposite of most forms of vicarious punishment (such as holding hostages, massive reprisals, family liability, blood feuds) whose point is to affect the motivation of the primary wrongdoers, not those who stand to be punished vicariously.

Another form of vicarious liability is the responsibility of employers ("masters") to compensate victims of the negligence or even, in some cases, the deliberate wrongdoing of their employees ("servants"), even when the employee is acting without, or in direct defiance of, the explicit orders of his boss, and the boss committed no negligence in hiring the employee in the first place, or in supervising, instructing, or outfitting him. Here, indeed, "the sins of the servant are visited upon the master." If my dog bites you, the biting is imputed to him, the liability to me.[6] Similarly, if the driver of my delivery truck, while doing his job, puts a dent in your fender or a crease in your skull, the liability to enforced compensation is mine, not his. (*His* liability is to *me;* he is now subject to being fired.) The rationale of this universal but once highly controverted practice is clear enough. If an accident victim has only a truck driver to sue, he may end up paying most of his disastrous medical expenses himself. The employer, having a "deeper pocket," is a more competent compensator; and, moreover, since he has *control* over the selection of employees for dangerous work, the rule will make him more careful in his assignment of tasks. It may be unfair to him to make him pay for an accident that was not his fault, but it would impose an even greater hardship and injustice to put the burden mainly on the shoulders of the equally faultless accident victim. And, again, there are means open to employers of anticipating and redistributing losses caused by their employees' negligence.

Still another form of vicarious liability derives from the relation of *suretyship*. A bonding company may insure an employer against the dishonesty of a new employee for a fee that may be paid by either employer or employee. If the employee commits embezzlement and makes his escape, the fault, guilt, agency, and causation all belong to the employee, but the liability to make good the losses is the innocent surety's. Similarly, the guarantor of another's debt pays if the other fails; and the poster of bail forfeits, if the bailed prisoner fails to make appearance.

Vicarious liability through authorization, hierarchy, mastership, and suretyship can thus be rational, in the sense that they rest on intellectually respectable, if not always convincing, rationales. Most of what has passed as vicarious criminal liability in human history is otherwise. Holmes traced the origin of both civil and criminal liability to certain animistic conceptions common to the Hebrews, Greeks, Romans, and Germans, and apparently to all human cultures at a certain stage in their development. The instrument of harm, whether it were a tool, a weapon, a tree, an ox, a slave, or a child, was regarded as the immediate and "natural" object of vengeance. It was "noxal," that is, accursed, and had to be forfeited to the victim, or his family, to be torn apart and annihilated. Later the principle of composition was adopted, and the owner of the noxal instrument could buy off its victim as an alternative to forfeiture. Nevertheless, in the early centuries of all major legal systems, inanimate objects and animals were "punished"; and the related practices of blood feud, noxal surrender, and substitute sacrifice flourished.

There are more refined forms of vicarious criminal liability for which a more plausible case can be made, although even these "rational" forms are rarely defensible as just. The imposition of punitive vicarious liability arrangements upon a community is always a desperate measure, justifiable at best only in extreme circumstances. I have in mind the taking of hostages by a wartime army of occupation (condemned by The Hague Convention of 1907 but practiced by Germans in two world wars) and stepped-up military reprisals for terrorism or atrocity directed at populations that surely include the innocent as well as the guilty. These cruel practices arouse angry resistance and thus tend to be self-defeating; and, in any case, they are examples of acts of war, rather than rules of a system of criminal law.

Could there be circumstances, in less desperate times, in which authorization, hierarchy, mastership, or suretyship, admittedly plausible bases for noncriminal liabilities, could also be the ground for criminal punishment? Under our present law, a principal will be coresponsible with his agent when the latter commits a criminal act at the former's direction or with his advance knowledge or subsequent ratification. The criminal punishment of superiors for actions done *entirely* on their own by subordinates, however, would be a barbarous regression in normal times. Criminal suretyship is a more difficult matter. I can imagine a voluntary system of suretyship that would permit fathers to arrange in advance to undergo punishment instead of their sons in case the latter committed crimes. Such a system could have some incidental merits among its preponderant disadvantages: deterrence and development of family solidarity. And it makes more sense than certain cosmic systems of criminal law in which the children answer for the sins of their fathers instead of the other way round.

There is an important point about all vicarious punishment: Even when it is reasonable to separate liability from fault, it is only the liability that can be passed from one party to another. In particular, *there can be no such thing as vicarious guilt.* Guilt consists in the intentional transgression of prohibition, "a violation of a specific taboo, boundary, or legal code, by a definite voluntary act." [7] In addition, the notion of guilt has always been essentially connected with the idea of "owing payment." The guilty party must "pay" for his sins, just as a debtor is one who must correct his moral imbalance by repayment. To be guilty is to be out of balance, or unredeemed, stained or impure. The root idea in guilt, then, is to be an appropriate person to make atonement, penance, or self-reproach, in virtue of having intentionally violated a commandment or prohibition. There have been extensions of this idea both through morbid superstition and natural analogy, but flawed intention, transgression, and needed atonement are still its central components. [8]

Now when an innocent man is punished for what a guilty man has done, he is treated *as if* he were himself guilty. There may be a rational point, and perhaps even justice, in certain circumstances, in doing this. Yet even though criminal liability can transfer or extend vicariously from a guilty to an innocent party, it obviously cannot be literally true that the guilt transfers as well. For guilt to transfer literally, action and intention too must transfer literally. But to say of

an innocent man that he bears another's guilt is to say that he had one (innocent) intention and yet another (guilty) one, a claim which upon analysis turns out to be contradictory. I think that theologians and others have found it easy to talk of vicarious guilt only because the concept of guilt has always had the double sense of actual sin, on the one hand, and payment, atonement, redemption, and such, on the other; and of course it is at least logically intelligible for concepts of the latter kind to transfer. In short, liability can transfer, but not agency, causation, or fault (the components of "contributory fault"), and certainly not guilt.

COLLECTIVE LIABILITY

In the remainder of this essay, we shall focus our attention on collective-responsibility arrangements. In principle, these can be justified in four logically distinct ways. Whole groups can be held liable even though not all of their members are at fault, in which case collective responsibility is still another form of liability without contributory fault similar to those discussed above; or, second, a group can be held collectively responsible through the fault, contributory or *noncontributory,* of each member; or, third, through the contributory fault of each and every member; or, finally, through the collective but *nondistributive* fault of the group itself. This section will be concerned only with the first of these forms, the collective liability that is one interesting subspecies of that vicarious liability which in turn is one interesting subspecies of strict liability.

Collective liability, as I shall use the term, is the vicarious liability of an organized group (either a loosely organized, impermanent collection or a corporate institution) for the actions of its constituent members. When the whole group as such is held responsible for the actions of one or some of its members, then, from the point of view of any given "responsible" individual, *his* liability in most cases will be vicarious.

Under certain circumstances, collective liability is a natural and prudent way of arranging the affairs of an organization, which the members might well be expected to undertake themselves, quite voluntarily. This expectation applies only to those organizations (usually small ones) where there is already a high degree of *de facto* solidarity. Collective responsibility not only expresses the solidarity but also strengthens it; thus it is a good thing to whatever extent the preexistent solidarity was a good thing. Where prior solidarity is absent, collective liability arrangements may seek their justification through the desperate prior *need* for solidarity.

When does a group have "solidarity"? Three intertwined conditions, I think, must be satisfied to some degree. There has to be first of all, a large *community of interest* among all the members, not merely a specific overlap of shared specialized interests, of the sort that unite the members of a corporation's board of directors, for example, no matter how strong. A community of interest exists between two parties to the extent that each party's integrated set of interests contains as one of its components the integrated interest-set of the other. Obviously, this will be difficult to arrange in large and diverse groups. A husband, for example, might have as his main interests (whose fulfillment as a harmonious set constitutes his *well-being*) his health, his material possessions, his professional reputation, his professional achievement, *and* the well-being (also defined in terms of an integrated set of interests) of his wife and his children. His interests would thus include or contain the interests of several other people. If those other persons' interests, in a precisely similar way, were to embrace his, then there would be between them a perfect community of interest. Secondly, such "community" is often associated with bonds of sentiment directed toward common objects, or of reciprocal affection between the parties. (R. B. Perry defined "love" as an interest in the interests of someone else). Thirdly, solidarity is ordinarily a function of the degree to which the parties share a common lot, the extent to which their goods and harms are necessarily collective and indivisible. When a father is jailed, his whole family shares the disgrace and the loss of his provisions. There is no hurting one member without hurting them all; and because of the way their interests are related, the successes and satisfactions of one radiate their benefits to the others.

Individuals normally pool their liabilities when they share a common cooperative purpose, and each recognizes in the others complementary abilities of a useful or necessary kind. Thus salesmen combine with administrators to become business partners, pooling their talents and sharing their risks. Joint authorships are often cases of mutual ghost-writing, where each party stands answerable for the joint product of their several labors. Athletic team members must all win or all lose together: Victory is not the prize of individual merit alone, nor is defeat linked to "contributory fault." Similarly, in underground conspiracies and desperate dangerous undertakings, the spirit of "all for one and one for all" is not merely a useful device; it is imposed by the very nature of the enterprise. What makes collective liability natural in such cases is that parties who are largely of one mind to begin with are led (or forced) by circumstances to act in concert and share the risk of common failure or the fruits of an indivisible success.

There have been times in the history of civilization when group solidarity was a more common thing, and more easily arranged, than today. In many places, including Northern Europe, the ultimate unit of legal responsibility has been not the individual, but the clan, the kinship group, or the immediate family; and only a couple of centuries ago the English common law still applied to married couples the "fiction of conjugal unity." Only since the passage of Married Women's Acts in the 1840's have married women in America had a legal identity separate, in many kinds of legal situations, from that of their husbands. The world has without a doubt been getting steadily more individualistic in this respect, and it is no wonder. Change is faster, leading at any given time to more continual novelty and consequent greater diversity. Political parties, religious groups, and fraternal associations can no longer count on perfect uniformity and general solidarity across a whole spectrum of attitudes and convictions. And how much harder it is today to be a marriage broker (even with computers) than in other more static ages, when persons were more easily interchangeable and common values could be taken for granted!

De facto solidarity, then, is less easily come by today, even within small family groups. And because it is, there is no longer much point in treating a wife, for example, as part of a single corporate person with her husband. Wives today can own their own property, bargain and trade with their husbands, sign contracts on their own, and sue and be sued in their own names. Still, some of the conditions making for *de facto* solidarity (such as the common lot, and indivisible goods and evils) are necessarily present in every marriage; and when these are reinforced by shared or contained interests and mutual affection, the solidarity that renders joint liabilities reasonable will also be present. When fates are shared, they must be pooled in any case. Where the plural possessive "our" more naturally comes to the lips than the singular "mine," then to enter joint bank accounts and other forms of collective liability is only to certify the given and destroy artificial inconvenience.

There is perhaps no better index to solidarity than vicarious pride and shame. These attitudes occur most frequently in group members on behalf of the larger group, or of some other member(s) of the larger group, of which they are a part. Individuals sometimes feel proud of ashamed of their families, ancestors, countries, or races; and all or most of those who belong to groups may feel pride or shame over the achievements or failures of single members of their groups. Some writers have in effect denied that pride (and presumably shame) can ever be authentically vicarious; and there is no doubt that the appearance of vicariousness can often be explained away. Parental pride in the achievements of a son may be the consequence of a belief that those achievements reflect the influence of the parent, so that it is really pride at "what I have created in my son." This sort of interpretation may be possible in some cases, but it obviously cannot explain the son's filial pride in the achievements of his parents or grandparents. In this connection, H. D. Lewis speaks of "the presumption that we ourselves, having been subject to the same influences, are not without a measure of the qualities for which others of our group are noted." [9] No doubt many occurrences of filial pride and shame can be traced to this source, but clearly it cannot account for the immigrant's pride in the "American way of life" or the war opponent's feeling ashamed "to wear the same uniform" as those he believes have committed atrocities. Of course, the latter may be something different from shame, namely, mortification at being associated by others with actions of which one disapproves and of which one is totally innocent. Normal embarrassment, like pride at what one has helped others to do or be and pride over one's qualities presumptively shared with conspicuously worthy other persons, is a self-centered atti-

tude; an authentically vicarious feeling, if there can be such a thing, must be based on the doings or qualities of others considered entirely on their own account, unrelated to any doings or qualities of the principal.

H. D. Lewis provides a clue when he speaks of the phenomenon of sympathetic identification: "Our interest in those with whom we have special ties of affection will enable us to follow their success with a glow of satisfaction as if it were our own." [10] If this is what authentically vicarious pride is like, it is a phenomenon of the same order as sympathetic pain or compassion. Indeed, any feeling one person can experience can be experienced vicariously by some other imaginatively sensitive person. What we want, however, is not so much an account of vicarious or imaginative *sharing* alone as an account that will also apply to vicarious unshared or substitute feeling. Here too sympathy, I think, is the key. When someone near to me, about whom I care, makes a fool of himself before others, I can feel embarrassed for him, even though he feels no such thing himself. Yet when some total stranger or some person I despise behaves similarly, my reaction will be indifference or pity or contempt—reactions that are not vicarious. Compare "I am proud (or ashamed) because of you" with "I am proud (or ashamed) for you." The former is like taking partial credit (or blame); the latter is like congratulating (or condemning from an internal or sympathetic judgment point). We are inclined to congratulate (or "condemn fraternally") only when we feel some degree of solidarity with the other parties. The solidarity is a necessary condition of the vicarious emotion, which is in turn an index to the solidarity.

I think this account helps explain some puzzling variations. It is natural, for example, that an American Negro should feel solidarity with all other Negroes and speak of what has been done to "the black man" by "the white man" and what the moral relations between "the" black man (all black men) and "the" white man (all white men) ought to be. But I, for one, am quite incapable of feeling the same kind of solidarity with all white men, a motley group of one billion persons who are, in my mind, no more an "organization" than is the entire human race as such. I certainly feel no bonds to seventeenth-century slave traders analogous to those ties of identification an American Negro must naturally feel with the captured slaves. Precisely because of this failure of imagination, I can feel no shame on *their* behalf. Similarly, a European, appalled by American foreign policy, will feel anger or despair, but not vicarious shame unless he has some sentimental attachment to the United States. An American with like views will be ashamed of his country. Indeed, one cannot be intensely ashamed of one's country unless one also loves it.

Collective-responsibility arrangements are most likely to offend our modern sensibilities when the liabilities are to criminal punishment. Yet there was a time when primitive conditions required that the policing function be imposed on local groups themselves through a system of *compulsory universal suretyship.* Among the early Anglo-Saxons, the perfectly trustworthy man was he who did not stray from the village where his many kin resided, for they were his sureties who could guarantee his good conduct. In contrast, the stranger far from his kindred had nothing to restrain him, and since his death would excite no blood feud, he had no legal protection against the assaults of other.[11] With the development of Christian feudalism, the ancient system of kindred liability broke down, for churchmen without kin or local tie began to appear among suspicious villagers, and "as time went on, many men who for one reason or another moved away from their original environments and sought their fortunes elsewhere . . . could not depend on ties of kindred to make them law-worthy and reputable."[12] Hence a new system of compulsory suretyship, based on neighborhood rather than kin was developed. Everyone was *made* "law-worthy and reputable" by being assigned to a neighborhood group every member of which was an insurer of his conduct. If an offender was not produced by his surety group to answer criminal charges, a fine was levied on each member of the group, and sometimes liability to make compensation as well.

Now this may strike us as a barbarous expedient of a primitive people who had no conception of individual justice; but I think that is too severe a judgment. The frankpledge system was a genuine system of criminal law: There was nothing arbitrary, *ad hoc,* or *ex post facto* about it. It was also a system of compulsory group self-policing in an age when there were no professional police.

Moreover, it reinforced a preexisting group solidarity the like of which cannot occur in an era of rapid movement like our own. And most important, the system worked; it prevented violence and became generally accepted as part of the expected natural order of things.

Yet surely there is no going back to this kind of collective responsibility. H. Gomperz concluded an essay by claiming: "That men can be held responsible solely for individual conduct freely willed is certainly wrong; it mistakes a principle characteristic of individualistic ages for an eternal law of human nature."[13] I agree that the principle of individual responsibility is not an "external law"; but Gomperz misleadingly suggests a kind of historical relativism according to which individualistic and collectivistic ages alternate like styles in ladies' skirts. On the contrary, the changes that have come with modern times have dictated quite inevitably that the one principle replace the other, and no "alternation" is remotely foreseeable, unless massive destruction forces the human race to start all over again in tiny isolated farming settlements. Under modern conditions the surety system would not work in the intended way, for the surety groups, being subject to rapid turnover, would lack the necessary cohesion and solidarity to exert much influence or control over their members. It is more difficult now to keep a watchful eye on our neighbors, since we no longer spend the better part of every day working in adjacent fields with them. Moreover, we no longer impose a duty on all citizens to raise the hue and cry upon discovery of a crime, drop their work, arm themselves, and join the hunt, on pain of penalty to their whole surety group. Now we say that detection and pursuit of criminals is the policeman's job. He gets paid for it, not us; and he is much more able to do it well. Besides, we all have other things to do.

But we have paid a price in privacy, which will get steadily stiffer, for the principle of individual criminal responsibility. The technical devices that make modern police work possible are reaching the point where they will make inspection of every person's life and history possible only minutes after a police official desires it. In olden times a man could not wonder for long whether he was his neighbor's keeper, for the voice of authority would instruct him unmistakably that he'd damn well better be. Today we prefer not to become involved in the control of crime, with the result that those who are charged with the control of crime become more and more involved with us.

In summary, collective criminal liability imposed on groups as a mandatory self-policing device is reasonable only when there is a very high degree of antecedent group solidarity and where efficient professional policing is unfeasible. Furthermore, justice requires that the system be part of the expected background of the group's way of life and that those held vicariously liable have some reasonable degree of *control* over those for whom they are made sureties. It is because these conditions are hardly ever satisfied in modern life, and not because individual liability is an eternal law of reason, that collective criminal responsibility is no longer an acceptable form of social organization.

So much for collective responsibility as a form of *liability without fault.* People often have other models in mind, however, when they speak of "collective responsibility."

LIABILITY WITH
NONCONTRIBUTORY FAULT

Various faults can exist in the absence of any causal linkage to harm, where that absence is only a lucky accident reflecting no credit on the person who is at fault. Where every member of a group shares the same fault, but only one member's fault leads to any harm, and that not because it was more of a fault than that of the others, but only because of independent fortuities, many outsiders will be inclined to ascribe collective liability to the whole group. Other outsiders may deny the propriety of holding even a faulty or guilty person liable for harm that was not "his fault"; but for a group member himself to take this public stand would be an unattractive piece of self-righteousness. It would be more appropriate for him to grieve, and voluntarily make what amends he can, than to insist stubbornly on the noncontributory character of his fault, which was a matter of pure lucky chance.

In this kind of situation we have a handy model for the interpretation of extravagant hyperboles about universal responsibility. One man drinks heavily at a party and then drives home at normal (high) speeds, injuring a pedestrian along the way. The claim that we are all guilty of this crime, interpreted in a certain way, is only a small exaggeration, for it is a very common practice, in which perhaps *most* of us participate, to drive above posted speed limits at night and also to drive in our usual fashion to and from parties at which we drink. Most of us are "guilty" of this practice, although only the motorist actually involved in the accident is guilty of the resultant injury. He is guilty *of* or *for* more than we are, and more harm is his fault; but it does not necessarily follow that he is more guilty or more at fault than the rest of us.

Now there are some character faults that are present to some, though not the same, degree in almost everyone. These flaws sometimes cause enormous amounts of harm. There is some point in saying that all those who share the flaws, even those who have had no opportunity to do mischief by them, are "responsible" when harm results, in the sense that they are morally no better than those whose fault contributed to the harm and are, therefore, properly answerable for the way they are, if only to their own consciences. There is even a point in the exaggeration that ascribes the common fault to everyone without exception, when in fact there are exceptions; for this may serve to indicate that serious and dangerous faults are far more common than is generally believed and may exist in the least suspected places. Since character flaws are dispositions to act or feel in improper ways in circumstances of various kinds, we may never know of a given man that he has the fault in question until circumstances of the appropriate kind arise; and they may never arise.

Can liability of the noncontributorily faulty be morally palatable? Criminal punishment of whole groups of fault-sharers would for a dozen reasons be impracticable. We have no way of confirming statements about what a man with a given character structure would do if the circumstances were different; so if we are determined to avoid punishing the genuinely faultless, we had better wait until the circumstances *are* different. In any case, the larger and more diverse the group of alleged fault-sharers, the less likely it is that they all share—or share to anything like the same degree—the fault in question. If, nevertheless, the fault is properly ascribed distributively to a group of great size, the probability increases that the fault is common also to judge, jury, and prosecutor. Moral uncertainties of this kind are not likely to be present when we have evidence linking the fault of an individual to some harmful upshot. Those luckier ones who share the fault but escape the causal link to harm must, from the point of view of criminal justice, simply be left to profit from their luck. But when we leave political-legal contexts, the case for causation as a necessary condition of liability weakens considerably. The law will neither punish B nor force him to compensate C for the harm caused by A's fault, when B is as prone as A to the fault in question; but that is no reason why private individuals should refrain from censuring or snubbing B to the same extent as A, or why B should not hold himself to account.

CONTRIBUTORY GROUP FAULT: COLLECTIVE AND DISTRIBUTIVE

Sometimes we attribute liability to a whole group because of the contributory fault of each and every member. Group responsibility, so conceived, is simply the sum of all the individual responsibility. Since each individual is coresponsible for the harm in question, no one's responsibility is vicarious. Nevertheless, problems are raised by three kinds of situations: first, where large numbers of people are independently at fault without any concert or communication between them; second, where the harm is caused by a joint undertaking of numerous persons acting cooperatively; and, third, where the harm is to be ascribed to some feature of the common culture consciously endorsed and participated in by every member of the group.

Suppose a man swimming off a public beach that lacks a professional lifeguard shouts for help in a voice audible to a group of one thousand accomplished swimmers lolling on the beach; and yet no one moves to help him, and he is left to drown. The traditional common law imposes no liability, criminal or civil, for the harm in this kind of case. Among the reasons often given are that, if liability were imposed on one, it would, in all consistency, have to be imposed on the whole vast group and that, if a duty to rescue drowning swimmers were imposed on every accomplished swimmer in a position to help, the results would be confusing and chaotic, with hoards of rescuers getting in each other's way and no one quite sure he is not violating the law by not entering the struggle quickly and ardently enough. On the other hand, so the argument goes, if each feels a duty to mitigate the dangerous confusion, there could be an Alphonse-Gaston exchange of courteous omissions on a large and tragic scale. This rationale has always seemed disingenuous to me. I see no reason why legal duties should not correspond here with moral ones: Each has a duty to attempt rescue so long as no more than a few others have already begun their efforts. In short, everyone should use his eyes and his common sense and cooperate as best he can. If no one makes any motion at all, it follows that no one has done his best within the limits imposed by the situation, and *all* are subject at least to blame. Since all could have rescued the swimmer, it is true of each of them that, but for *his* failure to attempt rescue in the circumstances that in fact obtained, the harm would not have occurred. It may be awkward to charge all one thousand persons with criminal responsibility, but the difficulties would be no greater than those involved in prosecuting a conspiracy of equal size. As for civil liability, the problems are even less impressive: The plaintiff (widow) should simply be allowed to choose her own defendants from among the multitudes who were at fault—those, no doubt, with the "deepest pockets."

The second kind of case exemplifying group fault distributable to each member is that where the members are all privy to a crime or tort as conspirators or accomplices or joint tortfeasors. In complicated crimes, *complicity* is ascribed unavoidably to persons whose degree of participation in the crime is unequal. The common law, therefore, divides guilty felons into four categories, namely, "perpetrators," "abettors," "inciters" (all three of these are "accomplices"), and "criminal protectors," so that one may be guilty of a given crime either as its principal perpetrator (and even perpetration is a matter of degree, abettors counting as "principals in the second degree") or as accessories, that is, inciters or protectors. Thus one can be guilty, as an accessory, even of crimes that one is not competent to perpetrate. A woman, for example, may be found guilty of rape, as an abettor or inciter to the man, who must, of course, be the principal perpetrator of the crime on some other woman.

Suppose C and D plan a bank robbery, present their plan to a respected friend A, receive his encouragement, borrow weapons from B for the purpose, hire E as getaway driver, and then execute the plan. Pursued by the police, they are forced to leave their escape route and take refuge at the farm of E's kindly uncle F. F congratulates them, entertains them hospitably, and sends them on their way with his blessing. F's neighbor, G, learns of all that has happened, disapproves, but does nothing. Another neighbor, H, learns of it but is bribed into silence. On these facts, A, B, C, D, E, and F are all guilty of the bank robbery— C and D as perpetrators, A and B as inciters,[14] E as an abettor, and F as a protector. G is guilty of the misdemeanor called "misprision of felony," and H of the misdemeanor called "compounding a felony." On the other hand, if J, an old acquaintance of C and D, sees them about to enter the bank, notices suspicious bulges in their pockets, surmises that they are up to no good, yet does nothing out of simple reluctance to "get involved," he is not legally guilty. Yet he is certainly subject to blame; and, as moralists, we might decide this marginal case differently than the lawyers and brand him a kind of "moral accessory" before the fact, "morally guilty," though to a lesser degree than the others. We can afford to have stricter standards of culpability than the lawyers, since no formal punishment will follow as a result of *our* verdicts and we do not have to worry about procedural complexities.

Part of the problem of determining degrees of responsibility of individuals in joint undertakings, where the responsibility is not vicarious, is assessing the extent of each individual's *contribution* to the undertaking. This involves assessment of various incommensurable dimensions of contribution—degrees of initiative, difficulty or causal crucialness of assigned subtasks, degrees of authority, percentage of derived profit, and so on. Although these matters cannot be settled in any mathematical way, rough and ready answers suggest themselves to common sense, and the legal categories of complicity have proved quite workable. The more difficult problems require estimates of *voluntariness*. Do I carry my own share of "moral guilt" for the Vietnamese abomination as a consequence of my payment of war taxes? Is my position morally analogous to that of B, the "inciter" in the bank robbery example? In avoid-

ing protest demonstrations, am I guilty of "cooperating" with evil, perhaps on the model of J, F, G, or H? The answers to those questions are difficult, I think, not because the (minute) extent of my causal contribution is not easily measurable, but because it is difficult to know how strict should be the standards of voluntariness for cases like this. Since nonpayment of taxes is a crime, the payment of war taxes is less than fully voluntary. To go to prison merely to avoid being associated, however indirectly, with some evil is to adopt the heroic path. The man who "cooperates" with crime under duress is surely in a different position from the man who cooperates, like H, as a result of a bribe or, like J, out of sloth or cowardice. Yet whether the threat of legal punishment is sufficient duress to excuse "cooperation" with authorities again depends on numerous factors, including the degree of the evil and the probabilities of its alleviation with and without the contemplated resistance. In any case, mere nonresistance does not count as "cooperation" unless various other conditions are fulfilled. Where those conditions are conspicuously unfulfilled, as in Nazi Germany, then nonresistance is entirely involuntary, since its only alternative is pointless self-sacrifice.

The third interesting case of distributive group fault is that which adheres to a group's folkways yet somehow reflects upon every member of the group. Even Dwight Macdonald concedes that there are "folk activities" that a group "takes spontaneously and as a whole ... which are approved by the popular mores" and which are not merely "things done by sharply differentiated sub-groups."[15] Nazi acts of violence against Jews, Macdonald argued, were not genuine folk activities in this sense. In contrast, the constant and widespread acts of violence "against Negroes throughout the South, culminating in lynchings, may be considered real "people's actions," for which the Southern whites bear collective responsibility [because] the brutality ... is participated in, actively or with passive sympathy, by the entire white community."[16] The postbellum Southern social system, now beginning to crumble, was contrived outside of political institutions and only winked at by the law. Its brutalities were "instrumentalities for keeping the Negro in his place and maintaining the supraordinate position of the white caste."[17] Does it follow from this charge, however, that "Southern whites [*all* Southern whites] bear collective responsibility?" I assume that ninety-nine percent of them, having been shaped by the prevailing mores, wholeheartedly approved of these brutalities. But what of the remaining tiny fraction? If they are to be held responsible, they must be so vicariously, on the ground of their strong (and hardly avoidable) solidarity with the majority. But suppose a few hated their Southern tradition, despised their neighbors, and did not think of themselves as Southerners at all? Then perhaps Macdonald's point can be saved by excluding these totally alienated souls altogether from the white Southern community to which Macdonald ascribes collective responsibility. But total alienation is not likely to be widely found in a community that leaves its exit doors open; and, in a community with as powerful social enforcement of mores as the traditional Southern one, the alienated resident would be in no happier a position than the Negro. Collective responsibility, therefore, might be ascribed to all those whites who were not outcasts, taking respectability and material comfort as evidence that a given person did not qualify for the exemption.

CONTRIBUTORY GROUP FAULT: COLLECTIVE BUT NOT DISTRIBUTIVE

There are some harms that are ascribable to group faults but not to the fault of every, or even *any,* individual member. Consider the case of the Jesse James train robbery. One armed man holds up an entire car full of passengers. If the passengers had risen up as one man and rushed at the robber, one or two of them, perhaps, would have been shot; but collectively they would have overwhelmed him, disarmed him, and saved their property. Yet they all meekly submitted. How responsible were they for their own losses? Not very. In a situation like this, only *heroes* could be expected to lead the self-sacrificial charge, so no individual in the group was at fault for not resisting. The whole group, however, had it within its power to resist successfully. Shall we say, then, that the group was collectively but not distributively at fault? Can the responsibility of a group be more than the sum of the responsibility of its members? There is surely a point in affirming so. There was, after all, a flaw in the way the group

of passengers was organized (or unorganized) that made the robbery possible. And the train robbery situation is a model for a thousand crises in the history of our corporate lives. No individual person can be blamed for not being a hero or a saint (what a strange "fault" that would be!), but a whole people can be blamed for not producing a hero when the times require it, especially when the failure can be charged to some discernible element in the group's "way of life" that militates against heroism.

One would think that, where group fault is nondistributive, group liability must be so too, lest it fall vicariously on individual members who are faultless. But, for all overt unfavorable responses, group liability is inevitably distributive: What harms the group as a whole necessarily harms its members. Hence if the conditions of justifiable collective liability—group solidarity, prior notice, opportunity for control, and so on—are not satisfied, group liability would seem unjustified.

An exception, however, is suggested by the case where an institutional group persists through changes of membership and faultless members must answer for harms caused, or commitments made, by an earlier generation of members. Commitments made in the name of an organized group may persist even after the composition of the group and its "will" change. When, nevertheless, the group reneges on a promise, the fault may be that of no individual member, yet the liability for breach of contract, falling on the group as a whole, will distribute burdens quite unavoidably on faultless members. Consider the philosophy department which debated whether to pass a graduate student on his preliminary examinations. The main argument against doing so was that passing him would commit the department to the supervision of the student's dissertation, and no one who knew this particular student was willing to read his thesis. The affirmative carried when two members volunteered to direct the dissertation themselves. One year later, however, one of these sponsors died, and the other took employment elsewhere. Thus *no member* was willing to supervise this student, and the department as a whole had to renege on its promise. No member felt personally bound by the promises of his departed colleagues, which had been made to the student in no one's name but the department's. No legal action, of course, was possible; but if the department had been *forced* to honor its word, this would have been an excellent example of nondistributive group fault (the departmental reneging) and consequent group liability of a necessarily distributive kind.

There is a different sense of "responsibility," and an important one, in which groups can be responsible collectively and distributively for traits (including faulty traits) in the group structure and history that can be ascribed to no given individual as their cause. Sigmund Freud[18] once raised the question whether individuals are "responsible" for their dreams and then astonishingly answered the question in the affirmative. Freud did not mean, however, that dreams are intentionally *acted out* or *caused* by the dreamer, or that they are, in any sense, the dreamer's *fault*, or that the dreamer is *liable* to censure or punishment or to self-directed remorse or guilt for them. What he did mean was that a person's dreams represent him faithfully in that they reveal in some fundamental way what sort of person he is. Freud was denying that dreams are "the meaningless product of disordered mental activity" or the work of "alien spirits." Rather, they have genuine psychological significance. Hence everyone must "take responsibility" for his dreams and not disown or repudiate them; and this is simply to "own up" to even the unpretty aspects of one's self as truly one's own.

Those who have read such works as Richard Hofstadter's *Paranoid Style in American Politics*[19] can hardly fail to be struck by the similarity between the social historian's revelations about the nation and the psychoanalyst's revelations about the individual. Both dredge up experiences from the past that are held to reveal persisting dispositions, trends, and "styles" of response that might otherwise be unknown to the subject. To deny the reality or significance of the child that still lives in the man, or of the early settlers whose imprint is still upon the nation, is to "deny responsibility" for traits that are truly one's own. When a nation's voices fail to acknowledge its own inherited character, the possibilities of understanding and rational control are just so far diminished, and the consequences for faultless individual citizens (as for the neurotically benighted individual in the other case) can be

devastating. But the responsibility I mention here is no kind of agency, causation, fault, or liability; it would less misleadingly, though somewhat awkwardly, be called "representational attributability."

NOTES

1. *Leviathan,* ed. Michael Oakeshott (Oxford: Basil Blackwell, 1946), Part 1, Ch. 16, 105.
2. *The Concept of Representation* (Berkeley and Los Angeles: University of California Press, 1967), 19.
3. *Ibid.,* 122.
4. *Leviathan,* Part 2, Ch. 18, 113.
5. The limits of "fictitious attribution" (the phrase is from Hobbes) are clearly marked out by A. Phillips Griffiths in "How Can One Person Represent Another?", *Proceedings of the Aristotelian Society,* Supp. 34 (1960), 187–224, and by Pitkin, *The Concept of Representation,* 49–54.
6. W. D. Falk, "Intention, Motive and Responsibility," *Proceedings of the Aristotelian Society,* Supp. 19 (1945), 249.
7. H. M. Lynd, *On Shame and the Search for Identity* (New York: Science Editions, 1961), 23.
8. I have been discussing guilt in the sense of one very special way of being *at fault.* Guilt, in this sense, is usually a necessary condition for guilt in a different sense, namely, that of "criminal liability." The model of guilt in the latter sense is the legal condition brought into existence by an authoritatively pronounced verdict in a criminal court. Guilt in this sense is analogous to the state of civil liability also created by authoritative judicial pronouncement as the end product of a civil suit. To be guilty in the sense of criminally liable is to be properly subject to the imposition of punitive sanctions, just as to be civilly liable is to be properly subject to legal pressure to make pecuniary compensation for harm. To call a man guilty of a crime is either to report that he has been authoritatively pronounced guilty or else to express one's own quite unofficial opinion that the conditions of criminal liability have in fact been satisfied so that an official verdict of "guilty" is or was called for.
Almost always in criminal law the *conditions* of criminal liability (that is, of "guilt" in one sense) include the requirement that the defendant intentionally acted (or omitted to act) in a way proscribed (or enjoined) by law (that is, that he was guilty in the other, "at fault" sense of "guilt"). But there is no conceptual necessity that intentional transgression be a condition of guilt (liability). There is no logical contradiction in the rule that permitted German citizens to be found "guilty" of having a Jewish grandparent, or in the rule that makes even bellhops guilty of "possessing" drugs when they carry a hotel guest's bags to his room, or in rules permitting the punishment of "criminal negligence," or in rules creating "strict liability" in criminal law. In Shirley Jackson's famous short story "The Lottery," the "winner" of an annual lottery is customarily stoned to death by his neighbors. The absurdity of calling the randomly selected sacrificial victim "guilty," I submit, is a moral, not a logical or conceptual absurdity. The condition of criminal liability in this case is not so much being at fault as being unlucky; but, in the sense of "guilt" under consideration, there is no contradiction in saying that a defendant was faultless but guilty nevertheless, providing he satisfied the conditions for liability specified by some rule. The only limit to the possibility of guilt in this sense is the requirement that there be *some conditions or other* for guilt; but the conditions need not include any kind of fault.
9. "Collective Responsibility," *Philosophy,* 23 (1948), 7.

10. *Ibid.*, 8.

11. L. T. Hobhouse, *Morals in Evolution* (London: Chapman & Hall, 1951), 81.

12. S. B. Chrimes, *English Constitutional History* (London: Oxford University Press, 1953), 77.

13. "Individual, Collective, and Social Responsibility," *Ethics,* 69 (1943), 342.

14. "An inciter . . . is one who, with *mens rea*, aids, counsels, commands, procures, or encourages another to commit a crime, or with *mens rea*, supplies him with the weapons, tools, or information needed for his criminal purpose." Rollin

M. Perkins, *Criminal Law* (Brooklyn: The Foundation Press, 1957), 558.

15. *Memoirs of a Revolutionist* (New York: Meridian, 1958), 45.

16. *Loc.cit.* (written in 1945).

17. John Dollard, *Caste and Class in a Southern Town,* as quoted *ibid.,* 45.

18. See *The Collected Papers of Sigmund Freud,* ed. Philip Rieff, BS 189 V, *Therapy and Technique* (New York: Collier Books, 1963), 223–226.

19. (New York: Alfred A. Knopf, 1965.)

A. M. HONORÉ

Law, Morals and Rescue*

A woman, viciously attacked, lies bleeding in the street. Fifty people pass by on the other side. A man destroys his barn to prevent a fire spreading to his neighbor's property. The neighbor refuses to compensate him. A young potholer foolishly becomes trapped below ground. A more experienced man, coming to his aid, breaks a leg. When we contemplate facts such as these, three questions seem to confront us concerning law, morals, and their interrelation. The first is about the shared morality of our society. Is there in modern industrial society, which is the only one most of us know, a shared attitude of praise or condemnation, encouragement, or dissuasion about helping those in peril? If so, two further points arise. Should the law, with its mechanisms of inducement, rewards, and compensation, be used to encourage what the shared morality treats as laudable and discourage what it reprobates? Should the law, thirdly, go further and, by the use of threats and penalties, "enforce" morality, as

the saying goes? These, it seems, are the main issues. In part they concern matters which, in England at least, have lately stirred up a passionate debate.[1] is it justifiable to use the mechanism of criminal law to "enforce" the shared morality, for instance in matters of sex? Greeks and Trojans have sallied forth and the clash of arms has rung out. Our concern, however, is with something wider and different: not sex, not only "enforcement," not only crime. I shall have a word, later on, to say in criticism of the use of the word "enforce" in this context. If we pass it for the moment, it yet remains true that "enforcement" is only part of what the law can do in the Good Samaritan situation. Apart from criminal sanctions, the law can encourage or discourage compliance with the shared morality by the use of techniques drawn from tort, contract, and restitution. Even "enforcement" is not confined to criminal law, because tort law, too, can be used to impose an obligation to aid others.

Our concern is not only wider but different from that of the jurists by whose brilliant and elevated jousting we have been entertained. They have debated whether some parts of the law which coincide with common morality should be

*"Law, Morals and Rescue," by Antony M. Honoré, from the book *The Good Samaritan and The Law,* ed. by James M. Ratcliffe (New York: Doubleday & Co., Inc., 1966), pp. 225–42, copyright © 1966 by James M. Ratcliffe. Reprinted by permission of Doubleday & Company, Inc.

scrapped. We, on the other hand, wish to know whether parts of morality, at present outside the law, should be incorporated in it. (I mean here Anglo-American law and not those systems in which this has already come about.) Some people feel that the intrusion of law into the private sphere of sex is indecent and outrageous. Others feel outraged by the failure of the law to intrude in relation to rescue and rescuers. Is the refusal to "enforce" the moral obligation to help others itself a moral offense, of which lawyers and legislators have been guilty in the English-speaking world this hundred years? Does the affront of this refusal bring the law and lawyers into disrepute? Should the law encourage or even insist on Do-Goodery? Or would this be an intrusion into yet another private sphere, not of sex, but of conscience?

Clearly we have a moral issue on our hands, and one which is concerned not with the "enforcement" of morals but with its nonenforcement. A number of writers, following Bentham[2] and Mill,[3] have advocated a legal obligation to rescue. Ames[4] and Bohlen[5] put forward an earnest plea to the same effect. But, though they mentioned, they did not closely analyze the moral issues. It is with these that I shall be principally concerned.

I THE SHARED MORALITY IN MATTERS OF RESCUE

An essential preliminary to the survey of the larger vistas of law and morals is to clear our minds about our moral views in the matter of aid to those in peril. By "our moral views" I mean the shared or common morality. Obviously this is not the same as the statement of what people actually do in a given society—the common practice of mankind. Their actions may fall short of their moral ideals and pretensions. Nor is it the same as that which an individual may accept for himself as morally obligatory. There is a distinction between that which the individual accepts for himself and that which he regards as being of general application. A man may think he has higher ideals, a stricter sense of obligation or duty, than the ordinary run of men could well be expected to entertain. This cherished personal morality, it seems to me, is no part or ingredient of the shared morality, though it may come, in

time, to spread to others and so to influence the shared morality.

The shared morality consists, rather, of those moral ideals and duties or obligations which the bulk of the community regard as applying to persons generally. But is the notion, defined, anything more than a figment? Ought we to refrain from speculating about its content until social surveys have determined whether it really exists? I think one must frankly concede that the results of properly conducted surveys would be far more authoritative than the guesses of moralists or lawyers. The survey which Messrs. Cohen, Robson, and Bates sought to ascertain the moral sense of the Nebraska community on parent-child relations[6] is, no doubt, a forerunner of what will, in time, become common practice. The shared morality of which I am speaking is not, however, quite what the Nebraska inquiry was attempting to ascertain. In that inquiry "community values" were defined as the "choices, expressed verbally, which members of the community feel the law-making authorities ought to make if confronted with alternative courses of action in specified circumstances."[7] These choices surely represent opinion as to legislation on moral issues rather than the shared morality itself. They tell us what people think legislators should do, not what they think ordinary citizens should do. No doubt there is a close, even a very close, connection between the two. Our view of what the law should be will be powerfully shaped by our notions of right and wrong, of what is desirable and what objectionable, but surely the two cannot without more be identified? It must a priori be an open question whether people who share moral ideas also think that these should be mirrored in the law. If they do, that is also a fact susceptible of and demanding confirmation by a properly conducted survey.

It remains doubtful, therefore, whether a suitable technique has yet been evolved for testing the existence and content of the shared morality of a community. Certainly the results are not yet to hand in a usable form. In the meantime, life does not stand still. Decisions must be reached with the aid of such information and intuition as we may possess. We cannot shirk the question of what our shared morality says about rescues and rescuers on the excuse that one day, we hope, a truly reliable answer will be available.

It is unwise in thinking about the shared morality to treat morality as an undifferentiated mass. For instance, there is a distinction between moral ideals and moral duties.[8] This is not the same as the previous distinction between a man's personal morality and the morality which he regards as of general application. Of course, a connection exists. A person may accept as an obligation for himself what he thinks of merely as an ideal for others. Broadly speaking, moral ideals concern patterns of conduct which are admired but not required. To live up to them is praiseworthy but not exigible. Moral duties, on the other hand, concern conduct which is required but not admired. With an important exception, to which I shall come, merely to do one's duty evokes no comment. Moral duties are pitched at a point where the conformity of the ordinary man can reasonably be expected. As a corollary, while it is tolerable, if deplorable, to fall short of the highest ideals, it is not permissible to neglect one's duties.

Certain virtues, notably altruism and generosity, depend on absence of obligation. It is not altruistic to pay one's debts, or generous to support one's parents (in the latter case the duty may in Anglo-American law be merely moral, but this makes no difference). Other virtues seem to hover between the status of ideals and duties. Is this, perhaps, true of the "neighborliness" which the parable of the Good Samaritan is meant both to illustrate and to inculcate? According to Matthew[9] and Mark,[10] the precept "love your neighbor as yourself" expresses a "commandment" and presumably imposes an obligation. Luke,[11] in contrast, treats it as pointing the way to perfection or "eternal life," a moral ideal. It may be that giving aid to those in peril is sometimes an ideal, sometimes a duty. At least three situations demand separate treatment:

1   The first is the rescue undertaken by one who has a professional or quasi-professional duty to undertake rescues. A fireman or life-saver is a professional rescuer. Doctors, nurses, and other members of the medical profession have a duty to save life, which, at times, demands that they should give help in an emergency. A priest must comfort the dying, a policeman must stop acts of violence. Besides these true professionals, there are what one may call devoted amateurs; for instance, experienced mountaineers or potholers, who hold themselves out as ready to effect rescues and, I am told, often welcome the chance to display their skills. Strictly speaking, none of these are "volunteers." They are only doing what they are bound by their calling or public profession to do. A doctor is not praised for coming promptly to the scene of an accident; that is only what we expect. He would be blamed if he delayed or refused to come. But this morally neutral reaction is appropriate only when the rescuer acts without risk or serious inconvenience to himself. If the fireman, policeman, or life-saver risks life or limb to help the imperiled, he deserves and receives praise, because there is an element of self-sacrifice or even heroism in his conduct, though what he does is clearly his duty. Heroism and self-sacrifice, unlike altruism, can be evinced both by those who do their duty and those who have no duty to do.

2   The second is the rescue undertaken by one who has special ties with the person imperiled. Family links, employment, and other associative ties may generate a duty to come to the help of a class of persons more limited than those whom the professional or professed rescuer is bound to assist. It is a parent's duty to snatch his child from the path of an oncoming automobile, an employer's to rescue the workman who has been trapped in the factory machine. It may well be their duty to risk their own safety should that prove necessary. Like the professional rescuer, they can expect no encomium merely for helping, but if they risk themselves they merit commendation.

3   The third situation is that of a person not bound by his profession or by special links with the person imperiled to come to his aid. Even in this case, common opinion would, perhaps, see a limited duty to assist when this is possible without risk or grave inconvenience to the rescuer. "It is undoubtedly the moral duty," an American judge has said, "of every person to extend to others assistance when in danger, to throw, for instance, a plank or rope to the drowning man or make other efforts for his rescue, and if such efforts should be omitted by anyone when they could be made without imperilling his own life, he would, by his conduct, draw upon himself the censure and reproach of good men."[12] Common humanity, then, forges between us a link, but a weak one. The duty stops short at the brink of

danger. Samaritans, it is held, must be good, but need not be moral athletes.

It is in this third situation alone, when the rescuer, bound by no professional duty or special tie to the person imperiled, exposes himself to danger, that we really call him a "volunteer." I appreciate that in Anglo-American law the notion of the "volunteer" has been at times twisted beyond recall. In order to deny the rescuer a remedy, the doctrine of voluntary assumption of risk has sometimes been extended to bar those who were merely doing their duty or responding to an appeal for help.[13] Conversely, in order to afford the rescuer a remedy, courts have at other times treated the altruist as if he were simply doing his plain duty and concluded that his action was a necessary consequence of the hazard and so of the fault of the person who created it.[14] But this is just legal fiction.

If this moral morphology is reasonably accurate, we have four types of rescuer and nonrescuer to contend with. The first is the priest or Levite who passes by on the other side. The second, in ascending order of excellence, is the man who does no more than he is bound to do, whether his duty arises from his profession, from some special link with the person imperiled, or from common humanity. The third is he who, in doing his duty, exposes himself to risk: possibly a hero. The fourth is the true volunteer altruistically exposing himself to danger to help those to whom he is bound by no special tie: perhaps a hero, too.

What should the law have to say to them?

II   THE MYTH OF NONINTERVENTION

First, should the law encourage or discourage the rescuer, or should it remain neutral? Members of my generation remember nonintervention as the name of a policy which, during the Spanish Civil War, ensured the victory of the side which cheated most. It was called by Talleyrand a metaphysical conception, which means very much the same thing as intervention. So with the intervention of law in the sphere of morals. There is no neutrality. If the law does not encourage rescue, it is sure to discourage it. If it does not compensate, it will indirectly penalize. If the rescuer who suffers injury or incurs expense or simply expends his skill goes without compensation, the law, so far as it influences conduct at all, is discouraging rescue.

Perhaps one day sociology will devise means of discovering whether people are really influenced in what they do by the thought of legal remedies. In the meantime, it would be altogether too facile to assume that they are not. A doctor living near a dangerous crossroads is continually called to minister to the victims of the road. The injured are unconscious or, if conscious, are in no mood to contract or to fill in National Health cards. Will the doctor come more readily and care for them more thoroughly if he knows he will be paid? If so, he is a man, not an angel. A mountain guide with a hungry family is called to rescue a foolish climber trapped on the north face of the Eiger. Does anyone imagine him to be indifferent to the question how his family will be kept if he is killed?

The law cannot stay out of the fight and, if it cannot, there is surely a strong case for compensating the rescuer. To do so will be in the interests of those who might be saved. The community applauds the Good Samaritan. So the law, if it encourages rescue, is helping to satisfy the interests of individuals and the wants of the community. If we think of law as being, among other things, a social service designed to maximize welfare and happiness, this is exactly what the law ought to do. One department of the law's service to society will be its moral service, which it performs by encouraging with the appropriate technical remedies whatever is morally approved and discouraging what is condemned.

Unquestionably there are limits to this function of the law. I will deal with only three. The most obvious is the limit set by oppression. If the encouragement of the shared morality and the discouragement of its breach would be a hardship to some without sufficient corresponding benefit to them or to others, the law should not endorse it. The fact that racial prejudice is approved in a given community does not mean that the courts must hold leases to Negroes in white residential areas void. But the encouragement of rescue will oppress neither rescuer nor rescued. The rescued benefits from being saved, and even if he is compelled to compensate the rescuer he will be, by and large, better off. It is true that compensation may be burdensome and I should not care to argue that civil remedies are necessarily less harsh than punishment. If an uninsured person has to pay heavy damages, he is worse off than if he were fined, for the fine, unlike the damages, is geared to his means. But this fact depends on the rules about assessment of damages in Anglo-American law, and these might be changed. It would be no hardship to suggest that the rescuer should receive compensation, if necessary, from the person imperiled, in accordance with the latter's means: *in id quod facere potest,* as the Roman formula ran.

Another limit or supposed limit may be set by the principle that virtue should be its own reward. Strictly speaking, I doubt if this applies to proposals for compensation as opposed to rewards. Still, the doctor's claim to be paid for his ministrations to the unconscious victim of a road accident may be called a claim for reward. Would it be an inroad on his virtue that he was entitled to be paid? Surely the argument is obtuse. No one is compelled to claim a reward he does not want. The doctor, like the finder of lost property, can preserve immaculate his moral idealism if he wishes. No one can be compelled to be compensated.

A third limit concerns the border line between altruism and meddling. Of course we do not want our next-door neighbor to rescue the baby every time he screams or to interrupt our family quarrels. But this merely shows that the received morality draws the line at officiousness. The test of what is officious will usually be whether the intending rescuer would reasonably suppose that his help will be welcome. If the victim objects or would be expected to object, the rescuer should abstain. But this can hardly apply to those victims who are too young or too deranged to know their own interests, and one might justify the rescue of a person attempting suicide (in a jurisdiction in which suicide is not a crime) on the ground that those who attempt it often lack a settled determination in the matter.

The line will be difficult to draw exactly, but lawyers are professional line-drawers. The relevant factors are easy enough to list: the gravity of the peril, the chances of successful intervention, the attitude of the victim, and the likelihood that another better-qualified rescuer will act.

None of the three limits mentioned seems to alter the proposition that the law would be a poor thing if it did not in general encourage rescue.

The means available to do this are essentially the compensation of the rescuer for expenses and injury and the rewarding of his services. It is convenient to take these separately.

1   *Injury.* No immediate difficulty is felt if the rescuer is covered by a personal accident policy or an insurance scheme connected with his employment, as would usually be true of firemen and other professional rescuers. There will still remain the question whether the insurer should be entitled to shift the loss to the person responsible for the peril. Certainly it makes for simplicity if he cannot.

When there is no insurance cover the problem is: Where should the compensation come from? Most people would be inclined to place it in the first instance on the person through whose fault the peril arose, whether the person imperiled or another. In order to justify making the person imperiled liable when he had been at fault, Bohlen argued that the basis of liability was the tendency of the defendant's conduct to cause the rescuer to take the risk involved in the attempted rescue.[15] If "cause" is to be taken seriously, this suggests that the rescuer who acts under a sense of obligation would recover for his injury, while the pure altruist would not, because the latter's act is a fresh cause. Yet altruism is not less but more worthy of the law's encouragement than the conscientious performance of one's duty. If in *Carnea v. Buyea*[16] the plaintiff who snatched the defendant from the path of the runaway automobile had been unrelated to the defendant, could that reasonably have been a ground for denying him a recovery? Surely the remedy should not be confined to cases where the peril "causes" the rescue, but should extend to those in which it merely prompts the rescuer.

Other writers and courts rely on foreseeability as the ground of liability. This, too, is open to objection. Suppose an intrepid but foolhardy explorer is stranded in an area where rescue is atrociously difficult and rescuers scarce. By the heroism of a James Bond he is saved. Surely the fact that rescue could not be foreseen makes no difference to Bond's claim for compensation? Is not the real basis of liability the twofold fact that the person imperiled has created a risk from which he wishes to be saved (whether he thinks rescue likely or not) and that his peril has prompted another to come to his aid (whether it has "caused" him to do so or not).

I have been dealing with the rationale of the imperiled person's duty to compensate the rescuer when the former is at fault. Legally speaking, this is the case that has evoked discussion, because it said that the person in peril owes himself no duty. When the peril is created by a third person, the objection is inapplicable. If the third person is at fault, he should be liable to compensate the rescuer for the reasons already given. If no one is at fault, it still remains a question whether compensation should be payable by either the person imperiled or the state. A remedy against the innocent person in peril can be justified either, if he is saved, on the ground that he has benefited at the rescuer's expense and should not take the benefit without paying the cost of its procurement or (whether he is saved or not) on the ground of unauthorized agency. The guiding notion of this (the Roman *negotiorum gestio* and the French *gestion d'affaire*) is that the agent, acting without the principal's authority, nevertheless does what the principal might be presumed to want done, when it is impracticable to obtain his consent. (If there is actual consent, for instance, if the person in peril calls for help, so much the easier, legally speaking, to justify giving a remedy.)[17]

Anglo-American law, in contrast with civil systems, is impregnated with the maxim, "Mind your own business," though recently there have been signs of a change. If we outflank the maxim by asserting that, to a limited extent, the peril of one is the business of all, it seems fair to make the person imperiled, though free from fault, indemnify the rescuer albeit only so far as his means reasonably permit.

None of the headings so far mentioned may afford an adequate remedy to the rescuer. In that case a state compensation scheme might well fill the gap. If the state is to compensate the victims of crimes of violence, as is now done in England,[18] why not compensate the equal heroism of those who suffer injury in effecting rescues?

2 *Expenses.* In principle the same rules should apply to expenses incurred by the rescuer as to injuries received by him. Two points may be noted. One is that the expense of organizing a rescue may nowadays be enormous. Suppose the Air Force presents the lost mariner with a bill for gasoline, maintenance of aircraft, wages of crew, and so on, perhaps incurred over several days of search. The crushing liability must be mitigated by having regard for the mariner's probably slender means. The other point is that in Anglo-American law there is a traditional reluctance to grant tort actions for negligence when the loss suffered is merely pecuniary. The rescuer who incurs expense but suffers no physical injury may thus find the way barred. It seems that courts will have to extend the bounds of the tort of negligence and the law of restitution if adequate remedies are to be supplied without legislative intervention. These are already some signs that this is happening.[19]

3 *Rewards.* The moral objections to rewarding altruism, we saw, are misconceived. But is there a positive case to be made in favor of rewarding rescuers? In practice, outstanding acts of courage in effecting rescue are marked by the award of medals and decorations. Many persons saved from danger would think themselves morally bound to offer something to their rescuers. But a legal claim to be paid is usually voiced only by the professional rescuer, especially the self-employed, who may spend much time and energy in this way. Take our friend the doctor who lives near an accident black spot. It is mere fiction to say that the unconscious victim impliedly contracts to pay for treatment.[20] Two other theories are possible: one, that payment is less a true reward than compensation for loss of profitable time; the other, that the person in peril, if he could have been consulted, would have agreed to pay for the treatment because medical services are normally paid for. The second theory, unlike the first, has a narrow range, because it does not extend to a rescuer whose services are normally given free.

III   A LEGAL DUTY TO AID THOSE IN PERIL?

My third question raises an issue concerning what is usually called the "enforcement" of morals. The use of this word is, I think, apt to mislead. Literally speaking, the law cannot force citizens to do anything, but only to submit to deprivation of freedom, or to having their money taken from them. Even if "enforcement" is taken, as it normally is, in an extended sense, the notion that morality is enforced by law carries with it the false implication that it is not enforced apart from law. Yet the chief agent for enforcing morality is public opinion. If the approval or disapproval of family and friends is not visited on those who conform or rebel, the conduct in question is not part of the shared morality. Few people, I imagine, would rather incur the censure of family and friends than pay a sum of damages or a fine. This should lead us to suspect that the law, when it imposes a duty to do what the shared morality already requires, is not enforcing but *reflecting, reinforcing,* and *specifying* morality.

There are strong reasons, I think, why the law should reflect, reinforce, and specify, at least that segment of the shared morality which consists in moral duties owed to others. The first is the advantage to those who stand to benefit. It is true that legal incentives probably influence no more than a tiny minority, but they certainly influence some. A driver sees the victim of a highway accident bleeding by the roadside. He knows he ought to stop, but is tempted to drive on in order to keep an assignment. The thought that there is a law requiring him to stop may pull him up short.

Even if the impact of the law is confined to a few, there is a special reason for reinforcing the duty to aid persons in peril. Peril means danger of death or serious injury or, at the least, of grave damage to property. The more serious the harm to be averted, the more worthwhile it is to save even a handful of those who would otherwise suffer irretrievable injury or death.

Secondly, there are some reasons for holding that the law ought in general to mirror moral obligations. In doing so, it ministers to an expectation entertained by the majority of citizens. The lawyer is, perhaps, so used to rules which permit men to flout their moral duties that he is at times benumbed. Promises made without consideration are not binding. A promisor can normally not be compelled to perform his promise but only to pay damage. Children need not support their parents. Samaritans need not be good. When we first learned these rules in law school, I daresay we were a little shocked, but the shock has worn off. It has not worn off the layman.

There are several elements in the sense of shock which laymen feel at the permissive state of the law in regard to moral duties. First, there is the "sense of injustice" of which Edmund Cahn has spoken.[21] If the law permits others to do with impunity that which I am tempted to do, but resist, what is the point of my resistance to temptation? The moral-breaker, like the unpunished lawbreaker, secures an unjust advantage at my expense.

A second element in the layman's sense of shock is the feeling that the law, like an overpermissive father, has set its standard too low. Just as a child loses respect for a father who allows him to back out of his promises, so the community will fail to respect the law which does likewise. It is, I imagine, another of those indubitable and unprovable commonplaces which are the very meat of jurisprudence that people's attitudes to particular laws often depend on their reverence for the law as a whole. If so, the failure of the law to reflect and reinforce moral duties undermines other, quite distinct laws. It may not be sensible for people to think of law in this way as a single, personified whole, but apparently they do.

A third element in the layman's sense of shock is the feeling that the guiding hand has failed. People to some degree expect a lead from the law, not merely threats and incentives. Rules of law which mirror moral duties have, among other things, an educative function. They formulate, in a way which, though not infallible, is yet in a sense authoritative, the content of the shared morality. They specify morality by marking, with more precision than the diffused sense of the people can manage, the minimum that can be tolerated.

The law cannot make men good, but it can, in the sphere of duty at least, encourage and help them to do good. It not only can but should reinforce the sanctions of public opinion, for the reasons given, unless it would be oppressive or impracticable to do so. I need say little of the practicability of imposing a duty to aid those in peril. France, Germany, and other countries have tried it out and found that it works reasonably well. But would it be oppressive? The mere fact that the majority is shocked at certain conduct does not, in my view, justify them in imposing civil or criminal liability unless there is also a balance of advantage in doing so. Difficult as it may be to strike a balance, we have in the case of rescue to add to the evils of injustice, disrespect, and want of guidance (should the law impose no duty to act) the possible benefit of those in peril if such duty is imposed. Then we must subtract the hardship of making people conform to accepted standards of neighborliness or suffer penalties. If the balance is positive, the law not merely may, but should, intervene. It has been urged that there is something peculiarly irksome in requiring people to take positive action as opposed to subjecting them to mere prohibitions. Why this should be so is a mystery. Perhaps we have a picture of Joe lounging in an armchair. It is more effort for him to get up than to stay where he is. But this is not how the law operates. Prohibitions are usually imposed because there is a strong urge or temptation to disregard them. To control the violent impulses of our nature is surely more arduous than to overcome the temptation selfishly to leave others in the lurch. Certainly there are important spheres, for instance, taxation and military service, where the law does not shrink from demanding positive action. Why should it do so in the law of rescue?

If it is argued that to require aid to be given to those in peril saps the roots of altruism by diminishing the opportunities for its exercise, the reply would be that the proposal is merely to impose a legal duty in situations where morality already sees one. Those who go beyond their moral duty will also be going beyond their legal duty. They lose no occasion for displaying altruism, merely because the law reflects a situation which *de facto* already exists.

The apparent objections to the introduction of a legal duty to rescue hardly withstand scrutiny. Perhaps the most substantial of them, in Anglo-American law, is simply tradition. Self-reliance, the outlook epitomized in the words, "Thank you, Jack, I'm all right," an irrational conviction that because law and morals do not always coincide there is some virtue in their being different,[22] all combine to frustrate the promptings of moral sensibility. One cannot but sense in some judicial utterances a certain pride in the irrational, incalculable depravity of the law, as if this demonstrated its status as an esoteric science, inaccessible to the common run of mankind. As the Russians said of Stalin: a monster, but ours. I will quote one or two.

"The only duty arising under such circumstance [that is, when one's employee catches her hand and wrist in a mangle] is one of humanity and for a breach thereof the law does not, so far as we are informed, impose any liability."[23]

Hence, there is no need to help her to free her hand. "With purely moral obligations the law does not deal. For example, the priest and the Levite who passed by on the other side were not, it is supposed, liable at law for the continued suffering of the man who fell among thieves, which they might and morally ought to have prevented or relieved."[24] In the case from which the quotation is taken, it was held to be no legal wrong for a mill owner to allow a boy of eight to meddle with dangerous machinery, in which his hand was crushed. Indeed, the boy was guilty of committing a trespass when he touched the machinery.

Two thousand years ago a Jewish lawyer demanded a definition of the term "neighbor." This makes him, I suppose, an analytical jurist. Whether the tale of the Samaritan answered his perplexities we cannot say. But he would surely have been astonished had he been informed that there were two answers to his question, one if he was asking as a lawyer, another if he was asking as a layman. To him, neighbor was neighbor and duty, duty. Perhaps this ancient lawyer's tale has a moral for law and lawyers today.

NOTES

1. P. Devlin, *The Enforcement of Morals* (Maccabaean Lecture, 1958), reprinted in *The Enforcement of Morals* (Oxford U. P., 1965); W. Friedmann in 4 *Natural Law Forum* (1964), 151; H. L. A. Hart, *Law, Liberty and Morality* (Oxford U. P., 1963); L. Henkin in 63 *Col. L. Rev.* (1963) 393; G. Hughes in 71 *Yale L. J.* (1961) 622; M. Ginsberg in 1964 *British Journal of Criminology*, 283; A. W. Mewett in 14 *Toronto L. J.* (1962) 213; E. Rostow in 1960 *Cambridge L. J.* 174 reprinted in *The Sovereign Prerogative* (Yale U. P., 1962); N. St. John-Stevas, *Life, Death and the Law* (1961); R. S. Summers in 38 *New York U. L. Rev.* (1963), 1201; B. Wootton, *Crime and the Criminal Law* (Stevens, 1963), 41.

2. J. Bentham, *Principles of Morals and Legislation,* 323 ("Who is there that in any of these cases would think punishment misapplied?").

3. J. S. Mill, *On Liberty,* Introduction ("There are also many positive acts for the benefit of others, which he may rightfully be compelled to perform . . . such as saving a fellow-creature's life").

4. J. B. Ames, *Law and Morals, supra,* pp. 1–21.

5. F. Bohlen, *The Moral Duty to Aid Others As a Basis of Liability, 56 U. Pa. L. Rev.* (1908) 215, 316.

6. J. Cohen, R. A. H. Robson, and A. Bates, *Ascertaining the Moral Sense of the Community,* 8 *Journal of Legal Education* (1955–56) 137.

7. *Ibid.*

8. E. Cahn, *The Moral Decision* (1956), 39.

9. Matthew 22:34.

10. Mark 12:28.

11. Luke 10:25.

12. U.S. v. Knowles (1864) 26 Fed. Cas. 801.

13. Cutler v. United Dairies (1933) 2 K.B. 297.

14. Pollock, *Torts* (15th ed.), 370; Haynes v. Harwood (1953) 1 K.B. at 163; Morgan v. Aylen (1942)1 All E.R. 489; Baker v. Hopkins (1959) 1 W.L.R. 966.

15. F. Bohlen, *Studies in the Law of Tort,* 569 n. 33.

16. 271 App. Div. 338. 65 N.Y.S. 2d 902 (1946).

17. Brugh v. Bigelow (1944) 16 N.Y.S. 2d 902 (1946).

18. Assessed by the Criminal Injuries Compensation Board (1964).

19. Hadley Byrne v. Heller (1964) A.C. 465.

20. Cotnam v. Wisdom 83 Ark. 601, 104 S.W. 164. 119 Am. St. R. 157 (1907); Greenspan v. Slate 12 N.J. 426, 97 Atl. 2d 390 (1953).

21. E. Cahn, *The Sense of Injustice* (1949); *The Moral Decision* (1956).

22. Historicus (Sir W. Harcourt), *Some Questions of International Law* (1863), 76, cited in R. Pound, *Law and Morals* (1924), 40. The argument that there is value in moral experiments does not apply to experiments in leaving others in the lurch.

23. Allen v. Hixson 36 S.E. 810 (1900).

24. Buch v. Amory Manufacturing Co. 69 N.H. 247; 44 Atl. 809 (1897).

P E O P L E v. Y O U N G

Appellate Division, New York Supreme Court, 1961*

BREITEL, Justice.

The question is whether one is criminally liable for assault in the third degree if he goes to the aid of another who he mistakenly, but reasonably, believes is being unlawfully beaten, and thereby injures one of the apparent assaulters. In truth, the seeming victim was being lawfully arrested by two police officers in plain clothes. Defendant stands convicted of such a criminal assault, for which he received a sentence of 60 days in the workhouse, the execution of such sentence being suspended.

Defendant, aged 40, regularly employed, and with a clean record except for an $8 fine in connection with a disorderly conduct charge 19 years before in Birmingham, Alabama, observed two middle-aged men beating and struggling with a youth of 18. This was at 3:40 P.M. on October 17, 1958 in front of 64 West 64th Street in Manhattan. Defendant was acquainted with none of the persons involved; but believing that the youth was being unlawfully assaulted, and this is not disputed by the other participants, defendant went to his rescue, pulling on or punching at the seeming assailants. In the ensuing affray one of the older men got his leg locked with that of defendant and when defendant fell the man's leg was broken at the kneecap. The injured man then pulled out a revolver, announced to the defendant that he was a police officer, and that defendant was under arrest. It appears that the youth in question had played some part in a street incident which resulted in the two men, who were detectives in plain clothes, seeking to arrest him for disorderly conduct. The youth had resisted, and it was in the midst of this resistance that defendant came upon the scene.

At the trial the defendant testified that he had known nothing about what had happened before he came upon the scene; that he had gone to his aid because the youth was crying and trying to pull away from the middle-aged men; and that the older men had almost pulled the trousers off the youth. The only detective who testified states, in response to a question from the court, that defendant did not know and had no way of knowing, so far as he knew, that they were police officers or that they were making an arrest.

Two things are to be kept sharply in mind in considering the problem at hand. The first is that all that is involved here is a criminal prosecution for simple assault (Penal Law, § 244), and that the court is not concerned with the incidence of civil liability in the law of torts as a result of what happened on the street. Second, there is not here involved any question of criminal responsibility for interfering with an arrest where it is known to the actor that police officers are making an arrest, but he mistakenly believes that the arrest is unlawful.

*210 N.Y.S. 2d 358 (1961)

Assault and battery is an ancient crime cognizable at the common law. It is a crime in which an essential element is intent (1 Wharton's Crim.Law and Proc. [Anderson Ed. 1957] § 329 et seq.; 1 Russell on Crime [11th Ed.] p. 724). Of course, in this state the criminal law is entirely statutory. But, because assault and battery is a "common-law" crime, the statutory provisions, as in the case of most of the common-law crimes, do not purport to define the crime with the same particularity as those crimes which have a statutory origin initially (Penal Law, § 240 et seq.). One of the consequences, therefore, is that while the provisions governing assault, contained in the Penal Law, refer to various kinds of intent, in most instances the intent is related to a supplemental intent, in addition to the unspecified general intent to commit an assault, in order to impose more serious consequences upon the actor (for example, Penal Law § 240). In some instances, of course, the intent is spelled out to distinguish the prohibited activity from what might otherwise be an innocent act or merely an accidental wrong (for example, Penal Law § 242, subds. 1 and 2).

It is in this statutory context that it was held in People v. Katz, 290 N.Y. 361, 49 N.E.2d 482, that in order to sustain a charge of assault in the second degree, based upon the infliction of grievous bodily harm, not only must there be a general intent to commit unlawful bodily harm but there must be a ['specific intent", that is, a supplemental intent to inflict grievous bodily harm. The case therefore does provide an interesting parallel analysis forwarding the idea that assault is always an intent crime even when the statute omits to provide expressly for such general intent, as is the case with regard to assault in the third degree (Penal Law, § 244). Even Russell notes that, "It has been the general practice of the legislature to leave unexpressed some of the mental elements of crime" (op. cit., p. 74).

With respect to intent crimes, under general principles, a mistake of fact relates as a defense to an essential element of the crime, namely, to the *mens rea* (1 Wharton, op. cit., § 157; 1 Russell, op. cit., pp. 75–85). The development of the excuse of mistake is a relatively modern one and is of expanding growth (1 Bishop on Criminal Law [9th Ed.] p. 202, et seq., esp. the exhaustive and impassioned footnote which commences at p. 206 and continues through to p. 214; see, Shorter v. People, 2 N.Y. 193). But the defense was already on the march at the time of Blackstone (4 Blackstone, Comm. § 27, see esp. the footnote discussion to that section in the Jones Ed. [1916]). Russell, supra, details the tortuous development of the defense and the long road travelled between treating it as a species of involuntary conduct until it was finally recognized as a negation of criminal intent, thus ranging from the older view that criminal liability should depend upon "objective moral guilt", rather than, as in the modern thinking, upon subjective intent, that is, *mens rea*.

Mistake of fact, under our statutes, is a species of excuse rather than a matter of justification. Consequently, reliance on section 42[1] of the Penal Law which relates exclusively to justification is misplaced. Section 42 would be applicable only to justify a third party's intervention on behalf of a victim of an unlawful assault, but this does not preclude the defense of mistake which is related to subjective intent rather than to the objective ground for action. It is interesting that in tort at the common law excuse was provable under the general issue while justification must have been specially pleaded (1 Bacon, Abr. [1868] tit. Assault and Battery [C] p. 374). While the distinctions between excuse and justification are often fuzzy, and more often fudged, in the instance of section 42 its limited application is clear from its language.

It is in the homicide statutes in which the occasions for excuse or justification are made somewhat clearer (see Penal Law, §§ 1054, 1055); but the distinction is still relevant with respect to most crimes. In homicide it is made explicitly plain that the actor's state of mind, if reasonable, is material and controlling (id. § 1055, penult. par. 1). It does not seem rational that the same reasonable misapprehension of fact should excuse a killing in seeming proper defense of a third person in one's presence but that it should not excuse a lesser personal injury.

In this State there are no discoverable precedents involving mistake of fact when one intervenes on behalf of another person and the prosecution has been for assault, rather than homicide. (The absence of precedents in this state and many others may simply mean that no enforcement agency would prosecute in the situations that must have occurred.) No one would dispute, however, that a mistake of fact would provide a defense if the prosecution were for homicide. This divided approach is sometimes based on the untenable distinction that mistake of fact may negative a "specific" intent required in the degrees of homicide but is irrelevant to the general intent required in simple assault, or, on the even less likely distinction, that the only intent involved in assault is the intent to touch without consent or legal justification (omitting the qualification of unlawfulness). The last, of course, is a partial confusion of tort law with criminal law, and even then is not quite correct (Restatement, Torts, §§ 63–75).

There have been precedents elsewhere among the states (6 C.J.S. Assault and Battery § 93; Am.Dig. System: Assault and Battery [Century Ed.], § 98 [Dec. Dig.] § 68). There is a split among the cases and in the jurisdictions. Most hold that the rescuer intervenes at his own peril (for example, State v. Ronnie, 41 N.J.Super. 339, 125 A.2d 163; Commonwealth v. Hounchell, 280 Ky. 217, 132 S.W.2d 921), but others hold that he is excused if he acts under mistaken but reasonable belief that he is protecting a victim from unlawful attack (for example, Kees v. State, 44 Tex.Cr.R. 543, 72 S.W. 855; Little v. State, 61 Tex.Cr.R. 197, 135 S.W. 119; Brannin v. State, 221 Ind. 123, 46 N.E.2d 599; State v. Mounkes, 88 Kan. 193, 127 P. 637). Many of the cases which hold that the actor proceeds at his peril involve situations where the actor was present throughout, or through most, or through enough of the transaction and, therefore, was in no position to claim a mistake of fact. Others arise in rough situations in which the feud or enmity generally to the peace officer is a significant factor. Almost all apply unanalytically the rubric that the right to intervene on behalf of another is no greater than the other's right to self-defense, a phrasing of ancient but questionable lineage going back to when crime and tort were not yet divided in the common law—indeed, when the right to private redress was not easily distinguishable from the sanction for the public wrong (Russell, op. cit., p. 20, et seq.).

It would protract the discussion and be bootless to detail all the cases, or even to make further illustrative selection. In England, however, it is interesting to observe, a defendant who intervened mistakenly in a proper arrest by peace officers has been held liable, not for assault, but under a specific statute related to police officers acting in the execution of their duty, and which, the courts construed, did not require knowledge on the part of the third party in order to make him responsible (Regina v. Forbes and Webb [1865] 10 Cox C.C. 362; Rex v. Maxwell and Clinchy [1909] 73 J.P. 77, 2 C.R.App. Rep.26 C.C.A.; 1 Russell, op. cit., pp. 764–766). Of course, in this state, too, there is an express crime for interfering with a lawful arrest (Penal Law, § 242, subd. 5). It is a felony and requires a "specific" intent to resist the lawful apprehension. So that here we have rejected the policy adopted in England expressly making innocent interference with a lawful arrest a crime.

The modern view, as already noted, is not to impose criminal responsibility in connection with intent crimes for those who act with good motivation, in mistaken but reasonable misapprehension of the facts. Indeed, Prosser would not even hold such a person responsible in tort (Torts [2d Ed.] pp. 91–92). He makes the added argument that "if an honest mistake is to relieve the defendant of liability when he thinks that he must defend himself, his meritorious defense of another should receive the same consideration." (Restatement, Torts, supra, § 76, also exculpates an actor for intervention on behalf of a third person where the actor has a reasonable belief that the third person is privileged and that such intervention is necessary. No-

tably, the Restatement sharply limits the persons on whose behalf the actor may intervene, but this, of course, is in the area of civil liability and, as already noted, there are those who would extend the privilege.)[2]

More recently in the field of criminal law the American Law Institute in drafting a model penal code has concerned itself with the question in this case. Under section 3.05 of the Model Penal Code the use of force for the protection of others is excused if the actor behaves under a mistaken belief (Model Penal Code, Tent.Draft No. 8, May 9, 1958.)[3]

The comments by the reporters on the Model Penal Code are quite appropriate. After stating that the defense of strangers should be assimilated to the defense of oneself the following is said:

"In support of such a ruling, it may perhaps be said that the potentiality for deterring the actor from the use of force is greater where he is protecting a stranger than where he is protecting himself or a loved one, because in the former case the interest protected is of relatively less importance to him; moreover the potential incidence of mistake in estimating fault or the need for action on his part is increased where the defendant is protecting a stranger, because in such circumstances he is less likely to know which party to the quarrel is in the right. These arguments may be said to lead to the conclusion that, in order to minimize the area for error or mistake, the defendant should act at his peril when he is protecting a stranger. This emasculates the privilege of protection of much of its content, introducing a liability without fault which is indefensible in principle. The cautious potential actor who knows the law will, in the vast majority of cases, refrain from acting at all. The result may well be that an innocent person is injured without receiving assistance from bystanders. It seems far preferable, therefore, to predicate the justification upon the actor's belief, safeguarding if thought necessary against abuse of the privilege by the imposition of a requirement of proper care in evolving the belief. Here, as elsewhere, the latter problem is dealt with by the general provision in Section 3.09." (Model Penal Code, Tent.Draft No. 8, supra, at p. 32.)[4]

Apart from history, precedents, and the language distinctions that may be found in the statutes, it stands to reason that a man should not be punished criminally for an intent crime unless he, indeed, has the intent. Where a mistake of relevant facts is involved the premises for such intent are absent. True, there are occasions in public policy and its implementation for dispensing with intent and making one responsible for one's act even without immediate or intentional fault. This is generally accomplished by statute, and generally by statute which expressly dispenses with the presence of intent. Thus, it may well be that a Legislature determine that in order to protect the police in their activities and to make it difficult to promote false defenses one may proceed against a police officer while acting in the line of duty only at one's peril, as do the English, *vide* supra. But this is not a part of the intent crime of assault as it existed under common law or as it exists today under the statutes.

Indeed, if the analysis were otherwise, then the conductor who mistakenly ejects a passenger for not having paid his fare would be guilty of assault, which is hardly the case (1 Bishop, op. cit., pp. 202–203). So, too, a police officer who came to the assistance of a brother police officer would be guilty of assault if it should turn out that the brother police officer was engaged in making an unlawful arrest or was embarked upon an assault of his own private motivation (cf. Reeves v. State, Tex.Cr. App., 217 S.W. 2d 19).

It is a sterile and desolate legal system that would exact punishment for an intentional assault from one like this defendant, who acted from the most commendable motives and without excessive force. Had the facts been as he thought them, he would have been a hero and not condemned as a criminal actor. The dearth of applicable precedents—as distinguished from theoretical generalizations never, or rarely, applied—in England and in most of the states demonstrates that the benevolent intervenor has not been cast as a pariah. It is no answer to say that the policeman should be called when one sees an injustice. Even in the most populous centers, policemen are not that common or that available. Also, it ignores the peremptory response to injustice that the good man has ingrained. Again, it is to be noted, in a criminal proceeding one is concerned with the act against society, not with the wrong between individuals and the right to reparation, which is the province of tort.

Accordingly, the judgment of conviction should be reversed, on the law, and the information dismissed.

Judgment of conviction reversed upon the law and the information dismissed. All concur except VALENTE and EAGER, JJ., who dissent and vote to affirm in a dissenting opinion by VALENTE, J. Order filed.

VALENTE, Justice (dissenting).

We are concerned on this appeal with a judgment convicting defendant of the crime of assault in the third degree in violation of Section 244, subd. 1, of the Penal Law. The defendant assaulted a plain-clothes police officer, while the latter was attempting to effect a lawful and proper arrest of another. We are to determine whether the defendant's ignorance of the officer's police status and his erroneous belief that the detective was a civilian committing an unjustified assault upon the other person—who was a complete stranger to the defendant—excuses the crime. The majority of the Court, in reversing the judgment of conviction, holds that defendant's mistake removes the element of intent necessary for a criminal act.

I dissent and would affirm the conviction because the intent to commit a battery was unquestionably proven; and, since there was no relationship between defendant and the person whom the police officers were arresting, defendant acted at his peril in intervening and striking the officer. Under well-established law, defendant's rights were no greater than those of the person whom he sought to protect; and since the arrest was lawful, defendant was no more privileged to assault the police officer than the person being arrested.

Under our statutes a *specific* intent is necessary for the crimes of assault in the first and second degrees (Sections 240 and 242 of the Penal Law). See People v. Katz, 290 N.Y. 361, 49 N.E. 2d 482. Generally, the assaults contemplated by those sections were known as "aggravated" assaults under the common law. (1 Wharton's Crim.Law & Prac. [Anderson Ed. 1957] § 358.) However, assault in the third degree is defined by Section 244, subd. 1, of the Penal Law as an assault and battery not such as is specified in Sections 240 and 242. No specific intent is required under Section 244. All that is required is the knowledgeable doing of the act. "It is sufficient that the defendant voluntarily intended to commit the unlawful act of touching" (1 Wharton's op. cit. § 338, p. 685).

In the instant case, had the defendant assaulted the officer with the specific intent of preventing the lawful apprehension of the other person he would have been subject to indictment under the provisions of subdivision 5 of Section 242 of the Penal Law, which constitutes such an act assault in the second degree. But the inability to prove a specific intent does not preclude the People from establishing the lesser crime of assault in the third degree which requires proof only of the general intent "to commit the unlawful act of touching", if such exists.

There is evidently no New York law on the precise issue on this appeal. However, certain of our statutes point to the proper direction for solution of the problem. Section 42 of the Penal Law provides:

"An act, otherwise criminal, is justifiable when it is done to protect the person committing it, or another whom he is bound to protect, from inevitable and irreparable personal injury. . . ."

Similarly, Section 246, so far as here pertinent, provides:

"To use or attempt, or offer to use, force or violence upon or towards the person of another is not unlawful in the following cases:
. . . .
"3. When committed either by the party about to be injured or by another person in his aid or defense, in preventing or attempting to prevent an offense against his person, or a trespass or other unlawful interference with real or personal property in his lawful possession, if the force or violence used is not more than sufficient to prevent such offense".

These statutes represent the public policy of this State regarding the areas in which an assault will be excused or rendered "not unlawful" where one goes to the assistance of another. They include only those cases in which the other person is one whom the defendant "is bound to protect" (Sec. 42) or where the defendant is "preventing or attempting to prevent an offense against" such other person (Sec. 246). Neither statute applies to the instant case since the other person herein was one unlawfully resisting a legal arrest—and hence no offense was being committed against his person by the officer—and he was not an individual whom defendant was "bound to protect".

It has been held in other states that one who goes to the aid of a third person acts at his peril, and his rights to interfere do not exceed the rights of the person whom he seeks to protect. State v. Ronnie, 41 N.J. Super. 339, 125 A.2d 163; Griffin v. State, 229 Ala. 482, 158 So. 316; Commonwealth v. Hounchell, 280 Ky. 217, 132 S.W.2d 921; 6 C.J.S. Assault and Battery, § 93, p. 950; 1 Wharton's op. cit., § 352; 4 Am. Jur. Assault and Battery, § 54, p. 155. We need not consider to what extent that rule is modified by Section 42 of the Penal Law since there is no question here but that the person being arrested was not in any special relation to defendant so that he was a person whom defendant was "bound to protect". It follows then that there being no right on the part of the person, to whose aid defendant came, to assault the officer—the arrest being legal—defendant had no greater right or privilege to assault the officer.

The conclusion that defendant was properly convicted in this case comports with sound public policy. It would be a dangerous precedent for courts to announce that plain-clothes police officers attempting lawful arrests over wrongful resistance are subject to violent interference by strangers ignorant of the facts, who may attack the officers with impunity so long as their ignorance forms a reasonable basis for a snap judgment of the situation unfavorable to the officers. Although the actions of such a defendant, who acts on appearances, may eliminate the specific intent required to convict him of a felony assault, it should not exculpate him from the act of aggressive assistance to a law breaker in the process of wrongfully resisting a proper arrest.

I do not detract from the majority's views regarding commendation of the acts of a good Samaritan, although it may be difficult in some cases to distinguish such activities from those of an officious intermeddler. But opposed to the encouragement of the "benevolent intervenor" is the conflicting and more compelling interest of protection of police officers. In a city like New York, where it becomes necessary to utilize the services of a great number of plain-clothes officers, the efficacy of their continuing struggle against crime should not be impaired by the possibility of interference by citizens who may be acting from commendable motives. It is more desirable—and evidently up to this point the Legislature has so deemed it—that in such cases the intervening citizen be held to act at his peril when he assaults a stranger, who unknown to him is a police officer legally performing his duty. In this conflict of interests, the balance preponderates in favor of the protection of the police rather than the misguided intervenor.

The majority points to the recommendations of the American Law Institute in drafting a Model Penal Code which makes the use of force justifiable to protect a third person when the actor believes his intervention is necessary for the protection of such third person (Model Penal Code, Tent. Draft No. 8, § 3.05 [1(c)], p. 30). Obviously these are recommendations which properly are to be addressed to a legislature and not to courts. The comments of the reporters on the Model Penal Code, from which the majority quotes, indicate (p. 31) that in the United States the view is preserved in much state legislation that force may not be used to defend others unless they stand in a special relationship to their protector. The reporters state: "The simple solution of the whole problem is to assimilate the defense of strangers to the defense of oneself, and this the present section does". If this be so, then even under the Model Penal Code, since the stranger, who is being lawfully arrested, may not assault the officers a third person coming to his defense may not do so. In any event, the Model Penal Code recognizes that the law as it now stands requires the conviction of the defendant herein. Until the Legislature acts, the courts should adhere to the well-established rules applicable in such cases. Such adherence demands the affirmance of the conviction herein.

NOTES

1. The section reads as follows:

"§ 42. Rule when act done in defense of self or another

"An act, otherwise criminal, is justifiable when it is done to protect the person committing it, or another whom he is bound to protect, from inevitable and irreparable personal injury, and the injury could only be prevented by the act, nothing more being done than is necessary to prevent the injury."

2. It is interesting that Dean Prosser is now the Chief Reporter for the American Law Institute in the draft of Restatement, Torts, Second. Tentative Draft No. 1 [April 5, 1957] of Restatement, Torts, Second, deletes the limitations to section 76 restricting intervention on behalf of strangers. And in the comments it is stated, "There is no modern case holding that there is no privilege to defend a stranger."

3. The full text of subdivision 1 of section 3.05 reads as follows:

"*Section 3.05. Use of Force for the Protection of Other Persons.*

"(1) The use of force upon or toward the person of another is justifiable to protect a third person when:

"(a) the actor would be justified under Section 3.04 in using such force to protect himself against the injury he believes to be threatened to the person whom he seeks to protect; and

"(b) under the circumstances as the actor believes them to be, the person whom he seeks to protect would be justified in using such protective force; and

"(c) The actor believes that his intervention is necessary for the protection of such other person."

4. Equally valuable comments may be found at p. 17 of the same draft, and at p. 140 of Tent. Draft No. 4.

PEOPLE v. YOUNG

New York Court of Appeals, 1962*

Per Curiam. Whether one, who in good faith aggressively intervenes in a struggle between another person and a police officer in civilian dress attempting to effect the lawful arrest of the third person, may be properly convicted of assault in the third degree is a question of law of first impression here.

The opinions in the court below in the absence of precedents in this State carefully expound the opposing views found in other jurisdictions. The majority in the Appellate Division have adopted the minority rule in the other States that one who intervenes in a struggle between strangers under the mistaken but reasonable belief that he is protecting another who he assumes is being unlawfully beaten is thereby exonerated from criminal liability.* The weight of authority holds with the dissenters below that one who goes to the aid of a third person does so at his peril.*

While the doctrine espoused by the majority of the court below may have support in some States, we feel that such a policy would not be conducive to an orderly society. We agree with the settled policy of law in most jurisdictions that the right of a person to defend another ordinarily should not be greater than such person's right to defend himself. Subdivision 3 of section 246 of the Penal Law does not apply as no offense was being committed on the person of the one resisting the lawful arrest. Whatever may be the public policy where the felony charged requires proof of a specific intent and the issue is justifiable homicide, it is not relevant in a prosecution for assault in the third degree where it is only necessary to show that the defendant knowingly struck a blow.

In this case there can be no doubt that the defendant intended to assault the police officer in civilian dress. The resulting assault was forceful. Hence motive or mistake of fact is of no significance as the defendant was not charged with a crime requiring such intent or knowledge. To be guilty of third degree assault "It is sufficient that the defendant voluntarily intended to commit the unlawful act of touching" (1 Wharton's Criminal Law and Procedure [1957], § 338, p. 685). Since in these circumstances the aggression was inexcusable the defendant was properly convicted.

Accordingly, the order of the Appellate Division should be reversed and the information reinstated.

Froessel, J. (dissenting). The law is clear that one may kill in defense of another when there is reasonable, though mistaken, ground for believing that the person slain is about to commit a felony or to do some great personal injury to the apparent victim (Penal Law, § 1055); yet the majority now hold, for the first time, that in the event of a simple assault under similar circumstances, the mistaken belief, no matter how reasonable, is no defense.

Briefly, the relevant facts are these: On a Friday afternoon at about 3:40, Detectives Driscoll and Murphy, not in uniform, observed an argument taking place between a motorist and one McGriff in the street in front of premises 64 West 54th Street, in midtown Manhattan. Driscoll attempted to chase McGriff out of the roadway in order to allow traffic to pass, but McGriff refused to move back; his actions caused a

*11 N. Y. S. 2d 274 (1962)
*Citations omitted [Eds.].

crowd to collect. After identifying himself to McGriff, Driscoll placed him under arrest. As McGriff resisted, defendant "came out of the crowd" from Driscoll's rear and struck Murphy about the head with his fist. In the ensuing struggle Driscoll's right kneecap was injured when defendant fell on top of him. At the station house, defendant said he had not known or thought Driscoll and Murphy were police officers.

Defendant testified that while he was proceeding on 54th Street he observed two white men, who appeared to be 45 or 50 years old, pulling on a "colored boy" (McGriff), who appeared to be a lad about 18, whom he did not know. The men had nearly pulled McGriff's pants off, and he was crying. Defendant admitted he knew nothing of what had transpired between the officers and McGriff, and made no inquiry of anyone; he just came there and pulled the officer away from McGriff.

Defendant was convicted of assault third degree. In reversing upon the law and dismissing the information, the Appellate Division held that one is not "criminally liable for assault in the third degree if he goes to the aid of another whom he mistakenly, but *reasonably,* believes is being unlawfully beaten, and thereby injures one of the apparent assaulters" (emphasis supplied). While in my opinion the majority below correctly stated the law, I would reverse here and remit so that the Appellate Division may pass on the question of whether or not defendant's conduct was reasonable in light of the circumstances presented at the trial (Code Crim. Pro., §§ 543-a, 543-b).

As the majority below pointed out, assault is a crime derived from the common law (*People* v. *Katz,* 290 N. Y. 361, 365). Basic to the imposition of criminal liability both at common law and under our statutory law is the existence in the one who committed the prohibited act of what has been variously termed a guilty mind, a *mens rea* or a criminal intent.*

Criminal intent requires an awareness of wrongdoing. When conduct is based upon mistake of fact reasonably entertained, there can be no such awareness and, therefore, no criminal culpability. In *People ex rel. Hegeman* v. *Corrigan* (195 N. Y. 1, 12) we stated: "it is very apparent that the innocence or criminality of the intent in a particular act generally depends on the knowledge or belief of the actor at the time. An honest and *reasonable* belief in the existence of circumstances which, if true, would make the act for which the defendant is prosecuted innocent, would be a good defense." (Emphasis supplied.)

It is undisputed that defendant did not know that Driscoll and Murphy were detectives in plain clothes engaged in lawfully apprehending an alleged disorderly person. If, therefore, defendant *reasonably* believed he was lawfully assisting another, he would not have been guilty of a crime. Subdivision 3 of section 246 of the Penal Law provides that it is not unlawful to use force "When committed either by the party about to be injured or *by another person in his aid or defense, in preventing or attempting to prevent an offense against his person,* * * * if the force or violence used is not more than sufficient to prevent such offense" (emphasis supplied). The law is thus clear that if defendant entertained an "honest and reasonable belief" (*People ex rel. Hegeman* v. *Corrigan,* 195 N. Y. 1, 12 *supra*) that the facts were as he perceived them to be, he would be exonerated from criminal liability.

By ignoring one of the most basic principles of criminal law—that crimes *mala in se* require proof of at least general criminal intent—the majority now hold that the defense of mistake of fact is "of no significance." We are not here dealing with one of "a narrow class of exceptions" (*People* v. *Katz,* 290 N. Y. 361, 365, *supra*) where the Legislature has created crimes which do not depend on *criminal* intent but which are complete on the mere intentional doing of an act *malum prohibitum.** (9 N Y 2d 51, 58; *People* v. *Werner,* 174 N. Y. 132, *supra*).

There is no need, in my opinion, to consider the law of other States, for New York policy clearly supports the view that one may act on appearances reasonably ascertained, as does New Jersey.* Our Penal Law (§ 1055), to which I have already alluded, is a statement of that policy. The same policy was expressed by this court in *People* v. *Maine* (166 N. Y. 50). There, the defendant observed his brother fighting in the street with two other men; he stepped in and stabbed to death one of the latter. The defense was justifiable homicide under the predecessor of section 1055. The court held it reversible error to admit into evidence the declarations of the defendant's brother, made before defendant happened upon the scene, which tended to show that the brother was the aggressor. We said (p. 52): "Of course the acts and conduct of the defendant must be judged solely with reference to the situation as it was when he first and afterwards saw it." Mistake of relevant fact, reasonably entertained, is thus a defense to homicide under section 1055 (*People* v. *Governale,* 193 N. Y. 581, 588), and one who kills in defense of another and proffers this defense of justification is to be judged according to the circumstances as they appeared to him.*

The mistaken belief, however, must be one which is reasonably entertained, and the question of reasonableness is for the trier of the facts.* "The question is not merely what did the accused believe, but also, what did he have the right to believe?" (*People* v. *Rodawald,* 177 N. Y. 408, 427.) Without passing on the facts of the instant case, the Appellate Division had no right to

---

*Citations omitted [Eds.].

assume that defendant's conduct was reasonable, and to dismiss the information as a matter of law. Nor do we have the right to reinstate the verdict without giving the Appellate Division the opportunity to pass upon the facts (Code Crim. Pro., § 543-b).

Although the majority of our court are now purporting to fashion a policy "conducive to an orderly society", by their decision they have defeated their avowed purpose. What public interest is promoted by a principle which would deter one from coming to the aid of a fellow citizen who he has reasonable ground to apprehend is in imminent danger of personal injury at the hands of assailants? Is it reasonable to denominate, as justifiable homicide, a slaying committed under a mistaken but reasonably held belief, and deny this same defense of justification to one using less force? Logic, as well as historical background and related precedent, dictates that the rule and policy expressed by our Legislature in the case of homicide, which is an assault resulting in death, should likewise be applicable to a much less serious assault not resulting in death.

I would reverse the order appealed from and remit the case to the Appellate Division pursuant to section 543-b of the Code of Criminal Procedure "for determination upon the questions of fact raised in that court."

Chief Judge Desmond and Judges Dye, Fuld, Burke and Foster concur in Per Curiam opinion; Judge Froessel dissents in an opinion in which Judge Van Voorhis concurs.

Order reversed, etc.

BARBARA WOOTTON

Eliminating Responsibility*

THE FUNCTION OF THE COURTS: PENAL OR PREVENTIVE?

... Proposals for the modernisation of the methods by which the criminal courts arrive at their verdicts do not, however, raise any question as to the object of the whole exercise. Much more fundamental are the issues which arise after conviction, when many a judge or magistrate must from time to time have asked himself just what it is that he is trying to achieve. Is he trying to punish the wicked, or to prevent the recurrence of forbidden acts? The former is certainly the traditional answer and is still deeply entrenched both in the legal profession and in the minds of much of the public at large; and it has lately been reasserted in uncompromising terms by a former Lord Chief Justice. At a meeting of magistrates earlier this year Lord Goddard is reported to have said that the duty of the criminal law was to punish—and that reformation of the prisoner was not the courts' business.[1] Those who take this view doubtless comfort themselves with the belief that the two objectives are nearly identical: that the punishment of the wicked is also the best way to prevent the occurrence of prohibited acts. Yet the continual failure of a mainly punitive system to diminish the volume of crime strongly suggests that such comfort is illusory; and it will indeed be a principal theme of these lectures that the choice between the punitive and the preventive[2] concept of the criminal process is a real one; and that, according as that choice is made, radical differences must follow in the courts' approach to their task. I shall, moreover, argue that in recent years

*From Crime and the Criminal Law by Barbara Wootton (London: Sweet & Maxwell, Ltd., 1963), pp. 40–57 and 58–84. Reprinted by permission of the author and the publisher.

a perceptible shift has occurred away from the first and towards the second of these two conceptions of the function of the criminal law; and that this movement is greatly to be welcomed and might with advantage be both more openly acknowledged and also accelerated.

First, however, let us examine the implications of the traditional view. Presumably the wickedness which renders a criminal liable to punishment must be inherent either in the actions which he has committed or in the state of mind in which he has committed them. Can we then in the modern world identify a class of inherently wicked actions? Lord Devlin, who has returned more than once to this theme, holds that we still can, by drawing a sharp distinction between what he calls the criminal and the quasi-criminal law. The distinguishing mark of the latter, in his view, is that a breach of it does not mean that the offender has done anything morally wrong. "Real" crimes, on the other hand, he describes as "sins with legal definitions"; and he adds that "It is a pity that this distinction, which I believe the ordinary man readily recognises, is not acknowledged in the administration of justice." "The sense of obligation which leads the citizen to obey a law that is good in itself is," he says, "different in quality from that which leads to obedience to a regulation designed to secure a good end." Nor does his Lordship see any reason "why the quasi-criminal should be treated with any more ignominy than a man who has incurred a penalty for failing to return a library book in time."[2a] And in a personal communication he has further defined the "real" criminal law as any part of the criminal law, new or old, which the good citizen does not break without a sense of guilt.

Nevertheless this attempt to revive the lawyer's distinction between *mala in se* and *mala prohibita*—things which are bad in themselves and things which are merely prohibited—cannot, I think, succeed. In the first place the statement that a real crime is one about which the good citizen would feel guilty is surely circular. For how is the good citizen to be defined in this context unless as one who feels guilty about committing the crimes that Lord Devlin classifies as "real"? And in the second place the badness even of those actions which would most generally be regarded as *mala in se* is inherent, not in the physical acts themselves, but in the circum-

stances in which they are performed. Indeed it is hard to think of any examples of actions which could, in a strictly physical sense, be said to be bad in themselves. The physical act of stealing merely involves moving a piece of matter from one place to another: what gives it its immoral character is the framework of property rights in which it occurs. Only the violation of these rights transforms an inherently harmless movement into the iniquitous act of stealing. Nor can bodily assaults be unequivocally classified as *mala in se;* for actions which in other circumstances would amount to grievous bodily harm may be not only legal, but highly beneficial, when performed by competent surgeons; and there are those who see no wrong in killing in the form of judicial hanging or in war.

One is indeed tempted to suspect that actions classified as *mala in se* are really only *mala antiqua*—actions, that is to say, which have been recognised as criminal for a very long time; and that the tendency to dismiss sundry modern offences as "merely quasi-crimes" is simply a mark of not having caught up with the realities of the contemporary world. The criminal calendar is always the expression of a particular social and moral climate, and from one generation to another it is modified by two sets of influences. On the one hand ideas about what is thought to be right or wrong are themselves subject to change; and on the other hand new technical developments constantly create new opportunities for antisocial actions which the criminal code must be extended to include. To a thoroughgoing Marxist these two types of change would not, presumably, be regarded as mutually independent: to the Marxist it is technical innovations which cause moral judgments to be revised. But for present purposes it does not greatly matter whether the one is, or is not, the cause of the other. In either case the technical and the moral are distinguishable. The fact that there is nothing in the Ten Commandments about the iniquity of driving a motor vehicle under the influence of drink cannot be read as evidence that the ancient Israelites regarded this offence more leniently than the contemporary British. On the other hand the divergent attitudes of our own criminal law and that of most European countries to homosexual practices has no obvious relation to technical development, and is clearly the expression of differing moral judgments, or at the least to different conceptions of the proper relation between morality and the criminal law.

One has only to glance, too, at the maximum penalties which the law attaches to various offences to realise how profoundly attitudes change in course of time. Life imprisonment, for example, is not only the obligatory sentence for noncapital murder and the maximum permissible for manslaughter. It may also be imposed for blasphemy or for the destruction of registers of births or baptisms. Again, the crime of abducting an heiress carries a potential sentence of fourteen years, while that for the abduction of a child under fourteen years is only half as long. For administering a drug to a female with a view to carnal knowledge a maximum of two years is provided, but for damage to cattle you are liable to fourteen years' imprisonment. For using unlawful oaths the maximum is seven years, but for keeping a child in a brothel it is a mere six months. Such sentences strike us today as quite fantastic; but they cannot have seemed fantastic to those who devised them.

For the origins of the supposed dichotomy between real crimes and quasi-crimes we must undoubtedly look to theology, as Lord Devlin's use of the term "sins with legal definitions" itself implies. The links between law and religion are both strong and ancient. Indeed, as Lord Radcliffe has lately reminded us, it has taken centuries for "English judges to realise that the tenets and injunctions of the Christian religion were not part of the common law of England";[3] and even today such realisation does not seem to be complete. As recently as 1961, in the "Ladies Directory" case, the defendant Shaw, you may remember, was convicted of conspiring to corrupt public morals, as well as of offences against the Sexual Offences Act of 1956 and the Obscene Publications Act of 1959, on account of his publication of a directory in which the ladies of the town advertised their services, sometimes, it would seem, in considerable detail. In rejecting Shaw's appeal to the House of Lords on the charge of conspiracy, Lord Simonds delivered himself of the opinion that without doubt "there remains in the courts a residual power to . . . conserve not only the safety but also the moral welfare of the state"; and Lord Hodson, concurring, added that "even if Chris-

tianity be not part of the law of England, yet the common law has its roots in Christianity."[4]

In the secular climate of the present age, however, the appeal to religious doctrine is unconvincing, and unlikely to be generally acceptable. Instead we must recognise a range of actions, the badness of which is inherent not in themselves, but in the circumstances in which they are performed, and which stretches in a continuous scale from wilful murder at one end to failure to observe a no-parking rule or to return on time a library book (which someone else may be urgently wanting) at the other. (Incidentally a certain poignancy is given to Lord Devlin's choice of this last example by a subsequent newspaper report that a book borrower in Frankfurt who omitted, in spite of repeated requests, to return a book which he had borrowed two years previously was brought before a local magistrate actually—though apparently by mistake—in handcuffs.[5]) But however great the range from the heinous to the trivial, the important point is that the gradation is continuous; and in the complexities of modern society a vast range of actions, in themselves apparently morally neutral, must be regarded as in varying degrees antisocial, and therefore in their contemporary settings as no less objectionable than actions whose criminal status is of greater antiquity. The good citizen will doubtless experience different degrees of guilt according as he may have stabbed his wife, engaged in homosexual intercourse, omitted to return his library book or failed to prevent one of his employees from watering the milk sold by his firm. Technically these are all crimes; whether or not they are also sins in a purely theological matter with which the law has no concern. If the function of the criminal law is to punish the wicked, then everything which the law forbids must in the circumstances in which it is forbidden be regarded as in its appropriate measure wicked.

Although this is, I think, the inevitable conclusion of any argument which finds wickedness inherent in particular classes of action, it seems to be unpalatable to Lord Devlin and others who conceive the function of the criminal law in punitive terms. It opens the door too wide. Still the door can be closed again by resort to the alternative theory that the wickedness of an action is inherent not in the action itself, but in the state of mind of the person who performs it. To punish people merely for what they have done, it is argued, would be unjust, for the forbidden act might have been an accident for which the person who did it cannot be held to blame. Hence the requirement, to which traditionally the law attaches so much importance, that a crime is not, so to speak, a crime in the absence of *mens rea*.

Today, however, over a wide front even this requirement has in fact been abandoned. Today many, indeed almost certainly the majority, of the cases dealt with by the criminal courts are cases of strict liability in which proof of a guilty mind is no longer necessary for conviction. A new dichotomy is thus created, and one which in this instance exists not merely in the minds of the judges but is actually enshrined in the law itself —that is to say, the dichotomy between those offences in which the guilty mind is, and those in which it is not, an essential ingredient. In large measure, no doubt, this classification coincides with Lord Devlin's division into real and quasi-crimes; but whether or not this coincidence is exact must be a question of personal judgment. To drive a car when your driving ability is impaired through drink or drugs is an offence of strict liability: It is no defence to say that you had no idea that the drink would affect you as it did, or to produce evidence that you were such a seasoned drinker that any such result was, objectively, not to be expected. These might be mitigating circumstances after conviction, but are no bar to the conviction itself. Yet some at least of those who distinguish between real and quasi-crimes would put drunken driving in the former category, even though it involves no question of *mens rea*. In the passage that I quoted earlier Lord Devlin, it will be remembered, was careful to include new as well as old offences in his category of "real" crimes; but generally speaking it is the *mala antiqua* which are held to be both *mala in se* and contingent upon *mens rea*.

Nothing has dealt so devastating a blow at the punitive conception of the criminal process as the proliferation of offences of strict liability; and the alarm has forthwith been raised. Thus Dr. J. Ll. J. Edwards has expressed the fear that there is a real danger that the "widespread practice of imposing criminal liability independent of any moral fault" will result in the criminal law being regarded with contempt. "The process of basing criminal liability upon a theory of absolute prohi-

bition," he writes, "may well have the opposite effect to that intended and lead to a weakening of respect for the law."[6] Nor, in his view, is it an adequate answer to say that absolute liability can be tolerated because of the comparative unimportance of the offences to which it is applied and because, as a rule, only a monetary penalty is involved; for, in the first place, there are a number of important exceptions to this rule (drunken driving for example); and, secondly, as Dr. Edwards himself point out, in certain cases the penalty imposed by the court may be the least part of the punishment. A merchant's conviction for a minor trading offence may have a disastrous effect upon his business.

Such dislike of strict liability is not by any means confined to academic lawyers. In the courts, too, various devices have been used to smuggle *mens rea* back into offences from which, on the face of it, it would appear to be excluded. To the lawyer's ingenious mind the invention of such devices naturally presents no difficulty. Criminal liability, for instance, can attach only to voluntary acts. If a driver is struck unconscious with an epileptic seizure, it can be argued that he is not responsible for any consequences because his driving thereafter is involuntary: indeed he has been said not to be driving at all. If on the other hand he falls asleep, this defence will not serve since sleep is a condition that comes on gradually, and a driver has an opportunity and a duty to stop before it overpowers him. Alternatively, recourse can be had to the circular argument that anyone who commits a forbidden act must have intended to commit it and must, therefore, have formed a guilty intention. As Lord Devlin puts it, the word "knowingly" or "wilfully" can be read into acts in which it is not present; although as his Lordship points out this subterfuge is open to the criticism that it fails to distinguish between the physical act itself and the circumstances in which this becomes a crime.[7] All that the accused may have intended was to perform an action (such as firing a gun or driving a car) which is not in itself criminal. Again, in yet other cases such as those in which it is forbidden to permit or to allow something to be done the concept of negligence can do duty as a watered down version of *mens rea*: for how can anyone be blamed for permitting something about which he could not have known?

All these devices, it cannot be too strongly emphasised, are necessitated by the need to preserve the essentially punitive function of the criminal law. For it is not, as Dr. Edwards fears, the criminal law which will be brought into contempt by the multiplication of offences of strict liability, so much as this particular conception of the law's function. If that function is conceived less in terms of punishment than as a mechanism of prevention these fears become irrelevant. Such a conception, however, apparently sticks in the throat of even the most progressive lawyers. Even Professor Hart, in his Hobhouse lecture on *Punishment and the Elimination of Responsibility,*[8] seems to be incurably obsessed with the notion of punishment, which haunts his text as well as figuring in his title. Although rejecting many traditional theories, such as that punishment should be "retributive" or "denunciatory," he nevertheless seems wholly unable to envisage a system in which sentence is not automatically equated with "punishment." Thus he writes of "values quite distinct from those of retributive punishment which the system of responsibility does maintain, and which remain of great importance even if our aims in *punishing* are the forward-looking aims of social protection"; and again "even if we *punish* men not as wicked but as nuisances . . ." while he makes many references to the principle that liability to punishment must depend on a voluntary act. Perhaps it requires the naïveté of an amateur to suggest that the forward-looking aims of social protection might, on occasion, have absolutely no connection with punishment.

If, however, the primary function of the courts is conceived as the prevention of forbidden acts, there is little cause to be disturbed by the multiplication of offences of strict liability. If the law says that certain things are not to be done, it is illogical to confine this prohibition to occasions on which they are done from malice aforethought; for at least the material consequences of an action, and the reasons for prohibiting it, are the same whether it is the result of sinister malicious plotting, of negligence or of sheer accident. A man is equally dead and his relatives equally bereaved whether he was stabbed or run over by a drunken motorist or by an incompetent one; and the inconvenience caused by the loss of your bicycle is unaffected by the question whether or not the youth who removed it had the intention

of putting it back, if in fact he had not done so at the time of his arrest. It is true, of course, as Professor Hart has argued,[9] that the material consequences of an action by no means exhaust its effects. "If one person hits another, the person struck does not think of the other as *just* a cause of pain to him. . . . If the blow was light but deliberate, it has a significance for the person struck quite different from an accidental much heavier blow." To ignore this difference, he argues, is to outrage "distinctions which not only underlie morality, but pervade the whole of our social life." That these distinctions are widely appreciated and keenly felt no one would deny. Often perhaps they derive their force from a purely punitive or retributive attitude; but alternatively they may be held to be relevant to an assessment of the social damage that results from a criminal act. Just as a heavy blow does more damage than a light one, so also perhaps does a blow which involves psychological injury do more damage than one in which the hurt is purely physical.

The conclusion to which this argument leads is, I think, not that the presence or absence of the guilty mind is unimportant, but that *mens rea* has, so to speak—and this is the crux of the matter—*got into the wrong place.* Traditionally, the requirement of the guilty mind is written into the actual definition of a crime. No guilty intention, no crime, is the rule. Obviously this makes sense if the law's concern is with wickedness: where there is no guilty intention, there can be no wickedness. But it is equally obvious, on the other hand, that an action does not become innocuous merely because whoever performed it meant no harm. If the object of the criminal law is to prevent the occurrence of socially damaging actions, it would be absurd to turn a blind eye to those which were due to carelessness, negligence or even accident. The question of motivation is *in the first instance* irrelevant.

But only in the first instance. At a later stage, that is to say, after what is now known as a conviction, the presence or absence of guilty intention is all-important for its effect on the appropriate measures to be taken to prevent a recurrence of the forbidden act. The prevention of accidental deaths presents different problems from those involved in the prevention of wilful murders. The results of the actions of the careless, the mistaken, the wicked and the merely unfortunate may be indistinguishable from one another, but each case calls for a different treatment. Tradition, however, is very strong, and the notion that these differences are relevant only after the fact has been established that the accused committed the forbidden act seems still to be deeply abhorrent to the legal mind. Thus Lord Devlin, discussing the possibility that judges might have taken the line that all "unintentional" criminals might be dealt with simply by the imposition of a nominal penalty, regards this as the "negation of law." "It would,"[10] he says, "confuse the function of mercy which the judge is dispensing when imposing the penalty with the function of justice. It would have been to deny to the citizen due process of law because it would have been to say to him, in effect: 'Although we cannot think that Parliament intended you to be punished in this case because you have really done nothing wrong, come to us, ask for mercy, and we shall grant mercy.' . . . In all criminal matters the citizen is entitled to the protection of the law . . . and the mitigation of penalty should not be adopted as the prime method of dealing with accidental offenders."

Within its own implied terms of reference the logic is unexceptionable. If the purpose of the law is to dispense punishment tempered with mercy, then to use mercy as a consolation for unjust punishment is certainly to give a stone for bread. But these are not the implied terms of reference of strict liability. In the case of offences of strict liability the presumption is not that those who have committed forbidden actions must be punished, but that appropriate steps must be taken to prevent the occurrence of such actions.

Here, as often in other contexts also, the principles involved are admirably illustrated by the many driving offences in which conviction does not involve proof of *mens rea*. If, for instance, the criterion of gravity is the amount of social damage which a crime causes, many of these offences must be judged extremely grave. In 1961, 299 persons were convicted on charges of causing death by dangerous driving, that is to say more than five times as many as were convicted of murder (including those found guilty but insane) and 85 per cent more than the total of convictions for all other forms of homicide (namely murder, manslaughter and infanticide) put together. It is,

moreover, a peculiarity of many driving offences that the offender seldom intends the actual damage which he causes. He may be to blame in that he takes a risk which he knows may result in injury to other people or to their property, but such injury is neither an inevitable nor an intended consequence of the commission of the offence: which is not true of, for example, burglary. Dangerous or careless driving ranges in a continuous series from the almost wholly accidental, through the incompetent and the negligent to the positively and grossly culpable; and it is quite exceptionally difficult in many of these cases to establish just what point along this scale any particular instance should be assigned. In consequence the gravity of any offence tends to be estimated by its consequences rather than by the state of mind of the perpetrator—which is less usual (although attempted murder or grievous bodily harm may turn into murder, if the victim dies) in the case of other crimes. In my experience it is exceptional (though not unknown) for a driving charge to be made unless an accident actually occurs, and the nature of the charge is apt to be determined by the severity of the accident. I recall, for example, a case in which a car driver knocked down an elderly man on a pedestrian crossing, and a month later the victim died in hospital after an operation, his death being, one must suppose, in spite, rather than because, of this. Thereupon the charge, which had originally been booked by the police as careless, not even dangerous, driving was upgraded to causing death by dangerous driving.

For all these reasons it is recognised that if offences in this category are to be dealt with by the criminal courts at all, this can only be on a basis of strict liability. This particular category of offences thus illustrates all too vividly the fact that in the modern world in one way or another, as much and more damage is done by negligence, or by indifference to the welfare or safety of others, as by deliberate wickedness. In technically simpler societies this is less likely to be so, for the points of exposure to the follies of others are less numerous, and the daily chances of being run over, or burnt or infected or drowned because someone has left undone something that he ought to have done are less ominous. These new complexities were never envisaged by the founders of our legal traditions, and it is hardly to be wondered at if the law itself is not yet fully adapted to them. Yet it is by no means certain that the last chapter in the long and chequered history of the concept of guilt, which is so deeply rooted in our traditions, has yet been written. Time was when inanimate objects—the rock that fell on you, the tree that attracted the lightning that killed you— were held to share the blame for the disasters in which they were instrumental; and it was properly regarded as a great step forward when the capacity to acquire a guilty mind was deemed to be one of the distinctive capacities of human' beings.[11] But now, perhaps, the time has come for the concept of legal guilt to be dissolved into a wider concept of responsibility or at least accountability, in which there is room for negligence as well as purposeful wrongdoing; and for the significance of a conviction to be reinterpreted merely as evidence that a prohibited act has been committed, questions of motivation being relevant only insofar as they bear upon the probability of such acts being repeated.

I am not, of course, arguing that all crimes should immediately be transferred into the strict liability category. To do so would in some cases involve formidable problems of definition—as, for instance, in that of larceny. But I do suggest that the contemporary extension of strict liability is not the nightmare that it is often made out to be, that it does not promise the decline and fall of the criminal law, and that it is, on the contrary, a sensible and indeed inevitable measure of adaptation to the requirements of the modern world; and above all I suggest that its supposedly nightmarish quality disappears once it is accepted that the primary objective of the criminal courts is preventive rather than punitive. Certainly we need to pay heed to Mr. Nigel Walker's reminder[12] that "under our present law it is possible for a person to do great harm in circumstances which suggest that there is a risk of his repeating it, and yet to secure an acquittal." In two types of case, in both of which such harm can result, the concept of the guilty mind has become both irrelevant and obstructive. In this lecture I have been chiefly concerned with the first of these categories—that of cases of negligence. The second category—that of mental abnormality—will be the theme of that which follows.

THE PROBLEM OF THE MENTALLY ABNORMAL OFFENDER

The problem of the mentally abnormal offender raises in a particularly acute form the question of the primary function of the courts. If that function is conceived as punitive, mental abnormality must be related to guilt; for a severely subnormal offender must be less blameworthy, and ought therefore to incur a less severe punishment, than one of greater intelligence who has committed an otherwise similar crime, even though he may well be a worse risk for the future. But from the preventive standpoint it is this future risk which matters, and the important question to be asked is not: Does his abnormality mitigate or even obliterate his guilt? but, rather, is he a suitable subject for medical, in preference to any other, type of treatment? In short, the punitive and the preventive are respectively concerned the one with culpability and the other with treatability.

In keeping with its traditional obsession with the concept of guilt, English criminal law has, at least until lately, been chiefly concerned with the effect of mental disorder upon culpability. In recent years, however, the idea that an offender's mental state might also have a bearing on his treatability has begun to creep into the picture— with the result that the two concepts now lie somewhat uneasily side by side in what has become a very complex pattern.

Under the present law there are at least six distinct legal formulae under which an accused person's mental state may be put in issue in a criminal case. First, he may be found unfit to plead, in which case of course no trial takes place at all, unless and until he is thought to have sufficiently recovered. Second, on a charge of murder (and theoretically in other cases also) a defendant may be found to be insane within the terms of the M'Naughten Rules, by the illogical verdict of guilty but insane which, to be consistent with the normal use of the term guilt, ought to be revised to read—as it once did—"not guilty on the ground of insanity." Third, a person accused of murder can plead diminished responsibility under section 2 of the Homicide Act, in which case, if this defence succeeds, a verdict of manslaughter will be substituted for one of murder.

Up to this point it is, I think, indisputable that it is the relation between the accused's mental state and his culpability or punishability which is in issue. Obviously a man who cannot be tried cannot be punished. Again, one who is insane may have to be deprived of his liberty in the interests of the public safety, but, since an insane person is not held to be blameworthy in the same way as one who is in full possession of his faculties, the institution to which he is committed must be of a medical not a penal character; and for the same reason, he must not be hanged if found guilty on a capital charge. So also under the Homicide Act a defence of diminished responsibility opens the door to milder punishments than the sentences of death and life imprisonment which automatically follow the respective verdicts of capital and noncapital murder; and the fact that diminished responsibility is conceived in terms of reduced culpability, and not as indicative of the need for medical treatment, is further illustrated by the fact that in less than half the cases in which this defence has succeeded since the courts have had power to make hospital orders under the Mental Health Act, have such orders actually been made.[13] In the great majority of all the successful cases under section 2 of the Homicide Act a sentence of imprisonment has been imposed, the duration of this ranging from life to a matter of not more than a few months. Moreover, the Court of Criminal Appeal has indicated[14] approval of such sentences on the ground that a verdict of manslaughter based on diminished responsibility implies that a "residue of responsibility" rests on the accused person and that this "residue of criminal intent" may be such as to deserve punishment—a judgment which surely presents a sentencing judge with a problem of nice mathematical calculation as to the appropriate measure of punishment.

Under the Mental Health Act of 1959, however, the notion of reduced culpability begins to be complicated by the alternative criterion of treatability. Section 60 of that Act provides the fourth and fifth of my six formulae. Under the first subsection of this section, an offender who is convicted at a higher court (or at a magistrates' court if his offence is one which carries liability to imprisonment) may be compulsorily detained in hospital, or made subject to a guardianship order, if the court is satisfied, on the evidence of two doctors (one of whom must have special experience in the diagnosis or treatment of mental disorders) that this is in all the circumstances the

most appropriate way of dealing with him. In the making of such orders emphasis is clearly on the future, not on the past: The governing consideration is not whether the offender deserves to be punished, but whether in fact medical treatment is likely to succeed. No sooner have we said this, however, than the old concept of culpability rears its head again. For a hospital order made by a higher court may be accompanied by a restriction order of either specified or indefinite duration, during the currency of which the patient may only be discharged on the order of the Home Secretary; and a magistrates' court also, although it has no similar power itself to make a restriction order, may commit an offender to sessions to be dealt with, if it is of the opinion that, having regard to the nature of the offence, the antecedents of the offender and the risk of his committing further offences if set at liberty, a hospital order should be accompanied by a restriction order.

The restriction order is thus professedly designed as a protection to the public; but a punitive element also, I think, still lingers in it. For if the sole object was the protection of the public against the premature discharge of a mentally disordered dangerous offender, it could hardly be argued that the court's prediction of the safe moment for release, perhaps years ahead, is likely to be more reliable than the judgment at the appropriate time of the hospital authorities who will have had the patient continuously under their surveillance.[15] If their purpose is purely protective all orders ought surely to be of indefinite duration, and the fact that this is not so suggests that they are still tainted with the tariff notion of sentencing—that is to say, with the idea that a given offence "rates" a certain period of loss of liberty. Certainly, on any other interpretation, the judges who have imposed restriction orders on offenders to run for ten or more years must credit themselves with truly remarkable powers of medical prognosis. In fairness, however, it should be said that the practice of imposing indefinite rather than fixed term orders now seems to be growing.

So, too, with the fifth of my formulae, which is to be found in a later subsection of section 60 of the same Act. Under this, an offender who is charged before a magistrates' court with an offence for which he could be imprisoned, may be made the subject of a hospital or guardianship order *without being convicted*, provided that the court is satisfied that he did the act or made the omission of which he is accused. This power, however (which is itself an extended version of section 24 of the Criminal Justice Act, 1948, and has indeed a longer statutory history), may only be exercised if the accused is diagnosed as suffering from either mental illness or severe subnormality. It is not available in the case of persons suffering from either of the two other forms of mental disorder recognised by the Act, namely psychopathy, or simple, as distinct from severe, subnormality. And why not? One can only presume that the reason for this restriction is the fear that in cases in which only moderate mental disorder is diagnosed, or in which the diagnosis is particularly difficult and a mistake might easily be made, an offender might escape the punishment that he deserved. Even though no hospital or guardianship order can be made unless the court is of opinion that this is the "most suitable" method of disposing of the case, safeguards against the risk that this method might be used for the offender who really deserved to be punished are still written into the law.

One curious ambiguity in this provision, however, deserves notice at this stage. Before a hospital order is made, the court must be satisfied that the accused "did the act, or made the omission with which he is charged." Yet what, one may ask, is the meaning, in this context, of "the act"? Except in the case of crimes of absolute liability, a criminal charge does not relate to a purely physical action. It relates to a physical action accompanied by a guilty mind or malicious intention. If then a person is so mentally disordered as to be incapable of forming such an intention, is he not strictly incapable of performing the act with which he is charged? The point seems to have been raised when the 1948 Criminal Justice Bill was in Committee in the House of Commons, but it was not pursued.[16] Such an interpretation would, of course, make nonsense of the section, and one must presume, therefore, that the words "the act" must be construed to refer solely to the prohibited physical action, irrespective of the actor's state of mind. But in that case the effect of this subsection would seem to be to transfer every type of crime, in the case of persons of severely disordered mentality, to the category of offences of absolute liability. In practice little use appears to be made of this provision (and in my experi-

ence few magistrates are aware of its existence); but there would seem to be an important principle here, potentially capable, as I hope to suggest later, of wider application.

The last of my six formulae, which, however, antedates all the others, stands in a category by itself. It is to be found in section 4 of the Criminal Justice Act of 1948, under which a court may make mental treatment (residential or nonresidential) a condition of a probation order, provided that the offender's mental condition is "such as requires and as may be susceptible to treatment," but is not such as to justify his being in the language of that day certified as "of unsound mind" or "mentally defective." Such a provision represents a very wholehearted step in the direction of accepting the criterion of treatability. For, although those to whom this section may be applied must be deemed to be guilty—in the sense that they have been convicted of offences involving *mens rea*—the only question to be decided is that of their likely response to medical or other treatment. Moreover, apart from the exclusion of insanity or mental defect, no restriction is placed on the range of diagnostic categories who may be required to submit to mental treatment under this section, although as always in the case of a probation order imposed on adults, the order cannot be made without the probationer's own consent. Nor is any reference anywhere made or even implied as to the effect of their mental condition upon their culpability. It is of interest, too, that, in practice, the use of these provisions has not been confined to what are often regarded as "pathological" crimes. Dr. Grünhut who made a study of cases to which the section was applied in 1953[17] found that out of a total of 636 probationers, 275 had committed offences against property, 216 sexual offences, ninety-seven offences of violence (other than sexual) and forty-eight other types of offence. Some of the property crimes had, it is true, "an apparently pathological background," but no less than 48 per cent were classified as "normal" acquisitive thefts.

All these modifications in the criminal process in the case of the mentally abnormal offender thus tend (with the possible exception of the 1948 Act) to treat such abnormality as in greater or less degree exculpatory. Their purpose is not just to secure that medical treatment should be provided for any offender likely to benefit from this, but rather to guard against the risk that the mentally disordered will be unjustly punished. Their concern with treatability, where it occurs, is in effect consequential rather than primary: The question—can the doctors help him? follows, if at all, upon a negative answer to the question: Is he really to blame?

Nowhere is this more conspicuous than in section 2 of the Homicide Act; and it was indeed from a study of the operation of that section that I was led nearly four years ago to the conclusion that this was the wrong approach; that any attempt to distinguish between wickedness and mental abnormality was doomed to failure; and that the only solution for the future was to allow the concept of responsibility to "wither away" and to concentrate instead on the problem of the choice of treatment, without attempting to assess the effect of mental peculiarities on degrees of culpability. That opinion was based on a study of the files of some seventy-three cases in which a defence of diminished responsibility had been raised,[18] which were kindly made available by the Home Office. To these have since been added the records of another 126 cases, the two series together covering the five and a half years from the time that the Act came into force down to mid-September 1962.

Before I pursue the implications of the suggestion that the concept of responsibility should be allowed to wither away, it may be well to ask whether anything in this later material calls for any modification of my earlier conclusion. I do not think it does. Indeed the experience of the past three and a half years seems to have highlighted both the practical and the philosophical difficulty—or as I would prefer to say the impossibility—of assessing other people's responsibility for their actions.

Some new issues have, however, arisen in the struggle to interpret the relevant section of the Act. Much legal argument has, for example, been devoted to the effect of drink upon responsibility. The Act, as you may remember, provides that a charge of murder may result in a conviction for manslaughter if the accused was suffering from "such abnormality of mind (whether arising from a condition of arrested or retarded development of mind or any inherent causes or induced by disease or injury) as substantially impaired his

responsibility for his acts." Accordingly, it has been suggested that the transient effect of drink, if sufficient to produce a toxic effect upon the brain, might amount to an "injury" within the meaning of the Act. Alternatively (in the picturesque phrase of one defence counsel) drink might "make up the deficit" necessary to convert a preexistent minor abnormality into a substantial impairment of responsibility. None of these issues has yet been authoritatively decided. Sometimes the court has been able to wriggle out of a decision, as the Court of Criminal Appeal did when the "injury" argument was used on behalf of Di Duca,[19] on the ground that the particular offender concerned, whether drunk or sober, showed insufficient evidence of abnormality. Sometimes the opposite escape route has been available, as when the trial judge in the case of Dowdall,[20] while careful to emphasise that the section was not to be regarded as "a drunkard's charter," reminded the jury that two doctors had testified to the defendant's gross abnormality even apart from his admitted addiction to liquor. In Samuel's[21] case, on the other hand, in which the "deficit" theory was strongly argued in the absence of the jury, the judge clearly regarded it as inadmissible and made no reference to it in his summing up. But nearly two years later the Court of Criminal Appeal[22] concluded its judgment in Clarke's appeal with a statement that "the court wished to make it clear that it had not considered the effect of drink on a mind suffering from diminished responsibility. The court had not considered whether any abnormality of mind, however slight, would constitute a defence when substantially impaired by drink. That matter would have to be considered on another occasion."

After drink, insanity. A second complication has arisen in the problem of distinguishing between persons whose responsibility is merely diminished, and those who are deemed to be insane within the meaning of the M'Naughten Rules. Here there appears to be a division of opinion among the judges as to the right of the Crown to seek to establish insanity in cases in which the defence pleads only diminished responsibility. In two out of my earlier series of seventy-three cases in which this defence was raised, and in four of the later series of 126 cases, a verdict of guilty but insane was actually returned; and in at least half a dozen others in which this defence did succeed, the witnesses called by the Crown to rebut evidence of diminished responsibility sought to establish that the accused was in fact insane. Such a procedure was in keeping with the forecast of the Attorney-General in his speech on the Second Reading of the Homicide Bill.[23] "If," he said, "the defence raise any question as to the accused's mental capacity, and evidence is called to show that he is suffering from a serious abnormality of mind, then, if the evidence goes beyond a diminution of responsibility and really shows that the accused was within the M'Naughten Rules, it would be right for the judge to leave it to the jury to determine whether the accused was, to use the old phrase, 'guilty but insane,' or to return a verdict of manslaughter on the basis that, although not insane, he suffered from diminished responsibility. . . ." Nevertheless in the case of *Price* in 1962[24] the trial judge ruled that "if the Crown raises the issue of insanity and the jury find the accused guilty but insane, he cannot challenge the verdict in any higher court. . . . It seems to me," he said, "having regard to the serious consequences which would follow to a man if the Crown does succeed in raising the issue of insanity that the law cannot be, without an Act of Parliament, that a man should lose his right of appeal. In these circumstances I rule that the Crown is not entitled to invite the jury to consider the issue of insanity."

If this ruling is upheld, the result will be that the—at the best of times exceptionally difficult—distinction between insanity and diminished responsibility will be unlikely to be drawn on the merits of the case. For, except in extreme cases, the defence is always likely to prefer a plea of diminished responsibility to one of insanity, since if the latter succeeds indefinite detention necessarily follows, whereas on a conviction for manslaughter, which is the outcome of a successful defence of diminished responsibility, the court has complete discretion to pass whatever sentence it thinks fit. Persons who may be insane within the meaning of the M'Naughten Rules are therefore always likely to be tempted to plead diminished responsibility. Yet if they do, the jury will, if the analogy of the judgment in *Price's* case is followed, be precluded from hearing evidence as to their possible insanity and so arriving at an informed judgment on the issue of diminished responsibility versus insanity.

These developments can only be said to have added to the prevailing confusion. One other step has, however, been taken, which does at least aim at clarification. In the early days of the Act's operation juries were generally given little guidance as to the meaning of diminished responsibility. Judges did not ordinarily go beyond making sure that the members of the jury were familiar with the actual words of the section, which they were then expected to interpret for themselves. In 1960, however, in allowing the appeal of Patrick Byrne, the Birmingham Y.W.C.A. murderer, the Court of Criminal Appeal[25] attempted a formulation of the meaning of diminished responsibility on which judges have subsequently been able to draw in their directions to juries. In the words used by the Lord Chief Justice in this judgment "abnormality of mind" must be defined widely enough "to cover the mind's activities in all its aspects, not only the perception of physical acts and matters, and the ability to form a rational judgment as to whether an act is right or wrong, but also the ability to exercise willpower to control physical acts in accordance with that rational judgment." Furthermore, while medical evidence on this issue was said to be "no doubt of importance," it was not necessarily conclusive and might be outweighed by other material. Juries might also legitimately differ from doctors in assessing whether any impairment of responsibility could properly be regarded as "substantial"; and to guide them on this last point it was suggested that such phrases as "partial insanity" or on "the borderline of insanity" might be possible interpretations of the kind of abnormality which would substantially impair responsibility.

How far this helps may be a matter for argument. In the following year, in the case of Victor Terry, the Worthing bank murderer, Mr. Justice Stable adopted the original course of handing the jury a transcript of the (exceptionally voluminous) medical evidence instead of attempting to sum this up himself; but this procedure did not commend itself to the Court of Criminal Appeal,[26] although the court's disapproval did not go so far as to result in the condemned man's appeal being allowed or save him from being hanged. Certainly for my part I cannot think that anyone can listen to, or read, the sophisticated subtleties in which legal disputations about degrees of responsibility persistently flounder and founder without reaching the paradoxical conclusion that the harder we try to recognise the complexity of reality, the greater the unreality of the whole discussion. Indeed it is hardly surprising that in practice most of these subtleties probably pass over the heads of juries, whose conclusions appear to be reached on simpler grounds. At least two-thirds of those persons in whose cases a defence of diminished responsibility has succeeded have produced some serious evidence of previous mental instability such as a history of previous attempts at suicide, or of discharge from the Forces on psychiatric grounds, or of some trouble for which psychiatric advice has been sought, while a much higher proportion, though not medically diagnosed, are thought by relatives to be in some way peculiar. On the other hand, well under half of those in whose case a defence of diminished responsibility was not successful appear to have had any history of mental instability. It would seem that juries, clutching perhaps at straws, are disposed to take the view that a previous history of mental disturbance indicates (on the balance of probability, which is all that they have to establish) subsequent impairment of responsibility. And in the remaining cases, in which there is no such history, the concept of diminished responsibility seems to be dissolving into what is virtually the equivalent of a mitigating circumstance. Certainly in many of the more recent cases it is difficult to establish the presence of mental abnormality unless by the circular argument that anybody who commits homicide must, by definition, be unbalanced. It was surely compassion rather than evidence of mental abnormality which accounted for the success of a defence of diminished responsibility in the case of the major who found himself the father of a Mongol baby and, after reading up the subject of Mongolism in his public library, decided that the best course for everybody concerned would be to smother the child. And in the not infrequent cases in which a defence of diminished responsibility has succeeded, when homicide has resulted from such common human motives as sexual jealousy or the desire to escape from pecuniary embarrassment, it is hard not to believe that juries were moved more by the familiarity, than by the abnormality, of the offender's mental processes.

The most important development of the past few years lies, however, in the fact that the impossibility of keeping a clear line between the wicked and the weak-minded seems now to be officially admitted. In the judgment of the Court of Criminal Appeal on Byrne's appeal, from which I have already quoted, the Lord Chief Justice frankly admitted that "the step between 'he did not resist his impulse,' and 'he could not resist his impulse' " was one which was "incapable of scientific proof. *A fortiori,*" the judgment continues, "there is no scientific measurement of the degree of difficulty which an abnormal person finds in controlling his impulses. These problems which in the present state of medical knowledge are scientifically insoluble the jury can only approach in a broad commonsense way."

Apart from admiration of the optimism which expects common sense to make good the deficiencies of science, it is only necessary to add that the problem would seem to be insoluble, not merely in the present, but indeed in any, state of medical knowledge. Improved medical knowledge may certainly be expected to give better insight into the origins of mental abnormalities, and better predictions as to the probability that particular types of individuals will in fact "control their physical acts" or make "rational judgments"; but neither medical nor any other science can ever hope to prove whether a man who does not resist his impulses does not do so because he cannot or because he will not. The propositions of science are by definition subject to empirical validation; but since it is not possible to get inside another man's skin, no objective criterion which can distinguish between "he did not" and "he could not" is conceivable.

Logic, experience and the Lord Chief Justice thus all appear to lead to the same conclusion—that is to say, to the impossibility of establishing any reliable measure of responsibility in the sense of a man's ability to have acted otherwise than as he did. After all, every one of us can say with St. Paul (who, as far as I am aware, is not generally suspected of diminished responsibility) "the good that I would I do not: but the evil which I would not, that I do."

I have dealt at some length with our experience of diminished responsibility cases under the Homicide Act because taken together, the three facts, first, that under this Act questions of responsibility have to be decided before and not after conviction; second, that these questions fall to be decided by juries; and, third, that the charges involved are of the utmost gravity, have caused the relationship of responsibility to culpability to be explored with exceptional thoroughness in this particular context. But the principles involved are by no means restricted to the narrow field of charges of homicide. They have a far wider applicability, and are indeed implicit also in section 60 of the Mental Health Act. Unfortunately, up till now, and pending completion of the researches upon which I understand that Mr. Nigel Walker and his colleagues at Oxford are engaged, little is known of the working of this section. But it seems inevitable that if in any case a convicted person wished (as might well happen) to challenge the diagnosis of mental disorder which must precede the making of a hospital order, he would quickly be plunged into arguments about subnormality and psychopathy closely parallel to those which occupy so many hours of diminished responsibility trials.

At the same time the proposal that we should bypass, or disregard, the concept of responsibility is only too easily misunderstood; and I propose, therefore, to devote the remainder of this lecture to an attempt to meet some of the criticisms which have been brought against this proposal, to clarify just what it does or does not mean in the present context and to examine its likely implications.

First, it is to be observed that the term "responsibility" is here used in a restricted sense, much narrower than that which it often carries in ordinary speech. The measure of a person's responsibility for his actions is perhaps best defined in the words that I used earlier in terms of his capacity to act otherwise than as he did. A person may be described as totally irresponsible if he is wholly incapable of controlling his actions, and as being in a state of diminished responsibility if it is abnormally difficult for him to control them. Responsibility in this restricted sense is not to be confused with the sense in which a man is often said to be responsible for an action if he has in fact committed it. The questions: Who broke the window? and could the man who broke the window have prevented himself from doing so? are obviously quite distinct. To dismiss the second as unanswerable in no way diminishes the impor-

tance of finding an answer to the first. Hence the primary job of the courts in determining by whom a forbidden act has actually been committed is wholly unaffected by any proposal to disregard the question of responsibility in the narrower sense. Indeed the only problem that arises here is linguistic, inasmuch as one is accustomed to say that X was "responsible" for breaking the window when the intention is to convey no more than that he did actually break it. Another word is needed here (and I confess that I have not succeeded in finding one) to describe "responsibility" for doing an action as distinct from the capacity to refrain from doing it. "Accountable" has sometimes been suggested, but its usage in this sense is often awkward. "Instrumental" is perhaps better, though one could still wish for an adjective such perhaps as "agential" derived from the word "agent." However, all that matters is to keep firmly in mind that responsibility in the present context has nothing to do with the authorship of an act, only with the state of mind of its author.

In the second place, to discard the notion of responsibility does not mean that the mental condition of an offender ceases to have any importance, or that psychiatric considerations become irrelevant. The difference is that they become relevant, not to the question of determining the measure of his culpability, but to the choice of the treatment most likely to be effective in discouraging him from offending again; and even if these two aspects of the matter may be related, this is not to be dismissed as a distinction without a difference. The psychiatrist to whom it falls to advise as to the probable response of an offender to medical treatment no doubt has his own opinion as to the man's responsibility or capacity for self-control; and doubtless also those opinions are a factor in his judgment as to the outlook for medical treatment, or as to the probability that the offence will be repeated. But these are, and must remain, matters of opinion, "incapable," in Lord Parker's words, "of scientific proof." Opinions as to treatability, on the other hand, as well as predictions as to the likelihood of further offences can be put to the test of experience and so proved right or wrong. And by systematic observation of that experience, it is reasonable to expect that a body of knowledge will in time be built up, upon which it will be possible to draw, in the attempt to choose the most promising treatment in future cases.

Next, it must be emphasised that nothing in what has been said involves acceptance of a deterministic view of human behaviour. It is an indisputable fact of experience that human beings do respond predictably to various stimuli—whether because they choose to or because they can do no other it is not necessary to inquire. There are cases in which medical treatment works: there are cases in which it fails. Equally there are cases in which deterrent penalties appear to deter those upon whom they are imposed from committing further offences; and there are cases in which they do not. Once the criminal law is conceived as an instrument of crime prevention, it is these facts which demand attention, and from which we can learn to improve the efficiency of that instrument; and the question whether on any occasion a man could or could not have acted otherwise than as he did can be left on one side or answered either way, as may be preferred. It is no longer relevant.

Failure to appreciate this has, I think, led to conflicts between psychiatry and the law being often fought on the wrong ground. Even so radical a criminologist as Dr. Sheldon Glueck seems to see the issue as one between "those who stress the prime social need of blameworthiness and retributive punishment as the core-concept in crime and justice and those who, under the impact of psychiatric, psychoanalytic, sociological, and anthropological views insist that man's choices are the product of forces largely beyond his conscious control . . ."[27] Indeed Dr. Glueck's discussion of the relation of psychiatry to law is chiefly devoted to an analysis of the exculpatory effect of psychiatric knowledge, and to the changes that have been, or should be, made in the assessment of guilt as the result of the growth of this knowledge. In consequence much intellectual ingenuity is wasted in refining the criteria by which the wicked may be distinguished from the weak-minded. For surely to argue thus is to argue from the wrong premises: The real difference between the psychiatric and the legal approach has nothing to do with free will and determinism. It has to do with their conceptions of the objectives of the criminal process, with the question whether the aim of that process is punitive or preventive, whether what matters is to punish the wrongdoer or to set him on the road to virtue;

and, in order to take a stand on that issue, neither party need be a determinist.

So much for what disregard of responsibility does not mean. What, in a more positive sense, is it likely to involve? Here, I think, one of the most important consequences must be to obscure the present rigid distinction between the penal and the medical institution. As things are, the supposedly fully responsible are consigned to the former: Only the wholly or partially irresponsible are eligible for the latter. Once it is admitted that we have no reliable criterion by which to distinguish between those two categories, strict segregation of each into a distinct set of institutions becomes absurd and impracticable. For purposes of convenience offenders for whom medical treatment is indicated will doubtless tend to be allocated to one building, and those for whom medicine has nothing to offer to another; but the formal distinction between prison and hospital will become blurred, and, one may reasonably expect, eventually obliterated altogether. Both will be simply "places of safety" in which offenders receive the treatment which experience suggests is most likely to evoke the desired response.

Does this mean that the distinction between doctors and prison officers must also become blurred? Up to a point it clearly does. At the very least it would seem that some fundamental implications for the medical profession must be involved when the doctor becomes part of the machinery of law enforcement. Not only is the normal doctor-patient relationship profoundly disturbed, but far-reaching questions also arise as to the nature of the condition which the doctor is called upon to treat. If a tendency to break the law is not in itself to be classified as a disease, which does he seek to cure—the criminality or the illness? To the medical profession these questions, which I have discussed at length elsewhere,[28] must be of primary concern. But for present purposes it may be more relevant to notice how, as so often happens in this country, changes not yet officially recognised in theory are already creeping in by the back door. Already the long-awaited institution at Grendon Underwood is administered as an integral part of the prison system; yet the régime is frankly medical. Its purpose has been described by the Prison Commission's Director of Medical Services as the investigation and treatment of mental disorder generally recognised as calling for a psychiatric approach; the investigation of the mental condition of offenders whose offences in themselves suggest mental instability; and an exploration of the problem of the treatment of the psychopath. Recommendations for admission are to come from prison medical officers, and the prison itself is under the charge of a medical superintendent with wide experience in psychiatry.[29]

Grendon Underwood is (unless one should include Broadmoor which has, of course, a much narrower scope) the first genuinely hybrid institution. Interchange between medical and penal institutions is, however, further facilitated by the power of the Home Secretary to transfer to hospital persons whom, on appropriate medical evidence, he finds to be suffering from mental disorder of a nature or degree to warrant their detention in a hospital for medical treatment. Such transfers have the same effect as does a hospital order, and they may be (and usually are) also accompanied by an order restricting discharge. It is, moreover, of some interest that transfers are sometimes made quite soon after the court has passed sentence. Out of six cases convicted under section 2 of the Homicide Act in which transfers under section 72 were effected, three were removed to hospital less than three months after sentence. Although it is, of course, always possible that the prisoner has been mentally normal at the time of his offence and had only suffered a mental breakdown later, transfer after a relatively short period does indicate at least a possibility that in the judgment of the Home Secretary some mental abnormality may have been already present either at the time of sentence or even when the crime was committed.

The courts, however, seem to be somewhat jealous of the exercise of this power, which virtually allows the Home Secretary to treat as sick persons whom they have sentenced to imprisonment and presumably regard as wicked. Indeed it seems that, if a diagnosis of mental disorder is to be made, the courts hold that it is, generally speaking, their business, and not the Home Secretary's, to make it. So at least it would appear from the judgments of the Court of Criminal Appeal in the cases of Constance Ann James[30] and Philip Morris,[31] both of whom had been found guilty of manslaughter on grounds of diminished responsibility and had been sentenced to imprisonment.

In the former case, in which the evidence as to the accused's mental condition was unchallenged, the trial judge apparently had misgivings about the public safety and in particular the safety of the convicted woman's younger child whose brother she had killed. He therefore passed a sentence of three years' imprisonment, leaving it, as he said, to the appropriate authorities to make further inquiries so that the Secretary of State might, if he thought fit, transfer the prisoner to hospital under section 72 of the Mental Health Act. The appeal was allowed, on the ground that there was obviously no need for punishment, and that there were reasonable hopes that the disorder from which the woman suffered would prove curable. In the circumstances, though reluctant to interfere with the discretion of the sentencing court, the Court of Criminal Appeal substituted a hospital order accompanied by an indefinite restriction.

In Philip Morris' case, in which, however, the appellant was unsuccessful, the matter was put even more clearly. Again the trial judge had refused to make a hospital order on grounds of the public safety and, failing any vacancy in a secure hospital, had passed a sentence of life imprisonment. But on this the Court of Criminal Appeal commented as follows: "Although the discretion . . . is very wide indeed, the basic principle must be that in the ordinary case where punishment as such is not intended, and where the sole object of the sentence is that a man should receive mental treatment, and be at large as soon as he can safely be discharged, a proper exercise of the discretion demands that steps should be taken to exercise the powers under section 60 and that the matter should not be left to be dealt with by the Secretary of State under section 72."

These difficulties are, one may hope, of a transitional nature. They would certainly not arise if all sentences involving loss of liberty were indeterminate in respect of the type of institution in which the offender is to be detained: still less if rigid distinctions between medical and penal institutions were no longer maintained. The elimination of those distinctions, moreover, though unthinkable in a primary punitive system which must at all times segregate the blameworthy from the blameless, is wholly in keeping with a criminal law which is preventive rather than punitive in intention.

In this lecture and in that which preceded it I have tried to signpost the road towards such a conception of the law, and to indicate certain landmarks which suggest that this is the road along which we are, if hesitantly, already treading. At first blush it might seem that strict liability and mental abnormality have not much in common; but both present a challenge to traditional views as to the point at which, and the purpose for which, considerations of guilty intent become relevant; and both illustrate the contemporary tendency to use the criminal law to protect the community against damage, no matter what might be the state of mind of those by whom that damage is done. In this context, perhaps, the little-noticed provisions of section 60 (2) of the Mental Health Act, with its distinction between the forbidden act and the conviction, along with the liberal implications of section 4 of the Criminal Justice Act, with its emphasis on treatability rather than culpability, are to be seen as the writing on the wall. And perhaps, too, it is significant that Dr. Glueck, notwithstanding his immediate preoccupation with definitions of responsibility, lets fall, almost as if with a sign, the forecast that some day it may be possible "to limit criminal law to matters of behavior alone," and that in his concluding lecture he foresees the "twilight of futile blameworthiness."[32] That day may be still a long way off: but at least it seems to be nearer than it was.

NOTES

1. *The Observer,* May 5, 1963.
2. I use this word throughout to describe a system the primary purpose of which is to prevent the occurrence of offences, whether committed by persons already convicted or by other people . . .
2a. Devlin, Sir Patrick (now Lord), *Law and Morals* (University of Birmingham) 1961, pp. 3, 7, 8, 9.
3. Radcliffe, Lord, *The Law and Its Compass* (Faber) 1961, p. 12.

4. *Shaw* v. *Director of Public Prosecutions* [1961] 2 W.L.R. 897.
5. *The Times,* November 11, 1961.
6. Edwards, J. Ll. J., *Mens Rea in Statutory Offences* (Macmillan) 1955, p. 247.
7. Devlin, Lord, *Samples of Law Making* (O.U.P.) 1962, pp. 71–80.
8. Hart, H. L. A., *Punishment and the Elimination of Responsibility* (Athlone Press) 1962, pp. 27, 28. Italics mine.
9. *Op. cit.,* pp. 29, 30.
10. Devlin, Lord, *Samples of Law Making* (O.U.P.) 1962, p. 73.
11. There could be an argument here, into which I do not propose to enter, as to whether this capacity is not shared by some of the higher animals.
12. Walker, N., "Queen Victoria Was Right," *New Society,* June 27, 1963.
13. House of Lords Debates, May 1, 1963, col. 174.
14. *R.* v. *James* [1961] Crim.L.R. 842.
15. One curious feature of this provision is the fact that a hospital order can apparently be made on a diagnosis of mental disorder, even if the disorder has no connection with the offence. See the Court of Criminal Appeal's judgment in the unsuccessful appeal of *R.* v. *Hatt* ([1962] Crim.L.R. 647) in which the appellant claimed that his predilection for unnecessary surgical operations had no connection with his no less fervent passion for making off with other people's cars.
16. House of Commons Standing Committee A, February 12, 1948, col. 1054.
17. Grünhut, M., *Probation and Mental Treatment* (to be published in the Library of Criminology).
18. Wootton, Barbara, "Diminished Responsibility: A Layman's View" (1960) 76 *Law Quarterly Review* 224.
19. *R.* v. *Di Duca* [1959] 43 Cr.App.R. 167.
20. Unpublished transcript.
21. Unpublished transcript.
22. *R.* v. *Clarke* [1962] Crim.L.R.836.
23. House of Commons Debates, Vol. 560 (November 15, 1956), col. 1252.
24. *R.* v. *Price* [1962] 3 All E.R. 960.
25. *R.* v. *Byrne* (1960) 44 Cr.App.R. 246.
26. *R.* v. *Terry* (1961) 45 Cr.App.R. 180.
27. Glueck, Sheldon, *Law and Psychiatry* (Tavistock Publications) 1962, p. 6.
28. Wootton, Barbara, "The Law, The Doctor and The Deviant," *British Medical Journal,* July 27, 1963.
29. Snell, H. K. (Director of Medical Services, Prison Commission), "H. M. Prison Grendon," *British Medical Journal,* September 22, 1962.
30. *R.* v. *James* [1961] Crim.L.R. 842.
31. *R.* v. *Morris* (1961) 45 Cr.App.R. 233.
32. Glueck, Sheldon, *Law and Psychiatry* (Tavistock Publications) 1962, pp. 33, 147.

H. L. A. HART

Changing Conceptions of Responsibility*

I

This lecture is concerned wholly with criminal responsibility and I have chosen to lecture on this subject here because both English and Israeli law have inherited from the past virtually the same doctrine concerning the criminal responsibility of the mentally abnormal and both have found this inheritance embarrassing. I refer of course to the M'Naghten rules of 1843. In Israel the Supreme Court has found it possible to supplement these exceedingly narrow rules by use of the doctrine incorporated in s. 11 of the Criminal Code Ordinance of 1936 that an 'exercise of will' is necessary for responsibility. This is the effect of the famous case of *Mandelbrot* v. *Attorney General* [1] and the subsequent cases which have embedded Agranat J's construction of s. 11 in Israeli law. English lawyers, though they may admire this bold step, cannot use as an escape route from the confines of the M'Naghten rules the similar doctrine that for any criminal liability there must be a 'voluntary act' which many authorities have said is a fundamental requirement of English criminal law. For this doctrine has always been understood merely to exclude cases where the muscular movements are involuntary as in sleepwalking or 'automatism' or reflex action.[2] Nonetheless there have been changes in England; after a period of frozen immobility the hardened mass of our substantive criminal law is at points softening and yielding to its critics. But both the recent changes and the current criticisms of the law in this matter of criminal responsibility have taken a different direction from development in Israel and for this reason may be of some interest to Israeli lawyers.

*From *The Morality of the Criminal Law* by H. L. A. Hart (Jerusalem: Magnes Press, 1965). Reprinted as Chapter VIII of *Punishment and Responsibility: Essays in the Philosophy of Law* by H. L. A. Hart (New York and Oxford: Oxford University Press, 1967), pp. 186–209.

Let me first say something quite general and very elementary about the historical background to these recent changes. In all advanced legal systems, liability to conviction for serious crimes is made dependent, not only on the offender having done those outward acts which the law forbids, but on his having done them in a certain frame of mind or with a certain will. These are the mental conditions or 'mental elements' in criminal responsibility and, in spite of much variation in detail and terminology, they are broadly similar in most legal systems. Even if you kill a man, this is not punishable as murder in most civilised jurisdictions if you do it unintentionally, accidentally or by mistake, or while suffering from certain forms of mental abnormality. Lawyers of the Anglo-American tradition use the Latin phrase *mens rea* (a guilty mind) as a comprehensive name for these necessary mental elements; and according to conventional ideas *mens rea* is a necessary element in liability to be established *before* a verdict. It is not something which is merely to be taken into consideration in determining the sentence or disposal of the convicted person, though it may also be considered for that purpose as well.

I have said that my topic in this lecture is the recent changes in England on this matter, but I shall be concerned less with changes in the law itself than with changes among critics of the law towards the whole doctrine of the mental element in responsibility. This change in critical attitude is, I believe, more important than any particular change in the detail of the doctrine of *mens rea*. I say this because for a century at least most liberal minded people have agreed in treating respect for the doctrine of *mens rea* as a hallmark of a civilised legal system. Until recently the great aim of most critics of the criminal law has been to secure that the law should take this doctrine very seriously and wholeheartedly. Critics have sought its expansion, and urged that the courts should be required always to make genuine efforts, when a person is accused of crime, to determine before convicting him whether that person actually did have the knowledge or intention or the sanity or any other mental element which the law, in its definition of crimes, makes a necessary condition of criminal liability. It is true that English law has often wavered on this matter and has even quite recently flirted with the idea that it cannot really afford to inquire into an individual's actual mental state before punishing him. There have always been English judges in whom a remark made in 1477 by Chief Justice Brian of the Common Pleas strikes a sympathetic chord. He said 'The thought of man is not triable; the devil alone knoweth the thought of man.'[3] So there are in English law many compromises on this matter of the relevance of a man's mind to the criminality of his deeds. Not only are there certain crimes of 'strict' liability where neither knowledge, nor negligence is required for conviction, but there are also certain doctrines of 'objective' liability such as was endorsed by the House of Lords in the much criticized case of *The Director of Public Prosecutions* v. *Smith*[4] on which Lord Denning lectured to you three years ago.[5] This doctrine enables a court to impute to an accused person knowledge or an intention which he may not really have had, but which an average man would have had. Theories have been developed in support of this doctrine of 'objective liability' of which the most famous is that expounded by the great American judge, Oliver Wendell Holmes in his book *The Common Law.* Nonetheless generations of progressive minded lawyers and liberal critics of the law have thought of the doctrine of *mens rea* as something to be cherished and extended, and against the scepticism of Chief Justice Brian they could quote the robust assertion of the nineteenth-century Lord Justice Bowen that 'the state of a man's mind is as much a fact as the state of his digestion.'[6] And they would have added that for the criminal law the former was a good deal more important than the latter.

But recently in England progressive and liberal criticism of the law has changed its direction. Though I think this change must in the end involve the whole doctrine of *mens rea,* it at present mainly concerns the criminal responsibility of mentally abnormal persons, and I can best convey its character by sketching the course taken in the criticism of the law in this matter. The main doctrine of English law until recently was of course the famous M'Naghten Rules formulated by the Judges of the House of Lords in 1843. As everybody knows, according to this doctrine, mental abnormality sufficient to constitute a defence to a criminal charge must consist of three elements: First, the accused, at the time of his act, must have suffered from a defect of reason; secondly, this must have arisen from disease of the mind; thirdly, the result of it must have been that the accused did not know the nature of his act or that it was illegal. From the start English critics denounced these rules because their effect is to excuse from criminal responsibility only those whose mental abnormality resulted in lack of knowledge: in the eyes of these critics this amounted to a dogmatic refusal to acknowledge the fact that a man might know what he was doing and that it was wrong or illegal and yet because of his normal mental state might lack the capacity to control his action. This lack of capacity, the critics urged, must be the fundamental point in any intelligible doctrine of responsibility. The point just is that in a civilized system only those who *could have* kept the law should be punished. Why else should we bother about a man's knowledge or intention or other mental element except as throwing light on this?

Angrily and enviously, many of the critics pointed to foreign legal systems which were free of the English obsession with this single element of knowledge as the sole constituent of responsibility. As far back as 1810, the French Code simply excused those suffering from madness (démence) without specifying any particular connection between this and the particular act done. The German Code of 1871 spoke of inability or impaired ability to recognize the wrongness of conduct or to act in accordance with this recognition. It thus, correctly, according to the critics, treated as crucial to the issue of responsibility not knowledge but the capacity to conform to law. The Belgian Loi de Défence Sociale of 1930 makes no reference to knowledge or intelligence but speaks simply of a person's lack of ability as a consequence of mental abnormality to control his action. So till recently the great aim of the critics inspired by these foreign models was essentially to secure an amendment of the English doctrine of *mens rea* on this point: to supplement its purely cognitive test by a volitional one, admitting that a man might, while knowing that he was breaking the law, be unable to conform to it.

This dispute raged through the nineteenth century and was certainly marked by some curious features. In James Fitzjames Stephen's great *History of the Criminal Law*[7] the dispute is vividly presented as one between doctors and lawyers. The doctors are pictured as accusing the lawyers of claiming to decide a medical or scientific issue about responsibility by out-of-date criteria when they limited legal inquiry to the question of knowledge. The lawyers replied that the doctors, in seeking to give evidence about other matters, were attempting illicitly to thrust upon juries their views on what should excuse a man when charged with a crime: illicitly, because responsibility is a question not of science but of law. Plainly, the argument was here entrapped in the ambiguities of the word 'responsibility' about which more should have been said. But it is also remarkable that in the course of this long dispute no clear statements were made of the reason why the law should recognise any form of insanity as an excuse. The basic question as to what was at stake in the doctrine of *mens rea* was hardly faced. Is it necessary because punishment is conceived of as paying back moral evil done with some essentially retributive 'fitting' equivalent in pain? If so, what state of mind does a theory of retribution require a person punished to have had? Or is a doctrine of *mens rea* necessary because punishment is conceived as primarily a deterrent and this purpose would be frustrated or useless if persons were punished who at the time of their crime lacked certain knowledge or ability? Or is the doctrine to give effect not to a retributive theory but to principles of fairness or justice which require that a man should not be punished and so be used for the ends of others unless he had the capacity and a fair opportunity to avoid doing the thing for which he is punished? Certainly Bentham and Blackstone had something to say on these matters of fundamental principle, but they do not figure much in the century-long war which was waged by English reformers, sometimes in a fog, against the M'Naghten Rules. But what was clear in the fog was that neither party thought of calling the whole doctrine of *mens rea* in question. What was sought was merely amendments or additions to it.

Assault after assault on the M'Naghten Rules were beaten off until 1957. It cannot be said that the defenders of the doctrine used any very sharp rapiers in their defence. The good old English bludgeon which has beaten off so many reforms of English criminal law was enough. When Lord Atkin's Committee recommended in 1923 an addition to the M'Naghten Rules to cater for what it termed "irresistible impulse,' it was enough in the debate in the House of Lords[8] for judicial members to prophesy the harm to society which would inevitably flow from the amendment. Not a word was said to meet the point that the laws of many other countries already conformed to the proposal: nothing was said about the United States where a similar modification of the M'Naghten Rules providing for inability to conform to the law's requirement as well as defects in knowledge had been long accepted in several States without disastrous results. But in 1957, largely as a result of the immensely valuable examination of the whole topic by the Royal Commission on Capital Punishment[9] the law was amended, not as recommended by the Commission, but in the form of a curious compromise. This was the introduction of the idea borrowed from Scots law of a plea of diminished responsibility. S. 2 of the Homicide Act of 1957 provides that, on a murder charge, if what it most curiously calls the accused's 'mental responsibility' was 'substantially' impaired by mental abnormality, he could be convicted, not of murder, but only of manslaughter, carrying a maximum sentence of imprisonment for life. This change in the law was indeed meagre since it concerned only murder; and even here it was but a halfway house, since the accused was not excused from punishment but was to be punished less than the maximum. The change does not excuse from responsibility but mitigates the penalty.

A word or two about the operation of the new plea of diminished responsibility during the last six years is necessary. The judges at first tended to treat it merely as catering for certain cases on the borderlines of the M'Naghten Rules, not as making a major change. Thus Lord Goddard refused to direct the jury that under the new plea the question of capacity to conform to law and not merely the accused's knowledge was relevant.[10] But the present Lord Chief Justice in a remarkable judgment expressly stated that this was so, and a generous interpretation was given to the section so as to include in the phrase 'abnormality of mind' the condition of the psychopath. He said that it was important to consider not only the accused's knowledge but also his ability 'to exercise will power to control physical acts in accordance with rational judgment.'[11] However, the most remarkable feature of six year's experience of this plea is made evident by the statistics: Apprehensions that it might lead to large-scale evasions of punishment have been shown to be quite baseless. For since the Homicide Act almost precisely the same percentage—about 47 per cent —of persons charged with murder escaped conviction on the ground of mental abnormality as before. What has happened is that the plea of insanity under the old M'Naghten Rules has virtually been displaced in murder cases by the new plea.[12] Though satisfactory, in that the old fears of reform have not been realized, the plea certainly has its critics and in part the general change in attitude of which I shall speak has been accelerated by it.

II

I have said that the change made by the introduction of diminished responsibility was both meagre and half-hearted. Nonetheless it marked the end of an era in the criticism of the law concerning the criminal responsibility of the mentally abnormal. From this point on criticism has largely changed its character. Instead of demanding that the court should take more seriously the task of dividing lawbreakers into two classes— those fully responsible and justly punishable because they had an unimpaired capacity to conform to the law, and those who were to be excused for lack of this—critics have come to think this a mistaken approach. Instead of seeking an expansion of the doctrine of *mens rea* they have argued that it should be eliminated and have welcomed the proliferation of offences of strict liability as a step in the right direction and a model for the future. The bolder of them have talked of the need to 'bypass' or 'dispense with' questions of responsibility and have condemned the old efforts to widen the scope of the M'Naghten Rules as waste of time or worse. Indeed, their attitude to such reforms is like that of the Communist who condemns private charity in a capitalist system because it tends to hide the radical errors of the system and thus preserve it. By far the best informed, most trenchant and influential advocate of these new ideas is Lady Wootton whose powerful work on the subject of criminal responsibility has done much to change and, in my opinion, to raise, the whole level of discussion.[13]

Hence, since 1957 a new skepticism going far beyond the old criticisms has developed. It is indeed a skepticism of the whole institution of criminal punishment so far as it contains elements which differentiate it from a system of purely forward-looking social hygiene in which our only concern, when we have an offender to deal with, is with the future and the rational aims of the prevention of further crime, the protection of society and the care and if possible the cure of the offender. For criminal punishment, as even the most progressive older critics of the M'Naghten Rules conceived of it, is *not* mere social hygiene. It differs from such a purely forward-looking system in the stress that it places on something in the past: the state of mind of the accused as the time, not of his trial, but when he broke the law.

To many modern critics this backward-looking reference to the accused's past state of mind as a condition of his liability to compulsory measures seems a useless deflection from the proper forward-looking aims of a rational system of social control. The past they urge is over and done with, and the offender's past state of mind is only important as a diagnosis of the causes of his offence and a prognosis of what can be done now to counter these causes. Nothing in the past, according to this newer outlook, can in itself justify or be required to license what we do to the offender now; that is something to be determined exclusively by reference to the consequences to society and to him. Lady Wootton argues that if the aim of the criminal law is to be the prevention of 'socially damaging actions' not retribution for past wickedness, the conventional doctrine puts *mens rea* 'into the wrong place.'[14] *Mens rea* is on her view relevant only *after* conviction as a guide to what measures should be taken to prevent a recurrence of the forbidden act. She considers it 'illogical,' if the aim of the criminal law is prevention, to make *mens rea* part of the definition of a crime and a necessary condition of the offender's liability to compulsory measures.[15]

This way of thinking leads to a radical revision of the penal system which in crude outline and in its most extreme form is as follows: Once it has been proved in a court that a person's outward conduct fits the legal definition of some crime, this without proof or any *mens rea,* is sufficient to bring him within the scope of compulsory measures. These may be either of a penal or therapeutic kind or both; or it may be found that no measures are necessary in a particular case and the offender may be discharged. But the choice between these alternatives is not to be made by reference to the offender's past mental state—his culpability—but by consideration of what steps, in view of his present mental state and his general situation, are likely to have the best consequences for him and for society.

I have called this the extreme form of the new approach because as I have formulated it is generally applicable to all offenders alike. It is not a system reserved solely for those who could be classed as mentally abnormal. The whole doctrine of *mens rea* would on this extreme version of the theory be dropped from the law; so that the distinctions which at present we draw and think vital to draw before convicting an offender, between, for example, intentional and unintentional wrongdoing, would no longer be relevant at this stage. To show that you have struck or wounded another unintentionally or without negligence would not save you from conviction and liability to such treatment, penal or therapeutic, as the court might deem advisable on evidence of your mental state and character.

This is, as I say, the extreme form of the theory, and it is the form that Lady Wootton now advances.[16] But certainly a less extreme though more complex form is conceivable which would replace, not the whole doctrine of *mens rea,* but only that part of it which concerns the legal responsibility of the mentally abnormal. In this more moderate form of the theory, a mentally normal person would still escape conviction if he acted unintentionally or without some other requisite mental element forming part of the definition of the crime charged. The innovation would be that no form of insanity or mental abnormality would bar a conviction, and this would no longer

be investigated before conviction.[17] It would be something to be investigated only after conviction to determine what measures of punishment or treatment would be most efficacious in the particular case. It is important to observe that most advocates of the elimination of responsibility have been mainly concerned with the inadequacies or absurdities of the existing law in relation to mentally abnormal offenders, and some of these advocates may have intended only the more moderate form of the theory which is limited to such offenders. But I doubt if this is at all representative, for many, including Lady Wootton, have said that no satisfactory line can be drawn between the mentally normal and abnormal offenders: There simply are no clear or reliable criteria. They insist that general definitions of mental health are too vague and too conflicting; we should be freed from all such illusory classifications to treat, in the most appropriate way from the point of view of society, all persons who have actually manifested the behaviour which is the *actus reus* of a crime.[18] The fact that harm was done unintentionally should not preclude an investigation of what steps if any are desirable to prevent a repetition. This skepticism of the possibility of drawing lines between the normal and abnormal offenders commits advocates of the elimination of responsibility to the extreme form of the theory.

Such then are the essentials of the new idea. Of course the phrase 'eliminating responsibility' does sound very alarming and when Lady Wootton's work first made it a centre of discussion the columns of *The Times* newspaper showed how fluttered legal and other dovecotes were. But part at least of the alarm was unnecessary because it arose from the ambiguities of the word 'responsibility'; and it is, I think, still important to distinguish two of the very different things this difficult word may mean. To say that someone is legally responsible for something often means only that under legal rules he is liable to be made either to suffer or to pay compensation in certain eventualities. The expression 'he'll pay for it' covers both these things. In this the primary sense of the word, though a man is normally only responsible for his own actions or the harm he has done, he may be also responsible for the actions of other persons if legal rules so provide. Indeed in this sense a baby in arms or a totally insane person might be legally responsible—again, if the rules so provide; for the word simply means liable to be made to account or pay and we might call this sense of the word 'legal accountability.' But the new idea—the programme of eliminating responsibility—is not, as some have feared, meant to eliminate legal accountability: Persons who break the law are not just to be left free. What is to be eliminated are enquiries as to whether a person who has done what the law forbids was responsible at the time he did it and responsible in this sense does not refer to the legal status of accountability. It means the capacity, so far as this is a matter of a man's mind or will, which normal people have to control their actions and conform to law. In this sense of responsibility a man's responsibility can be said to be 'impaired.' That is indeed the language of s. 2 of the Homicide Act 1957 which introduced into English law the idea of diminished responsibility: it speaks of a person's *'mental'* responsibility and in the rubric to s. 2 even of persons 'suffering from' diminished responsibility. It is of course easy to see why this second sense of responsibility (which might be called 'personal responsibility') has grown up alongside the primary idea of legal accountability. It is no doubt because the law normally, though not always, confines legal accountability to persons who are believed to have normal capacities of control.

So perhaps the new ideas are less alarming than they seem at first. They are also less new, and those who advocate them have always been able to point to earlier developments within English law which seem to foreshadow these apparently revolutionary ideas. Lady Wootton herself makes much of the fact that the doctrine of *mens rea* in the case of normal offenders has been watered down by the introduction of strict liability and she deprecates the alarm this has raised. But apart from this, the courts have often been able to deal with mentally abnormal persons accused of crime without confronting the issue of their personal responsibility at the time of their offence. There are in fact several different ways in which this question may be avoided. A man may be held on account of his mental state to be unfit to plead when brought to trial; or he may be certified insane before trial; or, except on a charge of murder, an accused person might enter a plea of guilty with the suggestion that he should be put on probation with a condition of mental treatment.[19] In fact, only a very small percentage of the mentally abnormal have been dealt with under the M'Naghten Rules, a fact which is understandable since a successful plea under those Rules means detention in Broadmoor for an indefinite period and many would rather face conviction and imprisonment and so may not raise the question of mental abnormality at all. So the old idea of treating mental abnormality as bearing on the question of the accused's responsibility and to be settled before conviction, has with few exceptions only been a reality in murder cases to which alone is the plea of diminished responsibility applicable.

But the most important departure from received ideas incorporated in the doctrine of *mens rea* is the Mental Health Act, 1959, which expands certain principles of older legislation. S. 60 of this Act provides that in any case, except where the crime is not punishable by imprisonment or the sentence is fixed by the law (and this latter exception virtually excludes only murder), the courts may, after conviction of the offender, if two doctors agree that the accused falls into any of four specified categories of mental disorder, order his detention for medical treatment instead of passing a penal sentence, though it requires evidence that such detention is warranted. The four categories of mental disorder are very wide and include even psychopathic disorder in spite of the general lack of clear or agreed criteria of this condition. The courts are told by the statute that in exercising their choice between penal or medical measures to have regard to the nature of the offence and the character and antecedents of the offender. These powers have come to be widely used[20] and are available even in cases where a murder charge has been reduced to manslaughter on a plea of provocation or diminished responsibility.

Advocates of the programme of eliminating responsibility welcome the powers given by the Mental Health Act to substitute compulsory treatment for punishment, but necessarily they view it as a compromise falling short of what is required, and we shall understand their own views better if we see why they think so. It falls short in four respects. First the power given to courts to order compulsory treatment instead of punishment is discretionary, and even if the appropriate medical evidence is forthcoming the courts may still administer conventional punishment if they choose. The judges *may* still think in terms of responsibility, and it is plain that they occasionally do so in these cases. Thus in the majority of cases of conviction for manslaughter following on a successful plea of diminished responsibility, the courts have imposed sentences of imprisonment notwithstanding their powers under s. 60 of the Mental Health Act, and the Lord Chief Justice has said that in such cases the prisoner may on the facts be shown to have *some* responsibility for which he must be punished.[21] Secondly, the law itself still preserves a conception of penal methods, such as imprisonment, coloured by the idea that it is a payment for past wickedness and not just an alternative to medical treatment; for though the courts may order medical treatment or punish, they cannot combine these. This of course is a refusal to think, as the new critics demand we should think,[22] of punitive and medical measures as merely different forms of social hygiene to be used according to a prognosis of their effects on the convicted person. Thirdly, as it stands at present, the scheme presupposes that a satisfactory distinction can be drawn on the basis of its four categories of mental disorder between those who are mentally abnormal and those who are not. But the more radical reformers are not merely sceptical about the adequacy of the criteria which distinguish, for example, the psychopath from the normal offender: They would contend that there may exist propensities to certain types of socially harmful behaviour in people who are in other ways not abnormal and that a rational system should attend to these cases.

But fourthly, and this is most important, the scheme is vitiated for these critics because the courts' powers are only exercisable after the conviction of an offender and, for this conviction, proof of *mens rea* at the time of his offence is still required: The question of the accused's mental abnormality may still be raised before conviction as a defence if the accused so wishes. So the Mental Health Act does not 'bypass' the whole question of responsibility: It does not eliminate the doctrine of *mens rea*. It expands the courts' discretion in dealing with a convicted person, enabling them to choose between penal and therapeutic measures and making this choice in practice largely independent of the offender's state of mind at the time of his offence. Its great merit is that the mentally abnormal offender who would before have submitted to a sentence of imprisonment rather than raise a plea of insanity under the M'Naghten Rules (because success would mean indeterminate detention in Broadmoor) may now be encouraged to bring forward his mental condition after conviction, in the hope of obtaining a hospital order rather than a sentence of imprisonment.

The question which now awaits our consideration is the merits of the claim that we should proceed from such a system as we now have under the Mental Health Act to one in which the criminal courts were freed altogether from the doctrine of *mens rea* and could proceed to the use of either penal or medical measures at discretion simply on proof that the accused had done the outward acts of a crime. Prisons and hospitals under such a scheme will alike 'be simply "places of safety" in which offenders receive the treatment which experience suggests is most likely to evoke the desired response.'[23]

The case for adopting these new ideas in their entirety has been supposed by arguments of varying kinds and quality, and it is very necessary to sift the wheat from the chaff. The weakest of the arguments is perhaps the one most frequently heard, namely, that our concern with personal responsibility incorporated in the doctrine of *mens rea* only makes sense if we subscribe to a retributive theory of punishment according to which punishment is used and justified as an 'appropriate' or 'fitting' return for past wickedness and not merely as a preventive of antisocial conduct. This, as I have argued elsewhere,[24] is a philosophical confusion and Lady Wootton falls a victim to it because she makes too crude a dichotomy between 'punishment' and 'prevention.' She does not even mention a moral outlook on punishment which is surely very common, very simple and, except perhaps for the determinist, perfectly defensible. This is the view that out of considerations of fairness or justice to individuals we should restrict even punishment designed as a 'preventive' to those who had a normal capacity and a fair opportunity to obey. This is still an intelligible ideal of justice to the individuals whom we punish even if we punish them to protect society from the harm that crime does and not to pay back the harm that they have done. And it remains intelligible even if in securing this form of fairness to those whom we punish we secure a lesser measure of conformity to law than a system of total strict liability which repudiated the doctrine of *mens rea*.

But of course it is certainly arguable that, at present, in certain cases, in the application of the doctrine of *mens rea*, we recognize this principle of justice in a way which plays too high a price in terms of social security. For there are indeed cases where the application of *mens rea* operates in surprising and possibly dangerous ways. A man may cause very great harm, may even kill another person, and under the present law neither be punished for it nor subjected to any compulsory medical treatment or supervision. This happened, for example, in February 1961 when a United States Air Force sergeant,[25] after a drunken party, killed a girl, according to his own story, in his sleep. He was tried for murder but the jury were not persuaded by the prosecution, on whom the legal burden of proof rests, that the sergeant's story was false and he was accordingly acquitted and discharged altogether. It is worth observing that in recent years in cases of dangerous driving where the accused claims that he suffered from 'automatism' or a sudden lapse of consciousness, the courts have striven very hard to narrow the scope of this defence because of the obvious social dangers of an acquittal of such persons, unaccompanied by any order for compulsory treatment. They have produced a most complex body of law distinguishing between 'sane' and 'insane' automatism each with their special burdens of proof.[26] No doubt such dangerous cases are not very numerous and the risk of their occurrence is one which many people might prefer to run rather than introduce a new system dispensing altogether with proof of *mens rea*. In any case something less extreme than the new system might deal with such cases; for the courts could be given powers in the case of such physically harmful offences to order, notwithstanding an acquittal, any kind of medical treatment or supervision that seemed appropriate.

But the most important arguments in favour of the more radical system in which proof of the outward act alone is enough to make the accused liable to compulsory measures of treatment or punishment, comes from those who, like Lady Wootton, have closely scrutinized the actual working of the old plea of insanity and the plea of diminished responsibility introduced in 1957 by the Homicide Act into cases of homicide. The latter treats mental abnormality as an aspect of *mens rea* and forces the courts before the verdict to decide the question whether the accused's 'mental responsibility,' that is, his capacity to control his actions was 'substantially impaired' at the time of his offence when he killed another person. The conclusion drawn by Lady Wootton from her impressive and detailed study of all the cases (199 in number) in which this plea was raised down to mid-September of 1962, is that this question which is thus forced upon the courts should be discarded as unanswerable. Here indeed she echoes the cry, often in earlier years thundered from the Bench, that it is impossible to distinguish between an irresistable impulse and an impulse which was merely not resisted by the accused.

But here too if we are to form a balanced view we must distinguish between dubious philosophical contentions and some very good sense. The philosophical arguments (which I will not discuss here in detail) pitch the case altogether too high: They are supposed to show that the question whether a man could have acted differently is *in principle unanswerable* and not merely that in Law Courts we do not usually have clear enough evidence to answer it. Lady Wootton says that a man's responsibility or capacity to resist temptation is something 'buried in [his] consciousness, into which no human being can enter,'[27] known if at all only to him and to God: it is not something which other men may never know; and since 'it is not possible to get inside another man's skin'[28] it is not something of which they can ever form even a reasonable estimate as a matter of probability. Yet strangely enough she does not take the same view of the question which arises under the M'Naghten Rules whether a man knew what he was doing or that it was illegal, although a man's knowledge is surely as much, or as little, locked in his breast as his capacity for self control. Questions about the latter indeed may often be more difficult to answer than questions about a man's knowledge; yet in favourable circumstances if we know a man well and can trust what he says about his efforts or struggles to control himself we may have as good ground for saying

'Well he just could not do it though he tried' as we have for saying 'He didn't know that the pistol was loaded.' And we sometimes may have good general evidence that in certain conditions, for example infancy or a clinically definable state, such as depression after childbirth, human beings are unable or less able than the normal adult to master certain impulses. We are not forced by the facts to say of a child or mental defective, who has struggled vainly with tears, merely 'he usually cries when that happens.' We say—and why not? —'he could not stop himself crying though he tried as hard as he could.'

It must however be conceded that such clear cases are very untypical of those that face the Courts where an accused person is often fighting for his life or freedom. Lady Wootton's best arguments are certainly independent of her more debatable philosophical points about our ability to know what is locked in another's mind or breast. Her central point is that the evidence put before Courts on the question whether the accused lacked the capacity to conform to the law, or whether it was substantially impaired, at the best only shows the *propensity* of the accused to commit crimes of certain sorts. From this, she claims, it is a fallacy to infer that he could not have done otherwise than commit the crime of which he is accused. She calls this fallacious argument 'circular': We infer the accused's lack of capacity to control his actions from his propensity to commit crimes and then both explain this propensity and excuse his crimes by his lack of capacity. Lady Wootton's critics have challenged this view of the medical and other evidence on which the courts act in these cases.[29] They would admit that it is at any rate in part through studying a man's crimes that we may discern his incapacity to control his actions. Nonetheless the evidence for this conclusion is not merely the bare fact that he committed these crimes repeatedly, but the manner and the circumstances and the psychological state in which he did this. Secondly in forming any conclusion about a man's ability to control his action much more than his repeated crimes are taken into account. Antisocial behaviour is not just used to explain and excuse itself, even in the case of the psychopath, the definition of whose disorder presents great problems. I think there is much in these criticisms. Nonetheless the forensic debate before judge and jury of the ques-

tion whether a mentally disordered person could have controlled his action or whether his capacity to do this was or was not 'substantially impaired' seems to me very often very unreal. The evidence tendered is not only often conflicting, but seems to relate to the specific issue of the accused's power or capacity for control on a specific past occasion only very remotely. I can scarcely believe that on this, the supposed issue, anything coherent penetrates to the minds of the jury after they have heard the difficult expert evidence and heard the judge's warning that these matters are 'incapable of scientific proof.'[30] And I sympathize with the judges in their difficult task of instructing juries on this plea. In Israel there are no juries to be instructed and the judges themselves must confront these same difficulties in deciding in accordance with the principle of the *Mandelbrot* case whether or not the action of a mentally abnormal person who knew what he was doing occurred 'independently of the exercise of his will.'

Because of these difficulties I would prefer to the present law the scheme which I have termed the 'moderate' form of the new doctrine. Under this scheme *mens rea* would continue to be a necessary condition of liability to be investigated and settled before conviction except so far as it relates to mental abnormality. The innovation would be that an accused person would no longer be able to adduce any form of mental abnormality as a bar to conviction. The question of his mental abnormality would under this scheme be investigated only after conviction and would be primarily concerned with his present rather than his past mental state. His past mental state at the time of his crime would only be relevant so far as it provided ancillary evidence of the nature of his abnormality and indicated the appropriate treatment. This position could perhaps be fairly easily reached by eliminating the pleas of insanity and diminished responsibility and extending the provisions of the Mental Health Act, 1959 to all offences including murder. But I would further provide that, in cases where the appropriate direct evidence of mental disorder was forthcoming, the courts should no longer be permitted to think in terms of responsibility and mete out penal sentences instead of compulsory medical treatment. Yet even this moderate reform certainly raises some difficult questions requiring careful consideration.[31]

Many I think would wish to go further than this 'moderate' scheme and would join Lady Wootton in a demand for the elimination of the whole doctrine of *mens rea* or at least in the hope that it will 'wither away.' My reasons for not joining them consist of misgivings on three principal points. The first concerns individual freedom. In a system in which proof of *mens rea* is no longer a necessary condition for conviction, the occasions for official interferences with our lives and for compulsion will be vastly increased. Take, for example, the notion of a criminal assault. If the doctrine of *mens rea* were swept away, every blow, even if it was apparent to a policeman that it was purely accidental or merely careless and therefore not, according to the present law, a criminal assault, would be a matter for investigaion under the new scheme, since the possibilities of a curable or treatable condition would have to be investigated and the condition if serious treated by medical or penal methods. No doubt under the new dispensation, as at present, prosecuting authorities would use their common sense; but every considerable discretionary powers would have to be entrusted to them to sift from the mass the cases worth investigation as possible candidates for therapeutic or penal treatment. No one could view this kind of expansion of police powers with equanimity, for with it will come great uncertainty for the individual: Official interferences with his life will be more frequent but he will be less able to predict their incidence if any accidental or careless blow may be an occasion for them.

My second misgiving concerns the idea to which Lady Wootton attaches great importance: that what we now call punishment (imprisonment and the like) and compulsory medical treatment should be regarded just as alternative forms of social hygiene to be used according to the best estimate of their future effects and no judgment of responsibility should be required before we apply to a convicted person those measures, such as imprisonment, which we now think of as penal. Lady Wootton thinks this will present no difficulty as long as we take a firm hold of the idea that the purpose and justification of the criminal law is to prevent crime and not to pay back criminals for their wickedness. But I do not think ob-

jections to detaching the use of penal methods from judgments of responsibility can be disposed of so easily. Though Lady Wootton looks forward to the day when the 'formal distinction' between hospitals and prisons will have disappeared, she does not suggest that we should give up the use of measures such as imprisonment. She contemplates that 'those for whom medicine has nothing to offer'[32] may be sentenced to 'places of safety' to receive 'the treatment which experience suggests is most likely to evoke the desired responses,' and though it will only be for the purpose of convenience that their 'places of safety' will be separate from those for whom medicine has something to offer, she certainly accepts the idea that imprisonment may be used for its deterrent effect on the person sentenced to it.

This vision of the future evokes from me two different responses: One is a moral objection and the other a sociological or criminological doubt. The moral objection is this: If we imprison a man who has broken the law in order to deter him and by his example others, we are using him for the benefit of society, and for many people, including myself, this is a step which requires to be justified by (*inter alia*) the demonstration that the person so treated could have helped doing what he did. The individual according to this outlook, which is surely neither esoteric nor confused, has a right not to be used in this way unless he could have avoided doing what he did. Lady Wootton would perhaps dismiss this outlook as a disguised form of a retributive conception of punishment. But it is in fact independent of it as I have attempted to show: for though we must seek a moral licence for punishing a man in his voluntary conduct in breaking the law, the punishment we are then licensed to use may still be directed solely to preventing future crimes on his part or on others' and not to 'retribution.'

To this moral objection it may be replied that it depends wholly on the assumption that imprisonment for deterrent purposes will, under the new scheme, continue to be regarded by people generally as radically distinct from medical treatment and still requiring justification in terms of responsibility. It may be said that this assumption should not be made; for the operation of the system itself will in time cause this distinction to fade, and conviction by a court, followed by a sentence of imprisonment, will in time be assimilated to such experiences as a compulsory medical inspection followed by detention in an isolation hospital. But here my sociological or criminological doubts begin. Surely there are two features which, at present, are among those distinguishing punishment from medical treatment and will have to be stripped away before this assimilation can take place, and the moral objection silenced. One of these is that, unlike medical treatment, we use deterrent punishment to deter not only the individual punished but others by the example of his punishment and the severity of the sentence may be adjusted accordingly. Lady Wootton is very skeptical of the whole notion that we can deter in this way potential offenders and therefore she may be prepared to forego this aspect of punishment altogether. But can we on the present available evidence safely adopt this course for all crime? The second feature distinguishing punishment from treatment is that unlike a medical inspection followed by detention in hospital, conviction by a court followed by a sentence of imprisonment is a public act expressing the odium, if not the hostility, of society for those who break the law. As long as these features attach to conviction and a sentence of imprisonment, the moral objection to their use on those who could not have helped doing what they did will remain. On the other hand, if they cease to attach, will not the law have lost an important element in its authority and deterrent force—as important perhaps for some convicted persons as the deterrent force of the actual measures which it administers.

My third misgiving is this. According to Lady Wootton's argument it is a mistake, indeed 'illogical,' to introduce a reference to *mens rea* into the definition of an offence. But it seems that a code of criminal law which omitted any reference in the definition of its offences to mental elements could not possibly be satisfactory. For there are some socially harmful activities which are now and should always be treated as criminal offences which can only be identified by reference to intention or some other mental element. Consider the idea of an attempt to commit a crime. It is obviously desirable that persons who attempt to kill or injure or steal, even if they fail, should be brought before courts for punishment or treatment; yet what distinguishes an attempt which fails from an innocent activity is just the fact that

it is a step taken with the intention of bringing about some harmful consequence.

I do not consider my misgivings on these three points as necessarily insuperable objections to the programme of eliminating responsibility. For the first of them rests on a judgment of the value of individual liberty as compared with an increase in social security from harmful activities, and with this comparative judgment others may disagree. The second misgiving in part involves a belief about the dependence of the efficacy of the criminal law on the publicity and odium at present attached to conviction and sentence and on deterrence by example; psychological and sociological researches may one day show that this belief is false. The third objection may perhaps be surmounted by some ingenuity or compromise, since there are many important offences to which it does not apply. Nonetheless I am certain that the questions I have raised here should worry advocates of the elimination of responsibility more than they do; and until they have been satisfactorily answered I do not think we should move the whole way into this part of the Brave New World.

NOTES

1. (1956) 10 P.D. 281.
2. See Edwards, 'Automatism and Criminal Responsibility' 21 M. L. R. (1958), p. 375, and Acts of Will and Responsibility. Chap. IV, *supra*. The doctrine as now formulated descends from Austin, *Lectures in Jurisprudence*, Lectures XVIII and XIX.
3. *Year Book*, 17 Pasch Ed. IV. f. 1. pl. 2.
4. (1961) A. C. 290.
5. Denning, *Responsibility before the Law*, Jerusalem, 1961.
6. *Edgington* v. *Fitzmaurice* (1885), 29 Ch. D. 459.
7. Chap. XIX, Vol. II, 'On the Relation of Madness to Crime.'
8. 57 H. L. Deb. 443–76 (1924), 'if this Bill were passed very grave results would follow' (Lord Sumner, p. 459). 'What a door is being opened!' (Lord Hewart, p. 467). 'This would be a very dangerous change to make' (Lord Cave, p. 475).
9. Cmd. 8932 (1953).
10. *R.* v. *Spriggs* (1958), 1 Q. B. 270.
11. *R.* v. *Byrne* (1960), 44 Cr. App. Rep. 246.
12. For the statistics see *Murder: Home Office Research Unit Report*, H.M.S.O. 1961, Table 7, p. 10.
13. See her *Social Science and Social Pathology* (1959) esp. Chapter VIII on 'Mental Disorder and the Problem of Moral and Criminal Responsibility;' 'Diminished Responsibility: A Layman's View' 76 *L.Q.R.* (1960), p. 224; *Crime and the Criminal Law* (1963).
14. See *Crime and the Criminal Law*, p. 52. But she does not consider explicitly whether, even if the aim of the criminal law is to prevent crime, there are not moral objections to applying its sanctions even as preventives to those who lacked the capacity to conform to the Law. See *infra*, pp. 207–8.

15. Op. cit., p. 51.

16. In *Crime and the Criminal Law* she makes it clear that the elimination or 'withering away' of *mens rea* as a condition of liability is to apply to all its elements not merely to its provisions for mental abnormality. Hence strict liability is welcomed as the model for the future (op. cit., pp. 46–57).

17. Save as indicated *infra* p. 205, n. 31.

18. See Wootton, op. cit., p. 51.

19. In 1962 the number of persons over 17 treated in these ways were respectively 36 (unfit to plead), 5 (insane before trial), and 836 (probation with mental treatment). See *Criminal Statistics* 1962.

20. In 1962 hospital orders under this section were made in respect of 1187 convicted persons (*Criminal Statistics* 1962).

21. *R.* v. *Morris* (1961) 45 Cr. App. Rep. 185.

22. See Wootton, op. cit., pp. 79–80.

23. Wootton, op. cit., pp. 79–80.

24. 'Punishment and the Elimination of Responsibility,' Chap. VII, *supra.*

25. *The Times,* 18 February 1961 (Staff Sergeant Boshears).

26. See *Bratty* v. *Att. Gen. For Northern Ireland* (1961), 3 All E.R., 523 and Cross, 'Reflections on Bratty's Case' 78 *L.Q.R.* (1962), p. 236.

27. See 'Diminished Responsibility: A Layman's View' 76 *L.Q.R.* (1960), p. 232.

28. See *Crime and the Criminal Law,* p. 74.

29. See N. Walker, 'M'Naghten's Ghost,' *The Listener,* 29 Aug. 1963, p. 303.

30. Per Parker C. J. in *R.* v. *Byrne* (1960) 44 Cr. App. 246 at 258.

31. Of these difficult questions the following seem the most important.

(1) If the post-conviction inquiry into the convicted person's mental abnormality is to focus on his present state, what should a court do with an offender (a) who suffered some mental disorder at the time of his crime but has since recovered? (b) who was 'normal' at the time of the crime but at the time of his conviction suffers from mental disorder?

(2) The Mental Health Act does not by its terms require the court to be satisfied before making a hospital order that there was any causal connection between the accused's disorder and his offence, but only provides that the court in the exercise of its discretion shall have regard to the nature of the offence. Would this still be satisfactory if the courts were bound to make a hospital order if the medical evidence of abnormality is forthcoming?

(3) The various elements of *mens rea* (knowledge, intention, and the minimum control of muscular movements required for an act) may be absent either in a person otherwise normal or may be absent because of some mental disorder (compare the distinctions now drawn between 'sane' and 'insane' automatism). (See *supra,* p. 202). Presumably it would be desirable that in the latter case there should not be an acquittal; but to identify such cases where there were grounds for suspecting mental abnormality, some investigation of mental abnormality would be necessary before the verdict.

32. Op. cit., p. 79–80 ('places of safety' are in quotation markes in her text).

HYMAN GROSS

Mental Abnormality as a Criminal Excuse*

I

A person's mental condition at the time he engages in criminal conduct may relieve him from criminal liability. When this is the case, we say that he is not criminally liable because he was not a responsible person at the time of the offense. To say that one was not responsible in this sense is to assert the most personal of all excuses. What interests us is not something about the perfor-

*This essay has not been previously published. It is a section of a forthcoming book by the author.

mance but something about the actor. The actor is said not to have had available those personal resources that are necessary to qualify him as accountable for his conduct. Since he is not accountable he cannot be faulted for his conduct and so enjoys exemption from judgments of culpability.

Mental abnormality of a sort relevant to excusing exists, then, when mental resources necessary for accountability are lacking. There are four varieties of relevant abnormality: One is mental illness that, formerly in medical literature and still in legal literature, would be characterized as a *disease* of the mind, by virtue of a sufficiently definite pathology and sufficiently pronounced morbidity. Intoxication, whatever its source, is another variety. Mental defectiveness is a third sort of relevant abnormality, encompassing cases of serious deficiency mainly in intelligence but including deficiency of any mental capacity necessary to control behavior. Finally, there is a variety of abnormality that may be conveniently referred to as automatism, which includes behavioral phenomena diverse in origin but which all are instances of a gross separation of consciousness and action such as exists during hypnosis, somnambulism, and epileptic seizures.

Relevant impairments of mental capacity may have an orgin which is extrapsychic or intrapsychic. Drugs, alcohol, hypnotic suggestion, a blow on the head, emotional shock, an extra chromosome, or a brain tumor are all ways in which incapacitation may be produced by external interventions upon normal mental functioning. It is clear that a person may himself be responsible for some of these interventions by doing something to himself or allowing others to. When this is the case, he is deemed responsible for the resulting condition he is in, though not otherwise. Still, one's being responsible for his condition does not always entail being criminally liable for what he does while in that condition. If he suffers mental incapacitation sufficient for him not to be responsible, he is then treated as one who is not, regardless of his having been a responsible person with reference to putting himself in that condition. A person may ultimately cause himself to suffer sieges of delirium tremens by the gradual effects of his own alcoholic indulgence. Yet he is entitled to be treated as not responsible regarding acts done during those sieges no less than a person whose delusions have an origin utterly beyond his control. But if a person while responsible does things to put himself in a state of incapacitation in which harmful conduct is expectable—he intoxicates himself to a dangerous degree—he may be liable for that when the harm occurs or, even without it occurring, when he engages in conduct that threatens the harm. The reason is that incapacitating himself while still a responsible person is itself a dangerous act, and so may be regarded as culpable. Other examples would be persons who willingly submit to drugs or hypnosis under circumstances portending harm, or who place themselves in dangerous situations knowing they are epileptics or sleepwalkers prone to violence. Culpability in such cases properly extends only to conduct that produces the loss of capacity and not the further conduct that is engaged in while the person is not responsible. One person may kill another quite deliberately under delusions produced by drugs taken quite deliberately, yet culpability is not for deliberate killing because the accused is not responsible at all for his homicidal conduct but only for the act of taking the drugs. Not without some awkwardness in principle, the lesser culpability is usually reflected in the criminal law by liability for homicide of a lesser degree.

When mental impairment is intrapsychic in origin, the excuse based on it is received more charily. The same debilitation which would easily pass muster for an excuse if externally induced is regarded with skepticism when its origin is not palpably outside the mind of the actor. Initial suspicion is indeed warranted because of increased opportunity for deception. But even after genuineness of the psychopathology is established, there is often lingering skepticism regarding its significance for judgments of responsibility. This skepticism is justified to the extent that it reflects sound opinion that the actor was quite capable of doing otherwise in spite of his illness. But it is not justified when it reflects the belief that a person is in some measure responsible for his mental illness since its origins are within him and, unlike the case of mental abnormalities having identifiable physical causes, it pertains to him in an especially intimate way because of its purely psychic character. Holding a person responsible for his mental illness is in general even more unjust than holding him responsible for his physical illness. Such medical knowledge as we have bearing on the etiology of serious mental illness makes it quite clear that in most cases the sick person could not reasonably be expected to do such things as would probably have prevented the onset of his illness, while in the case of physical illness effective precautions often might quite easily have been taken.

II

It is not any mental abnormality that excuses. Even when the abnormality is of a kind that is relevant to responsibility, certain conditions of incapacitation must be met if there is to be an excuse. In the criminal law these conditions have been formulated as rules which govern the insanity defense. These rules look mainly to mental illness and defectiveness, but the conditions for excusing under them have a rationale which extends to mental abnormality of whatever variety. Four basic versions of this defense have developed in the criminal law and, as shall be shown, the conditions required by each are less dissimilar from those required by the others than would appear from the terms used in formulating each. The first version, which dominates among Anglo-American jurisdictions, turns out to be too meager. The second of these versions (which in some form is now the law in a third of the American jurisdictions and under the Model Penal Code) represents the most satisfactory statement. The third and fourth versions, though lending themselves to suitably restrictive interpretation, as they stand offer too great opportunity for unwarranted excuses and in fact are the versions most often preferred by those advocating unsound excuses. First, each version will be briefly scanned and then good reasons will be distinguished from bad among excuses of this sort. The concern here is only with why a person is not responsible, and so the very difficult medical questions having to do with exactly what states of abnormality leave a person in a condition in which he is not responsible will remain unexplored. Only the more basic question of what it means not to be responsible is taken up here. But without answers to that, one does not know what exculpatory significance, if any, to attach ultimately to the medical facts.

The first version of the insanity defense is represented by the M'Naghten rules. Stated in their original terms, these rules provide that a person has a defense of insanity if he did not know the nature and quality of the act he was doing, or did not know that it was wrong, because laboring under a defect of reason from disease of the mind. There was in the original M'Naghten rules a further proviso that, even if not so afflicted, a person would have a defense if at the time of his act he was suffering from an insane delusion about something such that if—but only if—it were in fact the case, it would furnish a defense. This part of the M'Naghten rules has been generally disregarded because of the limitation it places on delusions which may excuse, though as we shall see the right reason for ignoring the rule on these grounds has not been generally apprehended. There has been a continuing need for a rule extending the defense generally to all those who have insane delusions about the circumstances under which they act, and this requirement has encouraged strained applications of the remainder of the M'Naghten doctrine to cover such cases.

Despite variations in language and differences in fine points of interpretation, the gist of the M'Naghten formula has remained unchanged in the many jurisdictions that have adopted it since its introduction in England well over a century ago. Serious incapacitation may make it impossible for the actor to be sufficiently aware of what he is doing so that he could choose to do otherwise. It may deprive him of appreciation of the harmfulness of his conduct, or of appreciation of the harm itself, so that a normal disposition to restrain harmful conduct is not aroused. It may deprive him of the ability to comprehend the circumstances in which he acts and so make it impossible for him to choose not to do what under the circumstances is not justifiable. It may make him incapable of knowing that the law prohibits what he does, when only the fact of legal prohibition is a reason for not doing it. In any of these cases, because of a failure of personal resources he cannot help what he does.

The second version of the insanity defense consists of some form of M'Naghten to which is added an excuse based on grossly deficient inhibitory capacity. This additional part is usually referred to as the irresistible impulse rule, though any suggestion that the act need be impulsive to qualify would be seriously misleading. Under this provision, if the accused was incapable of restraining himself from doing what he knew he was doing and knew he ought not to be doing, he may invoke as an excuse his inability to exercise self-control.

The gravamen of this excuse is again the actor's helplessness in being unable to avoid doing or causing harm. The excuse is even stronger than the claim of compulsion that is asserted when one has been forced to do something harmful. Instead of succumbing to pressures which one is nevertheless able to resist, the person without significant capacity for inhibition is simply unable to resist. The excuse is sometimes misconceived, however, so that it is the untoward urge rather than the inhibitory failure which receives primary attention. This distorts the rationale of the excuse. We do not excuse because the actor wanted very desperately to do what he did. By itself powerful determination to do harm is not grounds for exemption from judgments of culpability. On the contrary, it is grounds for a judgment of greater culpability.

The third version of the insanity defense makes mental disease or defect, *when it produces criminal conduct,* the basis of an excuse for that conduct. This version has been adopted in four American jurisdictions (though recently discarded in the one that gave it the name by which it is best known), enjoys considerable psychiatric advocacy, and is generally referred to as the Durham rule. It relies heavily in practice on the same rationale of excuse as the previous version, but offers opportunities for the troublesome departures that will be discussed shortly.

A final version is constituted by those criminal insanity provisions in which mental derangement or deficiency at the time of the act is itself an excuse. The actor need only be seriously defective or not in possession of his faculties in order for his conduct in such a state to be excusable. Unlike the previous version, the relation between the abnormality and the criminal conduct is not of concern here so long as the two are contemporaneous. This version has in somewhat primitive forms preceded M'Naghten in the commom law and now appears in the criminal law of some civil law jurisdictions. It enjoys strong support among those of the medical profession who are interested in these forensic matters and is probably even more congenial to psychiatric views of the insanity defense than is the Durham version. As with Durham there is heavy reliance in practice on the same rationale of excuse that support M'Naghten and irresistible impulse; but again, as with Durham, opportunities for excusing on other grounds are made possible, and these call for careful investigation.

III

The preceding discussion has shown what grounds the law has recognized for an excuse of mental abnormality when the excuse is presented in its most dramatic form as the insanity defense. Many of those who favor the third or fourth version of the insanity defense think it a good defense simply that a person was mentally ill at the time of his criminal act, or that his criminal conduct was a result of the mental illness he suffered at the time. There are three important arguments here, one grounded in moral considerations regarding avoidance of cruelty, and the other two in exculpatory considerations thought to apply to sick persons.

The first contention is that it is wrong to punish a person *when he is sick.* It is generally regarded as inhumane to neglect the suffering of those who are in a debilitated condition and even more inhumane to inflict further suffering on them. It would therefore be barbarous if the criminal law not only withheld comfort and cure from the sick who are subject to its processes but imposed upon such persons a penal regime. Directed to present concerns, this principle of humane treatment clearly requires that a person mentally abnormal at the time of his crime not be subjected to punitive treatment while he continues to be in such a state, but that instead he receive medical treatment.

The principle of humane treatment is unquestionably sound and must be given full effect at all times. It does not, however, confer a cloak of immunity on persons who are sick when committing a crime. Conduct may be culpable even though the actor had chicken pox, pneumonia or multiple sclerosis. It may be culpable when the disorder is mental rather than physical. When a sick person's conduct is culpable, he is to be treated for his illness so long as it lasts by those in whose hands he is placed by virtue of liability for such culpable conduct. But liability for culpable conduct is not avoided by the mere fact of sickness. It is also true that even determination of liability to punishment must be postponed if the continuing illness of the accused makes impossible the proceedings necessary for a just determination of liability, and that those having custody of him must during this time abide by the imperatives of humane treatment. But again there is nothing in this to entitle the accused to exemption from liability.

A second argument derives from general requirements for culpability. It is wrong to punish someone *for being sick.* The reason is that in being sick a person has not done anything blameworthy. Since merely falling ill does not constitute culpable conduct, it may not be punished. (A person might indeed be rightly blamed for making himself sick, or allowing himself to become or to be made sick, and we might well decide that such conduct then deserves punishment when it was understood that the well-being of others depended upon the fitness of the one who became sick. In such a case there is culpability because the accused could have acted to prevent his illness.)

But insofar as a person is being punished for his conduct and not for his disorder, the requirement of culpability is not transgressed. Nevertheless, it is sometimes claimed that when a mentally disordered person is punished for his conduct, he is being punished for his disorder since the conduct is a symptom of it. Such claims are especially prominent in arguments advocating extension of a mental abnormality defense to those persons, often characterized as psychopaths or sociopaths, whose dedication to wrongdoing is especially strong and free of internal conflicts. This claim rests on a misunderstanding of what it means to be punished for something. A person may be punished for a criminal act and that act may in various other perspectives be viewed quite accurately as a symptom of his illness, or indeed of society's illness, as an act of dedicated self-sacrifice, or as an act to advance a socially worthwhile cause. Still in all these cases we are punishing him only for his culpable conduct. We may punish in spite of causes, motives, or intentions, so long as they do not furnish an excuse or other reason for not punishing.

The third argument is that it is wrong to punish someone for what he does *as a result of being mentally sick.* Unlike the previous argument, the position here is not that it is wrong to punish someone for the illness evidenced by criminal conduct, but rather that it is wrong to punish someone for his conduct when it is *produced* by the disorder. The criminal conduct is not viewed as part of a pattern of behavior such that if one so behaves one must by that very fact be judged to be abnormal. Rather the conduct is viewed as determined by the abnormality in the sense that but for the abnormality there would have been no warrant for expecting such conduct.

Treating the fact that conduct resulted from mental abnormality as a reason to excuse the conduct leaves us with no principle on which to rest the excuse. Exculpation by way of justification would indeed be warranted by a principle that what is morbidly determined is not wrong, but there are no good reasons for recognizing as a justifying principle the proposition that condemnation ought to be restricted to healthy determinations to act harmfully. It is true that a person's mental abnormality, if it is to excuse his criminal conduct, must in some significant way be related to that conduct as its cause. This may be put in an even stronger form by saying that we ought to excuse when, but only when, conduct is the "product" of abnormality in the sense that the abnormality is a sufficient condition for the conduct. In that case, but only in that case, the accused was unable to do otherwise because of the abnormality and so is entitled to be excused. It is not true that we ought to excuse simply because the wrong thing that was done would likely not have been done but for the abnormality. Otherwise we should have to excuse anyone who acted from some untoward tendency attributable to a mental abnormality whenever it is unlikely that he would have done the act if he were normal, even in cases where he was quite as capable of acting otherwise as is a normal person subject to the same tendency. This would mean that a bank employee ought to be excused when he embezzles money only because of powerful unconscious wishes to be caught which he could effectively have chosen not to succumb to, although another employee who embezzles only because tempted by healthy fantasies of a life of leisure ought not to be excused.

There is a fourth argument for not punishing wrongdoers who suffered from mental abnormality that in effect requires for an excuse too much rather than too little. It has eminent philosophical credentials and is to be found in the best legal circles as well. The argument derives from general considerations bearing on justification of punishment.

It is pointed out that prescribing punishment for what the insane do is futile since the threat of punishment can have no deterrent effect on such persons. Anyone, therefore, who considers the practice of punishment to be justified by its deterrent effect must hold punishment of the insane to be unjustified and, in fact, a purposeless infliction of suffering. It has been argued in reply that punishment of the insane may still have a deterrent effect on sane persons since it deprives them of hope of escaping punishment by successfully advancing fraudulent claims of having been insane at the time of their offense. That answer is good only to the extent that crimes are committed after decisions to commit them which include deliberation on possible legal tactics to avoid conviction. But since most crimes are committed without decisions of this sort, the deterrent effect of a threat of punishment that makes no allowance for insanity is in any event largely otiose.

There are, however, other answers to the "no deterrence" objection to punishing the insane that do not require belief in such fictitious deliberations by would-be criminals.

If it is being suggested that nondeterribility has been the rationale for the insanity defense in the law as it has developed, we may ask why the law does not refuse by the same rationale to punish those who were genuinely and blamelessly ignorant of the law they broke. Such persons were in a position indistinguishable from the insane with respect to the futility of prospective punishment, and so to punish them is equally a purposeless infliction of suffering. Yet, as we know, in the law as it stands such innocent ignorance does not excuse, and this inconsistency must raise doubts about this rationale for the insanity defense.

But there is a more cogent objection than one based on inconsistency. It is not the case that all, or perhaps even most, insane persons are incapable of being deterred by threat of punishment. Under the prevailing Anglo-American insanity defense, the M'Naghten rules, there is an excuse if the accused by virtue of a defect of reason from disease of the mind did not know he was doing what was wrong. The Model Penal Code similarly establishes as a defense a person's lack of substantial capacity to appreciate the criminality of his conduct (which means more than mere knowledge that it is criminally prohibited) as a result of mental disease or defect. There are many persons who fit these specifications in being unable to appreciate that what they do is wrong and in fact think it for some reason justified, yet are aware and in awe of the threat of punishment quite as much as normal persons. In some of the most notable cases of the insanity defense, the defendant committed murder under the delusion that he was carrying out a divine command, or was giving his due to a man believed to be very wicked, or was killing someone who was bent on harming him. Less dramatic but far more frequent are the family and sex intrigue homicides where the killing was done in a suitably extreme abnormal mental state—usually spoken of as temporary insanity—in which the accused was likewise at the time convinced that he was justified. There is no reason to believe that in general their abnormality rendered the accused in these insanity cases incapable of being deterred by the threat of punishment, though of course like many normal defendants they were not in fact deterred by it. There is, further, every reason to believe that certain abnormal persons who would be entitled to exoneration on grounds of insanity were in fact deterred, just as normal persons would be because the law has made the conduct they contemplated punishable. If these things were not so, the insanity defense could consist simply in establishing the one point that by reason of mental abnormality the accused could not at the time of his crime be deterred by the threat of punishment. In fact what distinguishes the sane from the insane under criminal law standards is the inability of the insane to appreciate the *culpability*, not the punishability, of their conduct. Because of their abnormality the insane cannot at the time apprehend what justifies condemnation of their conduct. Even though amenable to threats of punishment, they lack a resource of appreciation that is necessary if one is to have a reason apart from avoidance of punishment for not doing what the law prohibits. Punishing such persons is indeed a useless infliction of suffering, for it can not serve to uphold the standards that the criminal law exists to preserve.

There is one other argument against mental abnormality defenses that should be noted here. Again it is an argument that by implication requires too much rather than too little for excuse. Many persons who are mentally ill and have committed crimes are dangerous, yet the very abnormality that is evidence of his being dangerous serves to shield the accused from liability. Those who see confinement of dangerous persons as a principal purpose of the criminal law are particularly distressed by this, for in effect just those who are thought to be most properly the concern of the criminal law are allowed to escape its restraints.

The answer to this argument is that not all restraint by the state need be based on criminal liability. If a person is dangerous because of mental abnormality, he may be prevented from doing harm by noncriminal commitment regardless of whether his conduct provided a basis for criminal liability. It is true that persons usually are not found to be a menace for purposes of commitment unless they have done something which would at least provide the substance of a criminal charge. But it is still dangerousness of the person and not criminality of his conduct that warrants deprivation of liberty. Since determinations of dangerousness and determinations of criminal liability are independent matters, a defense of insanity to a criminal charge does not weigh against the accused's subsequent liability to commitment because he is dangerous. Conversely, elimination or postponement of the question of insanity when determining liability would result in branding as criminals persons, whether dangerous or not, who are not to blame for what they did.

IV

The rationale of excusing for mental abnormality may be summarized in this way. Certain forms of mental incapacity deprive a person of ability to act other than the way he does because resources for an effective choice are lacking. When a person lacks capacity to tell what he is doing, whether it is offensive, or what is likely to happen; or lacks capacity to appreciate its harmful significance, or to restrain himself, he is in such a condition. It is apparent that a person incapacitated in any of these ways lacks a resource necessary for control and so necessary for culpable conduct. It is for this reason that an excuse of mental abnormality preempts the field of excuse and makes excuses going directly to culpability inappropriate. There is no point in being concerned about whether something was intentional, when whether it is intentional or not the actor was not a responsible agent. And conversely, when there is a complement of those personal resources that are necessary for responsible conduct, there is a duty to draw upon such resources to avoid harmful conduct. It follows that when a normal person claims he did not at the time appreciate the significance of sticking a knife into another person—his mind was elsewhere—he offers a different kind of excuse than the mentally abnormal man who makes

the same claim. The normal man can only expect by showing less culpability to blunt an accusation of conduct of a higher degree of culpability—he didn't harm the victim knowingly, but only negligently through absent–mindedness in failing to pay attention to the dangers of what he was occupied in doing. But the man who establishes that his failure of appreciation was due to a lack of necessary mental resources exempts himself from any judgment of culpability.

The distinction and connections between lack of responsibility and mere lack of culpability are important with regard to several difficulties surrounding the insanity defense.

We have already mentioned the usually discarded third part of the original M'Naghten rule. It provided that even if the accused person who suffered a defect of reason from disease of the mind could know the nature and quality of his act, and even if he could know that what he was doing was wrong, he still might have a defense if at the time of his act he suffered from a delusion such that had it been a correct belief it would have afforded a defense. This part of the rule has been dropped, but not in order to exclude insanity defenses based on delusion; in fact, delusion cases have always been recognized as paradigms of criminal insanity and are allowed in all M'Naghten rule jurisdictions by strained interpretations of the other parts. It is the limitation upon the kinds of delusion which are acceptable that has been found objectionable. The usual argument is that the limitation leads to absurd results. For example, in accordance with conventional legal rules that preclude criminal jurisdiction for crimes of foreign nationals committed in foreign countries, a homicide defendant in England who in a delusion at the time of his crime believed himself to be Bluebeard reenacting one of his murders in France would have a good defense. But a homicide defendant also in England who in his similar delusion believed himself to be Jack the Ripper would not. Even when the rule has been confined to delusions which bear on exculpatory claims (typically provocation and self-defense), as undoubtedly it was intended to be by its original proponents, criticism has not abated though the reason for rejecting the rule is less clear.

It seems, in fact, that the original rule was a sound one based on the premises concerning the facts of mental abnormality which the M'Naghten judges accepted, but that these premises are incorrect. The mistake from which the rule proceeded has been characterized as the doctrine of partial insanity. It holds that a person whose insanity consists merely in delusions is still capable of choosing to act in conformity with the law that governed the situation as he perceived it. He therefore is to be held accountable for not acting in conformity with law as it would apply to the situation he perceived, though by virtue of his inability to perceive the situation correctly he could not be held accountable for breaking the law with respect to the situation as it actually was. However, according to better medical knowledge, the fact of the matter is that such persons in the grip of their delusions are normally so severely incapacitated that they cannot even choose to act otherwise. We therefore cannot hold them responsible when they act as their delusion dictates and so must consider them ineligible for blame. Questions about matters of culpability (usually matters of justification) which the original rule raises are for this reason superfluous.

A second problem concerns what is meant by "wrong" under the terms of the M'Naghten rule. If the accused, because of a defect of reason from disease of the mind, did not know that what he was doing was wrong he has a defense on grounds of insanity. The question which has persistently troubled courts both in England and the United States is whether the failure of knowledge required is of legal or of moral wrong. Does a psychotic person who knows murder is a crime but believes he may nevertheless commit it because divinely commanded have a defense? What about a mental defective who knows he is not supposed to hurt other people but cannot even comprehend what a criminal law is? The Model Penal Code speaks of the accused's lack of capacity to appreciate the criminality of his conduct, but the difficulty remains, for appreciating the criminality of conduct is not the equivalent of knowing that it has been made a crime. Indeed the final draft of the Code provision offers "wrongfulness" as an optional substitute for "criminality".

The difficulty is removed by recognizing that what is crucial is capacity to know, rather than knowledge; and that it is a capacity to know

something that is necessary for culpability. In a just legal system conduct ought not to be treated as legally culpable unless reasonable opportunity exists to become aware of its legal interdiction. Such opportunity for awareness has significance only if there also is ability to take advantage of it. That in turn depends on ability to appreciate the untowardness of conduct, ability to be aware of the range of normal concerns of the law, as well as the ability to become acquainted with the law itself. If there is disabling incapacity with respect to any of these necessary conditions the person incapacitated is not responsible, for to that degree he lacks ability to take advantage of the opportunity to become aware of criminal liabilities and so his conduct cannot be deemed culpable. It turns out, then, that it is misleading to ask whether legal or moral wrong is meant. The question to be answered is whether the accused was deprived of any abilities that are necessary to take advantage of the opportunity of becoming aware of criminal liability.

Another difficulty concerns the irresistible impulse defense. There has been great hesitation in legal circles in admitting as an excuse an inability to exercise self-restraint. It challenges common sense appreciation of behavior to assert that a person possessed of all the abilities necessary to control what he is doing, nevertheless does not have the self-control to choose effectively not to do it. The excuse is therefore often construed as a direct denial of culpability analoguous to external compulsion—he didn't mean to do that, he was forced to—rather than as a denial of responsibility by virtue of incapacity. The excuse so construed is then rejected as being too easy a way out for persons who either have not chosen to resist with sufficient determination powerful untoward urges or have failed to take precaution against succumbing to the urge and are therefore no less culpable than persons who lose their temper and, while in the grip of their rage, commit crimes.

But this excuse of no responsibility becomes plausible as understanding of human pathology advances, and it becomes increasingly clear that there are serious mental abnormalities which consist in inability either by repression or precaution to inhibit acting on certain urges. The claim of irresistible impulse is then no longer construed as one simply of not having effectively chosen to do otherwise, but rather more, as not having the personal resources that are necessary to choose effectively.

V

A stark separation according to mental abnormality of those who are responsible from those who are not seems at times unsatisfactory. We are bound to recognize that sometimes there is not sheer incapacity with regard to elements of control, yet there is deviation from normal capacities great enough to make desirable a limitation on accountability. Accordingly, there has developed in the law a doctrine of diminished (or partial) responsibility which, though still only little and narrowly accepted, offers a path for receiving into the law continuing insights respecting varieties of limited impairment bearing on control of conduct. The most notable legal recognition so far has been in the English Homicide Act of 1957, which reduces what otherwise would be murder to culpable homicide when the accused suffered from such abnormality of mind as "substantially impaired his mental responsibility" for his acts. The rationale for diminished responsibility is simple. If a person who is incapacitated is ineligible for blame, a person who is seriously impaired though not incapacitated is eligible to be blamed only within limits. While not utterly bereft of resources required for accountability, his resources of control are dimished to a point where full faulting according to the tenor of the conduct is inappropriate. But for reasons previously given, it would be a serious mistake to construe the defense of diminished responsibility as a declaration that the somewhat sick, simply because they are sick, ought not to be held to a liability as great as that of the healthy person. Indeed, perfectly healthy persons who have perfectly natural reactions that put them in an abnormal emotional state may rightly claim diminished responsibility. Typically, this is the case when a person acts under the influence of extreme anger or fear because provoked or threatened.

Mental abnormality may affect culpability in a more direct way, however, and some confusion about this has arisen in discussions of diminished responsibility. By virtue of his abnormality, a person may be unable to act in a way that is criminally culpable, or at least not as culpable as the conduct charged. Or, though capable of such conduct, he may simply not have been acting in the way charged but rather was acting in some other way dictated by his abnormal processes. In either case he may lodge an exculpatory claim that his conduct is different than alleged with respect to elements bearing on culpability, and he would rely on the evidence of his mental abnormality to establish this. Such an exculpatory claim in essence is no different from the sort that is appropriate when a normal person has not acted culpably, but the kind of argument which supports the claim is different. Instead of evidence indicating simply that the accused was engaged in a somewhat different enterprise than alleged, the evidence indicates that by virtue of his abnormal mental condition at the time, the accused could not or simply did not engage in the enterprise alleged. Two exculpatory claims are made in this way. Both of them have as their point what in the language of traditional criminal law theory would be called a lack of *mens rea.*

Suppose a prisoner attacks a guard with a knife and inflicts serious wounds. The prisoner is charged with first degree assault, an element of which is intent to cause serious physical injury. It is claimed on his behalf that he was at the time suffering severe paranoid anxieties which led him to misinterpret a routine warning as a sign that he was about to be attacked by the guard, and that he slashed at the guard only to fend off what he believed to be imminent blows. Evidence of his abnormal state would tend to show that he did not have the specific intent to cause serious physical injury. This would mean that while admittedly he exercised control in conducting an assault, he did not exercise control with regard to those features of it that produced the serious injury. The act done, therefore, was something less culpable than the act charged. The same would hold true for a person accused of burglary, which requires an intent to commit a felony, and who at the time of breaking and entering a home was in such a mental condition as to be incapable of having any definite further purpose.

The other challenge to culpability by way of abnormality does not concern the purpose which informs the act, but rather the earlier stages of planning the accomplishment of objectives and attending to the course of conduct while it is in progress. Such operational design and supervision as is referred to by "malice aforethought," "premeditation," "deliberation," "willfully," and "knowingly" may be beyond the accused's capacities or may simply be nonexistent by virtue of his abnormality. Powerful effects of intoxication or of lingering mental illness may render a person unable or unconcerned to form the plan or to remain in control of its execution, and so one is required to conclude that his homicidal attack was not designed with reference to the death of his victim. The Model Penal Code extends this variety of abnormality defense to all cases where evidence of mental disease or defect is relevant to the question of whether the accused had a required state of mind at the time of the crime, so that even recklessness or negligence may be disproved by evidence of appropriate abnormality.

In both of these "criminal intent" challenges based on mental abnormality, it is not responsibility that properly is said to be diminished. Culpability is what is really claimed to be diminished, and diminished to a point where the conduct is less culpable than is required for the offense charged.

VI

The excuse of insanity has presented far greater difficulties than any other for the criminal process. The main reason is that the point of the proceedings is lost sight of and confusion arises in deciding who may appropriately answer the very different kinds of questions involved, and also in deciding what the consequences of accepting or rejecting the excuse ought to be.

Much of the controversy in which medical and legal views of the insanity defense appear to be at odds results from a failure to appreciate that the law must ultimately be concerned not with who is sick but with whose conduct is excusable. Deciding that issue requires several subsidiary decisions that fall peculiarly within either medical or legal competence. There must, in the first place, be standards which set forth generally the nature of the incapacities that render a person not responsible. It is these standards that constitute the rules of the insanity defense, and deciding upon them is the responsibility of those with legislative and judicial authority who must make the law. It bears emphasis that what is called for here is not some general description of relevant clinical abnormalities in language lawyers are used to. What is required is a statement of the kinds of mental failures (due to mental illness or defectiveness)

that entitle us to conclude for purposes of criminal liability that the accused could not help doing what he did. Once there are such standards of mental abnormality, proceedings to judge the abnormalities of a particular defendant with reference to such standards are possible. Then it is the opinion of medical experts which must first be looked to in order to determine the nature of the defendant's debilitation and the extent to which it affects capacities necessary for responsible conduct. Such expert opinion may be critically examined by lawyers, as indeed any expert opinion may be in a legal proceeding to determine a disputed issue. But that is not a means of substituting an inexpert for an expert opinion, but only a way of ensuring that its acceptance is ultimately based on reason rather than authority. There is finally a decision of vast discretion that is normally made by the jury. It is a conclusion about whether, according to the expert account of the mental condition that is finally accepted, there is debilitation sufficient to excuse according to the legal standards. Asking psychiatrists for expert opinions about whether such standards of incapacity are met is asking them to perform a role which is not within their special professional competence. But the job to be done in making the ultimate determination does require specialized skill in sifting among psychiatric opinions to arrive at a sound appreciation of the defendant's mental condition with reference to those features that are significant for judgments of responsibility. The paramount procedural problem of the insanity defense is to combine this specialist's appreciation with the layman's considered views about when choices to act are no longer meaningful or even possible. There is for this reason a great deal to recommend in principle suggestions, such as H. L. A. Hart's, that we adopt an "apparently coarser grained technique of exempting persons from liability to punishment if they fall into certain recognized categories of mental disorder", on the model of exemption from liability for persons under a specified age. But the establishment of a comprehensive scheme of clear categories seems at the present state of medical art a remote prospect.

Another sort of misapprehension deflects concern from responsibility to other matters, at the cost of both justice and humaneness in the administration of the criminal law. It is assumed that determining the accused to be responsible and so liable to have his conduct judged culpable is a warrant for treating him punitively rather than therapeutically. But in fact, it is said, many persons who meet legal standards for responsible conduct are nevertheless quite sick and sending them to a prison rather than a hospital is uncivilized. It is urged that the mentally ill ought therefore not to be treated as criminally responsible.

The mistake here is in giving priority to existing institutional arrangements and then attempting to have rules of liability which are humane in their effect under those arrangements. A rational and morally concerned society designs its institutions to treat in a humane way those who are liable according to just principles of liability. When a person who is liable according to proper standards of responsibility and culpability is also sick, principles of humane treatment, which are in no way inferior moral considerations, require that he be treated as sick. To the extent that inappropriate treatment may at present be expected under existing institutional arrangements and regimes, that is cause for reform of institutional arrangements and regimes, not of the rules of criminal liability.

DURHAM v. UNITED STATES

United States Court of Appeals, D.C. Cir., 1954*

BAZELON, Circuit Judge.

Monte Durham was convicted of housebreaking,[1] by the District Court sitting without a jury. The only defense asserted at the trial was that Durham was of unsound mind at the time of the offense. We are now urged to reverse the conviction (1) because the trial court did not correctly apply existing rules governing the burden of proof on the defense of insanity, and (2) because existing tests of criminal responsibility are obsolete and should be superseded.[2]

I.

Durham has a long history of imprisonment and hospitalization. In 1945, at the age of 17, he was discharged from the Navy after a psychiatric examination had shown that he suffered "from a profound personality disorder which renders him unfit for Naval service." In 1947 he pleaded guilty to violating the National Motor Theft Act[3] and was placed on probation for one to three years. He attempted suicide, was taken to Gallinger Hospital for observation, and was transferred to St. Elizabeths Hospital, from which he was discharged after two months. In January of 1948, as a result of a conviction in the District of Columbia Municipal Court for passing bad checks, the District Court revoked his probation and he commenced service of his Motor Theft sentence. His conduct within the first few days in jail led to a lunacy inquiry in the Municipal Court where a jury found him to be of unsound mind. Upon commitment to St. Elizabeths, he was diagnosed as suffering from "psychosis with psychopathic personality." After 15 months of treatment, he was discharged in July 1949 as "recovered" and was returned to jail to serve the balance of his sentence. In June 1950 he was conditionally released. He violated the conditions by leaving the District. When he learned of a warrant for his arrest as a parole violator, he fled

*214 F. 2d 862 (1954). Excerpts only. The footnotes are numbered here as in the original.

to the "South and Midwest obtaining money by passing a number of bad checks." After he was found and returned to the District, the Parole Board referred him to the District Court for a lunacy inquisition, wherein a jury again found him to be of unsound mind. He was readmitted to St. Elizabeths in February 1951. This time the diagnosis was "without mental disorder, psychopathic personality." He was discharged for the third time in May 1951. The housebreaking which is the subject of the present appeal took place two months later, on July 13, 1951.

According to his mother and the psychiatrist who examined him in September 1951, he suffered from hallucinations immediately after his May 1951 discharge from St. Elizabeths. Following the present indictment, in October 1951, he was adjudged of unsound mind in proceedings under § 4244 of Title 18 U.S.C., upon the affidavits of two psychiatrists that he suffered from "psychosis with psychopathic personality." He was committed to St. Elizabeths for the fourth time and given subshock insulin therapy. This commitment lasted 16 months—until February 1953—when he was released to the custody of the District Jail on the certificate of Dr. Silk, Acting Superintendent of St. Elizabeths, that he was "mentally competent to stand trial and. . . . able to consult with counsel to properly assist in his own defense."

He was thereupon brought before the court on the charge involved here. The prosecutor told the court:

"So I take this attitude, in view of the fact that he has been over there [St. Elizabeths] a couple of times and these cases that were charged against him were dropped, I don't think I should take the responsibility of dropping these cases against him; then Saint Elizabeths would let him out on the street, and if that man committed a murder next week then it is my responsibility. So we decided to go to trial on one case, that is the case where we found him right in the house, and let him bring in the defense, if he wants to, of unsound mind at the time the crime was committed, and then Your Honor will find him on that, and in your decision send him back to Saint Elizabeths Hospital, and then if they let him out on the street it is their responsibility."

Shortly thereafter, when the question arose whether Durham could be considered competent to stand trial merely on the basis of Dr. Silk's ex parte statement, the court said to defense counsel:

"I am going to ask you this, Mr. Ahern: I have taken the position that if once a person has been found of unsound mind after a lunacy hearing, an ex parte certificate of the superintendent of Saint Elizabeths is not sufficient to set aside that finding and I have held another lunacy hearing. That has been my custom. However, if you want to waive that you may do it, if you admit that he is now of sound mind."

The court accepted counsel's waiver on behalf of Durham, although it had been informed by the prosecutor that a letter from Durham claimed need of further hospitalization, and by defense counsel that ". . . . the defendant does say that even today he thinks he does need hospitalization; he told me that this morning."[4] Upon being so informed, the court said, "Of course, if I hold he is not mentally competent to stand trial I send him back to Saint Elizabeths Hospital and they will send him back again in two or three months."[5] In this atmosphere Durham's trial commenced.

II.

. . . It has been ably argued by counsel for Durham that the existing tests in the District of Columbia for determining criminal responsibility, that is, the so-called right-wrong test supplemented by the irresistible impulse test, are not satisfactory criteria for determining criminal responsibility. We are urged to adopt a different test to be applied on the retrial of this case. This contention has behind it nearly a century of agitation for reform.

A. The right-wrong test, approved in this jurisdiction in 1882,[13] was the exclusive test of criminal responsibility in the District of Columbia until 1929 when we approved the irresistible impulse test as a supplementary test in Smith v. Unites States.[14] The right-wrong test has its roots in England. There, by the first quarter of the eighteenth century, an accused escaped punishment if he could not distinguish "good and evil," that is, if he "doth not know what he is doing, no more than. . . . a wild beast."[15] Later in the same century, the "wild beast" test was abandoned and "right and wrong" was substituted for "good and evil."[16] And toward the middle of the nineteenth century, the House of Lords in the famous M'Naghten case[17] restated what had become the accepted "right-wrong" test[18] in a form which has since been followed, not only in England[19] but in most American jurisdictions,[20] as an exclusive test of criminal responsibility:

". . . . the jurors ought to be told in all cases that every man is to be presumed to be sane, and to possess a sufficient degree of reason to be responsible for his crimes, until the contrary be proved to their satisfaction; and that, to establish a defence on the ground of insanity, it must be clearly proved that, at the time of the committing of the act, the party accused was labouring under such a defect of reason, from disease of the mind, as not to know the nature and qulaity of the act he was doing, or, if he did know it, that he did not know he was doing what was wrong."[21]

As early as 1838, Isaac Ray, one of the founders of the American Psychiatric Association, in his now classic Medical Jurisprudence of Insanity, called knowledge of right and wrong a "fallacious" test of criminal responsibility.[22] This view has long since been substantiated by enormous developments in knowledge of mental life.[23] In 1928 Mr. Justice Cardozo said to the New York Academy of Medicine: "Everyone concedes that the present [legal] definition of insanity has little relation to the truths of mental life."[24]

Medico-legal writers in large numbers,[25] The Report of the Royal Commission on Capital Punishment 1949–1953,[26] and The Preliminary Report by the Committee on Forensic Psychiatry of the Group for the Advancement of Psychiatry[27] present convincing evidence that the right-and-wrong test is "based on an entirely obsolete and misleading conception of the nature of insanity."[28] The science of psychiatry now recognizes that a man is an integrated personality and that reason, which is only one element in that personality, is not the sole determinant of his conduct. The right-wrong test, which considers knowledge or reason alone, is therefore an inadequate guide to mental responsibility for criminal behavior. As Professor Sheldon Glueck of the Harvard Law School points out in discussing the right-wrong tests, which he calls the knowledge tests:

"It is evident that the knowledge tests unscientifically abstract out of the mental make-up but one phase or element of mental life, the cognitive, which, in this era of dynamic psychology, is beginning to be regarded as not the most important factor in conduct and its disorders. In brief, these tests proceed upon the following questionable assumptions of an outworn era in psychiatry: (1) that lack of knowledge of the 'nature or quality' of an act (assuming the meaning of such terms to be clear), or incapacity to know right from wrong, is the sole or even the most important symptom of mental disorder; (2) that such knowledge is the sole instigator and guide of conduct, or at least the most important element therein, and consequently should be the sole criterion of responsibility when insanity is involved; and (3) that the capacity of knowing right from wrong can be completely intact and functioning perfectly even though a defendant is otherwise demonstrably of disordered mind."[29]

Nine years ago we said:
"The modern science of psychology. . . . does not conceive that there is a separate little man in the top of one's head called reason whose function it is to guide another unruly little man called instinct, emotion, or impulse in the way he should go."[30]

By its misleading emphasis on the cognitive, the right-wrong test requires court and jury to rely upon what is, scientifically speaking, inadequate, and most often, invalid[31] and irrelevant testimony in determining criminal responsibility.[32]

The fundamental objection to the right-wrong test, however, is not that criminal irresponsibility is made to rest upon an inadequate, invalid or indeterminable symptom or manifestation, but that it is made to rest upon *any* particular symptom.[33] In attempting to define insanity in terms of a symptom, the courts have assumed an impossible role,[34] not merely one for which they have no special competence.[35] As the Royal Commission emphasizes, it is dangerous "to abstract particular mental faculties, and to lay it down that unless these particular faculties are destroyed or gravely impaired, an accused person, whatever the nature of his mental disease, must be held to be criminally responsible. . . ."[36] In this field of law as in others, the fact finder should be free to consider all information advanced by relevant scientific disciplines.[37]

Despite demands in the name of scientific advances, this court refused to alter the right-wrong test at the turn of the century.[38] But in 1929, we considered in response to "the cry of scientific experts" and added the irresistible impulse test as a supplementary test for determining criminal responsibility. Without "hesitation" we declared, in Smith v. United States, "it to be the law of this District that, in cases where insanity is interposed as a defense, and the facts are sufficient to call for the application of the rule of irresistible impulse, the jury should be so charged."[39] We said:

". . . . The modern doctrine is that the degree of insanity which will relieve the accused of the consequences of a criminal act must be such as to create in his mind an uncontrollable impulse to commit the offense charged. This impulse must be such as to override the reason and judgment and obliterate the sense of right and wrong to the extent that the accused is deprived of the power to choose between right and wrong. The mere ability to distinguish right from wrong is no longer the correct test either in civil or criminal cases, where the defense of insanity is interposed. The accepted rule in this day and age, with the great advancement in medical science as an enlightening influence on this subject, is that the accused must be capable, not only of distinguishing between right and wrong, but that he was not impelled to do the act by an irresistible impulse, which means before it will justify a verdict of acquittal that his reasoning powers were so far dethroned by his diseased mental condition as to deprive him of the will power to resist the insane impulse to perpetrate the deed, though knowing it to be wrong."[40]

As we have already indicated, this has since been the test in the District.

Although the Smith case did not abandon the right-wrong test, it did liberate the fact finder from exlusive reliance upon that discredited criterion by allowing the jury to inquire also whether the accused suffered from an undefined "diseased mental condition [which] deprive[d] him of the will power to resist the insane impulse. . . ."[41] The term "irresistible impulse," however, carries the misleading implication that "diseased mental condition[s]" produce only sudden, momentary or spontaneous inclinations to commit unlawful acts.[42] As the Royal Commission found:

". . . . In many cases . . . this is not true at all. The sufferer from [melancholia, for example] experiences a change of mood which alters the whole of his existence. He may believe, for instance, that a future of such degradation and misery awaits both him and his family that death for all is a less dreadful alternative. Even the thought that the acts he comtemplates are murder and suicide pales into insignificance in contrast with what he otherwise expects. The criminal act, in such circumstances, may be the reverse of impulsive. It may be coolly and carefully prepared; yet it is still the act of a madman. This is merely an illustration; similar states of mind are likely to lie behind the criminal act when murders are committed by persons suffering from schizophrenia or paranoid psychoses due to disease of the brain.

We find that as an exclusive criterion the rightwrong test is inadequate in that (a) it does not take sufficient account of psychic realities and scientific knowledge, and (b) it is based upon one symptom and so cannot validly be applied in all circumstances. We find that the "irresistible impulse" test is also inadequate in that it gives no recognition to mental illness characterized by brooding and reflection and so relegates acts caused by such illness to the application of the inadequate right-wrong test. We conclude that a broader test should be adopted.[44]

In the District of Columbia, the formulation of tests of criminal responsibility is entrusted to the courts[45] and, in adopting a new test, we invoke our inherent power to make the change prospectively.[46]

The rule we now hold must be applied on the retrial of this case and in future cases is not unlike that followed by the New Hampshire court since 1870.[47] It is simply that an accused is not criminally responsible if his unlawful act was the product of mental disease or mental defect.[48]

We use "disease" in the sense of a condition which is considered capable of either improving or deteriorating. We use "defect" in the sense of a condition which is not considered capable of either improving or deteriorating and which may be either congenital, or the result of injury, or the residual effect of a physical or mental disease.

Whenever there is "some evidence" that the accused suffered from a diseased or defective mental condition at the time the unlawful act was committed, the trial court must provide the jury with guides for determining whether the accused can be held criminally responsible. We do not, and indeed could not, formulate an instruction which would be either appropriate or binding in all cases. But under the rule now announced, any instruction should in some way convey to the jury the sense and substance of the following: If you the jury believe beyond a reasonable doubt that the accused was not suffering from a diseased or defective mental condition at the time he committed the criminal act charged, you may find him guilty. If you believe he was suffering from a diseased or defective mental condition when he committed the act, but believe beyond a reasonable doubt that the act was not the product of such mental abnormality, you may find him guilty. Unless you believe beyond a reasonable doubt either that he was not

suffering from a diseased or defective mental condition, or that the act was not the product of such abnormality, you must find the accused not guilty by reason of insanity. Thus your task would not be completed upon finding, if you did find, that the accused suffered from a mental disease or defect. He would still be responsible for his unlawful act if there was no causal connection between such mental abnormality and the act.[49] These questions must be determined by you from the facts which you find to be fairly deducible from the testimony and the evidence in this case.[50]

The questions of fact under the test we now lay down are as capable of determination by the jury as, for example, the questions juries must determine upon a claim of total disability under a policy of insurance where the state of medical knowledge concerning the disease involved, and its effects, is obscure or in conflict. In such cases, the jury is not required to depend on arbitrarily selected "symptoms, phases or manifestations"[51] of the disease as criteria for determining the ultimate questions of fact upon which the claim depends. Similarly, upon a claim of criminal irresponsibility, the jury will not be required to rely on such symptoms as criteria for determining the ultimate question of fact upon which such claim depends. Testimony as to such "symptoms, phases or manifestations," along with other relevant evidence, will go to the jury upon the ultimate questions of fact which it alone can finally determine. Whatever the state of psychiatry, the psychiatrist will be permitted to carry out his principal court function which, as we noted in Holloway v. U.S., "is to inform the jury of the character of [the accused's] mental disease [or defect]."[52] The jury's range of inquiry will not be limited to, but may include, for example, whether an accused, who suffered from a mental disease or defect did not know the difference between right and wrong, acted under the compulsion of an irresistible impulse, or had "been deprived of or lost the power of his will. . . ."[53]

Finally, in leaving the determination of the ultimate question of fact to the jury, we permit it to perform its traditional function which, as we said in Holloway, is to apply "our inherited ideas of moral responsibility to individuals prosecuted for crime. . . .[54] Juries will continue to make moral judgments, still operating under the fundamental precept that "Our collective conscience does not allow punishment where it cannot impose blame."[55] But in making such judgments, they will be guided by wider horizons of knowledge concerning mental life. The question will be simply whether the accused acted because of a mental disorder, and not whether he displayed particular symptoms which medical science has long recognized do not necessarily, or even typically, accompany even the most serious mental disorder.[56]

The legal and moral traditions of the western world require that those who, of their own free will and with evil intent (sometimes called *mens rea*), commit acts which violate the law, shall be criminally responsible for those acts. Our traditions also require that where such acts stem from and are the product of a mental disease or defect as those terms are used herein, moral blame shall not attach, and hence there will not be criminal responsibility.[57] The rule we state in this opinion is designed to meet these requirements.

Reversed and remanded for a new trial.

NOTES

1. D.C. Code §§ 22–1801, 22–2201 and 22–2202 (1951).
2. Because the questions raised are of general and crucial importance, we called upon the Government and counsel whom we appointed for the indigent appellant to brief and argue this case a second time. Their able presentations have been of great assistance to us. On the question of the adequacy of prevailing tests of criminal responsibility, we received further assistance from the able brief and argument of Abram Chayes, *amicus curiae* by appointment of this Court, in Stewart v. United States, 94 U.S.App. D.C.—, 214 F.2d 879.
3. 18 U.S.C. § 408 (1946). 1948 Revision, 18 U.S.C. §§ 10, 2311–2313.
4. Durham showed confusion when he testified. These are but two examples:
"Q. Do you remember writing it? A. No. Don't you forget? People get all mixed up in machines.
"Q. What kind of a machine? A. I don't know, they just get mixed up.
"Q. Are you cured now? A. No, sir.
"Q. In your opinion? A. No. sir.
"Q. What is the matter with you? A. You hear people bother you.
"Q. What? You say you hear people bothering you? A. Yes.
"Q. What kind of people? What do they bother you about? A. (No response.)"
Although we think the court erred in accepting counsel's admission that Durham was of sound mind, the matter does not require discussion since we reverse on other grounds and the principles governing this issue are fully discussed in our decision today in Gunther v. United States, 94 U.S.App.D.C.—, 215 F.2d 493.
5. The court also accepted a waiver of trial by jury when Durham indicated, in response to the court's question, that he preferred to be tried without a jury and that he waived his right to a trial by jury.
13. 1882, 12 D.C. 498, 550, 1 Mackey 498, 550. The right-wrong test was reaffirmed in United States v. Lee, 1886, 15 D.C. 489, 496, 4 Mackey 489, 496.
14. 1929, 59 App.D.C. 144, 36 F.2d 548, 70 A.L.R. 654.
15. Glueck, Mental Disorder and the Criminal Law 138–39 (1925), citing Rex v. Arnold, 16 How.St.Tr. 695, 764 (1724).
16. Id. at 142–52, citing Earl Ferrer's case, 19 How.St.Tr. 886 (1760). One writer has stated that these tests originated in England in the 13th or 14th century, when the law began to define insanity in terms of intellect for purposes of determining capacity to manage feudal estates. Comment, *Lunacy and Idiocy—The Old Law and Its Incubus,* 18 U. of Chi.L. Rev. 361 (1951).
17. 8 Eng.Rep. 718 (1843).

18. Hall, Principles of Criminal Law 480, n. 6 (1947).
19. Royal Commission on Capital Punishment 1949–1953 Report (Cmd. 8932) 79 (1953) (hereinafter cited as Royal Commission Report).
20. Weihofen, *The M'Naghten Rule in Its Present Day Setting,* Federal Probation 8 (Sept. 1953); Weihofen, Insanity as a Denense in Criminal Law 15, 64–68, 109–47 (1933); Leland v. State of Oregon, 1952, 343 U.S. 790, 800, 72 S.Ct. 1002, 96 L.Ed. 1302.
"In five States the M'Naghten Rules have been in substance re-enacted by statute." Royal Commission Report 409; see, for example, "Sec. 1120 of the [New York State] Penal Law [McK.Consol. Laws, c. 40] [which] provides that a person is not excused from liability on the grounds of insanity, idiocy or imbecility, except upon proof that at the time of the commission of the criminal act he was laboring under such a defect or reason as (1) not to know the nature and quality of the act he was doing or (2) not to know that the act was wrong." Ploscowe, *Suggested Changes in the New York Laws and Procedures Relating to the Criminally Insane and Mentally Defective Offenders,* 43 J. Crim.L., Criminology & Police Sci. 312, 314 (1952).
21. 8 Eng.Rep. 718, 722 (1843). "Today, Oregon is the only state that requires the accused, on a plea of insanity, to establish that defense beyond a reasonable doubt. Some twenty states, however, place the burden on the accused to establish his insanity by a preponderance of the evidence or some similar measure of persuasion." Leland v. State of Oregon, supra, note 20, 343 U.S. at page 798, 72 S.Ct. 1002. Since Davis v. United States, 1895, 160 U.S. 469, 484, 16 S.Ct. 353, 40 L.Ed. 499, a contrary rule of procedure has been followed in the Federal courts. For example, in compliance with Davis, we held in Tatum v. Unites States, supra, note 8, 88 U.S. App.D.C. 386, 389, 190 F.2d 612, 615, and text, "as soon as 'some evidence of mental disorder is introduced, . . . sanity, like any other fact, must be proved as part of the prosecution's case beyond a reasonable doubt.' "
22. Ray, Medical Jurisprudence of Insanity 47 and 34 et seq. (1st ed. 1838). "That the insane mind is not entirely deprived of this power of moral discernment, but in many subjects is perfectly rational, and displays the exercise of a sound and well balanced mind is one of those facts now so well established, that to question it would only betray the height of ignorance and presumption." Id. at 32.
23. See Zilboorg, *Legal Aspects of Psychiatry* in One Hundred Years of American Psychiatry 1844–1944, 507, 552 (1944).
24. Cardozo, What Medicine Can Do For the Law 32 (1930).
25. For a detailed bibliography on Insanity as a Defense to Crime, see 7 The Record of the Association of the Bar of the City of New York 158–62 (1952). And see. for example, Alexander, the Criminal, the Judge and the Public 70 et seq. (1931); Cardozo, What Medicine Can Do For the Law 28 et seq. (1930); Cleckley, the Mask of Sanity 491 et seq. (2d ed.1950); Deutsch, The Mentally Ill In America 389–417 (2d ed.1949); Glueck, Mental Disorder and the Criminal Law (1925). Crime and Justice 96 et seq. (1936); Guttmacher & Weihofen, Psychiatry and the Law 218, 403–23 (1952); Hall, Principles of Criminal Law 477–538 (1947); Menninger, The Human Mind 450 (1937); Hall & Menninger, *"Psychiatry and the Law"—A Dual Review,* 38 Iowa L.Rev. 687 (1953); Overholser, The Psychiatrist and the Law 41–43 (1953); Overholser & Richmond, Handbook of Psychiatry 208–15 (1947); Ploscowe, *Suggested Changes in the New York Laws and Procedures Relating to the Criminally Insane and Mentally Defective Offenders,* 43 J.Crim.L., Criminology & Police Sci. 312, 314 (1952); Ray, Medical Jurisprudence of Insanity (1st

ed.1838) (4th ed.1860); Reik, *The Doc-Ray Correspondence: A Pioneer Collaboration in the Jurisprudence of Mental Disease,* 63 Yale L.J. 183 (1953); Weihofen, Insanity as a Defense in Criminal Law (1933), *The M'Naghten Rule in Its Present Day Setting,* Federal Probation 8 (Sept. 1953); Zilboorg, Mind, Medicine and Man 246–97 (1943), *Legal Aspects of Psychiatry,* American Psychiatry 1844–1944, 507 (1944).

26. Royal Commission Report 73–129.

27. The Committee on Forensic Psychiatry (whose report is hereinafter cited as Gap Report) was composed of Drs. Philip Q. Roche, Frank S. Curran, Lawrence Z. Freedman and Manfred S. Guttmacher. They were assisted in their deliberations by leading psychiatrists, jurists, law professors, and legal practitioners.

28. Royal Commission Report 80.

29. Glueck, *Psychiatry and the Criminal Law,* 12 Mental Hygiene 575, 580 (1928), as quoted in Deutsch, The Mentally Ill in America 396 (2d ed. 1949); and see, for example, Menninger, The Human Mind 450 (1937); Guttmacher & Weihofen, Psychiatry and the Law 403–08 (1952).

30. Holloway v. United States, 1945, 80 U.S.App.D.C. 3, 5, 148 F.2d 665, 667, certiorari denied, 1948, 334 U.S. 852, 68 S.Ct. 1507, 92 L.Ed. 1774.

More recently, the Royal Commission, after an exhaustive survey of legal, medical and lay opinion in many Western countries, including England and the United States made a similar finding. It reported: "The gravamen of the charge against the M'Naghten Rules is that they are not in harmony with modern medical science, which, as we have seen, is reluctant to divide the mind into separate compartments—the intellect, the emotions and the will—but looks at it as a whole and considers that insanity distorts and impairs the action of the mind as a whole." Royal Commission Report 113. The Commission lends vivid support to this conclusion by pointing out that "It would be impossible to apply modern methods of care and treatment in mental hospitals, and at the same time to maintain order and discipline, if the great majority of the patients, even among the grossly insane, did not know what is forbidden by the rules and that, if they break them, they are liable to forfeit some privilege. Examination of a number of guilty but insane [the nearest English equivalent of our acquittal by reason of insanity] was returned, and rightly returned, has convinced us that there are few indeed where the accused can truly be said not to have known that his act was wrong." Id. at 103.

31. See Guttmacher & Weihofen, Psychiatry and the Law 421, 422 (1952). The M'Naghten rules "constitute not only an arbitrary restriction on vital medical data, but also impose an improper onus of decision upon the expert witness. The Rules are unanswerable in that they have no consensus with established psychiatric criteria of symptomatic description save for the case of disturbed consciousness or of idiocy,. . . ." From statement by Dr. Philip Q. Roche, quited id. at 407. See also United States ex rel. Smith v. Baldi, 3 Cir., 1951, 192 F.2d 540, 567 (dissenting opinion).

32. In a very recent case, the Supreme Court of New Mexico recognized the inadequacy of the right-wrong test, and adopted what it called an "extension of the M'Naghten Rules." Under this extension, lack of knowledge of right and wrong is not essential for acquittal "if, by reason of disease of the mind, defendant has been deprived of or lost the power of his will. . . ." State v. White, N.M., 270 P.2d 727, 730.

33. Deutsch, The Mentally Ill in America 400 (2d ed.1949); Keedy, *Irresistible Impulses as a Defense in Criminal Law,* 100 U. of Pa.L.Rev. 956, 992 (1952).

34. Professor John Whitehorn of the Johns Hopkins Medical School, who recently prepared an informal memorandum on this subject for a Commission on Legal Psychiatry appointed by the Governor of Maryland, has said: "Psychiatrists are challenged to set forth a crystal-clear statement of what constitutes insanity. It is impossible to express this adequately in words, alone, since such diagnostic judgments involve clinical skill and experience which cannot wholly be verbalized. . . . The medical profession would be baffled if asked to write into the legal code universally valid criteria for the diagnosis of the many types of psychotic illness which may seriously disturb a person's responsibility, and even if this were attempted, the diagnostic criteria would have to be rewritten from time to time, with the progress of psychiatric knowlwdge." Quoted in Guttmacher & Weihofen, Psychiatry and the Law 419–20 (1952).

35. ". . . . the legal profession were invading the province of medicine, and attempting to install old exploded medical theories in the place of facts established in the progress of scientific knowledge." State v. Pike, 1870, 49 N.H. 399, 438.

36. Royal Commission Report 114. And see State v. Jones, 1871, 50 N.H. 369, 392–393.

37. Keedy, *Irresistible Impulse as a Defense in Criminal Law,* 100 U. of Pa.L. Rev. 956, 992–93 (1952).

38. See, for example, Taylor v. United States, 1895, 7 App.D.C. 27, 41–44, where we rejected "emotional insanity" as a defense, citing with approval the following from the trial court's instruction to the jury: "Whatever may be the cry of scientific experts, the law does not recognize, but condemns the doctrine of emotional insanity—that a man may be sane up until a moment before he commits a crime, insane while he does it, and sane again soon afterwards. Such a doctrine would be dangerous in the extreme. The law does not recognize it; and a jury cannot without violating their oaths." This position was emphatically reaffirmed in Snell v. United States, 1900, 16 App.D.C. 501, 524.

39. 1929, 59 App.D.C. 144, 146, 36 F.2d 548, 550, 70 A.L.R. 654.

40. 59 App.D.C. at page 145, 36 F.2d at page 549.

41. 59 App.D.C. at page 145, 36 F.2d at page 549.

42. Impulse, as defined by Webster's New International Dictionary (2d ed.1950), is:

"1. Act of impelling, or driving onward with *sudden* force; impulsion, esp., force so communicated as to produce motion *suddenly,* or *immediately. . . .*

"2. An incitement of the mind or spirit, esp. in the form of an *abrupt* and vivid suggestion, prompting some *unpremeditated* action or leading to unforeseen knowledge or insight; a *spontaneous* inclination. . . .

3. . . . motion produced by a *sudden* or *momentary* force. . . ." [Emphasis supplied.]

43. Royal Commission Report 110; for additional comment on the irresistible impulse test, see Glueck, Crime and Justice 101–03 (1936); Guttmacher & Weihofen, Psychiatry and the Law 410–12 (1952); Hall, General Principles of Criminal Law 505–26 (1947); Keedy, *Irresistible Impulse as a Defense in Criminal Law,* 100 U. of Pa.L.Rev. 956 (1952); Wertham, The Show of Violence 14 (1949).

The New Mexico Supreme Court in recently adopting a broader criminal insanity rule, note 32, supra, observed: ". . . insanity takes the form of the personality of the individual and, if his tendency is toward depression, his wrongful act may come at the conclusion of a period of complete lethargy, thoroughly devoid of excitement."

44. As we recently said, ". . . former common law should not be followed where changes in conditions have made it obsolete. We have never hesitated to exercise the usual judicial function of revising and enlarging the common law." Linkins v. Protestant Episcopal Cathedral Foundation, 1950,

87 U.S.App.D.C. 351, 355, 187 F.2d 357, 361, 28 A.L.R.2d 521. Cf. Funk v. United States, 1933, 290 U.S. 371, 381–382, 54 S.Ct. 212, 78 L.Ed. 369.

45. Congress, like most State legislatures, has never undertaken to define insanity in this connection, although it recognizes the fact that an accused may be acquitted by reason of insanity. See D.C. Code § 24–301 (1951). And as this court made clear in Hill v. United States, Congress has left no doubt that "common-law procedure, in all matters relating to crime . . . still continues in force here in all cases except where special provision is made by statute to the exclusion of the common-law procedure." 22 App. D.C. 395, 401 (1903), and statutes cited therein; Linkins v. Protestant Episcopal Cathedral Foundation, 87 U.S. App.D.C. at pages 354–55, 187 F.2d at pages 360–361; and see Fisher v. United States, 1946, 328 U.S. 463, 66 S.Ct. 1318, 90 L. Ed. 1382.

46. See Great Northern R. v. Sunburst Oil & Refining Co., 1932, 287 U.S. 358, 53 S. Ct. 145, 77 L.Ed. 360; National Labor Relations Board v. Guy F. Atkinson Co., 9 Cir., 1952, 195 F.2d 141, 148; Concurring opinion of Judge Frank in Aero Spark Plug Co. v. B. G. Corporation, 2 Cir., 1942, 130 F.2d 290, 298, and note 24; Warring v. Colpoys, 1941, 74 App.D.C. 303, 122 F.2d 642, 645, 136 A.L.R. 1025; Moore & Oglebay, *The Supreme Court, Stare Decisis and Law of the Case,* 21 Texas L.Rev. 514, 535 (1943); Carpenter, *Court Decisions and the Common Law,* 17 Col.L.Rev. 593, 606–07 (1917). But see von Moschzisker, *Stare Decisis in Courts of Last Resort.* 37 Harv.L.Rev. 409, 426 (1924). Our approach is similar to that of the Supreme Court of California in People v. Maughs, 1906, 149 Cal. 253, 86 P. 187, 191, where the court prospectively invalidated a previously accepted instruction, saying:

". . . we think the time has come to say that in all future cases which shall arise, and where, after this warning, this instruction shall be given, this court will hold the giving of it to be so prejudicial to the rights of a defendant, secured to him by our Constitution and laws, as to call for the reversal of any judgment which may be rendered against him."

47. State v. Pike, 1870, 49 N.H. 399.

48. Cf. State v. Jones, 1871, 50 N.H. 369, 398.

49. "There is no *a priori* reason why every person suffering from any form of mental abnormality or disease, or from any particular kind of mental disease, should be treated by the law as not answerable for any criminal offence which he may commit, and be exempted from conviction and punishment. Mental abnormalities vary infinitely in their nature and intensity and in their effects on the character and conduct of those who suffer from them. Where a person suffering from a mental abnormality commits a crime, there must always be some likelihood that the abnormality has played some part in the causation of the crime; and, generally speaking, the graver the abnormality, . . . the more probable it must be that there is a causal connection between them. But the closeness of this connection will be shown by the facts brought in evidence in individual cases and cannot be decided on the basis of any general medical principle." Royal Commission Report 99.

50. The court may always, of course, if it deems it advisable for the assistance of the jury, point out particular areas of agreement and conflict in the expert testimony in each case, just as it ordinarily does in summing up any other testimony.

51. State v. Jones, 1871, 50 N.H. 369, 398.

52. 1945, 80 U.S.App.D.C. 3, 5, 148 F.2d 665, 667.

53. State v. White, see n. 32, supra.

54. 80 U.S.App.D.C. at page 5, 148 F.2d at page 667.

55. 80 U.S.App.D.C. at pages 4–5, 148 F.2d at pages 666–667.

56. See text, supra, 214 F.2d 870–872.

57. An accused person who is acquitted by reason of insanity is presumed to be insane, Orencia v. Overholser, 1947, 82 U.S.App.D.C. 285, 163 F.2d 763; Barry v. White, 1933, 62 App.D.C. 69, 64 F.2d 707, and may be committed for an indefinite period to a "hospital for the insane." D.C.Code § 24–301 (1951).

We think that even where there has been a specific finding that the accused was competent to stand trial and to assist in his own defense, the court would be well advised to invoke this Code provision so that the accused may be confined as long as "the public safety and . . . [his] welfare" require. Barry v. White, 62 App.D.C. at page 71, 64 F.2d at page 709.

UNITED STATES v. BRAWNER

United States Court of Appeals, D.C. Cir., 1972*

Leventhal, Circuit Judge:

Passing by various minor disagreements among the witnesses, the record permits us to reconstruct the events of September 8, 1967, as follows: After a morning and afternoon of wine-drinking, appellant Archie W. Brawner, Jr. and his uncle Aaron Ross, went to a party at the home of three acquaintances. During the evening, several fights broke out. In one of them, Brawner's jaw was injured when he was struck or pushed to the ground. The time of the fight was approximately 10:30 p.m. After the fight, Brawner left the party. He told Mr. Ross that some boys had jumped him. Mr. Ross testified that Brawner "looked like he was out of his mind". Other witnesses who saw him after the fight testified that Brawner's mouth was bleeding and that his speech was unclear (but the same witness added, "I heard every word he said"); that he was staggering and angry; and that he pounded on a mailbox with his fist. One witness testified that Brawner said, "[I'm] going to get my boys" and come back, and that "someone is going to die tonight."

Half an hour later, at about eleven p.m., Brawner was on his way back to the party with a gun. One witness testified that Brawner said he was going up there to kill his attackers or be killed.

Upon his arrival at the address, Brawner fired a shot into the ground and entered the building. He proceeded to the apartment where the party was in progress and fired five shots through the closed metal hallway door. Two of the shots struck Billy Ford, killing him. Brawner was arrested a few minutes later, several blocks away. The arresting officer testified that Brawner appeared normal, and did not appear to be drunk, that he spoke clearly, and had no odor of alcohol about him.

After the Government had presented the evidence of its non-expert witnesses, the trail judge ruled that there was insufficient evidence on "deliberation" to go to the jury: accordingly, a verdict of acquittal was directed on first degree murder.

The expert witnesses, called by both defense and prosecution, all agreed that Brawner was suffering from an abnormality of a psychiatric or neurological nature. The medical labels were variously given as "epileptic personality disorder," "psychologic brain syndrome associated with a convulsive disorder," "personality disorder associated with epilepsy," or, more simply, "an explosive personality." There was no disagreement that the epileptic condition would be exacerbated by alcohol, leading to more frequent episodes and episodes of greater intensity, and would also be exacerbated by a physical blow to the head. The experts agreed that epilepsy *per se* is not a mental disease or defect, but a neurological disease which is often associated with a mental disease or defect. They further agreed that Brawner had a mental, as well as a neurological, disease.

Where the experts disagreed was on the part which that mental disease or defect played in the murder of Billy Ford. The position of the witnesses called by the Government is that Brawner's behavior on the night of September 8 was not consistent with an epileptic seizure, and was not suggestive of an explosive reaction in the context of a psychiatric disorder. In the words of Dr. Platkin of St. Elizabeths Hospital, "He was just mad."

The experts called by the defense maintained the contrary conclusion. Thus, Dr. Eugene Stanmeyer, a psychologist at St. Elizabeths, was asked on direct by counsel for defense, whether, assuming accused did commit the act which occurred, there was a causal relationship between the assumed act and his mental abnormality. Dr. Stanmeyer replied in the affirmative, that there was a cause and effect relationship.

Later, the prosecutor asked the Government's first expert witness Dr. Weickhardt: "Did you . . . come to any opinion concerning whether or not the crimes in this case were causally related to the mental illness which you diagnosed?" An objection to the form of the question was overruled. The witness then set forth that in his opinion there was no causal relationship between the mental disorder and the alleged offenses. Brawner claims that the trial court erred when it permitted a prosecution expert to testify in this manner. He relies

*471 F. 2d 969 (1972). Excerpts only. The footnotes are numbered here as in the original.

on our opinion in Washington v. United States, 129 U.S.App.D.C. 29, 390 F.2d 444 (1967).

INSANITY RULE IN OTHER CIRCUITS

The American Law Institute's Model Penal Code expressed a rule which has become the dominant force in the law pertaining to the defense of insanity. The ALI rule is eclectic in spirit, partaking of the moral focus of *M'Naghten,* the practical accommodation of the "control rules" (a term more exact and less susceptible of misunderstanding than "irresistible impulse" terminology), and responsive, at the same time, to a relatively modern, forward-looking view of what is encompassed in "knowledge."

For convenience, we quote again the basic rule propounded by the ALI's Model Penal Code:

A person is not responsible for criminal conduct if at the time of such conduct as a result of mental disease or defect he lacks substantial capacity either to appreciate the criminality [wrongfulness] of his conduct or to conform his conduct to the requirements of the law.

COMMENTS CONCERNING REASON FOR ADOPTION OF ALI RULE AND SCOPE OF RULE AS ADOPTED BY THIS COURT

In the foreglimpse stating that we had determined to adopt the ALI rule we undertook to set forth comments stating our reasons, and also the adjustments and understandings defining the ALI rule as adopted by this Court. Having paused to study the rulings in the other circuits, we turn to our comments, and to our reflections following the extensive, and intensive, exposure of this court to insanity defense issues.[9]

1. NEED TO DEPART FROM "PRODUCT" FORMULATION AND UNDUE DOMINANCE BY EXPERTS.

A principal reason for our decision to depart from the *Durham* rule is the undesirable characteristic, surviving even the *McDonald* modification, of undue dominance by the experts giving testimony. The underlying problem was identified, with stress on different facets, in the *Carter, Blocker* (concurring), and *Washington* opinions. The difficulty is rooted in the circumstance that there is no generally accepted understanding, either in the jury or the community it represents, of the concept requiring that the crime be the "product" of the mental disease.

When the court used the term "product" in *Durham* it likely assumed that this was a serviceable, and indeed a natural, term for a rule defining criminal responsibility—a legal reciprocal, as it were, for the familiar term "proximate cause," used to define civil responsibility.

But if concepts like "product" are, upon refinement, reasonably understood, or at least appreciated, by judges and lawyers, and perhaps philosophers, difficulties developed when it emerged that the "product" concept did not signify a reasonably identifiable common ground that was also shared by the nonlegal experts,[10] and the laymen serving on the jury as the representatives of the community.

The doctrine of criminal responsibility is such that there can be no doubt "of the complicated nature of the decision to be made—intertwining moral, legal, and medical judgments," see King v. United States, 125 U.S.App.D.C. 318, 324, 372 F.2d 383, 389 (1967) and *Durham* and other cases cited *supra,* note 6. Hence, as *King* and other opinions have noted, jury decisions have been accorded unusual deference even when they have found responsibility in the face of a powerful record, with medical evidence uncontradicted, pointing toward exculpation.[11] The "moral" elements of the decision are not defined exclusively by religious considerations but by the totality of underlying conceptions of ethics and justice shared by the community as expressed by its jury surrogate. The essential feature of a jury "lies in the interposition between the accused and his accuser of the commonsense judgment of a group of laymen, and in the community participation and shared responsibility that results from the group's determination of guilt or innocence." Williams v. Florida, 399 U.S. 78, 100, 90 S.Ct. 1893, 1906, 26 L.Ed.2d 466 (1970).

The expert witnesses—psychiatrists and psychologists—are called to adduce relevant information concerning what may for convenience be referred to as the "medical" component of the responsibility issue. But the difficulty—as emphasized in *Washington*—is that the medical expert comes, by testimony given in terms of a non-medical construct ("product"), to express conclusions that in essence embody ethical and legal conclusions. There is indeed, irony in a situation under which the *Durham* rule, which was adopted in large part to permit experts to testify in their own terms concerning matters within their domain which the jury should know, resulted in testimony by the experts in terms not their own to reflect unexpressed judgments in a domain that is properly not theirs but the jury's. The irony is heightened when the jurymen, instructed under the esoteric "product" standard, are influenced significantly by "product" testimony of expert witnesses really reflecting ethical and legal judgments rather than a conclusion within the witnesses' particular expertise.

It is easier to identify and spotlight the irony than to eradicate the mischief. The objective of *Durham* is still sound—to put before the jury the information that is within the expert's domain, to aid the jury in making a broad and comprehensive judgment. But when the instructions and appellate decisions define the "product" inquiry as the ultimate issue, it is like stopping the tides to try to halt the emergence of this term in the language of those with a central role in the trial—the lawyers who naturally seek to present testimony that will influence the jury who will be charged under the ultimate "product" standard, and the expert witnesses who have an awareness, gained from forensic psychiatry and related disciplines, of the ultimate "product" standard that dominates the proceeding.

The experts have meaningful information to impart, not only on the existence of mental illness or not, but also on its relationship to the incident charged as an offense. In the interest of justice this valued information should be available, and should not be lost or blocked by requirements that unnaturally restrict communication between the experts and the jury. The more we have pondered the problem the more convinced we have become that the sound solution lies not in further shaping of the *Durham* "product" approach in more refined molds, but in adopting the ALI's formulation as the linchpin of our jurisprudence.

The ALI's formulation retains the core requirement of a meaningful relationship between the mental illness and the incident charged. The language in the ALI rule is sufficiently in the common ken that its use in the courtroom, or in preparation for trial, permits a reasonable three-way communication—between (a) the law-trained, judges and lawyers; (b) the experts and (c) the jurymen—without insisting on a vocabulary that is either stilted or stultified, or conducive to a testimonial mystique permitting expert dominance and encroachment on the jury's function. There is no indication in the available literature that any such untoward development has attended the reasonably widespread adoption of the ALI rule in the Federal courts and a substantial number of state courts.

2. RETENTION OF McDONALD DEFINITION OF "MENTAL DISEASE OR DEFECT."

Our ruling today includes our decision that in the ALI rule as adopted by this court the term "mental disease or defect" includes the definition of that term provided in our 1962 en banc *McDonald* opinion, as follows:

[A] mental disease or defect includes any abnormal condition of the mind which substantially affects mental or emotional processes and substantially impairs behavior controls.

McDonald v. United States, 114 U.S.App.D.C. at 124, 312 F.2d at 851.

We take this action in response to the problem, identified by amicus comments of Mr. Dempsey and the D.C. Bar Association, that the ALI's rule, lacking definition of "mental disease or defect," contains an inherent ambiguity. These comments consider this a reason for avoiding the ALI rule. We find more merit in the suggestion of Mr. Flynn, counsel appointed to represent appellant, that the *McDonald* definition be engrafted on to the ALI rule.[12]

In our further discussion of ALI and *McDonald*, we shall sometimes refer to "mental disease" as the core concept, without specifically referring to the possibility of exculpation by reason of a non-altering "mental defect."

The *McDonald* Rule has helped accomplish the objective of securing expert testimony needed on the subject of mental illness, while guarding against the undue dominance of expert testimony or specialized labels. It has thus permitted the kind of communication without encroachment, as between experts and juries, that has prompted us to adopt the ALI rule, and hence will help us realize our objective. This advantage overrides the surface disadvantage of any clumsiness in the blending of the *McDonald* component, defining mental disease, with the rest of the ALI rule, a matter we discuss further below.

3. INTEREST OF UNIFORMITY OF JUDICIAL APPROACH AND VOCABULARY, WITH ROOM FOR VARIATIONS AND ADJUSTMENTS

Adoption of the ALI rule furthers uniformity of judicial approach—a feature eminently desirable, not as a mere glow of "togetherness," but as an appreciation of the need and value of judicial communication. In all likelihood, this court's approach under *Durham*, at least since *McDonald*, has differed from that of other courts in vocabulary more than substance. Uniformity of vocabulary has an important value, however, as is evidenced from the familiar experience of meanings that "get lost in translation." No one court can amass all the experience pertinent to the judicial administration of the insanity defense. It is helpful for courts to be able to learn from each other without any blockage due to jargon. It is an impressive virtue of the common law, that its distinctive reliance on judicial decisions to establish the corpus of the law furthers a multiparty conversation between men who have studied a problem in various places at various times.

The value of uniformity of central approach is not shattered by the circumstance that in various particulars the different circuits have inserted variations in the ALI rule. Homogeneity does not mean rigidity, and room for local variation is likely a strength, providing a basis for comparison,[13] not a weakness. Nor is the strength of essential uniformity undercut by the caution of our appointed amicus that the formulation of the ALI rule provides extremely broad flexibility.[14] Flexibility and ductility are inherent in the insanity defense, as in any judicial rule with an extensive range —say, negligence, or proximate cause—and the ALI rule permits appropriate guidance of juries.

In prescribing a departure from *Durham* we are not unmindful of the concern that a change may generate uncertainties as to corollaries of the change.[15] While the courts adopting the ALI rule have stated variations, as we have noted, these were all, broadly, in furtherance of one or more of the inter-related goals of the insanity defense:

(a) a broad input of pertinent facts and opinions
(b) enhancing the information and judgment
(c) of a jury necessarily given latitude in light of its functioning as the representative of the entire community.

We are likewise and for the same objectives defining the ALI rule as adopted by the court, with its contours and corollaries given express statement at the outset so as to minimize uncertainty. We postpone this statement to a subsequent phase of the opinion (see. 990 et seq.) in order that we may first consider other alternatives, for in some measure our adaptation may obviate or at least blunt objections voiced to the ALI rule.

4. CONSIDERATION AND REJECTION OF OTHER SUGGESTIONS

a. *Proposal to abolish insanity defense*

A number of proposals in the journals recommend that the insanity defense be abolished altogether.[16] This is advocated in the amicus brief of the National District Attorneys Association as both desirable and lawful.[17] The amicus brief of American Psychiatric Association concludes it would be desirable, with appropriate safeguards, but would require a constitutional amendment. That a constitutional amendment would be required is also the conclusion of others, generally in opposition to the proposal.[18]

This proposal has been put forward by responsible judges for consideration, with the objective of reserving psychiatric overview for the phase of the criminal process concerned with disposition of the person determined to have been the actor.[19] However, we are convinced that the proposal cannot properly be imposed by judicial fiat.

The courts have emphasized over the centuries that "free will" is the postulate of responsibility under our jurisprudence. 4 Blackstone's Commentaries 27. The concept of "belief in freedom of the human will and a consequent ability and duty of the normal individual to choose between good and evil" is a core concept that is "universal and persistent in mature systems of law."

Morissette v. United States, 342 U.S. 246, 250, 72 S.Ct. 240, 243, 96 L.Ed. 288 (1952). Criminal responsibility is assessed when through "free will" a man elects to do evil. And while, as noted in *Morissette,* the legislature has dispensed with mental element in some statutory offenses, in furtherance of a paramount need of the community, these instances mark the exception and not the rule, and only in the most limited instances has the mental element been omitted by the legislature as a requisite for an offense that was a crime at common law.

The concept of lack of "free will" is both the root of origin of the insanity defense and the line of its growth.[20] This cherished principle is not undercut by difficulties, or differences of view, as to how best to express the free will concept in the light of the expansion of medical knowledge. We do not concur in the view of the National District Attorneys Association that the insanity defense should be abandoned judicially, either because it is at too great a variance with popular conceptions of guilt[21] or fails "to show proper respect for the personality of the criminal [who] is liable to resent pathology more than punishment."[22]

These concepts may be measured along with other ingredients in a legislative re-examination of settled doctrines of criminal responsibility, root, stock and branch. Such a reassessment, one that seeks to probe and appraise the society's processes and values is for the legislative branch, assuming no constitutional bar. The judicial role is limited, in Justice Holmes's figure, to action that is molecular, with the restraint inherent in taking relatively small steps, leaving to the other branches of government whatever progress must be made with seven-league leaps. Such judicial restraint is particularly necessary when a proposal requires, as a mandatory ingredient, the kind of devotion of resources, personnel and techniques that can be accomplished only through whole-hearted legislative commitment.

To obviate any misunderstanding from our rejection of the recommendation of those proposing judicial abolition of the insanity defense, we expressly commend their emphasis on the need for improvement of dispositional resources and programs. The defense focuses on the kind of impairment that warrants exculpation, and necessarily assigns to the prison walls many men who have serious mental impairments and difficulties. The needs of society—rooted not only in humanity but in practical need for attempting to break the recidivist cycles, and halt the spread of deviant behavior—call for the provision of psychiatrists, psychologists and counselors to help men with these mental afflictions and difficulties, as part of a total effort toward a readjustment that will permit re-integration in society.

b Proposal for defense if mental disease impairs capacity to such an extent that the defendant cannot "justly be held responsible."

We have also pondered the suggestion that the jury be instructed that the defendant lacks criminal responsibility if the jury finds that the defendant's mental disease impairs his capacity or controls to such an extent that he cannot "justly be held responsible."

This was the view of a British commission,[23] adapted and proposed in 1955 by Professor Wechsler, the distinguished Reporter for the ALI's Model Penal Code, and sustained by some, albeit a minority, of the members of the ALI's Council.[24] In the ALI, the contrary view prevailed because of a concern over presenting to the jury questions put primarily in the form of "justice."

The proposal is not to be condemned out of hand as a suggestion that the jury be informed of an absolute prerogative that it can only exercise by flatly disregarding the applicable rule of law. It is rather a suggestion that the jury be informed of the matters the law contemplates it will take into account in arriving at the community judgment concerning a composite of factors.[25]

However, there is a substantial concern that an instruction overtly cast in terms of "justice" cannot feasibly be restricted to the ambit of what may properly be taken into account but will splash with unconfinable and malign consequences. The Government cautions that "explicit appeals to 'justice' will result in litigation of extraneous issues and will encourage improper arguments to the jury phrased solely in terms of 'sympathy' and 'prejudice.' "

Nor is this solely a prosecutor's concern.

Mr. Flynn, counsel appointed to represent defendant, puts it that even though the jury is applying community concepts of blameworthiness "the jury should not be left at large, or asked to find out for itself what those concepts are."

The amicus submission of the Public Defender Service argues that it would be beneficial to focus the jury's attention on the moral and legal questions intertwined in the insanity defense. It expresses concern, however, over a blameworthiness instruction without more, saying (Br. 19) "it may well be that the 'average' American condemns the mentally ill."[26] It would apparently accept an approach not unlike that proposed by the ALI Reporter, under which the justice standard is coupled with a direction to consider the individual's capacity to control his behavior. Mr. Dempsey's recommendation is of like import, with some simplification.[27] But the problem remains, whether, assuming justice calls for the exculpation and treatment of the mentally ill, that is more likely to be gained from a jury, with "average" notions of mental illness, which

is explicitly set at large to convict or acquit persons with impaired mental capacity according to its concept of justice.

The brief of the D.C. Bar Association as amicus submits that with a "justly responsible" formulation the test of insanity "would be largely swallowed up by this consideration." And it observes that the function of giving to the jury the law to be applied to the facts is not only the duty of the court, see Sparf v. United States, 156 U.S. 51, 102, 15 S.Ct. 273, 39 L.Ed. 343 (1895), but is also "a bedrock right of every citizen"—and, possibly, his "only protection," citing Justice Story in United States v. Battiste, 2 Sumn. 240, 244, Fed.Cas. No. 14,545 (C.C.D.Mass. 1835).

We are impressed by the observation of Professor Abraham S. Goldstein, one of the most careful students of the problem:

[The] overly general standard may place too great a burden upon the jury. If the law provides no standard, members of the jury are placed in the difficult position of having to find a man responsible for no other reason then their personal feeling about him. Whether the psyches of individual jurors are strong enough to make that decision, or whether the "law" should put that obligation on them, is open to serious question. It is far easier for them to perform the role assigned to them by legislature and courts if they know—or are able to rationalize—that their verdicts are "required" by law.[28]

Professor Goldstein was referring to the board "justice" standard recommended by the Royal Commission. But the problems remain acute even with the modifications in the proposal of the ALI Reporter, for that still leads to "justly responsible" as the ultimate and critical term.

There may be a tug of appeal in the suggestion that law is a means to justice and the jury is an appropriate tribunal to ascertain justice. This is a simplistic syllogism that harbors the logical fallacy of equivocation, and fails to take account of the different facets and dimensions of the concept of justice. We must not be beguiled by a play on words. The thrust of a rule that in essence invites the jury to ponder the evidence on impairment of defendant's capacity and appreciation, and then do what to them seems just, is to focus on what seems "just" as to the particular individual. Under the centuries-long pull of the Judeo-Christian ethic, this is likely to suggest a call for understanding and forgiveness of those who have committed crimes against society, but plead the influence of passionate and perhaps justified grievances against that society, perhaps grievances not wholly lacking in merit. In the domain of morality and religion, the gears may be governed by the particular instance of the individual seeking salvation. The judgment of a court of law must further justice to the community, and safeguard it against undercutting and evasion from overconcern for the individual. What this reflects is not the rigidity of retributive justice—an eye for an eye—but awareness how justice in the broad may be undermined by an excess of compassion as well as passion. Justice to the community includes penalties needed to cope with disobedience by those capable of control, undergirding a social environment that broadly inhibits behavior destructive of the common good. An open society requires mutual respect and regard, and mutually reinforcing relationships among its citizens, and its ideals of justice must safeguard the vast majority who responsibly shoulder the burdens implicit in its ordered liberty. Still another aspect of justice is the requirement for rules of conduct that establish reasonable generality, neutrality and constancy. Cf. L. Fuller, The Morality of Laws 33–94 (1964). This concept is neither static nor absolute, but it would be sapped by a rule that invites an ad hoc redefinition of the "just" with each new case.

It is the sense of justice propounded by those charged with making and declaring the law—legislatures and courts—that lays down the rule that persons without substantial capacity to know or control the act shall be excused. The jury is concerned with applying the community understanding of this broad rule to particular lay and medical facts. Where the matter is unclear it naturally will call on its own sense of justice to help it determine the matter. There is wisdom in the view that a jury generally understands well enough that an instruction composed in flexible terms gives it sufficient latitude so that, without disregarding the instruction, it can provide that application of the instruction which harmonizes with its sense of justice.[29] The ALI rule generally communicates that meaning. Wade v. United States, *supra*, 426 F.2d at 70–71. This is recognized even by those who might prefer a more explicit statement of the matter.[30] It is one thing, however, to tolerate and even welcome the jury's sense of equity as a force that affects its application of instructions which state the legal rules that crystallize the requirements of justice as determined by the lawmakers of the community. It is quite another to set the jury at large, without such crystallization, to evolve its own legal rules and standards of justice. It would likely be counter-productive and contrary to the larger interest of justice to become so explicit—in an effort to hammer the point home to the very occasional jury that would otherwise be too rigid—that one puts serious strains on the normal operation of the system of criminal justice.

Taking all these considerations into account we conclude that the ALI rule as announced is not productive of injustice, and we decline to proclaim the broad "justly responsible" standard.

5. ALI RULE IS CONTEMPLATED AS IMPROVING THE PROCESS OF ADJUDICATION, NOT AS AFFECTING NUMBER OF INSANITY ACQUITTALS

Amicus Dempsey is concerned that a change by this court from *Durham-McDonald* to ALI will be taken as an indication that this court intends that the number and percentage of insanity acquittals be modified. That is not the intendment of the rule adopted today, nor do we have any basis for forecasting that effect.

a. Statistical data concerning the use of insanity in criminal trials in this jurisdiction were presented in the December 15, 1966, Report of the President's Commission on Crime in the District of Columbia.[31] These data have been up-dated in Mr. Dempsey's brief, with the aid of data helpfully supplied by the United States Attorney's office. At least since *Durham* was modified by *McDonald*, insanity acquittals have run at about 2% of all cases terminated. In the seven years subsequent to *McDonald* jury verdicts of not guilty by reason of insanity averaged only 3 per annum.[32] In trials by the court, there has been an annual average of about 38 verdicts of not guilty by reason of insanity; these typically are cases where the Government psychiatrists agreed that the crime was the product of mental illness.[33] We perceive no basis in these data for any conclusion that the number of percentage of insanity acquittals has been either excessive or inadequate.

We have no way of forecasting what will be the effect on verdicts, of juries or judges, from the reduction in influence of expert testimony on "productivity" that reflects judgments outside the domain of expertise.[34] Whatever its effect, we are confident that the rule adopted today provides a sounder relationship in terms of the giving, comprehension and application of expert testimony. Our objective is not to steer the jury's verdict but to enhance its deliberation.[35]

b. Some judges have viewed the ALI test as going beyond *Durham* in enlarging the category of persons who may win acquittals.[36] The 1966 report of the President's Crime Commission (*supra* note 15) apparently concludes that the debate over *Durham* was stilled by *McDonald*, and that *Durham-McDonald* is not significantly different in content from the ALI test. In contrast, Mr. Dempsey is concerned that a person's ability to control his behavior could be "substantially impaired" by mental condition, thus qualifying the defense under *McDonald*, while still leaving him with "substantial capacity," rendering the defense unavailable under the ALI rule. We have no way of knowing whether psychiatrists giving testimony would draw such a distinction, and moreover there would be no difference in result unless one also indulges the assumption, which is dubious, that the jury would reason that the crime may have been the "product" of the mental condition of a man even though he retained substantial capacity.

In the last analysis, however, if there is a case where there would be a difference in result—and it would seem rare—we think the underlying freedom of will conception renders it just to assign responsibility to a person, even though his controls have been impaired, if his residual controls give him "substantial capacity" both to appreciate the wrongfulness of his conduct and to conform it to the requirement of law. Whether the ALI standard is to be given a narrow or broad conception rests not on abstract analysis[37] but on the application reflecting the underlying sense of responsibility of the jury, as the community's surrogate.[38]

6. ELEMENTS OF THE ALI RULE ADOPTED BY THIS COURT

Though it provides a general uniformity, the ALI rule leaves room for variations. Thus, we have added an adjustment in the *McDonald* definition of mental disease, which we think fully compatible with both the spirit and text of the ALI rule. In the interest of good administration, we now undertake to set forth, with such precision as the subject will permit, other elements of the ALI rule as adopted by this court.

The two main components of the rule define (1) mental disease, (2) the consequences thereof that exculpate from responsibility.

a. *Intermesh of components*

The first component of our rule, derived from *Mc-Donald,* defines mental disease or defect as an abnormal condition of the mind, and a condition which substantially (a) affects mental or emotional processes and (b) impairs behavioral controls. The second component, derived from the Model Penal Code, tells which defendant with a mental disease lacks criminal responsibility for particular conduct: it is the defendant who, as a result of this mental condition, at the time of such conduct, either (i) lacks substantial capacity to appreciate that his conduct is wrong, or (ii) lacks substantial capacity to conform his conduct to the law.

The first component establishes eligibility for an instruction concerning the defense for a defendant who presents evidence that his abnormal condition of the mind has substantially impaired behavioral controls. The second component completes the instruction and defines the ultimate issue, of exculpation in terms of whether his behavioral controls were not only substantially impaired but impaired to such an extent that he lacked substantial capacity to conform his conduct to the law.[39]

b. *The "result" of the mental disease*

The rule contains a requirement of causality, as is clear from the term "result." Exculpation is established not by mental disease alone but only if "as a result" defendant lacks the substantial capacity required for responsibility. Presumably the mental disease of a kleptomaniac does not entail as a "result" a lack of capacity to conform to the law prohibiting rape.

c. *At the time of the conduct*

Under the Ali rule the issue is not whether defendant is so disoriented or void of controls that he is never able to conform to external demands, but whether he had that capacity at the time of the conduct. The question is not properly put in terms of whether he would have capacity to conform in some untypical restraining situation—as with an attendant or policeman at his elbow. The issue is whether he was able to conform in the unstructured condition of life in an open society, and whether the result of his abnormal mental condition was a lack of substantial internal controls. These matters are brought out in the ALI's comments to § 4.01 of the Model Penal Code Tentative Draft #4, p. 158:

> The schizophrenic . . . is disoriented from reality; the disorientation is extreme; but it is rarely total. Most psychotics will respond to a command of someone in authority within the mental hospital; they thus have some capacity to conform to a norm. But this is very different from the capacity to conform to requirements that are not thus immediately symbolized by an attendant or policeman at the elbow. Nothing makes the inquiry into responsibility more unreal for the psychiatrist than limitation of the issue to some ultimate extreme of total incapacity, when clinical experience reveals only a graded scale with marks along the way.

d. *Capacity to appreciate wrongfulness of his conduct*

As to the option of terminology noted in the ALI code, we adopt the formulation that exculpates a defendant whose mental condition is such that he lacks substantial capacity to appreciate the wrongfulness of his conduct. We prefer this on pragmatic grounds to "appreciate the criminality of his conduct" since the resulting jury instruction is more like that conventionally given to and applied by the jury. While such an instruction is of course subject to the objection that it lacks complete precision, it serves the objective of calling on the jury to provide a community judgment on a combination of factors. And since the possibility of analytical differences between the two formulations is insubstantial in fact in view of the control capacity test, we are usefully guided by the pragmatic considerations pertinent to jury instructions.[40]

In adopting the ALI formulation, this court does not follow the *Currens* opinion of the Third Circuit, which puts it that the sole issue in every case is defendant's capacity to control his behavior, and that as a matter of analysis a person who lacks substantial capacity to appreciate the wrongfulness [criminality] of his conduct necessarily lacks substantial capacity to control his behavior. Like the other circuits, we resist the *Currens* lure of logic in order to make certain that the jury will give heed to the substantiality of a defense of lack of substantial capacity to appreciate wrongfulness, a point that may elude a jury instructed solely in terms of control capacity. In a particular case, however, defendant may have reason to request omission of the phrase pertaining to lack of capacity to appreciate wrongfulness, if that particular matter is not involved on the facts, and defendant fears that a jury that does not attend rigorously to the details of the instruction may erroneously suppose that the defense is lost if defendant appreciates wrongfulness. Here again, it is not enough to rely solely on logic, when a simple change will aid jury understanding. In such a case, if defendant requests, the judge should limit the instruction to the issue involved in that case, and charge that the jury shall bring in a verdict of not guilty if as a result of mental illness defendant lacked substantial capacity to conform his conduct to the requirements of the law.

e. *Caveat paragraph*

Section 4.01 of the Model Penal Code as promulgated by ALI contains in subsection (2) what has come to be known as the "caveat paragraph":

(2) The terms "mental disease or defect" do not include an abnormality manifested only by repeated criminal or otherwise anti-social conduct.

The purpose of this provision was to exclude a defense for the so-called "psychopathic personality."[41]

There has been a split in the Federal circuits concerning this provision. Some of the courts adopting the ALI rule refer to both subsections but without separate discussion of the caveat paragraph—as in the *Chandler* and *Blake* opinions. As to the decisions considering the point, those of the Second and Third Circuits conclude the paragraph should be retained (in *Freeman* and *Currens*), while the *Smith* and *Wade* decisions, of the Sixth and Ninth Circuits, conclude it should be omitted. The Sixth Circuit's position is (404 f.2d at 727, fn.8) that there is "great dispute over the psychiatric soundness" of the caveat paragraph. The *Wade* opinion considers the matter at great length and puts forward three grounds for rejecting the caveat paragraph: (1) As a practical matter, it would be ineffectual in keeping sociopaths out of the definition of insanity; it is always possible to introduce some evidence, other than past criminal behavior, to support a plea of insanity. (2) The criminal sanction ought not be sought for criminal psychopaths—constant recidivists—because such people should be taken off the streets indefinitely, and not merely for a set term of years. (3) Its third ground is stated thus (426 F.2d at 73):

It is unclear whether [the caveat paragraph] would require that a defendant be considered legally sane if, although the only overt acts manifesting his disease or defect were "criminal or otherwise anti-social," there arises from his acts a reasonable inference of mental derangement either because of the nature of the acts or because of credible medical or other evidence.

Our own approach is influenced by the fact that our rule already includes a definition of mental disease (from *McDonald*). Under that definition, as we have pointed out, the mere existence of "a long criminal record does not excuse crime." Williams v. United States, 114 U.S.App.D.C. 135, 137, 312 F.2d 862, 864 (1962). We do not require the caveat paragraph as an insurance against exculpation of the deliberate and persistent offender.[42] Our *McDonald* rule guards against the danger of misunderstanding and injustice that might arise, say, from an expert's classification that reflects only a conception[43] defining all criminality as reflective of mental illness. There must be testimony to show both that the defendant was suffering from an abnormal condition of the mind and that it substantially affected mental or emotional processes and substantially impaired behavioral controls.

In this context, our pragmatic approach is to adopt the caveat paragraph as a rule for application by the judge, to avoid miscarriage of justice, but not for inclusion in instructions to the jury.

The judge will be aware that the criminal and antisocial conduct of a—person on the street, in the home, in the ward—is necessarily material information for assessment by the psychiatrist. On the other hand, rarely if ever would a psychiatrist base a conclusion of mental disease solely on criminal and anti-social acts. Our pragmatic solution provides for reshaping the rule for application by the court as follows: The introduction or proffer of past criminal and anti-social actions is not admissible as evidence of mental disease unless accompanied by expert testimony, supported by a showing of the concordance of a responsible segment of professional opinion, that the particular characteristics of these actions constitute convincing evidence of an underlying mental disease that substantially impairs behavioral controls.

This formulation retains the paragraph as a "caveat" rather than an inexorable rule of law. It should serve to obviate distortions of the present state of knowledge that would constitute miscarriages of justice. Yet it leaves the door open—on shouldering the "convincing evidence" burden—to accommodate our general rule to developments that may lie ahead. It is the kind of imperfect, but not unfeasible, accommodation of the abstract and pragmatic that is often found to serve the administration of justice.

We do not think it desirable to use the caveat paragraph as a basis for instructions to the jury. It would be difficult for a juryman—or anyone else—to reconcile the caveat paragraph and the basic (*McDonald*) definition of mental disease if a psychiatrist testified that he discerned from particular past criminal behavior a pattern that established defendant as suffering from an abnormal condition of the mind that substantially impaired behavioral controls. If there is no such testimony, then there would be no evidence that mere misconduct betokens mental illness, it would be impermissible for defense counsel to present such a hypothesis to the jury, and there would be very little likelihood that a jury would arrive at such a proposition on its own. On the other hand, an instruction along the lines of the caveat paragraph runs the risk of appearing to call for the rejection of testimony that is based materially, but only partially, on the history of criminal conducts.

f. *Broad presentation to the jury*

Our adoption of the ALI rule does not depart from the doctrines this court has built up over the past twenty years to assure a broad presentation to the jury concerning the condition of defendant's mind and its consequences. Thus we adhere to our rulings admitting expert testimony of psychologists,[44] as well as psychiatrists, and to our many decisions contemplating that expert testimony on this subject will be accompanied by presentation of the facts and premises underlying the opinions and conclusions of the experts,[45] and that the Government and defense may present, in Judge Blackmun's words, "all possibly relevant evidence" bearing on cognition, volition and capacity.[46] We agree with the amicus submission of the National District Attorneys Association that the law cannot "distinguish between physiological, emotional, social and cultural sources of the impairment"—assuming, of course, requisite testimony establishing exculpation under the pertinent standard—and all such causes may be both referred to by the expert and considered by the trier of fact.[47]

Breadth of input under the insanity defense is not to be confused with breadth of the doctrines establishing the defense. As the National District Attorneys Association brief points out, the latitude for salient evidence of, for example, social and cultural factors pertinent to an abnormal condition of the mind significantly affecting capacity and controls, does not mean that such factors may be taken as establishing a separate defense for persons whose mental condition is such that blame can be imposed. We have rejected a broad "injustice" approach that would have opened the door to expositions of for example, cultural deprivation, unrelated to any abnormal condition of the mind.

We have recognized that "Many criminologists point out that even normal human behavior is in-

fluenced by such factors as training, environment, poverty and the like, which may limit the understanding and options of the individual." King v. United States, *supra,* 125 U.S.App.D.C.at 323, 372 F.2d at 388. Determinists may contend that every man's fate is ultimately sealed by his genes and environment, over which he has no control. Our jurisprudence, however, while not oblivious to deterministic components, utimately rests on a premise of freedom of will. This is not to be viewed as an exercise in philosophic discourse, but as a governmental fusion of ethics and necessity, which takes into account that a system of rewards and punishments is itself part of the environment that influences and shapes human conduct. Our recognition of an insanity defense for those who lack the essential, threshold free will possessed by those in the normal range is not to be twisted, directly or indirectly, into a device for exculpation of those without an abnormal condition of the mind.

Finally, we have not accepted suggestions to adopt a rule that disentangles the insanity defense from a medical model, and announces a standard exculpating anyone whose capacity for control is insubstantial, for whatever cause or reason. There may be logic in these submissions, but we are not sufficiently certain of the nature, range and implications of the conduct involved to attempt an all-embracing unified field theory. The applicable rule can be discerned as the cases arise in regard to other conditions—somnambulism or other automatisms; blackouts due, for example, to overdose of insulin; drug addiction. Whether these somatic conditions should be governed by a rule comparable to that herein set forth for mental disease would require, at a minimum, a judicial determination, which takes medical opinion into account, finding convincing evidence of an ascertainable condition characterized by "a broad consensus that free will does not exist." Salzman v. United States, 131 U.S.App.D.C. 393, 400, 405 F.2d 358, 365 (1968) (concurring opinion of Judge Wright).

MENTAL CONDITION, THOUGH INSUFFICIENT TO EXONERATE, MAY BE RELEVANT TO SPECIFIC MENTAL ELEMENT OF CERTAIN CRIMES OR DEGREES OF CRIME.

Our decision accompanies the redefinition of when a mental condition exonerates a defendant from criminal responsibility with the doctrine that expert testimony as to a defendant's abnormal mental condition may be received and considered, as tending to show, in a responsible way, that defendant did not have the specific mental state required for a particular crime or degree of crime—even though he was aware that his act was wrongful and was able to control it, and hence was not entitled to complete exoneration.

Some of the cases following this doctrine use the term "diminished responsibility," but we prefer the example of the cases that avoid this term (for example, note 57, *infra*), for its convenience is outweighed by its confusion: Our doctrine has nothing to do with "diminishing" responsibility of a defendant because of his impaired mental condition,[52] but rather with determining whether the defendant had the mental state that must be proved as to all defendants.

Procedurally, the issue of abnormal mental condition negativing a person's intent may arise in different ways: For example, the defendant may offer evidence of mental condition not qualifying as mental disease under *McDonald*. Or he may tender evidence that qualifies under *McDonald*, yet the jury may conclude from all the evidence that defendant has knowledge and control capacity sufficient for responsibility under the ALI rule.

The issue often arises with respect to mental condition tendered as negativing the element of premeditation in a charge of first degree premeditated murder. As we noted in Austin v. United States, 127 U.S. App.D.C. 180, 382 F.2d 129 (1967), when the legislature modified the common law crime of murder so as to establish degrees, murder in the first degree was reserved for intentional homicide done deliberately and with premeditation, and homicide that is intentional but "impulsive," not done after "reflection and meditation," was made murder only in the second degree. (127 U.S.App.D.C. at 187, 382 F.2d at 135).

An offense like deliberated and premeditated murder requires a specific intent that cannot be satisfied merely by showing that defendant failed to conform to an objective standard.[53] This is plainly established by the defense of voluntary intoxication. In Hopt v. Utah, 104 U.S. 631, 634, 26 L.Ed. 873 (1881), the Court, after stating the familiar rule that voluntary intoxication is no excuse for crime, said:

[W]hen a statute establishing different degrees of murder requires deliberate premeditation in order to constitute murder in the first degree, the question of whether the accused is in such a condition of mind, by reason of drunkenness or otherwise, as to be capable of deliberate premeditation, necessarily becomes a material subject of consideration by the jury.

In Bishop v. United States, 71 App.D.C. 132, 136, 107 F.2d 297, 301 (1939), Justice Vinson noted that while voluntary intoxication per se is no defense to guilt, "the stated condition of a defendant's mind at the time of the killing ... is now a proper subject for consideration, inquiry, and determination by the jury." Thus "voluntary intoxication will not excuse murder, but it may negative the ability of the defendant" as to premeditation, and hence effect "a reduction to second degree murder."

Enlarging on *Hopt* and *Bishop*, Judge Burger's opinion in Heideman v. United States, 104 U.S.App.D.C. 128, 131, 259 F.2d 943, 946 (1958), points out:

Drunkenness is not per se an excuse for crime, but nevertheless it may in many instances be relevant to the issue of intent. One class of cases where drunkenness may be relevant on the issue of intent is the category of crimes where specific intent is required. Robbery falls into this category, and a defendant accused of robbery is entitled to an instruction on drunkenness as bearing on intent if the evidentiary groundwork has been adequately laid.

As Judge Burger points out there must be a showing of drunkenness that does more than remove inhibitions, and is such an "incapacitating state" as to negate intent. But he also notes, citing *Hopt,* and *Bishop,* that a lesser state of drunkenness, insufficient to negate the specific intent required for robbery, may suffice to negate the premeditation required for first degree murder.

Neither logic nor justice can tolerate a jurisprudence that defines the elements of an offense as requiring a mental state such that one defendant can properly argue that his voluntary drunkenness removed his capacity to form the specific intent but another defendant is inhibited from a submission of his contention that an abnormal mental condition, for which he was in no way responsible, negated his capacity to form a particular specific intent, even though the condition did not exonerate him from all criminal responsibility.

In Fisher v. United States, 80 U.S.App.D.C. 96, 149 F.2d (1946), the court upheld the trial court's refusal to instruct the jury that on issues of premeditation and deliberation "it should consider the entire personality of the defendant, his mental, nervous, emotional and physical characteristics as developed by the evidence in the case." Justice Arnold's abbreviated opinion was evidently premised on two factors: (1) that the instruction confused the issue of insanity with the issue of deliberation; (2) that "To give an instruction like the above is to tell the jury they are at liberty to acquit one who commits a brutal crime because he has the abnormal tendencies of persons capable of such crimes." His opinion made no effort to come to terms with the *Hopt* opinion, stressed by Fisher's counsel.

Fisher went to the Supreme Court and there was affirmed, but on the limited ground of disinclination to "force" this court in a choice of legal doctrine for the District of Columbia, 328 U.S. 463, 66 S.Ct. 1318, 90 L.Ed. 1382 (1946). The Court said (at 476, 66 S.Ct. at 1325) that such a change was "more properly a subject for the exercise of legislative power or at least for the discretion of the courts of the District."

In *Stewart I,* Stewart v. United States, 94 U.S. App.D.C. 293, 214 F.2d 879 (1954) which issued only two weeks after *Durham* was announced, we said that "reconsideration of our decision in Fisher should wait until we can appraise the results [of Durham]." In Stewart v. United States, 107 U.S.App.D.C. 159, 275 F.2d 617 (1960), the court en banc again stated that more experience with *Durham* was required to evaluate *Fisher,* and the matter was appropriate for legislative consideration. That was *Stewart II.* [54]

Today we are again *en banc,* and we have the benefit of many years of experience with *Durham-McDonald.* We are changing the insanity rule, on a prospective basis, to take into account intervening scholarship and court opinions. As a corollary, we deem it appropriate to change the rule of *Fisher* on a prospective basis, and to accept the approach which the Supreme Court declined to "force" upon us in 1946, but which has been adopted by the overwhelming majority of courts that have recently faced the question. We are convinced by the analysis set forth in the recent opinions of the highest courts of California,[55] Colorado,[56] New Jersey,[57] Iowa,[58] Ohio,[59] Idaho,[60] Connecticut,[61] Nebraska,[62] New Mexico[63] and Nevada.[64] They have joined the states that spoke out before *Fisher*—New York, Rhode Island, Utah, Wisconsin and Wyoming.[65]

The pertinent reasoning was succinctly stated by the Colorado Supreme Court as follows:[66]

The question to be determined is not whether defendant was insane, but whether the homicidal act was committed with deliberation and premeditation. The evidence offered as to insanity may or may not be relevant to that issue. * * * "A claim of insanity cannot be used for the purpose of reducing a crime of murder in the first degree to murder in the second degree or from murder to manslaughter. If the perpetrator is responsible at all in this respect, he is responsible in the same degree as a sane man; and if he is not responsible at all, he is entitled to an acquittal in both degrees. However, ... *evidence of the condition of the mind* of the accused at the time of the crime, together with the surrounding circumstances, may be introduced, not for the purpose of establishing insanity, but to prove that the situation was such that a specific intent was not entertained—that is, *to show absence of any deliberate or premeditated design.*" (Emphasis in original.)

On the other side of the coin, very few jurisdictions which have recently considered this question have held to the contrary position.[67]

Intervening developments within our own jurisdiction underscore the soundness of a doctrine for consideration of abnormal mental condition on the issue of specific intent. In the *Fisher* opinion of 1946, the court was concerned lest such a doctrine "tell the jury that they are at liberty to acquit one who commits a brutal crime because he has the abnormal tendencies of persons capable of such crimes." That a man's abnormal mental condition short of legal insanity may be material as negativing premeditation and deliberation does not set him "at liberty" but reduces the degree of the

criminal homicide. Our 1967 opinion in *Austin, supra,* clarifies that even "a particularly frightful and horrible murder" may not be murder in the first degree, that "many murders most brutish and bestial are committed in a consuming frenzy or heat of passion, and that these are in law only murder in the second degree."[68] Indeed the action of the trial judge in acquitting defendant of first degree murder indicates how the refinement of *Austin* has undercut the *Fisher* approach. Though the defendant went back to get his gun,[69] the judge concluded that the evidence as a whole—including defendant's broken jaw, the blood streaming down his face, and his irrational pounding on the mailbox— did not establish a reasonable foundation for inferring a calculated, deliberate mind at the time of shooting. We are not called upon to consider whether that action was proper in this case; what we do take note of is the inevitable implication of *Austin.*

There has also been a material legislative development since both *Fisher* and *Stewart II.* In 1964, after extensive hearings, Congress enacted the Hospitalization of the Mentally Ill Act, which provides civil commitment for the "mentally ill" who are dangerous to themselves or others.[70] Both the terminology and the underlying conception of this statute reflected a deliberate change from the 1939 law and its use of the term "insanity," which prior to *Durham* tended to be equated to psychosis and to disorientations like delusions. The enlarged conception underlying the 1964 law has been accorded a "liberal construction"[71] for the protection of the community, going so far as to include commitment of a disturbed mental defective with behavioral reactions resulting in danger-productive behavior.[72] The law is broad enough to include not only mental illness requiring confinement in St. Elizabeths, but also conditions of mental illness calling for placement in nursing homes,[73] or, where appropriate, halfway houses or requirement of outpatient care.[74] These statutory provisions provide a shield against danger from persons with abnormal mental condition —a danger which in all likelihood bolstered, or even impelled, the draconic *Fisher* doctrine.

Further, to the extent that the 1970 law (*supra,* note 48) leads to a conviction of first degree murder when the evidence is in equipoise on the issue of insanity, there would be an additional miscarriage of justice if the evidence were not available for consideration as raising a reasonable doubt on the issue of premeditation and deliberation.

In providing for the admission and consideration of expert testimony on abnormal mental condition insufficient for complete exoneration, we insert some observations prompted by State v. Sikora, 44 N.J. 453, 210 A.2d 193 (1965), *supra,* note 57. The doctrine does not permit the receipt of psychiatric testimony based on the conception that mental disorder is only a relative concept and that the behavior of every individual is dictated by forces—ultimately, his genes and lifelong environment—that are unconscious and beyond his control. As we have already made clear, we are not embarked on enquiry that must yield to tenets of the philosophy of determinism. The law accepts free will and blameworthiness as a general premise. Expert psychiatric testimony negativing blameworthiness for a crime—whether on ground of general exoneration or lack of requisite specific intent—must rest on the premise of an exception due to abnormal mental condition.

Our rule permits the introduction of expert testimony as to abnormal condition if it is relevant to negative, or establish, the specific mental condition that is an element of the crime. The receipt of this expert testimony to negative the mental condition of specific intent requires careful administration by the trial judge. Where the proof is not offered in the first instance as evidence of exonerating mental disease or defect within the ALI rule the judge may, and ordinarily would, require counsel first to make a proffer of the proof to be adduced outside the presence of the jury. The judge will then determine whether the testimony is grounded in sufficient scientific support to warrant use in the courtroom, and whether it would aid the jury in reaching a decision on the ultimate issues.[75]

NOTES

9. Ten years ago Judge Burger said: "While the time span since 1954 is brief, our total study and collective ease consideration of the problem is equal perhaps to as much as a half century of case review of this problem in most jurisdictions." Blocker v. United States, 110 U.S.App.D.C. at 52, 288 F.2d at 864 (en banc, 1961) (concurring opinion).

10. A difference in language perception probably contributed to the development that psychiatric testimony concerning "product" causal relationship did not develop along the lines presaged by legal students of the problem. Early critiques in journals asserted that a but-for test of "product" would rarely, if ever, permit a psychiatrist to testify as to the existence of mental illness coexisting with a lack of "product" causal relationship to the crime. See, for example, Wechsler, The Criteria of Criminal Responsibility, 22 U.Chi.L.Rev. 367, 371 (1955); De Grazia. The Distinction of Being Mad, 22 U.Chi.L.Rev. 339, 343 (1955). Presumably, the force of this analysis was strengthened when "mental disease or defect" was defined and tightened in McDonald. As events have developed, however, it has become almost commonplace that psychiatrists testifying as to the presence of mental disease have nevertheless found an absence of "product" causal relation with the crime, or at least expressed substantial doubt as to such relationship. Perhaps more to the point, it has become commonplace for psychiatrists called by Government and defense to be in agreement on the mental disease aspects of their testimony and to differ on the issue of "product" relationship. This is not intended, in any way, as a criticism of any particular testimony. There is often a genuine and difficult

question as to the relationship between a particular mental disease and particular offense. What is our concern, however, is that the inherent difficulty of his core problem has been intensified, and the sources of confusion compounded, by a kind of mystique that came to surround the "product" test, and testimony cast in that language.

11. For example, Hawkins v. United States, 114 U.S. App.D.C. 44, 310 F.2d 849 (1962); Isaac v. United States, 109 U.S.App.D.C. 34, 284 F.2d 168 (1960).

12. This was also the suggestion of the National District Attorneys Association subject to caveats, as the test recommended if the court did not accept its submission that the insanity defense should be abolished entirely.

13. Compare New State Ice Co. v. Liebmann, 285 U.S. 262, 280, 52 S.Ct. 371, 76 L.Ed. 747 (1932) (dissenting opinion of Brandeis, J.).

14. Amicus points out that in Freeman the Second Circuit referred to the fact that the Third and Tenth Circuits "have employed their own language approaching the objectives of the Model Penal Code formulation," and then offered a discussion of guiding policy considerations, including Senator Dodd's espousal of an approach sending "marginal" cases to a hospital rather than prison, that, as amicus puts it, "strikes quite a different tone than, say, the analogous discussion of the Tenth Circuit in Wion."

15. See, for example, Report of President's D.C. Crime Commission at pp. 550 ff. A majority of the members of the Commission preferred the ALI rule, but were concerned lest departure from Durham-McDonald spawn confusion.

16. "[I]t may be that psychiatry and the other social and behavioral sciences cannot provide sufficient data relevant to a determination of criminal responsibility no matter what our rules of evidence are. If so, we may be forced to eliminate the insanity defense altogether, or refashion it in a way which is not tied so tightly to the medical model." Washington v. United States, 129 U.S.App.D.C. at 42, n. 33, 390 F.2d at 457 (1967).

17. It suggests that a mental condition be exculpatory solely as it negatives mens rea.

18. For example, Mr. Dempsey. To the same general effect is the position in the research memorandum from the University of Virginia Law School Research Group to Mr. Flynn, appellant's appointed counsel attached to his brief.

19. See for example, Burger, then Circuit Judge, Proceedings of the Sixth Annual Meeting of the National Conference of State Trial Judges, Chicago, Illinois, Aug. 9–11, 1963, quoted in Wion v. United States, 325 F.2d at 428, n. 10; Bazelon, Chief Judge, in Washington v. United States, 129 U.S.App.D.C. at 42, n. 33, 390 F.2d at 457 (1967); Haynesworth, Chief Judge, in en banc opinion in United States v. Chandler, 393 F.2d at 928 (1968); see also remarks of Chief Justice Weintraub (of New Jersey) in Insanity as a Defense—Panel Discussion, Annual Judicial Conference, Second Circuit, 37 F.R.D. 365, 369 (1964).

20. Davis v. United States, 160 U.S. 469. 484–485, 16 S.Ct. 353, 40 L.Ed. 499 (1895); Durham v. United States, supra, 94 U.S.App.D.C. at 242, 214 F.2d at 876.

21. Amicus argues that penal systems can only survive so long as they "accord substantially with the popular estimate of the enormity of guilt," citing 1 W. Lecky, History of the Rise and Influence of the Spirit of Rationalism in Europe 336–337 (1891).

22. Citing Harris, Respect for Persons in Ethics and Society 129–130 (R. DeGeorge ed. 1966).

23. In 1953 the British Royal Commission on Capital Punishment proposed: [A person is not responsible for his unlawful act if] at the time of the act the accused was suffering

from disease of the mind (or mental deficiency) *to such a degree that he ought not to be held responsible.*

24. The minority, together with the Reporter for the Model Penal Code (Professor Herbert Wechsler), propsed the following test of insanity:

A person is not responsible for criminal conduct if at the time of such conduct as a result of mental disease or defect his capacity either to appreciate the criminality of his conduct or to conform his conduct to the requirements of law is *so substantially impaired that he cannot justly be held responsible.*

This proposal appears as alternative (a) to paragraph (1) of Model Penal Code § 4.01 (Tent. Draft No. 4, 1955) (emphasis added).

25. See authorities cited *supra,* note 6.

26. See, for example, Szasz, Psychiatry, Ethics and the Criminal Law, 58 Colum.L.Rev. 183, 195 (1958) "[To] have a 'psychopathic' personality is only a more elegant way of expressing moral condemnation." See also, Star, "The Public's Ideas About Mental Illness" (National Opinion Research Center, 1955); H. Kalven and H. Zeisel, The American Jury 405 (1966).

27. He proposes (Br. 78) an instruction with this crucial sentence: "It is up to you to decide whether defendant had such an abnormal mental condition, and if he did whether the impairment was substantial enough, and was so related to the commission of the crime, *that he ought not be held responsible.*" (Emphasis added.).

28. A Goldstein, The Insanity Defense 81–82 (1967).

29. See H. Kalven and H. Zeisel. The American Jury (1966), passim, and particularly Chapters 5, 8, 12, 15 et seq. See also, Rifkind, Follow-up: The Jury. The Center Magazine 59, 64 (July, 1970).

30. See for example, the response of the Attorney General in Ramer v. United States, 390 F.2d 564, 575, n. 10 (9th Cir. en banc, 1968).

31. See ch. 7, section III: The Mentally Ill Offender, subsection "Experience Under the Durham Rule," at p. 534 ff of the Report, including Tables 1–10.

32. *McDonald* was decided in 1962. For fiscal years ending June 30, 1964–1970, there were 21 verdicts of not guilty by reason of insanity in trials by jury, 265 such verdicts in trials by court. These data appear in Appendix C of Mr. Dempsey's brief, as revised by submission of Sept. 21, 1971. Mr. Dempsey provides data on all terminations for fiscal 1964–1968. The data for these five years show 7537 terminations, and 194 verdicts of not guilty by reason of insanity. The other terminations are: 3500 verdicts of guilty on plea, 1567 verdicts of guilty after trial, and 629 verdicts of not guilty.

33. These trials are discussed in the amicus submission of David Chambers, consultant, who prepared a report on the John Howard Pavilion at St. Elizabeths Hospital, submitted to the Hospital and the National Institutes of Mental Health. Professor Chambers characterizes most insanity trials to the courts as more nearly comparable to the taking of guilty pleas—consisting of a stipulated statement of facts; a conclusory Hospital report that the crime was the product of mental illness; and brief supporting testimony from a single John Howard psychiatrist—all in a context of a "tacit or explicit understanding" that the defendant will not contest his indefinite commitment to the Hospital.

34. Any such analysis of the productivity testimony and verdicts nor only would require prodigious time and effort, but might well be inconclusive in view of the way experts testifying on the "product" issues come to diametric differences in the same trial.

35. We do not share the cynical view that treats the instruction as devoid of consequence. In a study of the reactions of more than a thousand jurors to two experimental trials involving a defense of insanity, it was found that juries deliberated significantly longer when instructed under *Durham* than under *M'Naghten.* Yet this did not undercut consensus; there was no significant difference in the percentages of hung juries. R. Simon, The Jury and the Defense of Insanity 213 *ff.* (1967).

36. See the opinion of Trask, J., for six of the 13 judges on the Ninth Circuit, in Wade v. United States, 426 F.2d 64, 75, 79.

37. Mr. Dempsey is concerned lest the ALI test assigns responsibility unless capacity has been reduced "to the vagrant and trivial dimensions characteristic of the most severe afflictions of the mind," *see* Wechsler, Codification of Criminal Law in the United States: The Model Penal Code, 68 Colum.L.Rev. 1425. 1443 (1968). But the application in fact will depend in the last analysis on the jury's application of community standards to the evidence adduced.

38. Even under *McDonald* the jury has frequently brought in a verdict of guilty, when the exculpatory rules would plainly permit, or even contemplate, a verdict of not guilty by reason of insanity. King v. United States, *supra.*

39. Defendant is also exculpated if he lacks substantial capacity to appreciate the conduct is wrongful.

40. In *M'Naghten's* case, 10 Cl. & F. 200, 211, 8 Eng.Rep. 718, 722 (H.L.1843), the majority opinion of Lord Chief Justice Tindal ruled that the jury should be instructed in terms of the ability of the accused "to know that he was doing an act that was wrong." adding: "If the question were to be put as to the knowledge of the accused solely and exclusively with reference to the law of the land, it might tend to confound the jury, by inducing them to be believe that an actual knowledge of the law of the land was essential in order to lead to a conviction."

When the question arose as to whether "wrong" means moral or legal wrong, the American courts split. One group, following *M'Naghten,* held the offender sane if he knew the act was prohibited by law. A second group, following the lead of Judge Cardozo in People v. Schmidt, 216 N.Y. 324, 110 N.E. 945, 948–950 (1915) ruled that, for example, the defense was available to a defendant who knew the killing was legally wrong but thought it morally right because he was so ordered by God. The issue is discussed and authorities collected in A. Goldstein, The Insanity Defense, and notes thereto. In Sauer v. United States, 241 F.2d 640, 649 (9th Circ. 1957), Judge Barnes summed up the practicalities: "[The] practice has been to state merely the word 'wrong' and leave the decision for the jury. While not entirely condonable, such practice is explained in large measure by an awareness that the jury will eventually exercise a moral judgment as to the sanity of the accused."

This issue rarely arose under *M'Naghten,* and its substantiality was reduced if not removed by the control capacity test, since anyone under a delusion as to God's mandate would presumably lack substantial capacity to conform his conduct to the requirements of the law.

We are not informed of any case where a mental illness left a person with capacity to appreciate wrongfulness but not a capacity to appreciate criminality. If such a case ever arises, supported by credible evidence, the court can then consider its correct disposition more meaningfully, in the light of a concrete record.

41. See Comments to Fourth Draft, p. 160:

6. Paragraph (2) of section 4.01 is designed to exclude from the concept of "mental disease or

defect" the case of so-called "psychopathic personality." The reason for the exclusion is that, as the Royal Commission put it, psychopathy "is a statistical abnormality: that is to say, the psychopath differs from a normal person only quantitatively or in degree, nor qualitatively: and the diagnosis of psychopathic personality does not carry with it any explanation of the causes of the abnormality." While it may not be feasible to formulate a definition of "disease," there is much to be said for excluding a condition that is manifested only by the behavior phenomena that must, by hypothesis, be the result of disease for irresponsibility to be established. Although British psychiatrists had agreed, on the whole, that psychopathy should not be called "disease," there is considerable difference of opinion on the point in the United States. Yet it does not seem useful to contemplate the litigation of what is essentially a matter of terminology: nor is it right to have the legal result rest upon the resolution of a dispute of this kind.

42.   We note that the Second Circuit adopted the caveat paragraph on the ground that

a contrary holding would reduce to absurdity a test designed to encourage full analysis of all psychiatric data and would exculpate those who knowingly and deliberately seek a life of crime. (*Freeman,* 357 F.2d at 625).

43.   See, for example, D. Abrahamsen, Who Are the Guilty? 125 (1952).

44.   Jenkins v. United States, 113 U.S. App.D.C. 300, 307 F.2d 637 (en banc, 1962) (assuming substantial experience in the diagnosis of disease in association with psychiatrists or neurologists).

45.   For example, the opinions in *Durham, Carter, McDonald* and *Washington,* and Judge Burger's concurring opinion in *Blocker.*

46.   Pope v. United States, 372 F.2d 710, 736 (8th Cir. 1967).

47.   The Association points out that "the effects of poverty, historical factors and prejudice may well have an adverse effect upon an individual's mental condition."

52.   Our doctrine is different from the doctrine of "partial responsibility" that permits a jury to find that a defendant's mental condition was such that he is only "partly responsible," and therefore entitled to a verdict reducing the degree of the offense. See Model Penal Code, Comments to Art. 201, app. B at 111 (Tentative Draft No. 9, 1959), quoting the English Homicide Act of 1957, 5 & 6 Eliz. 2, c. 11.

53.   The term "malice" in second degree murder has been extended to include recklessness where defendant had awareness of a serious danger to life and displayed wanton disregard for human life. Lee v. United States, 72 App.D.C. 147, 150–151, 112 F.2d 46, 49–50 (1949): Austin v. United States, *supra,* 127 U.S.AppD.C. at 184, 382 F.2d at 133; United States v. Dixon, 135 U.S.App.D.C. 401, 405, 419 F.2d 288, 292 (1969) (concurring opinion).

54.   There was no independent consideration in Stewart v. United States, 129 U.S.App.D.C. 303, 394 F.2d 778 (1968), which was not an en banc court, and merely cited the earlier cases.

55.   People v. Nicolaus, 65 Cal.2d 866, 56 Cal.Rptr. 635, 423 P.2d 787 (1967); People v. Goedecke, 65 Cal.2d 850, 56 Cal.Rptr. 625, 423 P.2d 777 (1967); People v. Ford, 65 Cal.2d 41, 52 Cal.Rptr. 228, 416 P.2d 132 (1966); People v. Conley, 64 Cal.2d 310, 49 Cal.Rptr. 815, 411 P.2d 795, 40 Cal.Rptr. 271, 394 P.2d 959 (1964); People v. Gorshen, 51 Cal.2d 716, 336 P.2d 492 (1959); People v. Wells, 33 Cal.2d 330, 202 P.2d 53 (1949).

56.   Schwickrath v. People. 159 Colo. 390, 411 P.2d 961 (1966); Gallegos v. People, 159 Colo. 379, 411 P.2d 956 (1966); Becksted v. People, 133 Colo. 72, 292 P.2d 189 (1956); Battalino v. People, 118 Colo. 587, 199 P.2d 897 (1948); Ingles v. People, 95 Colo. 518, 22 P.2d 1109 (1933).

57.   State v. Di Paolo, 34 N.J. 279, 168 A.2d 401 (1961), clarified in State v. Sikora, 44 N.J. 453, 210 A.2d 193 (1965).

58.   State v. Gramenz, 256 Iowa 134, 126 N.W.2d 285 (1964).

59.   State v. Nichols, 3 Ohio App.2d 182, 209 N.E.2d 750 (1965).

60.   State v. Clokey, 83 Idaho 322, 364 P.2d 159 (1961).

61.   State v. Donahue, 141 Conn. 656, 109 A.2d 364 (1954).

62.   Starkweather v. State, 167 Neb. 477, 93 N.W.2d 619 (1958).

63.   State v. Padilla, 66 N.M. 289, 347 P.2d 312 (1959).

64.   Fox v. State, 73 Nev. 241, 316 P.2d 924 (1957).

65.   New York, People v. Moran, 249 N.Y. 179, 163 N.E. 553 (1928); Rhode Island, State v. Fenik, 45 R.I. 309, 121 A. 218 (1923); Utah, State v. Green, 78 Utah 580, 6 P.2d 177 (1931); Wisconsin, Hempton v. State, 111 Wis. 127, 86 N.W. 596 (1901) and Wyoming, State v. Pressler, 16 Wyo. 214, 92 P. 806 (1907).

66.   Battalino v. People, 118 Colo. 587, 199 P.2d 897, 901 (1948).

67.   State v. Janovic, 101 Ariz. 203, 417 P.2d 527 (1966); Armstead v. State. 227 Md. 73, 175 A.2d 24 (1961); State v. Flint, 142 W.Va. 509, 96 S.E.2d 677 (1957); Ezzell v. State, 88 So.2d 280 (Fla.1956).

68.   127 U.S.App.D.C. at 189–190, 382 F.2d at 138–139.

69.   *See* Belton v. United States, 127 U.S.App.D.C. 201, 203, 382 F.2d 150, 152 (1967).

70.   78 Stat. 944 (1960), 21D.C.Code § 501 et seq.

71.   Millard v. Harris, 132 U.S.App. D.C. 146, 150, 406 F.2d 964, 968 (1968).

72.   In re Alexander, 124 U.S.App.D.C. 352, 372 F.2d 925 (1967).

73.   Lake v. Cameron, 124 U.S.App.D.C. 264, 364 F.2d 657 (1966).

75.   S.Rep.No.925, 88th Cong., 2d sess., 31 (1964).

Suggestions for Further Reading

Allen, F. A., *The Borderland of Criminal Justice* (1964)

American Law Institute, *Model Penal Code, Pt. I, Porposed Official Draft* (1962).

American Law Institute, *Restatement of the Law of Torts* (1934), and supplements (1948, 1954).

Anderson, J., "The Problem of Causality," *Australasian Jour. of Phil.,* Vol. 16, (1938), pp. 127–42.

Brant, Richard, "A Utilitarian Theory of Excuses," *Philosophical Review,* Vol. 78 (1969), pp. 337–361.

Cohen, M. R., "Moral Aspects of the Criminal Law," 49 *Yale L.J.* 987 (1940), pp. 128–129.

Comment, "Admissibility of Subjective Abnormality to Disprove Criminal Mental States," 12 *Stan. L. Rev.* 226 (1959), pp. 588–589.

Comment Note, "Mental or Emotional Condition as Diminishing Responsibility for Crime," 22 *A.L.R.* 3d 1228 (1968).

Dershowitz, Alan M., "Psychiatry in the Legal Process: A Knife That Cuts Both Ways," 4 *Trial* 29 (1968).

Edgerton, H., "Legal Cause," 72 *U. of Pa. L. Rev.,* 211–44, 343–75 (1924).

Feinberg, Joel, "Causing Voluntary Actions", in *Doing and Deserving* (1970), pp. 152–186.

Feinberg, Joel, "Crime, Clutchability, and Individuated Treatment," in *Doing and Deserving* (1970), pp. 252–71.

Feinberg, Joel, "What Is So Special About Mental Illness?" in *Doing and Deserving* (1970), pp. 272–92.

Feldbrugge, F. J. M. "Good and Bad Samaritans, A Comparative Study of Criminal Law Provisions Concerning Failure to Rescue," 14 *Am. J. Comp. L.* 630 (1966).

Fine and Cohen, "Is Criminal Negligence a Defensible Basis for Penal Liability?" 16 *Buffalo L. Rev.* 749 (1967).

Fingarette, H., "The Concept of Mental Disease in Criminal Law Insanity Tests," 33 *U. Chi. L. Rev.* 229 (1966).

Fitzgerald, P. J., "Voluntary and Involuntary Acts" in *Oxford Essays in Jurisprudence,* ed. A. G. Guest (1961).

Fletcher, George P., "Fairness and Utility in Tort Theory," 85 *Harv. L. Rev.* 537 (1972).

Fletcher, George P., "Theory of Criminal Negligence: A Comparative Analysis," 119 *U. Pa. L. Rev.* 401 (1971).

Friedrich, C. J., ed. *Nomos III. Responsibility* (1960).

Glover, Jonathan, *Responsibility* (1970)

Goldstein, A., *The Insanity Defense* (1967).

Goldstein, J., and Katz, J. "Abolish the 'Insanity Defense'—Why Not?" 72 *Yale L. J.* 853 (1963).

Green, L., "Are Negligence and 'Proximate' Cause Determined by the Same Text?" 1 *Texas L. Rev.,* 242–60, 423–45 (1923).

Gregory, C. O., "Proximate Cause in Negligence—A Retreat from Rationalization,'" 6 *Univ. of Chi. L. Rev.,* 36 (1938).

Griffiths, John, "Ideology in Criminal Procedure," 79 *Yale L. J.* 359 (1970).

Gross, Hyman, "Some Unacceptable Excuses," 19 *Wayne L. Rev.* 997 (1973).

Hall, J., *General Principles of Criminal Law 2d ed. (1960).*

Hall, J., "Negligent Behavior Should Be Excluded from Penal Liability," 63 *Colum. L. Rev.* 632 (1963).

Halleck, Seymour L., *Psychiatry and the Dilemmas of Crime* (1967).

Harper, F. V., "Liability Without Fault and Proximate Cause," 30 *Michigan L. Rev.,* 1001 (1932).

Hart, H. L. A., Review of *Crime and the Criminal Law* by Barbara Wootton, 74 *Yale L. J.* 1325 (1965).

Hart, H. L. A., *The Morality of the Criminal Law* (1964).

Hart, H. L. A., *Punishment and Responsibility* (1968).

Holmes, Oliver W., Jr., *The Common Law, Lectures I, II, III* (1881).

Howard, Colin, *Strict Liability* (1963).

Hughes, Graham, "Criminal Omissions," 67 *Yale L. J.* 590 (1958).

James, F., Jr. "The Nature of Negligence," 3 *Utah L. Rev.,* 275 (1953).

James, F., Jr. and R. F. Perry, "Legal Cause," 60 *Yale L. J.* 761 (1954).

Kadish, S. H., "The Decline of Innocence," 26 *Camb. L. J.* 273 (1968).

Kelsen, H., "Causality and Retribution," in *What is Justice?* (1957).

Kenny, Anthony, "Intention and Purpose," *Journal of Philosophy,* Vol. 63 (1966), pp. 642–651.

Lewis, H. D., "Collective Responsibility," *Philosophy,* Vol. 23 (1948), pp. 3–18.

Livermore, J. M. and P. E. Meehl, "The Virtues of M'Naghten," 51 *Minn. L. Rev.* 789 (1967).

Louisell, D. W. and G. C. Hazard, "Insanity as a Defense: The Bifurcated Trial," 49 *Calif. L. Rev.* 805 (1961).

Lyons, David, "On Sanctioning Excuses," *Journal of Philosophy,* Vol. 66 (1969), pp. 646–660.

Macaulay and Other Indian Law Commissioners, *A Penal Code Prepared by the Indian Law Commissioners* (1837).

Michael, J., and H. Wechsler, *Criminal Law and Its Administration* (1940).

Moreland, R., "Rationale of Criminal Negligence," 32 *Kentucky L. J.,* 1–40, 127–92, 221–61 (1943–44).

Morris, Herbert, ed., *Freedom and Responsibility* (1961).

Morris, Herbert, "Punishment for Thoughts," 49 *The Monist* 342 (1965).

Note, "Amnesia: A Case Study in the Limits of Particular Justice," 71 *Yale L. J.* 109 (1961).

Note, "Justification for the Use of Force in the Criminal Law," 13 *Stan. L. Rev.* 506 (1961).

Packer, H. "Mens Rea and the Supreme Court," (1962) *Sup. Ct. Rev.* 107.

Plamenatz, J., "Responsibility, Blame and Punishment" in *Philosophy, Politics, and Society* (ed. P. Laslett and W. G. Runciman, 1967).

Prosser, W. L., *Handbook of the Law of Torts,* 2d. ed. (1955).

Ratcliff, James M. ed., *The Good Samaritan and the Law* (1966).

Sayre, F. B., "Criminal Attempts," 41 *Harv. L. Rev.* 55 (1933).

Silber, J. "Being and Doing: A Study of Status Responsibility and Voluntary Responsibility," 35 *U. Chi. L. Rev.* 47 (1967).

Szasz, Thomas S., *Law, Liberty, and Psychiatry* (1962).

Wasserstrom, Richard, "H. L. A. Hart and the Doctrines of Mens Rea and Criminal Responsibility," 35 *U. Chi. L. Rev.* 92 (1967).

Wasserstrom, Richard "Strict Liability in the Criminal Law" 12 *Stan. L. Rev.* 730 (1960).

Wechsler, H. and J. Michael, "A Rationale of the Law of Homicide," 37 *Colum. L. Rev.* 701 (1937).

Williams, G., "Absolute Liability in Traffic Offenses," [1967] *Crim. L. Rev.* 194.

Williams, G., "Causation in Homicide," [1957] *Crim. L. Rev.* 429.

Williams, G., *The Mental Element in Crime* (1965).

Wootton, Barbara, "Diminished Responsibility: A Layman's View," 76 *Law Quarterly Review* (1960).

Wootton, Barbara, *Social Science and Social Pathology,* Part II (1959).